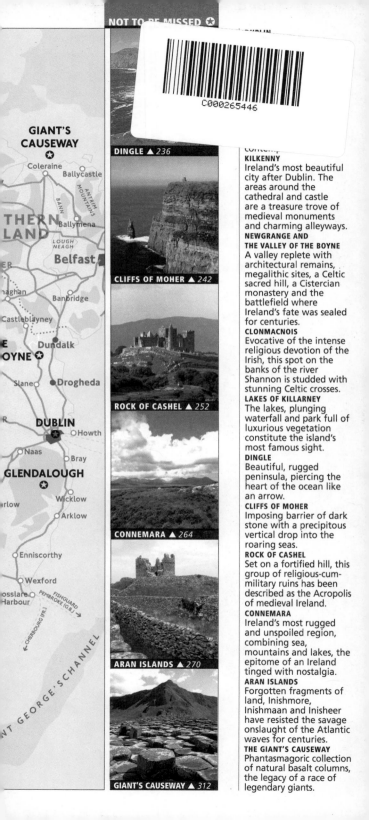

DINGLE ▲ 236

CLIFFS OF MOHER ▲ 242

ROCK OF CASHEL ▲ 252

CONNEMARA ▲ 264

ARAN ISLANDS ▲ 270

GIANT'S CAUSEWAY ▲ 312

KILKENNY
Ireland's most beautiful city after Dublin. The areas around the cathedral and castle are a treasure trove of medieval monuments and charming alleyways.

NEWGRANGE AND THE VALLEY OF THE BOYNE
A valley replete with architectural remains, megalithic sites, a Celtic sacred hill, a Cistercian monastery and the battlefield where Ireland's fate was sealed for centuries.

CLONMACNOIS
Evocative of the intense religious devotion of the Irish, this spot on the banks of the river Shannon is studded with stunning Celtic crosses.

LAKES OF KILLARNEY
The lakes, plunging waterfall and park full of luxurious vegetation constitute the island's most famous sight.

DINGLE
Beautiful, rugged peninsula, piercing the heart of the ocean like an arrow.

CLIFFS OF MOHER
Imposing barrier of dark stone with a precipitous vertical drop into the roaring seas.

ROCK OF CASHEL
Set on a fortified hill, this group of religious-cum-military ruins has been described as the Acropolis of medieval Ireland.

CONNEMARA
Ireland's most rugged and unspoiled region, combining sea, mountains and lakes, the epitome of an Ireland tinged with nostalgia.

ARAN ISLANDS
Forgotten fragments of land, Inishmore, Inishmaan and Inisheer have resisted the savage onslaught of the Atlantic waves for centuries.

THE GIANT'S CAUSEWAY
Phantasmagoric collection of natural basalt columns, the legacy of a race of legendary giants.

IRELAND

EVERYMAN GUIDES

● Encyclopedia section

■ **NATURE** The natural heritage: species and habitats characteristic to Ireland, annotated and illustrated by naturalist authors and artists.

HISTORY The impact of international events on local history, from the arrival of the first inhabitants to modern days, with key dates appearing in a timeline alongside the text.

ARTS AND TRADITIONS Customs and traditions and their continuing role in contemporary life.

ARCHITECTURE The architectural heritage, focusing on style and topology; a look at rural and urban buildings, and major civil, religious and military monuments.

AS SEEN BY PAINTERS A selection of paintings by different artists and schools from around the world, arranged chronologically or thematically.

AS SEEN BY WRITERS An anthology of texts, taken from works of writers from several periods and nationalities, arranged thematically.

▲ Itineraries

Each itinerary begins with a map of the area to be explored.

✪ **NOT TO BE MISSED** These sites should be seen at all cost. They are highlighted in gray in the margins.

★ **EDITOR'S CHOICE** Sites singled out by the editor for special attention.

INSETS On richly illustrated double pages, these insets turn the spotlight on subjects deserving more in-depth treatment.

◆ Practical information

All the travel information you will need before you go and when you get there.

USEFUL ADDRESSES A selection of hotels, restaurants, cafés, etc.

PLACES TO VISIT A handy table of addresses and opening times.

APPENDICES Bibliography, list of illustrations, index and glossary.

MAP SECTION Maps of areas covered by the guide, preceded by an index; these maps are marked out with letters and figures, making it easy for the reader to pinpoint a town, region or site.

◆ THE SOUTHWEST

◆ THE SOUTHWEST

Each map in the map section is designated by a letter. In the itineraries, all the sites of interest are given a grid reference (for example: ◆ **F** C1).

The itinerary map shows the main sites.

● ■ ▲ ◆
The above symbols within the text provides cross-references to a place or a theme discussed elsewhere in the guide.

The mini-map pinpoints the itinerary within the wider area covered by the guide.

▲ CONNACHT
ARAN ISLANDS

1 ROCK ISLAND   2 BRANNOCK ISLAND   3 DÚN MÓR   4 KILMURVEY   5 GORT NA GCAPALL   6 DÚN EOCHLA   7 CILL RÓNÁIN   8 KILLEANY   9 AIRPORT   INIS MEÁIN   10 DÚN CHONCHÚIR   11 DÚN FEARBHAÍ   12 AIRPORT   INIS OÍRR   13 DÚN FOININA   14 TEAMPULL CHOMHLÁIN   15 AIRPORT

◆ B A6-B6 F C1

THE ARAN ISLANDS
GRACE AMIDST BLEAKNESS ☉
Forgotten sentinels of the approach to Europe, the Aran Islands arch their dark backs, like monsters surging from the deep. If spending the night in Inishmore is not on the schedule, the best way to cover it is on a bicycle (which can be rented on all three of the islands), following the narrow roads leading to the strange outsize fortifications of Dún Aengus and even crossing over to the humble but unjustly neglected sister islands of Inishmaan and Inishere. (There are sea links between the mainland and the islands throughout the year, and between the three islands in the summer.)

BIRTH OF TOURISM
With easier access provided by the new steamer in 1891, the Aran Islands became a place of pilgrimage for numerous learned men. Archeologists and sociologists, botanists, politicians and nationalists (above all Patrick Pearse ● 61, who was so determined that the English flag should not fly over Inis Meáin), painters, film-makers, linguistic experts and writers (Hyde, MacNeill, Synge) were all enraptured by the haunting beauty of these unspoilt islands.

The Aran Islands lie in the ocean like a school of whales surveying Galway Bay. Geologically they are a ridge of carboniferous limestone, an extension of the Burren ▲ 242. The land is stony, scored with rocky valleys, and has almost no soil cover at all. Crops have had to be scratched from the dry, ungenerous surface of the islands, divided up into the tiny stone-walled fields known as "gardens". Nowadays the fourteen thousand inhabitants are able to improve their meager living with ever-growing tourism. This and fishing are their main sources of income. They remain Gaelic-speaking and immensely proud of their ancient island traditions. The impressive dry-stone forts (dúns) are the sturdiest, although perhaps not the earliest, testament to human life on the islands. The islanders are known to have been converted to Christianity early in the 6th century. Their courageous approach to the incredibly harsh island existence has inspired a number of writers, in particular John Millington Synge, who stayed here for long months at the turn of the 20th century. They were also inspiration for the American film director Robert Flaherty, maker of *Man of Aran*. A visit to the Aran Islands is a chance to see some unique and magnificent landscape, but also to step into a past world. The people seem hewn out of rock, wind and water: survivors from another age. In his poem "Lovers on Aran" Seamus Heaney expresses the ancient thrill of the islands: "Did sea define the land or land the sea . . . Each drew new meaning from the waves' collision. . . . Sea broke on land to full identity."

INIS MÓR (INISHMORE)
(From the jetty to the southern tip of the island.) Before coming to Cill Rónáin ▲ 242, there is a beach on the left called Trá na bhFrancach ("beach of the French"). A French ship sank here with all hands. A reminder of a happier event is the monument to mark the 1966 Atlantic crossing made in a rowing-boat by Ridgeway and Blythe.
CILL RÓNÁIN (KILRONAN) ✶. A Celtic cross has stood near the harbor since the late 19th century. It was carved by the father of Patrick Pearse ● 61 in honor of one of the island's curates, between 1881 and 1892, and symbolizes the modernization of the fishing industry. It is said that the curate wrote to the authorities in Dublin on the islanders' behalf: his telegram demanded either boats or coffins. The village has another reminder of the past in the form of a police station, now in ruins, once occupied by the British police. There is still a police station on the island, but now the police wear a different uniform. The Protestant church is also ruined, as no one has worshipped there since the 1930's.
TEAMPULL BHEANÁIN (ST BENEN'S CHURCH). Standing on a headland in Killeany Bay are the ruins of CAISLEÁN AIRCIN (Arkyn Castle). It replaced a 16th-century fortification and was probably built by Cromwell's supporters in 1652–3. Not far from Killeany, set on the side of a hill, are the foundations of the only ROUND TOWER on the island. On top of the hill is one of the smallest churches in Ireland, TEAMPULL BHEANÁIN. It was named after Saint Benen, one of

STONE WALLS
The islands are a like a checkerboard, criss-crossed with dry-stone walls enclosing fields often not much bigger than a pocket handkerchief. In order to grow any crops at all, over generations the islanders put down layers of rotted seaweed to fill out the almost non-existent soil.

270   271

☉ This symbol indicates a place not to be missed.

★ The star symbol signifies sites singled out by the editor for special attention.

◆ B A6-B6 F C1
This reference pinpoints the place's location on one of the maps at the back of the book.

● Encylopedia section

▲ Itineraries in Ireland

◆ Practical information

LEINSTER ▲ 139

The eastern province, opening onto the Irish Sea, was the prey of Viking, Norman and English invaders, who created prosperous cities: Wexford, Kilkenny and Dublin. The capital of Ireland, home to one in every three of the Republic's inhabitants, is the island's crowning glory and the conservatory of its architectural, literary, artistic and musical traditions. By contrast, Leinster, where the faint heartbeat of the medieval monastic cities can still be faintly heard, also contains the pastoral beauty of the Wicklow Mountains, the vast peat bogs of Offaly and the great plains of Meath and Westmeath.

MUNSTER ▲ 209

Ireland's largest province possesses three of the Republic's biggest cities and four of its biggest rivers. Its western coastline boasts the estuary of the Shannon, the archipelago's most majestic river. Its landscapes are marked by a striking diversity, from the craggy rocks of County Kerry to the fertile Golden Vale that dominates Cashel and the mineral, lunar landscape of the Burren. Washed by the Gulf Stream, this area enjoys a mild climate all the year round, making it a haven for migrating birds.

CONNACHT ▲ 255

This is the Cinderella of Ireland, the poorest province but also the most beautiful in its nobility and starkness, as well as being the Gaelic heartland and a fisherman's dream. Romantic Connemara and the sprinkling of islands on its rugged shores seem to stand in defiance of modernity, inviting visitors to relax and recharge their batteries. County Galway and County Mayo, the Sligo so beloved of the poet W.B. Yeats, Roscommon and demure Leitrim all provide a striking contrast with the Ireland of the "Celtic tiger" concentrated around Dublin.

ULSTER ▲ 291

Divided by an international frontier with painful implications, the northern province of Ireland contains nine counties – three in the Republic and six forming part of the United Kingdom. A bastion of Celtic identity, as seen from the countless architectural remains and the epic Red Branch cycle, it is also the focal point of a conflict, yet to be resolved, between two political and religious identities that have marked the landscape, lifestyles, economy, literature and history of this part of the island, and given Ireland one Nobel Prize for Literature (Seamus Heaney, 1995) and two Nobel Peace Prizes (Mairéad Corrigan and Betty Williams, 1976; David Trimble and John Hume, 1998).

● Encyclopedia section

■ NATURE
Ian Hill, Michael Viney
■ HISTORY
Pierre Joannon, Pierre-Yves Lambert,
Jean-Michel Picard
■ ARTS AND TRADITIONS
Paul Brennan, Peadar Duignan,
Pierre Joannon, Seamus O'Tuama
■ ARCHITECTURE
Jacques Briard, Peter Harbison,
Fidelma Mullane
■ IRELAND AS SEEN BY PAINTERS
Philippe Pilard

▲ Itineraries in Ireland

■ LEINSTER
Jacques Briard, Peter Harbison,
Pierre Joannon, Stephen Joannon,
Raymond Keaveney, Fiona Mc Laughin,
Seamus O'Tuama, Jean-Michel Picard,
James Scully, Patrick F. Wallace
■ MUNSTER
Stella Cherry, Seán Dunne,
Peter Harbison, Pierre Joannon,
Vladimir Léon, Seamus O'Tuama
■ CONNACHT
Paul Brennan, Mary E. Cawley,
John De Courcy, Peter Harbison,
Pierre Joannon, Peadar O'Dowd
■ ULSTER
Peter Harbison, Ian Hill, Pierre Joannon,
Fiona Mc Laughin, Éithne Verling

◆ Practical information

Solène Bouton, Françoise Connolly,
Martine Denisot, Jerome Holland

→ NUMEROUS SPECIALISTS AND ACADEMICS HAVE CONTRIBUTED TO THIS GUIDE.
ALL THE INFORMATION GIVEN HERE
WAS SUBMITTED FOR THEIR APPROVAL.

→ WE WOULD LIKE TO GIVE SPECIAL THANKS TO PETER HARBISON
(ARCHEOLOGIST, EDITOR OF *IRELAND OF THE WELCOMES* AND MEMBER
OF THE ROYAL IRISH ACADEMY), PIERRE JOANNON (CHIEF EDITOR OF *ÉTUDES
IRLANDAISES* AND PRESIDENT OF THE IRISH FUND OF FRANCE) AND FIDELMA
MULLANE (UDARÁS NA GAELTACHTA).

EVERYMAN GUIDES
Published by Everyman Publishers Plc

© 2001 Everyman Publishing Plc

Originally published in France by
Nouveaux-Loisirs, a subsidiary of
Editions Gallimard, Paris, 1994
© 1994 Editions Nouveaux-Loisirs.

First published 1995
Further editions, revised and updated:
September 1996, July 1998,
September 2001

Ireland – ISBN 1 84159 051 7

IRELAND
■ **EDITING**
Laure Raffaëlli *assisted by* Béatrice
Méneux, Odile Simon (Nature), Sabine
Rousselet
UPDATING: Solène Bouton,
France Bourboulon, Nicolas Christich
■ **PICTURE RESEARCH**
Élise Chleq (Paris),
Suzanne Bosman (Londres)
■ **DESIGN**
Olivier Brunot, Yann Leduc,
Michèle Bisgambiglia
and Philippe Canville (Nature)
■ **ILLUSTRATIONS**
NATURE
Anne Bodin, Frédéric Bony,
Jean Chevallier, Denis Clavreul,
Gismonde Curiace, François Desbordes,
Bernard Duhem, Claire Felloni,
Gilbert Houbre, Dominique Mansion,
François Place, Pascal Robin,
Frédérique Schwebel
ARTS AND TRADITIONS
Anne Bodin, Jean-Marie Guillou
ARCHITECTURE
Jean-Marie Guillou, Roger Hutchins,
Maurice Pommier, Claude Quiec,
Catherine Totems, Tony Townshend
ITINERARIES
Yvon Le Corre and Vincent Brunot,
Jean Chevallier, François Desbordes,
Jean-Marie Guillou, Alban Larousse,
Maurice Pommier, Pascal Robin
MAPS SECTION
Éric Gillion
Coloring: Claire Cormier,
Jean-Marc Lanusse, Catherine Totems
COMPUTER GRAPHICS
Patrick Alexandre, Paul Coulbois,
Martine Frouin-Marmouget (AFDEC),
Kristof Chemineau
■ **MAPS**
Édigraphie
■ **PHOTOGRAPHS**
Sonia Dourlot, Emmanuel Chaspoul,
Renata Holzbachova and Philippe Benet,
Benoît Juge, John Murray,
Dominique Zintzmeyer

Printed in Italy by Editoriale Lloyd

EVERYMAN GUIDES
Gloucester Mansions, 140a Shaftesbury Avenue,
London WC2H 8HD
guides@everyman.uk.com

Encyclopedia section

Ireland is as sweet as a new world, lapped by two expanses of water, and as fierce as a land that has withstood the onslaughts of the Atlantic for years. Its shores have already surrendered their weakest estates to the storms but men still wait with their small brightly colored boats in the shelter of a pier for the chance to bring in a meager catch. But Ireland's heart is not torn between the land and the sea: instead, it dances a jig in the pubs.

Photograph: Claddagh village, early 20th century.

The Emerald Isle's mysterious stones embrace an incredible architectural variety (standing stones, stone circles, dolmens, like the one at Legananny ▲ *307*, or funerary chambers), and there is a sacred geography in the choice of their sites which binds mankind to the land and the gods.

Photograph: Victorian ladies on the Legananny standing stone, early 20th century.

"During this morning walk in
Dublin, I continued to believe that
no matter where I looked
I would find traces of the faces, the
laughter and the voices which gave
birth to this city and whose buildings
and streets had a way of making you
feel that they belonged to you."
J.P. Donleavy, *My Ireland*

*Photograph: Grafton Street,
Dublin, 1904*

In the Monasterboice cemetery ▲ *198*, Muiredach's Cross (16 feet tall) is carved with scriptural scenes, showing episodes from the Old and New Testaments.

Nature

■ CLIMATE

The humidity of the climate lends itself to the appearance of some spectacular rainbows, especially in the southwest of Ireland.

Ireland's temperate, humid climate is due to prevailing southwesterly winds as well as the influence of the North Atlantic ocean current, the famous Gulf Stream. The perpetual motion of the air masses generates extremely unpredictable weather conditions, which can run the gamut from rain to blazing sunshine. The depressions coming in from the Atlantic make their presence felt throughout the year. Squalls of wind and rain sweep the northwest region of the island which is generally more windy and overcast than the southwest. In winter, extremely violent storms can blow in from the ocean shores, lashing Ireland with the full force of their fury.

Although snow never lasts long in Ireland, it does settle in the country's central mountainous regions. It is unusual in the south.

As they pass over Ireland, the depressions generate first southwesterly and then northwesterly winds.

ATLANTIC OCEAN

Clew Bay

Galway Bay

Burren

Shannon

Boggerah Mountains

PECTORAL SANDPIPER
This North American shorebird turns up in small numbers (up to twenty or so) in Ireland each fall.

BUFF-BREASTED SANDPIPER
This is the second most likely North American wader to be blown off course to Ireland in fall.

During the last ice age, Ireland was almost entirely covered with ice. Geological deposits carried by the drifting glaciers formed a composite layer over the many different types of the island's former bedrock. When the glaciers retreated, small hills of stone and clay, called drumlins, were formed. In some fairly shallow bays, like Clew Bay ▲ *279*, opposite, these small knolls formed islands.

"If you don't like the weather, wait a couple of minutes!" This saying illustrates the extremely changeable nature of the Irish climate, which sets the scene for some superb lighting effects.

Every winter, the storms carry salt water a long way inland. Due to the fierce westerly winds, the vegetation is flattened and even the trees are stunted.

STOAT

The stoat is one of the few species to have survived the ice age in Ireland where the subsequent severe rises in temperature and sea level were fatal to many animals.

Summer

Winter

The turning of the Earth deflects the winds westward over the Atlantic.

Warm air masses move up from the Gulf of Mexico along with the warm waters of the Gulf Stream (mauve arrows), causing fog and rain as they cool.

Donegal Bay

Spertin Mountains

Mourne Mountains

North Canal

Shannon

Wicklow Mountains

IRISH SEA

When the cold air coming down from the pole meets the tropical air rising northward, this creates depressions off the coast of Ireland. Before a depression, the weather is overcast and humid; afterward, it is colder and clearer, with showers and a northwesterly wind.

Less than 30 inches
30 to 40 inches
40 to 50 inches
50 to 60 inches
60 to 80 inches
More than 80 inches

In winter, rain can cause floods. The mountains receive over 6 feet of water per year.

The Irish summer is generally cool. Thanks to warm air moving in from Europe, the island enjoys some long warm spells.

19

GANNET
This bird's busy, noisy colonies
are one of the finest natural
sights on the Irish coastline.

The high cliffs on the Atlantic coast afford a
superb vantage point, over a distance of
164 feet, for watching the slow advance of the waves which
teem with underwater life. In spring, plankton (tiny marine
plants and animals that drift with the currents) flourishes:
this is the staple source of nourishment in the food chain
for the pelagic species. From the west and south coasts,
you can see dolphins, whales and basking sharks, while the
comings and goings of the seabirds, at the height of their
migration season in the fall and spring, bring the coastline
to life.

There are countless shoals of mackerel,
herring and cod at the point where the cold
waters of the Atlantic meet the warm currents
of the Gulf Stream.

BOTTLE-NOSED DOLPHIN
During the breeding season,
in summer, this dolphin goes
hunting in pods for shoals of mackerel,
which is its favorite food.
Some bays have their own resident
group of dolphins.

BLUE SHARK
This impressive
predator of the deep
with nocturnal habits
is harmless. It comes
in close to the coast
in summer to feast on
shoals of fish.

GREAT SKUA
A passage migrant to Ireland, this powerful seabird forces other seabirds to regurgitate their prey, then snatches it from them.

MANX SHEARWATER
This shearwater, a notable long-distance migrant which travels out over the Atlantic in winter as far as Canada, South America and South Africa, nests on some of the same islets as the petrels.

STORM PETREL
Every night in summer, tens of thousands of these tiny seabirds come to sit on their eggs in holes situated on islands off the west coast.

F. Desbordes

◄ COMMON SEAL
This is an inhabitant of the estuaries and bays whose sandbards, cut off by the channels, offer it refuge at low tide.

Young gray seal with white coat

GRAY SEAL
This large powerful seal eats about 13 lbs of fish per day. Its numbers are steadily increasing along Ireland's Atlantic coast.

MINKE WHALE
The Irish waters are a favorite haunt for this small whale which grows up to about 33 feet long.

BASKING SHARK
This giant cruises along the coastline, its mouth gaping at water level as it devours the plankton. It can grow up to 33 feet long.

LEATHERY TURTLE
This is the largest species of turtle and can grow up to 6 feet long and weigh up to 1,000 lbs. Its nesting sites are scattered throughout the tropics, but it may wander great distances and occasionally reaches Irish waters.

21

RAVEN
Most of the cliffs have their own resident pair of this largest of crows. They nest very early in the season.

SEA PINK
This plant decorates the clifftop grass with pinkish flower heads which are exposed to the wind and salt.

BLADDER CAMPION
Bladder campion favors bare environments, growing in windy places reminiscent of the mountain areas which are this type of plant's original habitat.

SHAG
Unlike its close relative the cormorant, from which it can be distinguished by its jaunty crest in the breeding season, the shag is almost entirely marine.

PUFFIN
Unlike some seabirds, such as gulls, this comical little member of the auk family does not regurgitate fish for its young, carrying it instead in its beak.

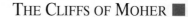

CHOUGH
Ireland's Atlantic shoreline is one of the few places in the British Isles that still provides a home for these acrobatic and handsome crows.

During the winter, waves lash Ireland's Atlantic coastline more fiercely than anywhere else in Europe. The eroded rocks rearing over the ocean are a spectacular sight. In spring and early summer, rocks jutting out from the steepest slopes are colonized by large numbers of nesting birds. Each species selects a favorite site where it will rear its young. The islands near the coastline are also home to large colonies of birds, which populate the clifftops or the crevices, avoiding the hustle and bustle of human life.

Cliffs of Moher

KITTIWAKE
Living far out to sea in winter, this dapper gull nests on the cliffs every spring. Its wingtips look as if they have been dipped in ink.

GUILLEMOT
Most abundant of the auks in Ireland, this bird breeds in dense noisy colonies on ledges of seacliffs, especially around the south and west coasts.

RAZORBILL
In spring, this relative of the guillemot likes to build its nest in nooks and crevices in the cliffs.

FULMAR
The first record of this Arctic petrel breeding in Ireland was in 1911, in Mayo; today there are about 32,000 breeding pairs.

Kittiwakes, clustered in colonies, build their deep nests with seaweed which they cement with their droppings to the steep ledges of the rock.

ROCKY STRAND

Despite being buffeted by the waves, the rocky shore is an extremely well balanced environment which provides permanent habitats for a wide variety of organisms.

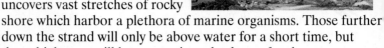

Twice a day, the ebb tide uncovers vast stretches of rocky shore which harbor a plethora of marine organisms. Those further down the strand will only be above water for a short time, but those higher up will have to wait twelve hours for the sea to submerge them once more. Each organism, however, is specially adapted to the length of time that the littoral zone where it makes its home is above water level. The diversity of locations is a result of the island's geographical position, in the area where the cold waters from the north meet the warm currents from the south.

ed algae
(arragheen)

Sponge

Oyster catcher

Mussels

Under water, the top of the rocks is usually covered in different types of algae. Their underside, however, starved of light, is home to a variety of animal life.

GOBY
In small rock pools, this voracious predator clings to the rock using its joined ventral fins, which form suction discs.

Fucus serratus

Laver
(*porphyra umbilicalis*)

Caragheen
(*Chondrus crispus*)

Cormorant

Calliblepharis ciliata

Sea urchin

Scallop

Oarweed
(*laminaria hyperborea*)

Velvet swimming crab

SUBLITTORAL ZONE
In the clear waters of the Atlantic, large brown seaweeds may grow as deep as 98 feet: their strong, flexible roots can withstand the pull of the waves. Many red seaweeds also grow here, forming water plant communities which provide shelter for fish and crabs.

VELVET SWIMMING CRAB
This crab's legs, which resemble paddles, enable it to move extremely fast.

EDIBLE CRAB
This summer visitor to rocky shores can be found in the deeper rock pools.

COMMON PERIWINKLES AND FLAT PERIWINKLES

These small sea snails move slowly across the surface of seaweed or rocks by means of an extended foot covered in mucus. Only the common periwinkle is edible.

Common periwinkle   Flat periwinkle

Xanthoria

Verrucaria lichen

THE SPLASH ZONE

Offering no shelter from the waves, this region is home to few plants and animals. Several types of lichen live here. In the higher areas, the lichen *Verrucaria*, which covers the surface of rocks, looks like tar stains.

Herring gull

Limpet

Barnacle

Brown algae
Pelvetia canaliculata
Bladder wrack
(*fucus vesiculus*)

Enteromorpha

Sea anemones

Pepper dulse
(*laurencia pinnatifida*)

BARNACLE
This crustacean feeds on minute planktonic organisms which it catches with its jointed legs.

LIMPET
Firmly fixed to the rock, this shellfish survives at low tide due to the water trapped in its shell.

Edible crab
Common prawn

MIDLITTORAL ZONE

This zone is home to the seaweed which marks the half-tide level. Occasionally, mussels colonize the top of rocks. Because of the pools, a number of seaweeds, fish and other organisms which are not well-suited to existence above water level can live quite far up the strand.

SEA ANEMONE
These predators unfurl their tentacles covered with stinging cells to paralyse their prey.

COMMON PRAWN
This is a scavenger in temporary rock pools; its fanlike tail enables it to escape backward.

EDIBLE SEA URCHIN
On the Atlantic coast, sea urchins use their spines to open up cavities in the rock.

STARFISH AND BRITTLE STARS
These carnivores feed on bivalves and can even open mussel shells.

25

WEXFORD BAY

Geese from Greenland and swans from Russia winter together in Wexford Harbour ▲ *181*.

Ireland possesses many wetlands which rank among some of the most important in Europe and provide a safe haven in winter for many waterfowl and shorebirds. These waterbirds, which have migrated from their breeding grounds in Canada, Greenland, Iceland, Northern Europe and Siberia, find abundant food in the estuaries and sounds which are sheltered from frost and always accessible. The nature reserve of Wexford Slobs provides a winter home for up to eight thousand white-fronted geese from Greenland (half of the world's population) which feed on cereals, unlifted potatoes, seeds and grass.

Young

Adult

WHITE-FRONTED GOOSE
Birds from the population that breeds in Greenland winter in Ireland.

Young

Adult

BEWICK'S SWAN
Breeding on the remote tundras of Arctic Russia, this wild swan winters in northwest Europe, arriving in Ireland in late fall.

Male   Female

Thousands of geese can be watched from the observation posts erected in Wexford.

WIDGEON
The most common wintering duck in Ireland can be found in large numbers on the banks of the River Shannon at the end of winter.

DUNLIN
This shorebird winters in large flocks, especially on the Shannon Estuary, Dundalk Bay, Strangford Lough, North Bull, Dublin and Cork Harbour.

BAR-TAILED GODWIT
This shorebird feeds on large worms, especially lugworms, in the ooze. In Wexford, when there are high spring tides it also forages for food in the flooded fields.

REDSHANK
Most redshanks that winter in Ireland once nested in Iceland. The largest numbers of this noisy shorebird occur in the autumn and spring migration peaks.

LAPWING
Large flocks of this atttractive shorebird winter in Ireland, particularly in the Wexford area.

BRENT GOOSE
This small sea goose, which is quite tame, sometimes frequents the roadsides in Dublin Bay, where it feeds.

SHORT-EARED OWL
This winter visitor is seen mainly on the east coast and hunts all kinds of rodents, mostly during the daytime.

PEREGRINE FALCON
This bird climbs to very high altitudes, then dives suddenly at great speed on small waders.

■ SANDY BEACHES

Sandhopper

The Irish coastline, although mainly rocky by nature, boasts some fine sandy beaches. Some of these, which consist of grains of quartz or granite carried by the rivers, are conducive to the formation of dunes. Dunes cover a total of 466 miles of the coastline. In Connacht, the beaches more often than not consist of tiny shells or fragments of calcareous algae. Although the Atlantic shoreline, which is particularly vulnerable to the wind and the currents, is not very hospitable to marine life, the northern bays, whose beaches are composed of finer deposits, provide a home for a wide variety of fauna.

Strands are long sandy beaches, bordered on the landward side by dunes where maritime plants, such as sea holly, grow.

Oyster catcher

Sanderling

Coiled casting excreted by the lugworm after it has extracted any food from

Black-headed gull

Green algae solidify the ooze.

Ragworm burrow

Scrobicularia

SOLE
Only when fully mature does the body of this fish flatten out sideways and its eyes change position.

COMMON SHRIMP
This shellfish changes color to blend in with its surroundings.

LUGWORMS AND RAGWORMS
These form the staple diet of waders.

Lugworm

Ragworm

The upper part of the ooze is home to many micro-organisms. Deeper down, it becomes darker in color due to the lack of oxygen.

OYSTER CATCHER
This bird's sturdy beak enables it to open mussels and other shellfish on which it feeds.

LITTLE TERN
This bird lays and buries its eggs on the beach.

Great black-headed gull

Herring gull

Young herring gull   Lesser black-backed gull

GULLS
These three species are frequent visitors to the estuaries, especially during migration. In winter, some lesser black-backed gulls abandon this environment to spend the winter months along the coasts of Spain and North Africa.

RINGED PLOVER
If anyone comes too close to this bird's nest, the adult is able to simulate a broken wing to create a diversion.

TURNSTONE
This bird turns over stones and seaweed in search of small invertebrates.

Marram grass

Herring gull

Tide mark

Ringed plover

Redshank

SHORE CRAB
This is a common sight on beaches; its shell displays a wide variety of colors and patterns.

Turret shell

Scallops

Cockle

Venus clam

Razor shell

While the worms travel through the ooze below by digging burrows, the shellfish above move around and feed with their retractable siphons.

Cockle

Netted dog whelks

Sunset shell

MASKED CRAB
This crustacean spends its life buried in fine sandy beaches.

Pullet shell

Razor shell

Lugworm

Pullet shell

Scrobicularia

29

The Burren, in County Clare, resembles a giant rock garden. It is one of the largest natural rocky sites in Ireland. Although the erosion of the hills and limestone plateaus was aggravated by pre-Christian farmers who grazed their goats and sheep here, nature has mitigated this ecological disaster by carpeting the rugged fissures with unusual plants. From May onward, the plants flower luxuriantly in combinations which are unique in Europe. Arctic and Mediterranean flora flower together; woodland flowers thrive out in the open and alpine species bloom by the edge of the ocean.

RED FOX
The fox is a mainly nocturnal animal, hunting small mammals.

PINE MARTEN
The pine marten, Ireland's rarest mammal, climbs trees with great agility when hunting its prey. The Burren is one of its last strongholds in the British Isles.

Botanists flock to the Burren ▲ *242*, which has made a name for itself for its variety of plant communities. Flowers native to the Atlantic coast, as well as the Arctic, grow side by side with southern orchids in its cracked chalky soil.

Peacock butterfly

Hart's tongue fern
(asplenium scolopendrium)

Pine marten

Irish saxifrage
(saxifraga rosacea)

Squinancywort
(asperula cynanchica)

The roots of certain plants penetrate deep into cracks in the rock where organic matter has accumulated.

Hoary rock-rose
(helianthenum canum)

Maidenhair fern
(adiantium capillus veneris)

ALPINE BEARBERRY
This plant can be found on the warm hillsides of the Burren.

BLOODY CRANESBILL
The anthers at the center of this magenta flower are turquoise.

BEE ORCHID
More than twenty species of orchids bloom in the Burren.

BURNET ROSE
This rose flowers in early summer. In the fall, its leaves turn deep red.

Female

Male

HEN HARRIER
This handsome bird of prey patrols at low altitudes in search of the small birds and rodents which form its diet. Its population has greatly declined since the 1970's.

SPRING GENTIAN
Originally an Alpine flower, this blooms from mid April to mid June.

MOUNTAIN AVENS
This Arctic plant carpets the limestone clifftops in May and June.

Fox

Blackthorn

STONECHAT
This non-migrant bird is a common sight in the Burren. It occurs mainly along the coast.

Male wheatear

Female wheatear

Male wheatear in flight

WHEATEAR
This bird nests in summer in the crevices of rocks on moors and in the mountains and migrates to Africa for winter.

31

■ THE BOGS

Over four centuries the area covered by peat bogs has greatly diminished. Nevertheless, some bogs in the hills still survive intact.

1600   1993

One-seventh of the island is not green, but brown. Ireland's most inhospitable landscapes lie above peat. Heavy rainfall, poor, badly drained soil, and a cool climate are the three main conditions which have favored the development of two types of bog. Topographical bogs are situated on the marshy lowlands at the center of the country and climatic bogs occupy the mountainsides and long stretches of the west coast. These latter are either blanket bogs or raised bogs.

Birch

Alder

Royal fern

Legall's gorse

Heather

Pondweed, the first type of plant to colonize water.

The bogs create a mosaic effect of deep pools, mossy lawns and heather-covered hills. This habitat forms a striking contrast with the surrounding countryside.

Blanket bogs, confined to the northwest of the country, have not been farmed to such an extent and are consequently better preserved.

The prevailing humidity in the bogs favors the growth of the royal fern.

RAISED BOGS
These form on land which is waterlogged and sheltered, two qualities which slow down the bacterial decomposition of the plants. They accumulate and, compressed, form layers of peat which can be as thick as 33 feet.

The peat, whose main characteristic is its lack of oxygen, functions as a preservative. Excavations have unearthed pollen, fabric and human bodies.

1980 Connemara National Park is created ▲ 268.

665 The land is cleared and farmed (cereals).

432 Saint Patrick arrives in Ireland. The bogs, which cover a large part of the land, are replaced by fields.

2000 BC The great pine forests dwindle and the milder, more humid climate encourages the formation of bogs.

2500 BC Forests of pine, ash and elm and heathland are predominant.

5000 BC The first farmers settle.

6000 BC Hazel bushes are predominant, oaks and elms begin to grow.

BOG FORMATION
The transformation of a pond into a bog is a centripetal process. Dead plants decompose very slowly, accumulating at the bottom and thereby forming peat (**1, 2, 3**). If the climate is mild and humid and evaporation is lower than the level of rainfall, a large dome of peat moss develops (**4, 5**).

Cushions of peat moss

Raised bog

Cut made to extract the peat

Bog formation zone

TOPOGRAPHIC BOG FORMATION
The bogs in central areas developed on top of lakes left behind by the glaciers, 10,000 years ago. After the stagnant water had become choked by floating plants, this swampy meadow was covered by ground plants.

BLANKET BOG
Formed directly over the mineral soil, this bog is only 6 to 20 feet deep. Its formation is linked to heavy rainfall (the average exceeds 47 inches per year). The moss plays a lesser role and the vegetation is thicker.

■ PLANTS AND WILDLIFE OF THE BOGS

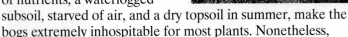

The white, fleecy tufts of cotton grass give the bogs an extraordinarily summery look.

The acidity of the peat, the lack of nutrients, a waterlogged subsoil, starved of air, and a dry topsoil in summer, make the bogs extremely inhospitable for most plants. Nonetheless, a wide variety of species can adapt to such extremes. Tufts of grass, sedge and rushes, as well as carnivorous plants, are concealed on the western hills which are thickly carpeted with peat moss. Few birds inhabit these areas, but some have a cryptic plumage which enables them to remain unseen when nesting on the ground.

VIVIPAROUS LIZARD
As the name implies, Ireland's only lizard gives birth to fully formed young. It feeds on insects and spiders.

BOG ASPHODEL
This plant carpets the bogs in thick clumps.

Spaghnum moss can store up to thirty times its weight in water.

BROWN HARE
This mammal, the most common on the bogs, browses on sedge and cotton grass.

Female

Male

RED DEER
Formerly a forest species, this can now be found in the vast bogs in the mountains, where it is protected.

Peat moss has no roots but absorbs the nutrients contained in rainwater. It stores water in the dead cells on its leaves.

CURLEW
The bogs provide a safe haven for this large shorebird with its beautiful wild, bubbling song. In winter, it frequents the estuaries.

KESTREL
A common sight in the bogs, this bird of prey hunts rodents, frogs and dragonflies by hovering.

Cotton grass

Cross-leaved heather

Bog pimpernel

LESSER BLADDERWORT
This carnivorous plant grows in boggy pools. Its leaves act like trapdoors to catch insects.

COMMON SUNDEW
This plant catches insects using the hairs on its leaves. These insects provide the nitrogen and phosphorus it needs.

FINE-LEAVED HEATHER
This grows in thick clumps on extremely dry soils.

HEATHER (LING)
The most common species of heather. Its frail stem offers little resistance to the wind.

In late summer, when the various plants are in full bloom, the bog becomes a kaleidoscope of magnificent colors.

FOUR-SPOTTED CHASER
This large species of dragonfly flies at high speed and in straight lines to catch insects in the bog.

EMPEROR MOTH
This attractive moth hovers over moorland and, in flight, displays the bold markings on its wings which resemble large eyes.

The dead moss slowly decomposes and turns into peat.

35

■ PEAT FARMING

Dry peat is used as a fuel called turf which is slow-burning and gives off an acrid smell.

For centuries, the Irish looked on the bogs as wild, damp areas, barely good enough for grazing. When the peat was cut, first on a small scale, then mechanized around 1930, it provided litter for cattle. It was also used in horticulture as an organic manure and, primarily, as an inexpensive fuel. From 1946, industrial cutting led to the drainage of this previously uncultivated land. Although at first glance the number of bogs seems to have remained unchanged, protected ecosystems are becoming increasingly few and far between.

The donkey, the beast of burden best suited to working in the bogs.

Peat bricks cut with the *slean*.

OPENING A PEAT BED
The surface vegetation and roots are cut away with a spade. This uncovers the first strip of peat.

CUTTING THE PEAT
The peat bricks are cut from narrow strips of peat and laid out on top of the bog.

DRYING
The waterlogged bricks are spread out at intervals to dry in the sun and wind.

STANDING
When they are firm enough, the bricks are stood on end to speed up the drying process.

PILING
The dry bricks are piled up and occasionally covered with straw. They then spend the winter on the bog.

THE ROLE OF THE DONKEY
Before machine-cutting, donkeys carried the peat in wicker panniers.

THE SLEDGE
Commonly used when the ground was uneven, this pannier on a wooden platform was pulled by a horse.

Modern machines, operated with tractors, extract long strips of peat, then compress and dry them.

Stumps from the prehistoric forest have been found under the cut peat.

ROPE MADE OF "BOG WOOD"
This rope is made from pine trees salvaged from the bogs and has the advantage of being waterproof. It was used to moor boats and secure bundles of straw. It also served to burn as torches.

The compressed peat bricks manufactured by Bord na Mona are sold as fuel.

Co. Armagh   Co. Antrim   Co. Galway

Wicker basket

The *slean*, a spade used for cutting and extracting the peat, is comprised of a narrow blade and a piece of metal at the side to stop the peat brick falling off. Its shape varies from one area to another, depending on the type of peat and the methods of extraction.

The machines owned by the national company, Bord na Mona, extract the peat on a large scale. Powdered peat is used for fuel in the country's thermal power stations.

TRANSPORTING THE PEAT
Nowadays, most of the bogs can be reached by tractor. Formerly, the peat had to be carried as far as the road in a basket or pannier.

PEAT STACKS
Peat stacks stand behind many homes in the countryside. They are constructed so that rainwater simply runs off the sides without being absorbed by the peat.

■ GARINISH ISLAND

The formal design of this Italian garden ▲ 226 provides an ideal setting for the luxuriant plants and bushes.

Created in the early 20th century by Joan Annan Bryce, the island's owner, and Harold Peto, architect and landscape designer, the garden on Garinish, has been state-owned since 1953. The island, which comes under the influence of the Gulf Stream, reaps the benefits of a particularly temperate, humid climate: the winters are not terribly severe and frost is virtually unheard of. Due to these exceptional conditions, in some ways reminiscent of subtropical regions, collections of flowers have been planted from all over the world.

CALLISTEMON
The flame-red hues of the various species of callistemon deck out the Italian garden in a cavalcade of color.

"YAKUSHIMANUM" RHODODENDRON
The island's soil is perfect for growing rhododendrons, including this miniature species from Japan.

"SINOGRANDE" RHODODENDRON
Originally from China and Tibet, this large species is covered with bell-shaped flowers.

"GOLDEN HORN" RHODODENDRON
This rhododendron ranks among the loveliest species and flowers in the section of the garden called "Happy Valley".

ROBIN AND BLACKBIRD
When the temperature is mild, the air is filled with the song of these non-migrant birds, even in the depths of winter.

The island's pools are home to many types of water lilies, which dapple the tranquil surface of the waters with light and color.

"DICKSONIA ANTARCTICA"
This tree fern, native to New Zealand, has a fibrous trunk and fronds, similar to a palm tree. It can grow as tall as 33 feet.

"EXMOUTH"
MAGNOLIA
GRANDIFLORA
Like all magnolias, this is frost-hardy. It flowers early.

"ASHFORD RED"
ABUTILON
This shrub, native to South America, belongs to the mallow family.

DATURA
This ornamental species belongs to the tomato and potato family.

EMBOTHRIUM
COCCINEUM
Known as "the Chilean fire bush", this species flowers in early summer.

HEDGEROWS AND DRY STONE WALLS

Near the sea, hedgerows and trees are few and far between so stone walls serve as havens for the fauna.

Thousands of miles of hedgerow wind their way across the farmland forming a leafy network of hawthorn bushes and tall grass, a sanctuary for birds and small mammals. On less fertile soil, in particular near the windswept west coast, the hedgerows are replaced by dry stone walls or earth and rubble embankments. The small enclosed fields, in part spared by pesticides and weedkillers, are home to countless wild flowers and insects. In Ireland, the roadsides are also of considerable ecological interest.

Male

YELLOW HAMMER
This bird is fond of building its nest in rough hedges.

LONG-TAILED TIT
This acrobatic passerine uses lichen, dry grass and feathers to build its extremely intricate nest.

SPARROWHAWK
The most common bird of prey in Ireland flies at low altitudes above the hedgerows hunting for birds such as finches and tits.

Jackdaw

BADGER
This member of the weasel family may dig its set beside the hedgerow at the side of quiet roads. It hunts for food at night.

Bank vole

HEDGEHOG
This insectivore lives discreetly in the hedgerows. When disturbed, it rolls itself into a ball of spines.

PYGMY SHREW
The smallest Irish mammal, this shrew feeds on beetles, spiders and woodlice.

BANK VOLE
This rodent feeds on bark, leaves and seeds.

RABBIT
This animal digs holes with secret exits in dry hedgerows.

LONG-TAILED FIELDMOUS
In fall, this animal sometimes makes its home in abandoned bird nests.

Ash

Willow
warbler

Yellow
hammer
(male)

Deep cavities in the
walls sometimes
contain enough soil
for ferns and moss to
grow side by side.

BLACKBERRY BUSH
Butterflies gather
nectar from its
flowers. In the fall,
birds, as well as mice,
foxes and other
mammals feast on its
berries.

WREN
This bird slips like a
mouse through the
hedgerows, hunting
for tiny insects
and spiders.

Stoat

RAGGED ROBIN
This plant's clusters
of raggedly cut pink
petals bring a splash
of color to the
marshy pastures near
roadsides.

Hazel bush

Hedgehog

Fern

COMMON GORSE
This plant's spiny leaves are
ideally suited to the dry, windy
environment of the verges of
Irish roads.

GIANT HOGWEED
This huge, stout-stemmed
wildflower, which grows
up to 16 feet tall at
roadsides, attracts
nectar-feeding insects.

41

Ireland is an archetypal stock farming country. Traditionally cattle from poor areas are reared side by side with top-class continental breeds. The counties of Galway and Donegal concentrate mainly on sheep, including some old breeds which are now in danger of becoming extinct. Last but not least, this country is renowned, and rightly so, for breeding both racing horses and draught horses, not to mention ponies for riding.

Fifty years ago, milk was still being churned by hand on Irish farms.

LANDRACE PIG
This pig is bred intensively to produce prolific stock and is more often battery-reared than free-range.

BURREN GOATS
There are goats running virtually wild in the most remote areas of Ireland's mountains, particularly in the Burren ▲ 242.

SAANEN GOAT
This Swiss breed has become very popular because a growing number of people in Ireland are developing a taste for its cheese and milk.

KERRY COW
The oldest breed of cow in Ireland, it is now protected in several herds. This hardy beast can still calve at the age of fourteen.

IRISH MOIL COW
Currently very few in number, this cow is now only found in Ulster. It has no horns.

At the country fairs of the past, the cattle boasted Hereford blood and still sported horns.

In Ireland, the donkey has traditionally been used as a beast of burden.

SUFFOLK SHEEP
Native to East Anglia (UK), this animal is currently being reared in Ireland for its prime quality meat and fine wool.

DOMESTIC DONKEY
This species from North Africa was imported on a large scale at the beginning of the 19th century, because the horses had been pressed into service by the British cavalry.

JACOB SHEEP
This multi-horned mountain sheep comes from Spain. Certain farmers breed it for its hard-wearing wool and its lean, tasty meat.

BLACKFACE SHEEP
This sheep, native to the Scottish Highlands, produces excellent lamb but its wool is of little commercial value.

CONNEMARA PONY
Introduced by the Celts, this pony, native to the Alps, has been crossbred with Arab and Spanish horses. This is an attractive, hardy breed.

IRISH HUNTER
The product of cross-breeding between a draught mare and a thoroughbred stallion, this is now the most popular horse in Ireland for riding and, particularly, jumping.

43

■ FRESHWATER FISHING

The adult salmon's ascent of fast-flowing rivers is a formidable ordeal.

Eels and salmon are migratory fish. The routes taken by eels span the entire north Atlantic as well as Arctic or subtropical seas, especially the Sargasso Sea.

Although the Irish are not great fish-eaters, their country is renowned for the abundance and quality of its fish: 8,700 miles of river and 1,554 square miles of lakes have made fishing a true way of life. Remarkable catches of salmon or trout, naturally, but also of char and eels are not unusual here. Although river salmon and trout are usually caught by flyfishing, they are also industrially farmed, but the meat of farmed fish never equals the delicacy of that of their cousins in the wild.

SALMON

Salmon can be caught from February to April, when large salmon journey upstream to breed; or from June to the end of August, when the grilses or young salmon migrate in their turn.

At dawn, trout forage for food in the clear water.

During the day, trout take refuge among the river's aquatic plants or under the overhanging banks.

Migration is a demanding ordeal, during which the fish rests sporadically in the still water of coves. They can also use drifting trunks and branches to protect themselves from the current and from predators.

THE TECHNIQUE OF FLYFISHING

The fisher is able to bait the fish, which thinks it is seeing a real insect alighting on the water, due to the swaying of the rod, the silk line and the lightness of the fly.

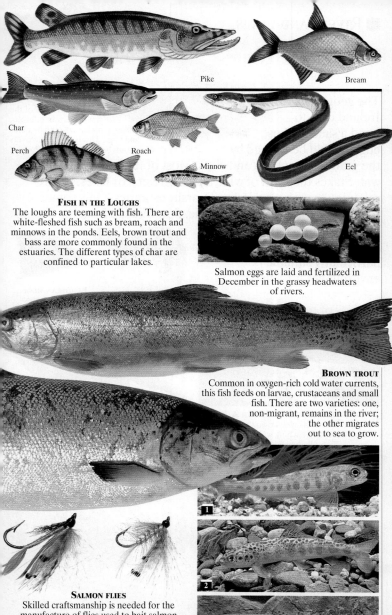

Pike

Bream

Char

Perch

Roach

Minnow

Eel

FISH IN THE LOUGHS
The loughs are teeming with fish. There are white-fleshed fish such as bream, roach and minnows in the ponds. Eels, brown trout and bass are more commonly found in the estuaries. The different types of char are confined to particular lakes.

Salmon eggs are laid and fertilized in December in the grassy headwaters of rivers.

BROWN TROUT
Common in oxygen-rich cold water currents, this fish feeds on larvae, crustaceans and small fish. There are two varieties: one, non-migrant, remains in the river; the other migrates out to sea to grow.

1

2

3

SALMON FLIES
Skilled craftsmanship is needed for the manufacture of flies used to bait salmon or trout.

Salmon have adapted to become small freshwater fish, but in the wild are extremely powerful sea creatures. The salmon fishing is the shortest of all the fishing seasons.

THE DEVELOPMENT OF THE SALMON
The young salmon (**1**) grow fast from April to July; at this stage they are called parrs (**2**). They then head out to sea, normally in April to May, aged between one and three years: these are smolts (**3**) and have a silvery skin. Their migration takes them west of Greenland and north of the Faroe Islands. Once they have become grilses (3 to 10 lbs) after a year, or salmon (6 to 60 lbs) after two to four years, they return to lay their eggs in the same river.

RIVERS AND LAKES

Mountain stream

Lough

Slow-moving river

Estuary

The geography of Ireland calls to mind a saucer whose edges would be formed by the granite mountains and cliffs. Most of the country's running water takes the form of wide alkaline rivers, or lakes, before rejoining the sea via winding, marshy estuaries. Only some waterways, which are more acidic, flow directly from the mountains into the ocean. Limestone-rich water is a particularly suitable environment for fish.

In the center of the country, carboniferous, limestone rock is covered by fields and bogs. This is where the rivers widen out, becoming tranquil loughs.

EUROPEAN MINK
This small nocturnal carnivore has now become extremely scarce throughout Europe.

CONNEMARA'S TORRENTIAL RIVER ▲ *264*
These limpid waters race down the limestone rocks before reaching wide rivers or alkaline lakes.

OTTER
An inhabitant of Ireland, this fish-eating carnivore was once widely hunted for its pelt.

Dipper

Otter

Brown trout

History

–9000	–6600	–4500	–2000		–500	0
First traces of man in Ireland	Mesolithic period	Megalithic civilization		Bronze Age	Celtic invasions	

Pre-Christian Ireland

First inhabitants

Excavations at Mount Sandel near Coleraine (County Derry) and at Lough Boora (County Offaly) have yielded evidence of human habitation in Ireland as early as 9000 BC. These Mesolithic peoples

were succeeded by Neolithic tribes (around 3500 BC); the megaliths, dolmens, and funerary chambers scattered at intervals along the Boyne ▲ *194* are attributed to them.

Between 2000 and 1700, a new wave of immigrants ushered in the Bronze Age, mining for copper in the counties of Cork and Kerry and working the gold that was extracted from the Wicklow Mountains.

The Celts

Around 500 BC, the Celts, or Gaels, invaded the island and subjugated its inhabitants. Their strong social, cultural, linguistic, artistic and religious identity set them apart, contrasting sharply with the political anarchy and violence endemic in Ireland (which had never been tempered by Roman invasion).

The island was bristling with small, warlike kingdoms governed by elected kinglets, or *Rí*, who were more inclined to fight than to unite in allegiance to an *Ard Rí* (High King). In the 4th century, they formed a federation of five main kingdoms corresponding, roughly, to the provinces of Ulster, Leinster, Munster,

Connacht and the counties of Meath and Westmeath. The two politico-religious capitals of Gaelic Ireland were Emain

Macha (Navan Fort ▲ *322*), the seat of the kings of Ulster, and Tara ▲ *191*, the seat of the kings of Meath and, later, of Ireland's *Ard Rí*.

Christian Ireland

"Island of scholars and saints"

Saint Patrick completed the island's evangelization in the 5th century. The patrician Church, originally episcopal and Roman, became Celtic and monastic in the 6th century. Columba (also known as Columcille), Ciarán, Brendan,

Comgal and Finian founded wealthy, monasteries whose fame drew scholars, nobles and men of letters from the continent. These centers of worship and culture promoted the arts, particularly calligraphy and illumination ▲ *150*. They trained missionaries who carried the Word of God into the world: Saint Fiacre near Meaux, Saint Kilian in Wurzburg, etc. The most famous was Saint Colombanus, the founder of Luxeuil Abbey.

303–304 Persecution of the Christians (Rome)	**455** Rome seized by the Vandals	**800** Charlemagne crowned Emperor in Rome	**1066** Battle of Hastings (England)	**1099** First crusade and the storming of Jerusalem
300	**600**	**900**	**1000**	**1200**

5TH CENTURY Evangelism of Saint Patrick	**550–650** Rise of Celtic monachism	**795** First Viking raids in Ireland	**1069** Norman invasion

VIKING INVASIONS

From 795, Scandinavian pirates plundered the islands and the settlements along the coast. These raiders became bolder: in 837, two fleets sailed up the Boyne and the Liffey. By the latter part of the 9th century, they had settled and founded fortified ports (at Dublin, Waterford and Cork, for example). The High King Brian Boru (right) tried to create a unified realm under his rule, crushing the Vikings and their Celtic allies at Clontarf in 1014. He was murdered immediately after the battle, however, and any possibility of a strong and united kingdom died with him.

REORGANIZATION OF THE CHURCH

Saint Malachy, Archbishop of Armagh, put an end to the Celtic particularism of the Irish church. The synods of Cashel (1101), Rath Breasail (1111) and Kells (1152) abolished local customs and set up the current Diocesan organization, placing the island's thirty-six bishops under the supervision of the four archbishops of Cashel, Tuam, Dublin and Armagh, the seat of Ireland's primate. The abbeys, brought under control once more, were handed over to the monastic orders ● 57.

CELTO-NORMAN IRELAND

AN UNFINISHED CONQUEST

In response to an appeal by the dethroned king of Leinster, Dermot MacMurrough, a company of Norman knights landed on the coast of Wexford in 1169, led by Richard FitzGilbert de Clare, Earl of Pembroke ("Strongbow"). A year later, Strongbow seized Dublin and assumed the crown of Leinster. In 1171, the Plantagenet king, Henry II, wary of Strongbow's ambitions, landed at Waterford (below) and made the Celtic leaders, Norman barons and princes of the Church acknowledge his suzerainty. For three centuries, Celts and Normans waged a bitter war: initially victorious, the Normans were gradually driven back by Aedh O'Connor, Art MacMurrough, Donald O'Neill and the Scotsman Edward Bruce.

SOCIAL AND LEGAL REVOLUTION

The Normans built castles and fortified villages ● 100 throughout Ireland. Cottage industries and trade developed. A central government was set up with a viceroy at its helm, who convoked a two-chamber parliament to vote on taxes, and legislate in areas not covered by English law. The king of England was finally, legally, the king of Ireland.

Irish mercenaries.

THE GREAT ANGLO-NORMAN HOUSES

Through their association with the Celts, the Norman invaders became increasingly Hibernized. In 1366, the colonial parliament passed the Statutes of Kilkenny, forbidding both intermarriage and the adoption of Irish names, dress, speech, and customs. Later, between 1394 and 1399, Richard II tried to bring down "the Irish enemies and English rebels", but ultimately failed. Power was now in the hands of three great families: the FitzGeralds of Desmond, the FitzGeralds of Kildare and the Butlers of Ormonde. Despite Poyning's Law (1494) which subjugated the Irish parliament to the Crown, Garret More, the eighth earl of Kildare, reigned supreme in Ireland from 1477 to 1513.

Richard II returning to England.

CONQUEST AND COLONIZATION

TUDOR MIGHT

In 1534, a revolt led by "Silken Thomas", Garret More's grandson, was put down by Henry VIII, who had Thomas beheaded in London. Having destroyed the influence of the FitzGeralds, Henry VIII tightened his grip on Ireland at the same time as he broke with Rome, dissolving the monasteries and setting himself up as the head of the Anglo-Norman Church (established as the Anglican Church of Ireland). Although Mary Tudor (right) was Catholic, she continued to appoint the Irish bishops and also supported the first attempts to colonize lands belonging to the O'Mores and the O'Connors, respectively re-named "Queen's County" and "King's County". Her half-sister, Elizabeth, who came to the throne in 1558, extended the Act of Supremacy to Ireland. Her reign was punctuated by violently suppressed revolts: the rebellion of Shane O'Neill in 1567, the double revolt of James FitzMaurice FitzGerald in 1579, and the uprising of Ulster in 1594, led by Hugh O'Neill, Earl of Tyrone, and Hugh O'Donnell, Earl of Tyrconnell. After their defeat at Yellow Ford in 1598, the English launched a campaign of systematic annihilation. In 1601, Lord Mountjoy crushed the Irish and their Spanish allies at Kinsale. O'Donnell emigrated while O'Neill was forced to sign the treaty of Mellifont in 1603, before his exile. The "Flight of the Earls" sealed Ulster's fate and sounded the knell on the old Gaelic civilization.

1453 Fall of Byzantium	**1492** Columbus discovers America	**1534** Henry VIII breaks with Rome, becomes head of the Church of England	**1588** Defeat of the Invincible Armada	**1598** Edict of Nantes	**1618–40** Thirty Years' War	**1649** Execution of Charles I
	1500		**1600**			**1700**
1494 Poyning's Law		**1541** Henry VIII acknowledged King of Ireland	**1558–1603** Elizabeth I suppresses Irish revolts		**1649–55** Cromwell colonizes Ireland	

Colonists massacred by the Irish, 1641.

JACOBITE AND CROMWELLIAN "PLANTATIONS"

ratified Cromwell's confiscations. James II, however, was less hostile toward them. Deposed in 1689 by his daughter Mary and his son-in-law William III of Orange, he attempted to reclaim his throne with the support of Louis XIV. He was defeated at the Battle of the Boyne in 1690 ▲ *194*. The Treaty of Limerick (1691) put an end to the war, although it did not prevent the defeated from being stripped of all their rights and property.

In May 1609, the Plantation Articles gave the colonists almost the whole of the province of Ulster which, it was hoped, would be transformed into a bastion of loyalty to the English crown. Although the dispossessed Irish citizens were not entirely driven out, this "planting" upset the physiognomy of the northeast of the island, which was never again at one with the rest of Ireland. The men of Ulster were quick to take advantage of the weakening of central power that occurred around the time of the English Civil War, rebelling and massacring a great many colonists. The military side of the revolt was organized by Owen Roe O'Neill, who crushed the English at Benburb (1646), and the political side by the Catholic Confederation of Kilkenny, a central government that was undermined by serious conflict from the start. In 1649, Charles I was beheaded and Cromwell landed in Ireland, mercilessly butchering the garrisons of Drogheda and Wexford. Violently quelling the rebellion, he tried to drive the Irish into the poor lands of the west ("to hell or Connaught"), and establish a military colonate in the rest of the country. Although this attempt to create a Puritan "plantation" failed, it nonetheless left the Irish more dispossessed and embittered than ever before. Their lot did not improve with the restoration of the Stuarts: Charles II

1776 Declaration of American Independence

1789 French Revolution

1815 Battle of Waterloo

1837 Queen Victoria ascends the English throne

1775

1800

1780–2 England grants Ireland free trade and parliamentary independence

1798 Failure of the revolt by the United Irishmen

1800 Act of Union passed

1829 Catholic emancipation

THE PROTESTANT NATION

THE PENAL LAWS

Under William III, Queen Anne and George I, the penal laws effectively outlawed Catholics from society. They saw their clergy exiled, lands confiscated, professions closed, education and political rights suspended. As a consequence. their military elite swelled the ranks of the Irish regiments in the service of France and Spain, while their ecclesiastical counterparts made their escape to Irish colleges on the continent.

THE PATRIOT PARTY

Colonial Ireland was upheld by two pillars: the minor Ulster Protestants, radical and nonconformist, and the "Ascendancy", the Anglican landed gentry who were very powerful in the south of the island. Comfortable in their supremacy, they began to object to the authority of the parent state. A "Patriot Party", under the leadership of high-ranking figures such as Henry Grattan, Flood and Lord Charlemont, made its presence felt

at the Dublin parliament. The revolt of the American colonies and the levy of a corps of Irish volunteers enabled the party to wrest free trade from England in 1780 and legislative independence for Dublin in 1782. Such were the achievements of the Patriot Party, which was committed to boosting industry and trade, but which came up against the twin stumbling blocks of parliamentary reform and Catholic emancipation.

REVOLUTIONARY FERVOR

The French Revolution galvanized the Presbyterian workers in Ulster and the Catholic middle classes in the South, whose most radical contingent founded the Society of United Irishmen in Belfast and Dublin in 1791. This provoked a preventive crackdown

Defeat at Vinegar Hill.

instituted by the Castle ▲ *167*, and the mobilization of the Orange Order ▲ *324* (supporters of Protestant supremacy); which, in turn, compelled the United Irishmen to seek aid from France. In 1798, part of Ulster and the Wicklow Mountains rose up in arms, before being hacked to pieces at Vinegar Hill ▲ *181*. The Protestant Theobald Wolfe Tone, the founding father of modern Irish Nationalism, won over the Directoire, which launched three unsuccessful expeditions. Captured and sentenced to death, Wolfe Tone slit his throat in prison. In 1800, the Act of Union between Ireland and Great Britain was passed, dealing the death blow to the Dublin parliament and creating the United Kingdom.

The great strike of 1913.

IRELAND UNDER THE UNION

THE LIBERATOR

Daniel O'Connell, nicknamed "the Liberator", enlisted the Church to fight under his banner, had himself elected to parliament (even though he was not eligible) and compelled the English parliament to pass a law in 1829 emancipating the Catholics. He organized mass meetings and attempted to bring about the repeal of the Union. At this point the government took action, and O'Connell and his followers were forced to back down.

REBELLIONS AND REFORMS

After O'Connell's death (1847), the torch of unrest was handed on to the romantic Young Ireland movement. This party stirred up a futile rebellion in 1848, while the island was struggling in the throes of the Great Famine ● 58. In 1858, the foundations of the Irish Republican Brotherhood (the Fenians) were laid, and the movement gathered support throughout the United States, England and Ireland. The failure of the Fenian rebellion of 1867 did not prevent this revolutionary movement from remaining active behind the scenes until shortly after World War One. From 1879 onward, the Protestant Charles Stewart Parnell took over at the helm of the reform movement. Skillfully embracing parliamentary debate, the agrarian demands of the Land League and the benevolent neutrality of the Fenians, he obtained the beginnings of land reform in 1881; but his campaign for self-government, or Home Rule, however, came up against the uncompromising hostility of both Presbyterian Ulster and the British Imperialist establishment. The ambitious land reform passed in 1903, twelve years after Parnell's death,

enabled Irish peasants to purchase the lands they were farming. At the same time, a great wave of cultural pride made itself felt, as evidenced by the Gaelic League ● 67, founded in 1893 by Douglas Hyde, by Sinn Féin, founded in 1905 by Arthur Griffiths, by the literary revival symbolized by William Butler Yeats ● 122 and by the advent of Irish trade unionism, set up by Larkin and Connolly (who were forced to deal with the lock-out of 1913 in Dublin).

Above right, James Larkin; left, James Connolly.

53

1931 The Statute of Westminster recognizes the freedom of the dominions within the Commonwealth

1939–45 World War Two

1914–18 World War One

1914   1920   1935   1950

1916 Nationalist uprising in Dublin

1919–21 Anglo-Irish War of Independence

1922 Birth of the Free State of Ireland

1949 Proclamation of the Republic of Ireland in Dublin

WE SERVE NEITHER KING NOR KAISER, BUT IRELAND!

HOME RULE

At the resumption of the debate in favor of Home Rule, Protestant Ulster looked set to start a civil war. Westminster accepted the principle of separate treatment for the six counties making up Northern Ireland, and passed a Home Rule Bill in 1912, which was immediately suspended for the duration of the war. On Easter Monday 1916 ● *60*, a handful of rebels seized the nerve centers of Dublin. They held out for a week, despite being outnumbered twenty to one. The execution of the leaders of the rebellion and the clumsy crackdown by the English paved the way for Sinn Féin to walk off with over two thirds of the Irish seats in the 1918 elections. The Anglo-Irish War of Independence broke out immediately afterward. Unable to "pacify" the country using strong-arm tactics, Lloyd George tackled the problem in two stages: in 1920, the six counties in the northeast were given home rule within the United Kingdom; and in 1921, the twenty-six nationalist counties became the Irish Free State.

Ulster volunteers on bikes, Irish volunteers on foot!

MODERN IRELAND

BUILDING THE STATE

The Irish Free State, which came into being in 1922, had to face a bitter civil war which raged until May 1923 ● *62*. The victorious government of William Thomas Cosgrave helped the country back on its feet and established its independence by joining the League of Nations and by negotiating increased powers of home rule for the dominions of the Commonwealth. In 1926, Eamonn De Valera, who had been defeated in the civil war, founded the Fianna Fáil party ("soldiers of destiny") and became the leader of the opposition; in 1932, he came to power. Apart from two short periods (1948–51 and 1954–7), he remained in power until 1959 when he became President. He severed the last constitutional links between Ireland and the Empire, stoically suffered the "economic war" of 1932–8, and in 1937 brought in a Catholic constitution, which was almost Republican. On the home front, he quelled any movements that challenged the authority of the State, played an active role within the League of Nations, and transformed Ireland's neutrality during World War Two into a true test of sovereignty.

ILLVSTRAZIONE DEL POPOLO

	1991	
1955 Warsaw Pact	**1989** Fall of the Berlin Wall	Dissolution of the USSR

1975

2000

1969 London sends troops into Northern Ireland	**1972** The Republic of Ireland and the United Kingdom join the EEC	**1985** Signing of the Agreement of Hillsborough	**1993** Downing Street Declaration

ECONOMIC MODERNIZATION

The postwar years were marked by a desire for political and economic change. The Republic was declared in 1949. Economic progress was boosted by industrialization, which involved the influx of foreign capital, the modernization of agricultural practices and the growth of the export market. This was to culminate in membership of the EEC, in 1973, which enabled Ireland to diversify its trade.

Eamonn De Valera (1882–1975).

THE NORTHERN IRELAND QUESTION

Northern Ireland, created by the English parliament and ratified by the 1925 border agreement, had within it various institutions whose discriminatory practices eventually triggered off a nonviolent campaign for civil rights. In 1969, however, this campaign fell foul of hostile Protestant extremists and local police. In 1970 the IRA rose again and unleashed a terrorist offensive against the Northern Irish State and the English presence there.

Protestant paramilitary groups were formed to meet violence with violence. In view of the deteriorating situation in Northern Ireland, Westminster sent in troops in 1969, suspended the local institutions in 1972 and imposed direct rule over the province, interrupted only by the brief interlude in 1973 when power was shared, in line with the Sunningdale Agreement. Since then, continuing Republican terrorism both in Northern Ireland, and on the mainland, and Loyalist sectarian attacks, the failure of crackdowns, however energetic, and the inability of Nationalist politicians and moderate Unionists to find any common ground, have forced the governments in London and Dublin to join forces to resolve the situation. In 1985, the Anglo-Irish Agreement, made at Hillsborough, institutionalized the Republic of Ireland's advisory role in controlling the crisis. At last, on December 15, 1993, a joint declaration by the English and Irish prime ministers, known as the Downing Street Declaration, recognized the Irish people's right to self-determination. On August 31, 1994, the IRA ordered a cease-fire, but the ensuing stalemate in the peace process led to a renewal of violence in February 1996. Nevertheless, elections took place on May 30, as planned, in a lead up to multiparty negotiations starting on June 10, 1996. Fresh impetus was given to the peace process with the election of a Labour government in the UK in 1997. The 1998 Good Friday Agreement, backed by a referendum, allowed a degree of self-rule in Northern Ireland, with the South dropping its constitutional claims. The start of the 21st century has seen a slight increase in terrorist activity, and negotiations remain tense, but there seems to be a real drive for peace both sides of the border.

The spread of Christianity in western Europe initially took place in areas where the Romans had settled. Unlike Britain (where Christian communities had been established as early as the beginning of the 3rd century), Ireland had never been occupied by the Roman armies and did not discover Christianity until around the middle of the 4th century. The Irish came into contact with the new faith through trading and raids. Not only did the tribal chieftains bring back gold, silver and other personal treasures from their pillaging in Britain and on the continent, but they also took prisoners who were sold as slaves. Among their numbers were Christians who continued to practice their religion unhindered, and gained followers.

PALLADIUS
In 431, Pope Celestine I (above) sent a bishop, Palladius the Gaul, to Ireland to set up an episcopal organization to instruct and supervise people who had already become Christians. His activity seems to have been confined to the southern half of the island, where he certainly helped to familiarize its people with the practices of the Roman church.

SAINT PATRICK
(above and left) Patrick the Gaul (c. 415–93) was abducted at the age of sixteen by Irish warriors and sold as a slave. He spent six years in captivity in the Mayo area before managing to escape. He then made a career for himself within the church, possibly staying in Gaul before being ordained as a bishop.

SAINT PATRICK'S EVANGELIZATION

Originally sent to Ulster, Patrick returned to western Ireland, without official permission, to preach to the peoples with whom he had been imprisoned. It was not until the end of the 6th century that Bishop Patricius began to be worshipped as an apostle of Ireland. Although at first he was venerated on the northeast coast, in the 7th century he became the patron saint of Armagh's powerful monastic organization, whose expansion was linked to the political fortunes of the dynasty of the Uí Néills, great kings of Ireland at Tara ▲ 191.

THE EARLY CHURCH

Although the transition from the old Celtic religion to the new Christian faith was not made without opposition, there was no bloodshed. The tribal chieftains forged close links first with the bishops, and later with the abbots of the large monasteries. By the 7th century, most of the members of the former learned classes, along with the most important tribal chieftains, had become Christians.

THE GOLDEN AGE OF MONASTERIES

The monastic movement, introduced in Ireland during Patrick's lifetime, had become the main method of structuring the Irish Church in the 8th and 9th centuries. Large monasteries (Armagh, Bangor, Iona, Kildare, Clonmacnois) were actual cities, centers of culture and trade. They also took over from the pagan necropolises in so far as the kings now chose to be buried within their holy walls. The intense lifestyle of these wealthy monasteries lent itself to the creation of some magnificent works of art in which Christian themes were integrated with motifs inspired by the Celtic style ▲ 151 or by Germanic gold and silver work.

Between 1845 and 1847, the potato harvests were ruined by the blight. A famine of great proportions descended on the peasantry whose sole means of subsistence was potatoes. The English government intervened halfheartedly before giving up at the enormity of the catastrophe. It is estimated that around one million Irish citizens died of starvation, typhus, scurvy and dysentery. Hundreds of thousands of emigrants took to the seas to escape the horror of a ravaged country: those who survived the crossing were confronted with poverty and the hostility of the indigenous population.

THE STATE'S RESPONSE

Robert Peel's Tory government tried to import maize, control prices and solve unemployment by starting some large public works projects. It was not enough. John Russell's Liberal cabinet, opposed to any interventionism, made the Anglo-Irish landowners

"CABBAGE GARDEN REVOLUTION"

Fired by aspirations for a new beginning for their people, the Nationalists in the Young Ireland Movement launched a revolt during the famine, but this came to an unfortunate end on July 29, 1848, in a Ballingary cabbage garden.

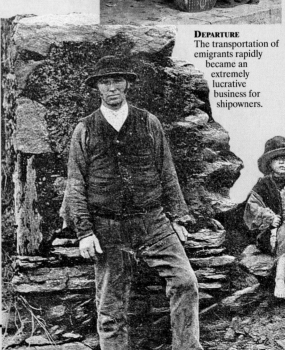

DEPARTURE

The transportation of emigrants rapidly became an extremely lucrative business for shipowners.

responsible for helping the people. Some went bankrupt; others mercilessly evicted their peasants. The soup kitchens and the aid distributed by the charities proved woefully inadequate.

THE IRISH DIASPORA

Braving storms, poverty, disease, hostility and exploitation, the Irish emigrated, putting down roots in all English-speaking countries. It is now estimated that seventy million members of the Irish diaspora are scattered throughout the world. An estimated forty-two million of these live in the United States alone.

IRISH AMERICANS

They helped to build roads and railways and, with the passing years, succeeded in controlling the American Federation of Labor, the Catholic Church, and the electoral machinery of the Democratic Party which was to make John F. Kennedy president.

A NEW AGE

The great famine bled dry Ireland's poor population. Between 1847 and 1857, it dropped from 8 to 6½ million inhabitants. It also swelled the wave of emigration which swept eight million Irish from their native land between 1801 and 1921, and it destroyed large-scale land ownership without improving the lot of the exploited peasants. Most importantly, it created a new Irish nation beyond the seas, strong and thirsty for revenge: a tragic birth for the Ireland of the modern era.

IRISHMEN AVENGE THE LUSITANIA
JOIN AN IRISH REGIMENT TO-DAY

World War One forced back the specter of civil war by sending Orangemen and Nationalist militiamen to the front. Only a few diehards declared they would serve neither "king nor kaiser, but Ireland". On Monday, April 24, 1916 a secret military committee ordered around one thousand poorly armed rebels to storm Dublin's key buildings. It took no less than sixteen thousand soldiers supported by artillery to dislodge them after a week of street-fighting. Sixteen leaders of the uprising were shot. At first hostile to this insane and violent takeover, the Irish people were rapidly won over by the wild daring of these men, and by their courage in the face of the English firing squads.

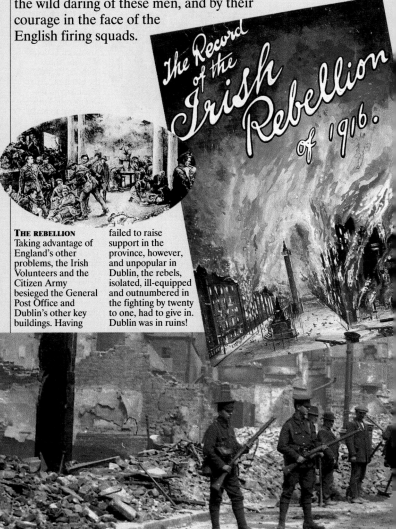

The Record of the Irish Rebellion of 1916.

THE REBELLION Taking advantage of England's other problems, the Irish Volunteers and the Citizen Army besieged the General Post Office and Dublin's other key buildings. Having failed to raise support in the province, however, and unpopular in Dublin, the rebels, isolated, ill-equipped and outnumbered in the fighting by twenty to one, had to give in. Dublin was in ruins!

THE MOTIVES
Knowing that defeat was inevitable, what were the rebels hoping to gain? The "realists" believed that their belligerent status would enable Ireland to take part in future peace talks; the "idealists" intended this bloody protest to prove that conquest could not on any account be recommended or accepted.

THE PROTAGONISTS
Patrick Pearse (below, left) dreamt of a free, Gaelic Ireland. James Connolly (below, center) and Constance Markievicz (right) ▲ *286* wanted to take part in the "European revolt of the proletariat" against the war, as advocated by Lenin. Tom Clarke (below, right) embodied the old insurrectionary tradition inherited from the Irish Republican Brotherhood.

EAMONN DE VALERA
The last leader of the revolt to lay down his arms, De Valera (right) had his death sentence commuted to life imprisonment. Freed in 1917, he took up the reins of the illicit government and rose to power in 1932. Prime Minister, then President, he was to embody the fortunes of independent Ireland.

CRACKDOWN
The sentences imposed by the court martial were 16 executions, 3,226 arrests and 1,862 imprisonments in England and Wales. The prison camps became "universities for rebels" while public opinion turned against the authorities.

Signatures on
the 1921 treaty.

Sinn Féin won a landslide victory at
the 1918 elections, established an
Irish Parliament and declared
independence. The IRA started
the war of liberation.

Outflanked, London called out the
veterans of the Great War to restore order, but
their methods permanently alienated them
from the people. Having partitioned off
Northern Ireland, Lloyd George signed a treaty
with the moderate factions of Sinn Féin, granting
Southern Ireland Dominion Status. This was
unacceptable to Republican extremists, and they
rejected the agreement. In June 1922 a bitter civil
war broke out which devastated Dublin before
inflaming the whole province. The Free State's army
suppressed the centers of resistance without further ado,
forcing the Republicans to lay down their arms in May 1923.

THE ILLICIT PARLIAMENT

Having won 73 of the
105 Irish seats in the
1918 elections, Sinn
Féin convoked its
members of parliament
at Mansion House in
Dublin on January 21,
1919: they formed an
Irish parliament (Dáil
Éireann) with De
Valera as President,
proclaimed
independence,
launched an appeal to
the free nations of the
world and voted in
favor of a democratic
program. A provisional
government was
appointed.

THE IRA

When diplomacy
failed, the Dáil
Éireann's army
opened guerrilla
warfare on Dublin
(where they deployed
mobile commando
units), and in the
countryside with
"flying columns", the
most famous of which
was Tom Barry's West
Cork Column.

The crackdown
Attached to the Royal Irish Constabulary, the Black and Tans and the Auxiliaries (all former officers and soldiers from the trenches) spread terror throughout the country, burning towns and villages. Well-armed, lacking in discipline, they traveled around in Crossley trucks or Austin armored cars.

Michael Collins
He galvanized the IRA and neutralized enemy intelligence. A negotiator of the 1921 treaty, President of the Provisional Government and Commander-in-Chief of the national army, he died in an ambush in 1922.

The Treaty
The compromise treaty of December 1921 caused a rift between Sinn Féin and the IRA. The supporters of the agreement, led by Griffiths and Collins, were elected by plebiscite; their opponents, led by De Valera and Brugha, refused to admit defeat.

Civil War
Civil war broke out on June 28, 1922, first in Dublin, devastated by another week-long bloodbath, then in the countryside, where the Free State's army hunted down the Republican "irregulars". Once Liam Lynch, the military leader of the rebellion had been been killed, De Valera ordered a ceasefire on May 24, 1923.

EASTER WEEK REPEATS ITSELF
THE I.R.A. STILL DEFENDS THE REPUBLIC

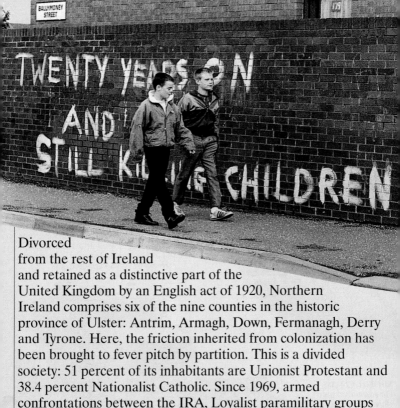

Divorced
from the rest of Ireland
and retained as a distinctive part of the
United Kingdom by an English act of 1920, Northern
Ireland comprises six of the nine counties in the historic
province of Ulster: Antrim, Armagh, Down, Fermanagh, Derry
and Tyrone. Here, the friction inherited from colonization has
been brought to fever pitch by partition. This is a divided
society: 51 percent of its inhabitants are Unionist Protestant and
38.4 percent Nationalist Catholic. Since 1969, armed
confrontations between the IRA, Loyalist paramilitary groups
and British peace-keeping forces have claimed three thousand
lives. For want of a consensus between the communities,
London and Dublin have combined forces to try and restore
peace in this trouble-stricken province.

A DIVIDED SOCIETY
Hostile to any
thought of
reunification, the
majority Unionist
party commandeered
the State machinery
and treated members
of the Catholic
minority as second-
class citizens. In the
mid-1960's, the latter
staged a peaceful
march, demanding
their rights. The
violence of the
Protestant response,
in the summer of
1969, helped
reactivate the IRA,
forcing Westminster
to take control of
administration and
introduce the
necessary reforms.

Republican terrorism,
official counter-
measures and Loyalist
paramilitaries plunged
the province into
chaos.

From top to bottom: Hume, Paisley and Adams.

SUMMER OF 1969
The Catholic ghetto of the Bogside in Derry ▲ 318 was fortified and became a "no-go area"; in Belfast, British soldiers intervened. Westminster tried to outlaw discrimination.

A CLIMATE OF COOPERATION
Most solutions presuppose a prior agreement between Dublin and London. That was the tenor of the Thatcher-FitzGerald agreements (1985) and of the joint declaration by John Major and Albert Reynolds (1993).

A CONSENSUS REACHED
Disparaged by the Democratic Unionist Party of the Reverend Ian Paisley, who again cried treason, the Good Friday Agreement was negotiated under the auspices of London, Dublin and Washington. It marks the desire of the SDLP (then led by John Hume), David Trimble's Ulster Unionist Party and Gerry Adams' Sinn Féin to come to a compromise. Approved by a referendum both sides of the border, it introduced a coalition government, made up of representatives of all the main parties, and the formulation of a North-South Council. At the same time, the South gave up its constitutional claims to the North. Although by no means the end of troubles in Northern Ireland, the Agreement marked an important stage in the negotiations for peace.

● THE IRISH LANGUAGE

bunreaċt na héireann 1937-1987

Agus ar mbeit dúinn
dá cur romainn an
maiteas poiblide do
cur ar agaid maille
le Crihonnaċt agus
le hIonnracas
agus le Caręannaċt

ÉIRE 28

Irish is sometimes referred to as "Gaelic", but so is the Scottish language. To be more accurate, the term "Irish Gaelic" should be used to describe the language spoken in Ireland. "Gaelic" is actually derived from the word "Gael", the name given to the Celts. The Irish word for their language is "Gaedhilge" ("Gaelige", after the spelling reform of 1945, which was designed to abolish a certain number of letters which were written but not pronounced).

ORIGINS

Irish is a Celtic language, and therefore has Indo-European roots. It has been used in Ireland since the 4th century. Since then the language has passed through several distinct linguistic periods: the proto-Irish of the ogham inscriptions (4th to 7th century), the Old Irish found in commentaries (8th to 9th century), Middle Irish (around 900–1200) and Modern Irish (since 1200). Old Irish is one of the earliest languages to appear in western Europe.

OGHAM STONES
The name of these strange standing stones dotted around Ireland bears close similarities to that of the Celtic god of writing, Ogmios. They probably marked the site of a grave. Dating, it seems, from the beginning of Christian times (4th century) to the 7th century, they are found primarily in the counties of Cork and Kerry. In oghamic writing, each letter is formed by using straight or oblique lines, appearing on either side of the stone's edge. Each letter is composed of between one and five strokes. The inscription is read from the top and, more often than not, it bears a person's name, as well as that of their father.

ANCIENT IRISH LITERATURE

The main body of ancient Irish literature is made up of epic legends which in many cases date back to the Old Irish period, at least as far as the written tradition is concerned. These legends speak of an aristocratic and warlike society in which the individual person was subordinate to the clan. In this society, the poet enjoyed a privileged status on a par with lawyers, doctors and musicians. The lives of the Irish saints also introduced a type of character similar to the epic hero.

IRISH ON THE WANE

FROM OLD IRISH TO MODERN IRISH

During the late Middle Ages, Ireland had a profound cultural influence on Great Britain and the continent. At the time of the Viking invasions (10th century), the Irish became more inward-looking, which led to a simplification of the language (Middle Irish). Although the Anglo-Norman invasions did not cause Irish to be eradicated, they brought about a fresh simplification (Modern Irish). Despite the attempts of English sovereigns (such as Henry VIII, for example) to oust the Irish language from the island, the whole of the Irish population was still speaking Gaelic until the Great Famine of 1845
● 58.

Douglas Hyde and Eoin MacNeill, founders of the Gaelic League.

DOUGLAS HYDE

A poet and man of letters, Hyde was born in Sligo in 1860. After studying at Trinity College ▲ *148*, he founded an Irish literary society in 1891 in London and became President of the one in Dublin the following year. This sensitized him to the importance of Irish as a ferment of national unity, and, in line with this principle, he founded the Gaelic League in 1893. He finally left the League in 1915 and started a political career which culminated in his becoming President in 1938.

GRADUAL DISAPPEARANCE

While the wealthy farmers of Ireland were becoming anglicized, among the poorer peasants, mortality and emigration were taking their toll; consequently the Irish language declined more quickly in the wealthiest areas. In 1800, it is estimated that half of the population (5 million people) still spoke Irish. Fifty years later, according to the census taken after the Great Famine, there were 1½ million Irish speakers; in 1911, only an eighth remained.

THE GAELIC REVIVAL

THE FOUNDATION OF THE GAELIC LEAGUE

Several learned societies sprang up during the 19th century in an attempt to check the decline of the language. The most active of these was the Gaelic League ("Conradh na Gaedhilge"), founded on July 31, 1893, under the presidency of the poet Douglas Hyde. From this time onward, some people linked the political movement for national liberation with the linguistic struggle for the "restoration" of the Irish language and Celtic culture. This idea gained a great deal of support, even from a number of Anglo-Irish Protestants and Dublin intellectuals. Many learned to speak Irish (like Synge ● *123*) and occasionally even wrote in Irish (such as Patrick Pearse, the future hero of 1916 ● *61*). This Nationalist movement was banned in 1915.

SUPPORT POLICIES

Since independence in 1921, the various governments have all enforced a policy of support for Gaelic (recognized as the first national language by Article 8 of the 1937 Constitution): used in official documents, Gaelic is a compulsory subject on the curriculum of primary and secondary schools and, until very recently, on that of state examinations, in particular for entrance to jobs in the civil service. This means that many English-speaking Irish people have a "smattering" of Irish and say that they speak it whenever a census is taken. This policy of support for the language has occasionally led to excesses; for example, money has been found to fund the translation of a great number of foreign books. In order to revive the Irish language for all occasions, some neologisms have had to be coined to make up for its cultural backwardness, and certain towns and villages that have long been anglicized have now had their original Gaelic name restored.

IRISH LANGUAGE MEDIA

Four radio stations (*Raidio na Gaeltachta*) broadcast throughout the country (92.6–94.4 FM). The major national channels, RTE Radio and Radio 2, and the television channels, broadcast very few programs in Irish, apart from a daily news bulletin. The written press is small and not widely available: four fairly specialized monthly publications, a weekly, *Anois* ("Now"), printed in Dublin, as well as a daily newspaper *Lá* ("Day"), printed in Belfast.

THE "GAELTACHT"

Irish is still spoken in the *Gaeltacht*, areas mainly encompassing parts of the counties of Cork, Kerry, Galway (Aran, Connemara), Mayo and Donegal. These remote regions are on the periphery economically. The people who live there now are encouraged to stay by a continued policy of social support and grants awarded for education and economic initiatives. Since 1956, there has been a *Gaeltacht* ministry, responsible for protecting the Irish-speaking areas.

THE "GAELTACHT"
After the 1991 census, there were 1,095,830 Irish-speaking people out of 3,367,000 inhabitants over three years of age. But the population of the *Gaeltacht* in 1981 was 58,000 inhabitants and again only 75 percent of the people in these districts were Irish-speaking.

Map of Irish-speaking areas in 1851 and 1981.

LINGUISTIC ASPECTS

TRADITIONAL WRITING

The Irish alphabet is derived from the medieval Irish scribal tradition. In fact, it is a product of so-called "Irish semi-uncial" writing, used in Latin manuscripts from Ireland. Several sets of "Gaelic" block letters were perfected in the 17th century.

But for some twenty years now, Irish has mainly been printed using the Latin alphabet. (The Irish alphabet is the same as the French or English alphabet, but does not include the letters j, k, q, v, w, x, y or z).

PHONETICS

There is a discrepancy between writing and pronunciation which may at first disconcert the uninitiated. The phonetic system contrasts palatal (front) consonants with non-palatal consonants. These are marked by a preceding vowel, *e* or *i*, which is not pronounced: *fáilte* ("welcome") is pronounced *fa.lt'e* (*l'*,*t'* are palatal consonants, as indicated by the *i*). The system also contrasts occlusive consonants and spirant consonants (indicated by an *h* or a superscribed dot in the *cló Gaelach* – the traditional written form). Moreover, the same word may start sometimes with an occlusive consonant or at others with a spirant consonant: nominative, *an Ghaeltacht* ("the Gaeltacht"); genitive, *Aire na Gaeltachta* ("the Gaeltacht Minister").

BILINGUALISM
Telefon (telephone) can be understood immediately by any non-speaker, but *bruscar* ("litter") poses a little more of a problem. Take care in the toilets not to confuse *fir* ("men") with *mná* ("women"). Road signs are usually bilingual. However, in the Gaelic-speaking areas of the *Gaeltacht*, the English translations are often painted over.

Arts and traditions

The important Irish holidays, in the North as in the South, are actually professions of faith and statements of identity which expose the contradictions and frictions that have been shaped by history. St Patrick's Day, March 17, is a day of rejoicing for the local Irish people as well as for the seventy million descendants of Irish blood scattered throughout the world. On this day, green (the national, or even Nationalist, color) is accorded particular pride of place. In Northern Ireland, on July 12, it is orange, the symbolic color of Unionism, which spreads like wildfire through the streets during this important holiday. "The Twelfth" is a celebration of the victory of William of Orange at the Battle of the Boyne.

"GOD SAVE ULSTER"
To the accompaniment of the high-pitched bagpipes, drowned out by the muffled rolling of the *lambeg* drums, the members of the Orange lodges file past in their bowler hats, with rolled umbrellas on their arms and regalia on their chests. Orange, the prevailing color, mingles with the red, white and blue of the Union Jack, while multicolored banners bearing the heads of Queen Victoria, Carson and William of Orange flutter above the crowds. Drinking heavily, singing hymns and declaring their dogged determination to stay British, the Orangemen are probably trying as much to put their own minds at ease as to remind the outside world that peace is impossible without them.

"THE TWELFTH"
This is the militant Orangeman's day. Every year, the loyal "sons and daughters of Ulster" enthusiastically and flamboyantly celebrate their loyalty to "Crown and Constitution". Quite apart from its political and denominational angle, "The Twelfth" reflects a lasting attachment to local Northern-Irish traditions.

The shamrock (three-leafed clover) was used by Saint Patrick ● *56* to illustrate and explain the Holy Trinity – the mystery of one God divided into three coexisting, consubstantial and coeternal persons – to the Celts of Ireland.

"St Patrick's Day is an important symbol for all Irish people. It reconciles our many distinct cultural traditions and influences. It instils in us a feeling of hope and pride at the richness of our heritage."

Mary Robinson

ST PATRICK'S DAY

This day is not just the most important national holiday in Ireland, it is also a holiday for Irish people all over the world. This is the day when the United States turns green! In New York, parades create a holiday mood all day. On March 17, continuing a time-honored tradition, the *taoiseach* (Ireland's prime minister) goes to Washington to present a Waterford crystal dish filled with shamrocks to the president of the United States, who never fails to seize this opportunity to remember he has Irish blood in his veins! Back across the water in Dublin, where 350,000 people gather to celebrate the occasion, St Patrick's Day is an excuse for some jubilant, colorful reunions between Irish people who stayed at home and their expatriate friends and relatives, all marching together in close order behind brass bands. In this way, they can "return to their roots", and reassert an Irish identity that is not nearly as shaky as some might claim.

Bones

The famous English composer Arnold Bax (1883–1953) apparently declared that "of all the antiquities in the world Ireland possesses the most varied and beautiful music". This tradition is more alive today than ever before, and although the successors of the Gaelic bards are continuing to give Irish life a certain rhythm, even now, they have also been a source of delight for the rest of the world for over thirty years. The aim of the *Comhaltas Ceoltóirí Éireann*, an organization for Irish musicians founded in 1951, was to promote traditional music. And with countless musical events under its belt, it can pride itself on a mission accomplished.

THE CELTIC HARP

The Celtic harp, which has been around since the Gael period, is now the emblem of Ireland. It is the instrument played by the poets, the *filid*, who were admired both for their scholarship and their music. Stripped of their social role by the Normans, and persecuted by the English, the harpists survived various acts of repression to make a comeback at the festivals in Belfast in the late 18th century.

A HERITAGE REVISITED

In the early 1960's, the composer Seán O'Riada (1931–71) and his group, *Ceoltóirí Chualann*, popularized representative tunes and instruments such as the *uilleann* pipes, elbow pipes operated with the right arm (below); the fiddle, a violin without a chin rest played by bowing very quickly; and the *bodhrán*, a drum made of goatskin stretched over a beechwood frame.

Traditional groups also include different types of diatonic and chromatic accordions, concertinas (smaller than the accordion), tin whistles, metal pipes with six holes, transverse flutes, and even bones; nowadays spoons are also knocked against one another to produce a rhythm.

Accordion

Celtic harp

Bodhrán

Uilleann pipes

KEY VENUES
The success of traditional music led to the creation of many festivals, the most important of which, the *Fleadh Cheoil na hÉireann*, is held every year in a different village. But, above all, music is a sociable pursuit and so it can often be heard in the pubs or even in the street, coming into direct contact with the people.

Tin whistles

Concertina

AND TRADITIONAL MUSIC BECAME FOLK . . .
In the 1970's, groups such as the *Chieftains*, the *Dubliners*, *Planxty*, *Dé Dannann*, *Moving Hearts* (with Christie Moore) and Van Morrison (below) took a fresh look at traditional music, adapted to more contemporary rhythms by *Clannad* (left).

AND FOLK BECAME ROCK . . .
The punk phenomenon contributed to the evolution of folk, and Irish rock made an appearance in the late 1970's. *U2* (above), the true ambassadors of "Celtic rock" today, have become one of the leading rock bands in the world. Other major figures on the current musical scene are Chris de Burgh, the *Pogues*, the *Hothouse Flowers*, Sineád O'Connor, *Frank and Walters*, *Divine Comedy* and *The Cranberries*.

In Ireland, *Guinness* filling a glass is "liquid poetry" and knowing how to drink it is "a serious matter, which requires almost as much effort as staying sober".

The oldest pub in Ireland is said to be around eight hundred years old. Because of the advances made in agriculture, brewing and distilling in the 17th and 18th centuries, alcohol production escalated, ushering in a golden age of public houses in the mid-19th century (there were fifteen thousand licenses in 1850). Acquiring a public house in those days was one way of acquiring an education. This "licensed place of worship" (Flann O'Brien) contained a mishmash of all aspects of the country's life, whether poetic or polemic, cultural or political.

In former times, pubs frequently doubled as grocers' shops.

Typical pubs have a bar (at which you can stand) and a lounge (where you can sit down).

When closing time is imminent, the bartender will call out "Last orders, please!" to remind drinkers that it is time to order their last drinks and get ready to leave.

74

Tradition dictates that women do not drink in the bar, but times are changing.

When drinks are bought in rounds, everyone takes turns to pay.

In Dublin, it is said that the statue of Parnell points in the direction of the nearest pub.

Ireland is a country of story-telling, and pub raconteurs enjoy spinning a yarn.

75

The Romans despised beer, the vulgar "barley wine" which Christians associated for many years with the pagans lost in the cold and foggy reaches of the North. Nonetheless, the Christian monks were the first to brew beer. To get into the Church's good books, Ireland's first lay brewers cleverly chose a patron saint: Colombanus. As the legend goes, the latter introduced beer-making skills to many European monasteries during the 6th century. Today, Ireland is the world's thirtieth largest producer of beer . . . and the fifth largest consumer.

"WATER, MALT AND HOPS"

Barley, the best cereal for brewing, has to be malted so that the starch it contains can be converted into sugar, ready to be fermented and converted, in turn, into alcohol and carbon dioxide. The malt obtained in this way is ground into flour which, mixed with hot water in enormous vats (mashing), has its solid residue (mash) filtered out. The liquid obtained (wort) is heated with the hops at a temperature higher than 212ºF. Once it has been cooled, yeasts are added and it is left to ferment. The "green beer" then goes through a resting stage before being racked into barrels or bottled.

GUINNESS

Guinness, with its famous black and gold label, produces four million pints per day; and nearly eight million pints are drunk every day throughout the world. This international company also has interests in the whiskey, spirits and champagne industries.

THE SERVING OF STOUT

This is a true ritual, a favorite with the Irish: the pint is pulled very slowly and the glass is filled in two stages so that a creamy head is formed. Then the "most natural of drinks" is left to stand for several minutes before being quaffed.

STOUT, ALE AND LAGER

The manner of fermentation determines the type of beer. Top fermentation, the oldest method, produces full-bodied beers with a strong flavor. In Ireland these include ale, an English beer which is amber-colored (light or dark, as the case may be); and stout, also of English origin (formerly porter), but made famous in 1824 by the beer invented by Arthur Guinness, using strongly roasted malt. Bottom fermentation is used to produce the extremely popular lager beer. And Guinness created the harp label accordingly.

MURPHY'S, BEAMISH AND SMITHWICK'S

The two other Irish stouts, *Murphy's* (1792) and *Beamish* (1858), are proud to flaunt their southern origins. In Cork, local patriotism requires that you down a pint of *Murphy's* rather than *Guinness*, the capital's stout. *Smithwick's* (created in Kilkenny in 1710) is an ale produced by the Guinness group.

"Of all the wines, Irish is the best", maintained Peter the Great, Tsar of Russia. He was talking about Irish whiskey, "the blessed elixir of the gods", since it was the Irish monks, on their return from the Holy Land in around AD 600 who came up with the secrets of its distillation. The main ingredients of this drink, called *uisce beatha* ("water of life" in Gaelic), are pure water and barley. The drink was enthusiastically taken up by the Anglo-Norman invaders who anglicized its name to "whiskey" and helped popularize it on both sides of the Irish Sea.

MANUFACTURE

During malting, the germination of some of the barley is provoked, then halted when it is dried in a kiln. The barley, either malted or unmalted, is then ground and mixed with cooled boiled water, so that the enzyme diastase in the malt can convert the starch in the unmalted barley into fermentable sugar. This fermentation produces a brownish liquid called wash, which, after about three days, undergoes the first distillation in a pot still or column still. The vapor which is given off is condensed to produce low wines. Once these are distilled, they produce an alcohol called feints, which, when this in turn is distilled, finally results in Irish whiskey. This is matured in oak casks for at least three years, and often for twelve or fifteen years, before being blended and bottled.

"I suppose what makes Irish whiskey
and Irish Guinness so good, is the
curative properties of Liffey water."
Brendan Behan

"SLÁINTE!"

There are many ways to drink Irish whiskey. In cold weather, order an "Irish coffee", a mixture of whiskey, coffee and cream invented by Joe Sheridan in Shannon, or a "hot Irish", made with boiling water, lemon, cloves, cinnamon and brown sugar. You can also drink it in cocktails or "on the rocks". But the best way to savor its velvety flavor is to drink it at room temperature, neat or diluted with a little still water. Whatever the case, do not ignore the tradition of the round, which still prevails here, and which will prompt you to take up the chorus of the famous song, *The Wild Rover*: "I've been a wild rover for many a year and I spent all my money on whiskey and beer . . ."

DISTILLERIES

In the 18th century, there were two thousand stills in operation in Ireland. Everyone profited by this except the Treasury. So the government decided to grant licenses only to the largest distilleries. This was the start of the modern distilling industry, which has never completely stamped out the illicit stills that even today produce *poteen*, contraband whiskey strong enough to fell a herd of aurochs. It was at this time that the Irish whiskey giants appeared: Bushmills, the first recorded distillery which opened its doors in 1608; Jameson, founded by John Jameson in 1780; Power, created by James Power in 1791; Midleton, which produces *Paddy*, set up by the Murphy brothers in 1825; Tullamore, which started production in 1829. In 1966, these big names merged to create the Irish

Distillers group which has brought Irish whiskey to the fore.

79

● The "Travellers"

The "tinkers" now live on the fringes of Irish society, often despised and usually ignored. Only a very few, divorced from their background, can be found dotted among the pages of Irish literature. They prefer the term "travellers" or "travelling people" to that of "tinkers", which they find insulting. These children of an Irish society that has long disappeared are no relation whatsoever to the gypsies on the continent. But, as is also the case with the latter, people have tried on occasion to romanticize their life . . . a life which is actually extremely hard. However, those who once traveled the country's roads in their thousands enjoyed a certain symbiotic relationship with the rural world. Since the mid-20th century, two phenomena have profoundly altered their way of life: rural depopulation and the urbanization of the countryside. This marginal, nomadic minority was once again deprived of its roots when it had to adapt to a sedentary life on the outskirts of towns.

On the roads

In the 19th century, the "travellers" abandoned ditches for tents, then tents for carts or wagons at the beginning of the 20th century. Before 1960, most still lived in groups of two to four families in brightly decorated horse-drawn caravans, now exchanged for mobile homes.

The language of Shelta, derived from Gaelic, and still spoken by the elderly, enabled the "travellers" to communicate with each other without being understood by outsiders.

ODD JOBS OF DAYS GONE BY
Descended from the wandering craftsmen of olden times, from peasants evicted from their lands or from poor people reduced to begging, the "travellers" went in search of odd jobs, following a route laid down by tradition. Their role in society, which was at that point essentially rural, was well-defined.

They would take on all kinds of jobs: repairing broken objects, working tin (the word "tinker" originally described a tinsmith), selling horses, sweeping chimneys, peddling knick-knacks and begging.

On November 1, 1884, in Thurles, Michael Cusack founded the Gaelic Athletic Association (G.A.A.) to revive the national sports that had been ousted by those "imported from abroad", and to boost national identity. Its impact was so great that every district now has its own division. Gaelic football and hurling teams (which now boast around 300,000 members, exclusively made up of amateurs), play for the glory of their county and the delight of the 70,000 spectators who attend the finals.

GAELIC FOOTBALL

A cross between football and rugby, Gaelic football is known for its high, accurate passes, its long kicks and its extremely violent tackles. Thirty players (fifteen players per team) join battle on a field measuring approximately 459 feet by 262 feet. The ball, smaller than a football, is dribbled by either hand or foot. The match falls into two thirty-minute halves. Each team has a goalkeeper, six defenders, two center-field players and six attackers. The goals are similar to those in rugby except that there is a net below the crossbar. The aim is therefore to score a goal, worth three points, by kicking the ball into the net below the crossbar, which is 10 feet above the ground, or to score a point by kicking the ball over the top of the crossbar.

RUGBY

The Irish claim that they invented rugby and "who else but compatriots of Yeats, and Synge, O'Casey, Wilde and Shaw would have been crazy enough to invent . . . this game which bears such a strong resemblance to the windswept, rugged wastes of Connemara" (Jean Lacouture)! In the 1860's, the sport was played in the universities and the predominantly Protestant public schools, before becoming an established activity in Catholic schools in the 1900's. Nowadays, sportsmen from the Republic and from Northern Ireland will play on the same teams.

"ALL-IRELAND FINALS"

The finals of the hurling and Gaelic football championships take place in September, in Croke Park (Dublin), where the G.A.A. has its headquarters.

HURLING

Hurling is a type of hockey played on turf and is regarded as the most exciting field sport because of the skill and the strength it demands. Hurling has several points in common with Gaelic football: the number of players, the size of the pitch and the principle of goal-scoring. Each player uses a hurley (*camán*, in Irish), a flat stick made of ash with a wide base. The size of the hurley may vary depending on the height of the player, but is usually around 3 feet. The ball (*sliothár*), which is slightly larger than a tennis ball, has a cork center and is covered with well-sewn leather. It can travel as fast as 68 miles per hour. There is also a version of hurling for women: *camogie*, with teams of thirteen players on a smaller pitch.

Irish cooking, which is wholesome and plentiful, uses prime quality products. The basic ingredient of Irish stew, the "national dish", used to be goat or kid, as no farmer would have sacrificed his young lambs. Today, Irish stew is prepared with free-range lamb, potatoes and onions. You can supplement these ingredients, to the horror of the purists, with carrots and swedes. Countless recipes agree on one point: a good Irish stew should be thick and creamy.

INGREDIENTS
2 lb neck of lamb, 8 onions, 1–1½ pints water, 2¼ lb potatoes, chopped parsley, thyme, salt and pepper. Optional: 1 lb swedes, 12 oz carrots, 1 *bouquet garni*.

1. Begin by boning the meat, cut into fairly large chunks and trim the fat.

4. Repeat the same procedure with the rest of the ingredients until the dish is full. Add the water and position the *bouquet garni*.

5. Cover with a sheet of foil and a lid. Cook in the oven at 250ºF/Gas Mark 4 or leave to simmer over a low heat for around 2 hours. Stir occasionally to prevent the stew from sticking; add more water if it gets too dry.

SODA BREAD

8 oz/2 cups wheat flour, 1 lb/4 cups wholemeal flour, 1 teaspoon salt,
1 teaspoon bicarbonate of soda, 1 pint milk

1. Mix the dry ingredients in a bowl and make a hollow in the center. Pour in a little milk.

2. Stir gently with a wooden spoon. Continue adding the milk to obtain a loose dough which is not too sticky.

3. Sprinkle the work surface with flour and knead the dough to obtain a ball around 2 inches thick.

4. Place the ball on a board sprinkled with flour and, using a buttered knife, make a cross-shaped cut in the top of the bread. Bake in the oven for around 40 minutes at 400°F/Gas Mark 6.

Pierce with a skewer to check it is thoroughly cooked.

5. Leave to cool for 4 to 6 hours before cutting. It can also be enjoyed spread with salted butter.

2. Peel and slice the potatoes and onions into small rounds. Arrange a layer of potatoes at the bottom of a dish, add parsley, thyme, onions, and if required swedes and carrots.

3. Add the chunks of meat and season with salt and pepper.

6. An Irish stew can be prepared several hours beforehand. It often tastes better after reheating. Soda bread is the ideal accompaniment for this lamb stew.

● IRISH SPECIALTIES

SALMON
Salmon, whether smoked over oak or grilled, is the most prestigious dish served at the Irish table. It is always accompanied by brown bread spread with salted butter.

BEER
Ireland is a major producer of good-quality beers, many of them with an international reputation. They include *Guinness, Murphy's* and *Beamish* (stouts), *Smithwick's* (ale) and *Harp* (lager).

WHISKEY
There are now more than ten brands of Irish whiskey, including: *John Power, Jameson, Bushmills, Tullamore* and *Paddy*. Last but not least, there are whiskey cream liqueurs such as *Bailey's* and *Irish Mist*.

BLACK PUDDING
Black pudding is, with bacon and eggs, the main ingredient in the Irish breakfast.

JEWELRY
The silversmiths are above all famous for jewelry inspired by Celtic motifs. Lovers may be tempted to buy the Claddagh ring, an ancient symbol of fidelity.

TEA
The Irish drink a great deal of this "west-European nectar". *Barry's Tea* is the largest manufacturer.

GLASSWARE
Irish crystal is the best in the history of fine glassware (since 1715). The crystal glassworks at Waterford are now the largest in the world.

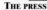

CLOTHING
Originally made in Donegal, tweed is a woven woolen cloth used for making jackets and the famous caps. Aran sweaters are knitted using undyed wool produced from Connemara sheep.

THE PRESS
There are four national daily morning newspapers in the Republic of Ireland: *The Irish Independent, The Irish Times, The Irish Examiner* and *The Star*; two daily evening newspapers: *The Evening Herald* and *The Evening Echo*; six Sunday newspapers: *The Sunday Business Post, The Sunday Independent, The Sunday Tribune, The Sunday Times, The Sunday World* and *Ireland on Sunday*. In Northern Ireland, apart from the British press, there are three main dailies: *The Belfast Telegraph, The Irish News* and *The Ulster News Letter*.

MUSICAL INSTRUMENTS
Some of these are peculiar to Ireland such as the tin whistle, a pipe often tuned to D, and the *bodhrán*, a traditional drum.

Architecture

● Megaliths

PORTAL TOMBS
Portal tombs, which date from between 4000 and
3500 BC, have an enormous roofing stone, often sloping
(like the one at Proleek ▲ *199*), supported by
several uprights.

You will find an incredible array of prehistoric
architecture in Ireland, which boasts in the
region of one thousand megaliths. Appearing
quite late, they rank among the finest in
Europe. Portal tombs, probably the most
ancient of them all, are the most widespread in the island. Court
cairns, wedge tombs and passage tombs are often grouped
together in vast necropolises, as in the Boyne Valley where the
famous Newgrange tumulus measures 305 feet in diameter
and 38 feet high.

NEWGRANGE ▲ *196*
A 62-foot-long passage
leads to a corbeled
chamber 20 feet high,
framed by three small
lower chambers at the
sides. The monument
was once surrounded
by a circle of standing
stones, of which
only twelve
survive.

PASSAGE TOMBS
Passage tombs are the
finest examples of
megalithic
monuments, often
grouped together in
commanding
necropolises like the
one at Carrowkeel
▲ *288*, County Sligo
(plan right) and
particularly in the
Boyne Valley at
Newgrange, Dowth
and Knowth. They
date from between
3300 and 2500 BC.

CARVINGS
Ireland is a treasure house of megalithic art.
The main motifs are spirals, diamonds, suns
and arcs, not to mention human feet
and bizarre "rib cages".

CARROWKEEL
These dolmens
have a central
chamber with three
side recesses and a
passage with stepped
capstones.

COURT CAIRNS, OR COURT TOMBS

Court cairns have a long chamber, sometimes compartmented, entered through a large ritual forecourt bordered by dry-stone walls. They date from the mid-Neolithic period between around 3800 and 3500 BC. The one at Schanballyedmond, County Tipperary, was surrounded by a rectangular group of ritual timber posts embedded in the ground, level with the first of the cairn's stones.

CREEVYKEEL ▲ 286

This court cairn has a small compartmented dolmen opening onto an oval court in addition to two other small dolmens placed back to back, one opening northward, the other southward. Together, the group forms a trapezoid cairn buttressed by a facing wall.

WEDGE TOMBS

Wedge tombs, whose shape and form become progressively narrower from front to back, were built mainly in the west of Ireland between around 3300 and 2500 BC.

DOLMEN IN ISLAND

(County Cork) This is a good example of a wedge tomb with a long rectangular chamber surrounded by a double line of stones in the shape of a "U". Holes dug for a circle of timber posts have been found around the perimeter of the monument.

Different types
of palisade.

Unlike the Mediterranean races, the Celtic-speaking peoples of
Ireland never acquired a taste for city life. From the Iron Age to
the late Middle Ages, secluded farmsteads were the most
popular Irish dwelling. At Craggaunowen, Ferrycarrig and in the
Ulster History Park, archeological excavations have given a
much clearer picture of daily life during this period than has
been obtained solely from visible remains. The two most
common types of dwelling were the ring-fort (or *rath*, in Gaelic)
and the *crannóg*, both circular in shape.

HOUSES
Inside the *crannógs*, houses were generally
round, with trellis walls made of a mixture of
wattle and daub, and probably a thatched
roof, or a roof made of reeds. Within
the ring-fort, houses were often made
of stone and had weight-bearing
walls: a single post, in the
center, could be enough to
support the roof.

"CRANNÓGS", ARTIFICIAL ISLANDS
Very popular around the 7th
century, *crannóg*s were built on
lakes, usually not far from the bank,
in shallow water. A layer of stones,
tree trunks and branches was
assembled, held in place by a
rampart of posts driven into the bed
of the lake. The platform created in
this way was covered with a surface of
earth and sand and protected by
a wooden palisade.

A *Crannóg* is sometimes
reached by a causeway, bridge
or gangplank at low tide, but more
often than not the crossing had to be
made by means of a boat of hollowed-
out tree trunks.

2 **3** **4**

COMMUNAL OVEN

Made of branches and dried mud.

Made of stone.

THE PALISADE
1. Interwoven posts and branches.
2. Dry-stone embankment.
3. Stone embankment topped with posts and branches.
4. Earth embankment topped with posts. The fence stopped livestock getting out and wolves getting in.

RING-FORTS
These circular forts were surrounded by a wall, usually made of earth or stone (as was the case in the west of the country, where this material was easily obtainable). There are more than thirty thousand ring-forts in Ireland.

DÚN AENGUS ▲ 273
Few ring-forts grew to the size of Dún Aengus, which sits on the edge of a cliff overlooking the Atlantic Ocean. It takes the form of a semicircle of roughly concentric walls made of dry limestone masonry, with stairways leading to the top. It is still not known when and why this structure was built.

MILLSTONE

During the first three centuries following the advent of Christianity in Ireland, monasteries and churches were largely built of timber. After 800, however, the Irish developed a taste for the grandeur and durability of stone structures, and used stone more and more, at least for churches and crosses, saving the timber for the monk's lodgings which were more temporary.

ORATORIES
The Oratory of Gallarus ▲ 238 is a good example of how the corbel principle, used in building the *clocháin* ("beehive huts", so-called because of their rounded shape) ▲ 236, was successfully applied to a rectangular plan.

MONASTERIES
The first monasteries, whose boundaries were demarcated by a circular earth embankment containing the church and the monks' huts, were not very extensive. Between the 8th and 9th centuries, a second enclosure, reserved for the laity connected with the monastery, was often added. Sometimes, as at Nendrum ▲ 306 (opposite), there was also a third enclosure, where the craftsmen lived and worked.

EARLY CHURCHES
Churches continued to be small as late as the 12th century, even when they were made of stone, probably because they were merely reproductions of the older wooden churches they had just superseded. The church on St MacDara's Island ▲ 265 (above) is a good example of this. It displays two of the typical features of early Irish churches: the antae, which prolong the south and north walls beyond the east and west gable-ends; and the stone roof, probably derived from shingle roofs.

ROUND TOWERS
Constructed between 950 and 1200, these towers were probably useful for taking bearings. The door, between 7 and 10 feet above the ground, suggests that the tower may have been used for defense and also for storing treasure. However, its Irish name, *cloigtheach* ("bell house") implies a more peaceful purpose.

DOORWAY OF GALLARUS ORATORY
The door, swinging on a wooden hinge, was unusual in that it opened horizontally.

1. DURROW
2. CASTLEDERMOT
3. AHENNY
4. KILFENORA

ASSEMBLING THE CROSSES

Tenon and mortise joints were used to assemble the cross and base, as well as the shaft, the top and the crowning element, when they were not made all of a piece. The Ahenny cross (**4**) was copied from a complex wooden cross comprised of many parts, fixed together by wooden or metal rivets.

SCRIPTURAL CROSSES

The themes, taken from the Old and New Testaments, were chosen to illustrate the Bible and Church dogmas and to excite the piety of onlookers. There are striking similarities between the composition of these scenes and those found on frescos in continental churches: these crosses may have taken the place of the frescos that the small, gloomy churches of Ireland were not able to show off to their best advantage.

It was in the center and east of the country that the art of Celtic crosses reached its zenith (at Kells, Monasterboice, Clonmacnois and Durrow, for example).

MONASTERY LAYOUT

The surrounding wall sheltered the churches, initially made of timber or peat, topped by a thatched roof, then subsequently (after 800) made of stone with a timber or stone roof; crosses made of wood, then stone; round towers soaring as high as 98 feet and, last but not least, the houses and the scriptorium, usually made of timber.

THE ROMANESQUE
STYLE

The most widespread ornament is the palmette (**2**), occasionally stylized and combined with chevrons (**1**), which can also be found alone (**3**). On the capitals, carved heads with plaited hair are interwoven with zoomorphic motifs. **1**

There was no decoration in stone churches in Ireland until the 12th century. The Romanesque style, probably introduced by the English, drew its sources from the French churches along the pilgrims' route to Compostela. The relics of founding saints drew the Irish pilgrims like a magnet, so it may have been for them that the first Romanesque churches were built. With a few exceptions, ornamentation was reserved for the windows, the west porch and the chancel-arch separating the choir from the nave.

EARLY ROMANESQUE
The early 12th-century Cormac's Chapel has three porches (there is no porch on the western façade), as well as bands of blind arcading on the outer side walls, and two towers over the arms of the transept: distinctive features that make this building unique. Its stone roof is virtually the only feature to be imitated in Ireland.

LATE ROMANESQUE Characteristic features of Romanesque churches dating from the end of the 12th century included a rectangular nave and smaller choir without a transept, decorated porches, an embellished chancel-arch rising between the nave and the choir, and a small, rarely ornamented, east window. The roof was usually timber, occasionally thatched, but hardly ever stone.

Cormac's Chapel (1127–34) ▲ 253, at Cashel, is probably the earliest genuine Romanesque church in Ireland. It bears the stamp of English (far more than continental) influences.

Kilmalkedar Church, Dingle Peninsula ▲ 239.

2

3

4

THE DOORWAY
The porch at Clonfert ▲ *202 (below)* has a doorway surrounded by engaged piers, crowned by an architrave flanked by a triangular gable.

THE ARCHES
The arches of the doorway and the chancel-arch are adorned with carvings of geometric motifs and interlacing animal ornaments which continue from one block of stone to another.

THE GABLE
This boasts two distinct styles: a blind arcade embellished by heads reminiscent of Celtic "severed heads", and a geometric motif suggesting a chevron ornament.

Jamb (detail): 15th-century statue of a saint.

Voussoir

Capital

THE GREAT ABBEYS

Religious architecture changed drastically during the 12th and early 13th centuries, when ecclesiastical orders from the continent arrived in Ireland. The small churches scattered here and there in monastic cities were replaced by monasteries, huge structures creating veritable religious cities in which the monastery buildings formed a whole with the church. This change was ushered in by the Cistercians, an order introduced in Ireland in 1142 by Saint Bernard of Clairvaux, at the request of Saint Malachy. They brought in new rules for monastic life and for the architecture of the establishments they set up.

FRANCISCAN PLAN

FRANCISCAN PLAN
In the 15th century, the foremost builders among monks were the Franciscans. They had, moreover, started to erect priories and convents as early as the 13th century. The long, narrow churches often had chapels or a single transept on the south side, as well as high, slender towers over the arms of the transept.

FRANCISCAN TOWER

CISTERCIAN TOWER

CISTERCIAN PLAN
(above)
Cistercian buildings are positioned around the square or rectangular courtyard of the cloister. The church, on the north side, is cruciform in plan (**1**) and, over the crossing of the transept, there is a wide, squat tower (**2**), sometimes added in the 15th century. Around the courtyard runs an arcade (**3**); the chapterhouse (**4**), perpendicular to the cloister, is on the east side; the refectory (**5**) is on the south side. The kitchens (**6**) and the storehouses (**7**) are located to the west of the refectory and are on the first floor, while the dormitory is on the second floor (**8**).

The purpose of the crenelations on monastery towers was more decorative than defensive.

Cistercian abbey at Greyabbey ▲ *306*.

FUNERARY MONUMENTS
In the 15th century, families who were privileged enough to bury their dead within the abbey walls erected large monuments in honor of their deceased relatives. The top of the tombs was often decorated with carvings, while figures of saints adorned the outside. At Kilconnell (County Galway), for example, two French saints (Denis and Louis) appear on the tomb of an unknown family.

THE LAVABO
The Cistercian Rule insisted that monks washed their hands before and after meals. The octagonal lavabo at Mellifont ▲ 198 was built for this purpose. Below its ogive vault, there would have been a spring fed by a nearby stream by dint of an underground system of pipes.

● CASTLES

Tower house.

In 1169, the Normans landed in
Ireland. In order to enforce their dominion
over lands conquered by force of arms, they built fortifications
called "motte-and-baileys": wooden towers (*bretesche*) erected
on top of mounds of earth and, at their base, the lower
wards where the soldiers were billeted (and
probably the livestock was kept), the
whole area surrounded on occasion by
a fosse. Nevertheless, even before 1200,
the Normans were gradually replacing these fortifications with
strong stone castles which were often extremely large and
sometimes surrounded by a moat. It was not until the 15th and
16th centuries that the Irish erected their own type of
fortification: the tower house.

NORMAN CASTLES
When their motte-
and-baileys had fallen
into a state of
disrepair, the
Normans launched an
extensive building

campaign to replace
them: they built
stronger stone keeps
which were either

rectangular (Trim
▲ *190*), polygonal
(Athlone ▲ *208*),
or round (Dundrum
▲ *307*).

In the 17th century,
the entrance to
Limerick Castle wa
flanked by two
sturdy machicolate
twin towers. In
those days, the
castle could be
reached by
means of a
drawbridg

**LIMERICK
CASTLE ▲** *249*
This is built
to the plan
favored by the
Normans in the
early 13th
century: a
roughly
rectangular bailey
surrounded by
curtain walls and
defended by
cylindrical towers
erected at each
corner.

The northeast tower
was replaced in 1611 by
a rectangular bastion
capable of taking the
weight of five or six
pieces of artillery.

Bull's-eye window of a fortified tower.

The vault of the ceiling was often constructed over a brushwood trellis, which held the stones in place until the arch was completed.

1. Mortar
2. Arch
3. Brushwood trellis
4. Temporary timber props

OPENINGS

Narrow windows protected the occupants from arrow-fire. Missiles could be hurled onto the attacking forces from additional defenses situated at roof level above the main entrance or at the corners.

IRISH FORTIFIED TOWERS

These towers, smaller than a Norman castle, usually had three stories, linked by a spiral staircase just inside the main entrance. The tower was often surrounded by a high wall which kept the enemy out and meant that the livestock could be penned in at night.

TUDOR-STYLE MANOR HOUSES (17th century) These buildings were intended more for comfort than defense, as can be seen by their many large windows. However, despite this, they still displayed some defensive features. At Portumna ▲ *200*, there is a square tower at either corner of the main body of the building, from which cannon could be fired. The doorways were often decorated in the Renaissance style, but muskets could be fired on attackers through narrow loopholes concealed beside the door.

● FORTIFICATIONS

After the 17th century, it was the English who built
fortifications in Ireland, in a bid to protect themselves from the
natives and to safeguard against the ever-present danger of
attack by sea: after all, the island could have served as a gateway
into England for France; but either these invasions did not take
place, or else they ended in failure.

**FORTIFICATIONS
WITH BASTIONS**
From 1600, the
English revived the
defensive system of
fortified towns being
used in Europe; the
finest example of this
in Ireland is Charles
Fort ▲ 223, protected
both by sea and by
land. The star-shaped
fort is comprised of
polygonal bastions
(**1**), designed to fire
from all sides, curtain
walls (**2**), separated
by a fosse (**3**) from a
covered way with
traverses (**4**) and a
glacis (**5**).

**URBAN
FORTIFICATIONS**
Throughout medieval
Europe, thick walls,
furnished with
variously shaped
bastions, were built
around the cities as a
defense against
cannonades. One of
the last towns to erect
fortifications of this
nature was Derry in
1613 ▲ 319. Its city
walls were comprised
of an outer wall,
6 feet thick, which
stood in front of a
rampart made of
earth 13 feet thick.
These were protected
by eight bastions, two
platforms and four
gatehouses with
drawbridges,
indicating the new
town's cruciform axis:
four streets leading
from a central square
to the city gates.

THE SHANNON FORTIFICATIONS

To guard against possible attacks from the west, the English erected fortifications along the Shannon during the last two decades of the 19th century, including the Martello tower at Banagher ▲ *201* and the far more sophisticated defenses at Shannonbridge ▲ *202* (right). This square battery on the Shannon was a variation on the Martello tower.

THE LOCATION OF MARTELLO TOWERS

Most of the Martello towers were built along the east coast, and in such a way that each one was in sight of the last.

CANNON

A long-range cannon, mounted on an arm able to swivel 360°, was installed on the roof of Martello towers.

MARTELLO TOWERS

In the early 19th century, the English built Martello towers along the most exposed stretches of the coast. These were modeled on the Genoese towers that they had been unable to capture when they had attempted to take Corsica in 1794. Their name was derived from a corruption of the name "Mortella" (a village in Corsica). The only entrance to these self-contained round towers with extremely thick walls was on the first floor, and they required very few men to defend them.

101

Straw or reeds made the best roofing materials. Rye, corn, oat and barley straw was widely used, but nowadays reeds are the most common material.

The traditional Irish house is a powerful symbol, a testament to past societies. Its characteristic size and shape have remained unchanged from the Neolithic period to the present day: one single story, a thatched roof, and a rectangular plan. It is built along precise lines, ensuring the sturdiness of the house, which may vary in length but not in breadth.

SECURING THE THATCHED ROOF WITH ROPES

The *sugán* (twisted straw or hay) is attached to a stone, timber or iron peg under the eaves of the façade (**1**), then the ball of *sugán* (*ceirtlín*) is thrown over the ridge (a difficult and strenuous task) so that the *sugán* can be attached to a peg on the back wall. The roofer obtains a criss-cross mesh of *sugán*, which he then attaches firmly to the gable ends (**2**).

TYPICAL PLANS

There are two main styles. In the center and east of Ireland, the fireplace and the doorway are aligned, a porch inside separating the doorway from the hearth. The roof is hipped, or has four sloping sides.

Ceirtlín: a large ball of twisted straw or hay (*sugán*).

"Path" of the *sugán*.

Knots in the criss-cross mesh of *sugán*.

In the west and north of Ireland, the fireplace and the doorway are not in line. The hearth may often be at the far end of the house, sometimes in the gable end. These houses have gable or double-sloped roofs. There is usually a front door and a back door, on opposite sides.

Reed   Corn   Rye   Barley

1

2

Rods shaped like hairpins (*scollop*) used to secure the thatch (**2**).

Rods made of willow or hazel (around 3 feet long) for the thatch frame (**1**).

Peat sod (top layer of the bog) for the sloping sides.

Roofing peat

INTERIOR
The kitchen is the focus of all activity. The furniture (beds, chairs, sideboard) is positioned against the dividing wall. The hearth has its own accessories made of black iron: hook or pot-hanger, pots and pans, stove and kettle, cluttered around the fireplace, where a peat fire burns.

SCALLOP THATCHING
The rods forming the frame are placed on the surface. Rain may rot the rods and the thatch.

TIED THATCHING
Widespread on the west coast, because of the strong winds, but above all as a result of the tough economic climate.

DIFFERENT TYPES OF ROOFING

SCALLOP THATCHING

TIED THATCHING

THRUST THATCHING
This is the best method, using high-quality straw or reeds.

SLATE ROOFS
Carboniferous limestone rock, like Liscannor stone from the north of County Clare ▲ *240*, makes excellent roofing.

The term "Georgian" covers a classical architectural style, fashionable in Ireland during the reigns of the three Georges between 1714 and 1820, at a time when country residences were being modeled on city styles. The type of Italian Renaissance villa built by Palladio served as a model for manor houses built between 1725 and 1750: a tall central building linked to smaller wing buildings by a short colonnade. Later on, the neoclassical style reigned supreme, deriving its colonnaded porticos and its liking for carvings from antiquity.

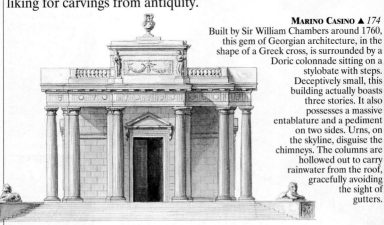

MARINO CASINO ▲ *174*
Built by Sir William Chambers around 1760, this gem of Georgian architecture, in the shape of a Greek cross, is surrounded by a Doric colonnade sitting on a stylobate with steps. Deceptively small, this building actually boasts three stories. It also possesses a massive entablature and a pediment on two sides. Urns, on the skyline, disguise the chimneys. The columns are hollowed out to carry rainwater from the roof, gracefully avoiding the sight of gutters.

EMO COURT ▲ *182*
James Gandon, the leading exponent of Irish neoclassicism in the late 18th century, who built the Four Courts ▲ *146* and the Custom House ▲ *144* in Dublin, designed Emo Court in the 1790's.

Its plan is rectangular and both façades are formed of a central block with three ornamental fronts linked by a balustrade to the buildings which jut out on either side and which are decorated by carvings depicting the arts. The central dome was not completed until 1860.

DOORWAYS

Dublin is renowned for its Georgian doorways. Made of wood, often paneled and painted in bright colors, they are surrounded by a classical doorcase, flanked by columns, occasionally topped by small windows. The style of the capitals varies greatly. The entablature is crowned by a semi-circular fanlight; the extent and lavishness of its decoration gives some measure of the owner's imagination.

BALCONIES

Many of the Georgian terraces had elliptical wrought-iron balconies, adorned with classical motifs which were generally geometric (Greek borders) or floral (garlands, lyres, etc).

RUSSBOROUGH HOUSE ▲ 184

Like a long stage set, its façade stretching for 787 feet, Russborough was designed by Castle and Bindon around 1740 in the style of the Irish Palladian villas. The central block, with its portico crowned by a pediment, is slightly set back from the two shorter buildings which are linked to it by a colonnade. A court at each end is entered through a tall arch made of rusticated stone.

TOWNHOUSES

In the Dublin of the 1740's, huge stone residences were built, ushering in the neoclassical style. Rather than these few isolated buildings, however, the houses which belonged to the minor nobility were more typical of urban Georgian style: redbrick, four-story buildings with recessed doorways and windows whose proportions gradually altered. These houses were built in terraces, sometimes forming a square around a central park. They were often copied, on a more modest scale, in country towns.

Georgian decoration is characterized by an abundance of ornaments, made of stone or wood for architectural embellishment and stucco for interiors. Stuccowork, already being practiced as early as 1620, reached the height of its popularity in the 18th century, with high-reliefs depicting human figures, festoons, garlands and other *putti*, introduced by the Swiss Lafranchini brothers. In the middle of the century, Robert West nudged stuccowork toward a Rococo style, teeming with fruit, flowers, and birds. Later, Michael Stapleton returned to more understated bas-reliefs: dancing figures for friezes, garlands, urns and cameos.

Wooden furniture was often carved with naturalistic floral motifs.

Georgian ornamentation displayed countless details borrowed from classical architecture: Greek borders, palmettes, rosettes linked by garlands and bucraniums.

Bas-relief human figures often depicted mythological subjects.

Rococo stuccoworkers liked to use swirling plant-like volutes for high-reliefs.

Oval cameos were also extremely popular and depicted portraits or full-length figures inspired by mythology. They were flanked on either side by garlands, thereby forming a continuous motif, extremely popular in the 1770's.

Among the most characteristic motifs of the Georgian style were lion heads, with drapery, rosettes and all types of garlands.

Ireland
as seen by painters

| 1 | 2 |

| 3 |

The "English landscape" was invented in the 18th century: important landowners, no longer satisfied with building and restoring their houses, wanted to shape the countryside around them in equal measure. If painters were supposed to imitate nature, then landscape gardeners were supposed to imitate art. Influenced by Edmund Burke's theories of esthetics, GEORGE BARRET (1728/32–84) produced works reflecting both the sublime: *Stormy Landscape*; and the beautiful: *The Waterfall at Powerscourt* (1760) (**3**). PHILIP HUSSEY (1713–83) was reputedly a sailor before he became a painter, learning his second trade while working on the figureheads for sailing ships. His *Interior with members of a family* (around 1750) (**2**) depicts the salon of a bourgeois house, probably belonging to a family of the Ascendancy. The painting is directly related to the "conversation piece" genre: the portrait of a family or group of friends practicing the art of conversation in a salon or garden (as seen in the works of Francis Hayman and the young Gainsborough), especially in *The Grosvenor Family*. This is a group portrait for which everyone poses as if for a photograph a century or so later. This blend of social ostentation and outward simplicity can also be found, but in a more intense form, in *The Vere Foster Family* (**1**), painted by WILLIAM ORPEN (1878–1931) around 1907. The artist is unequivocally, and not without humor, quoting Gainsborough and the *Portrait of Mr and Mrs Andrews*: the hunting rifle held by the male protagonist is as much a social symbol as a realistic object. Unlike Gainsborough, however, Orpen only suggests the landscape. According to Bruce Arnold, his biographer, the work was unfinished and, indeed, the Foster family do seem to be posing in front of a studio backdrop. Orpen, gifted and worldly, spent more of his time living in London than in Ireland and, like Sir John Lavery, was carrying on the tradition, in the 20th century, of gaining a reputation as an artist by painting portraits of influential people in society. In 1902, in his play *Cathleen Ni Houlihan*, William Butler Yeats personified Ireland as an old beggar-woman transformed into a radiant young beauty when she finds a man who is prepared to die for her. Twenty years later, SIR JOHN LAVERY (1856–1941) painted a romantic picture of Cathleen ● *107*, lending her the features of his wife, Hazel, who was born in Chicago. The idea of using an American beauty to personify Ireland was rather controversial: however, it was given the official stamp of approval when she appeared on the bank notes of the Free State.

109

"Anyone who has not lived for weeks among these grey clouds and waters cannot understand my delight in laying eyes on the red garments worn by the women."

J. M. Synge

William Butler Yeats was fond of declaring that an artist's work must have a homeland. In painting *A Connemara Girl* (**1**), AUGUSTUS BURKE (1849–91) had, in his way, anticipated this belief. Possibly influenced by French painting, which throughout the 19th century had developed a rural theme (in the work of painters as different and as ill-matched as Rosa Bonheur, Jules Breton, Jules Sébastien-Lepage and above all Jean-François Millet and Camille Pissarro), Burke depicted the innocent beauty of a young girl with her goats, set against the backdrop of a sunset and a tranquil ocean. A vision? This painting shares similarities with the work of Puvis de Chavannes. The work of PAUL HENRY (1876–1958) evokes a completely different mood. Painting at the same time as Jack Butler Yeats, he devoted several sets of canvases to daily life in the west: *Launching the Currach* (**4**), *The Potato Pickers* (**2**), and *Connemara Landscape* (**3**) create strong, simple images. Too simple, in the eyes of his critics.

| 1 | 2 | 3 |

| 4 |

JACK·B·YEATS

One might be tempted to say of Jack Butler Yeats (1871–1957), son of John, the portrait painter (1839–1922), and younger brother of William (1865–1939) ▲ *284*, that he was in an ideal position to depict "Irishness" in art. For Jack, like Synge ▲ *123*, "Irishness" was to be found on the northwest coast. Jack exhibited his drawings of *Life in the West* in 1899 and Synge published *The Aran Islands* in 1907. Portraits of peasants, fishermen, scenes in the grocer's, or in court; pen-and-ink drawings, often enhanced by watercolors . . . . *Life in the West of Ireland* (1912) (**4**) contains a collection of pictures that must have seemed extremely exotic in Belfast or Dublin. In 1913, G.A. Birmingham published *Irishmen All* which Jack illustrated with a dozen or so portraits, executed in oils, of Irish "types"such as the priest, the politician, the publican, the pastor (**3**). The bold outlines of the characters and objects were set in representative landscapes. However, Yeats was not just concerned with producing an eye-witness account of reality. He made many sketches and placed great emphasis on the role of memory and imagination in his creative work. In the 1920's, Yeats' painting style became more flowing, his strokes became broader and the outlines disappeared, as can be seen, for example, in *The Island Funeral* (1923) (**2**). He gradually abandoned subjects taken from the west and focused his attention on Dublin, as can be seen in *The Liffey Swim* (1923) (**1**).

G. Courbet

In Trouville, in 1865, GUSTAVE COURBET met Johanna Hefferman, mistress of the Anglo-American painter, James Abbott McNeill Whistler, who had painted her in 1863 in *The White Girl*, now owned by the National Gallery of Art in Washington. *La Belle Irlandaise* (**1**, **2** detail) was given various titles: *Portrait de Jo, Femme irlandaise, Femme d'Irlande*. Ireland comes up every time: the young woman's beauty, like her red hair, whose luxuriance is emphasized by the gesture of her right hand, seems quintessentially "Irish". A woman at the mirror. Vanity? Anxiety? More metaphorically, searching for an identity? Several months later, Courbet painted his scandalous *Sommeil*: two naked women, intertwined. One woman is a brunette, the other a redhead. The "beautiful Irishwoman" again shows her face.

LUCIAN FREUD (born in 1922) is one of the leading names of London's art world. Herbert Read, the historian and art critic, has summed up this artist as being steadfastly representational, "the Ingres of Existentialism": a description that encapsulates both the artist's technical mastery and the atmosphere of anxiety exuded by his works. In *Two Irishmen* (**3**), two men strike a pose. Although this composition has an apparent solidity, it still knocks us off-balance: the man sitting down is painted from above, while the man standing up seems to be viewed from below, creating an off-center effect. One of them is looking straight at us, the other is not. An almost photographic view of the city can be seen through the window. Energy, melancholy, solitude. Terseness is also one of the characteristic features of Lucian Freud's art.

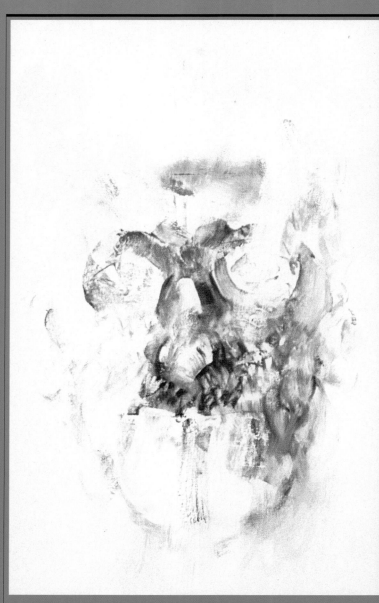

Louis Le
Brocquy (born
in Dublin in 1916) has
won international
acclaim after several
decades of unflagging
work on a sequence
of portraits of
legendary Irish
writers, including
William Butler Yeats,
James Joyce (above)
and Samuel Beckett.
An aggrieved
contingent will
protest that Irish
painting is still taking
a back seat to its
literature. What is
undeniable is that Le
Brocquy's "surreal"
portraits stay with the
observer. The art
critic Richard
Kearney has rightly
called attention to the
"insomniac" quality
of this painting. And
the poet John
Montague has
contributed the
observation that, in
its hypnotic
whiteness, the canvas
becomes a modern
"Saint Veronica's
veil". It is no longer a
portrait, it has
become an
apparition.

Ireland
as seen by writers

HISTORY

THE TUATHA DE DANAAN

There is a rich tradition of storytelling amongst the Celtic peoples of Ireland. Many have never been written down but are passed from generation to generation by word of mouth in the long, dark winter nights.

❝Long ago the Tuatha De Danaan came to Ireland in a great fleet of ships to take the land from the Fir Bolgs who lived there. These newcomers were the People of the Goddess Danu and their men of learning possessed great powers and were revered as if they were gods. They were accomplished in the various arts of druidry, namely magic, prophecy and occult lore. They had learnt their druidic skills in Falias, Gorias, Findias and Murias, the four cities of the northern islands.

When they reached Ireland and landed on the western shore, they set fire to their boats so that there would be no turning back. The smoke from the burning boats darkened the sun and filled the land for three days, and the Fir Bolgs thought the Tuatha De Danaan had arrived in a magic mist.

The invaders brought with them the four great treasures of their tribe. From Falias they brought Lia Fail, the Stone of Destiny. They brought it to Tara and it screamed when a rightful king of Ireland sat on it. From Gorias they brought Lugh's spear. Anyone who held it was invincible in battle. From Findias they brought Nuada's irresistible sword. No one could escape it once it was unsheathed. From Murias they brought the Dagda's cauldron. No one ever left it hungry.

Nuada was the king of the Tuatha De Danaan and he led them against the Fir Bolgs. They fought a fierce battle on the Plain of Moytura, the first one the Tuatha De Danaan fought in a place of that name. Thousands of the Fir Bolgs were killed, a hundred thousand in all, and among them their king, Eochai Mac Erc. Many of the Tuatha De Danaan died too, and their king, Nuada, had his arm severed from his body in the fight.

In the end the Tuatha De Danaan overcame the Fir Bolgs and routed them until only a handful of them survived. These survivors boarded their ships and set sail to the far-scattered islands around Ireland.

When the Fir Bolgs had fled, the Tuatha De Danaan took over the country and went with their treasures to Tara to establish themselves as masters of the island.❞

MARIE HEANEY, *OVER NINE WAVES*
A BOOK OF IRISH LEGENDS,
PUB. FABER AND FABER, LONDON AND BOSTON, 1994

ON THE IRISH

Strabo (c. 63 BC–after AD 21), the Greek geographer, historian and philosopher, never actually visited Britain but gleaned his information from the writings of Caesar.

❝Besides some small islands round about Britain, there is also a large island, Ierne, which stretches parallel to Britain on the north, its breadth being greater than its length. Concerning this island I have nothing certain to tell, except that its inhabitants are more savage than the Britons, since they are man-eaters as well as heavy eaters, and since, further, they count it an honourable thing, when their fathers die, to devour them, and openly to have intercourse, not only with the other women, but also with their mothers and sisters; but I am saying this only with the understanding that I have no trustworthy witnesses for it; and yet, as for the matter of man-eating, that is said to be a custom of the Scythians also, and in cases of necessity forced by sieges, the Celti, the Iberians, and several other peoples are said to have practised it.**

STRABO, *GEOGRAPHY*, TRANS. H.L. JONES,
LONDON AND NEW YORK, 1930

THE IRISH DIET
English traveler Fynes Moryson (1526–1617) was horrified by the standard of food he encountered.

Touching the Irish dyet, Some Lords and Knights, and Gentlemen of the English-Irish, and all the English there abiding, having competent meanes, use the English dyet, but some more, some lesse cleanly, few or none curiously, and no doubt they have as great and for their part greater plenty then the English, of flesh, fowle, fish, and all things for food, if they will use like Art of Cookery. Alwaies I except the Fruits, Venison, and some dainties proper to England, and rare in Ireland. And we must conceive, that Venison and Fowle seeme to be more plentiful in Ireland, because they neither so generally affect dainty foode, nor so diligently search it as the English do. Many of the English-Irish, have by little and little been infected with the Irish filthinesse, and that in the very cities, excepting Dublyn, and some of the better sort in Waterford, where the English continually lodging in their houses, they more retaine the English diet. The English-Irish after our manner serve to the table joynts of flesh cut after our fashion, with Geese, Pullets, Pigges and like rosted meats, but their ordinary food for the common sort is of Whitmeates, and they eate cakes of oates for bread, and drinke not English Beere made of Mault and Hops, but Ale. At Corck I have seene with these eyes, young maides starke naked grinding of Corne with certaine stones to make cakes thereof, and striking of into the tub of meale, such reliques thereof as stuck on their belly, thighes and more unseemely parts. And for the cheese or butter commonly made by the English Irish, an English man would not touch it with his lippes, though hee were halfe starved; yet many English inhabitants make very good of both kindes. In Cities they have such bread as ours, but of a sharpe savour, and some mingled with Annisseeds, and baked like cakes, and that onely in the houses of the better sort.

FYNES MORYSON, *AN ITINERARY, VOLUME III*,
PUB. JAMES MACLEHOSE AND SONS, GLASGOW, 1908

A WELL-EATEN CHILD IS BETTER THAN TWO UNDERFED
Born in Ireland of English parents, Jonathan Swift (1667–1745) departed for England following his ordination. Forced to return to Ireland in search of a better situation he finally accepted a position at St Patrick's Cathedral, Dublin. Forerunner of Joyce for his love of words and creative use of the English language, Swift is one of the great satirists. His novel "Gulliver's Travels" was published in 1726. The administration of Ireland by the English provided a perfect target and in the following extract Swift offers blackly ironic solutions to the problems of poverty and overpopulation in Ireland following the famine.

**I have been assured by a very knowing American of my acquaintance in London, that a young healthy Child well Nursed is at a year Old a most delicious nourishing and wholesome Food, whether Stewed, Roasted, Baked, or Boiled; and I make no doubt that it will equally serve in a Fricasie, or a Ragoust.
I do therefore humbly offer it to publick consideration, that of the Hundred and twenty thousand Children, already computed, twenty thousand may be reserved for

Breed, whereof only one fourth part to be Males; which is more than we allow to Sheep, black Cattle, or Swine, and my Reason is, that these Children are seldom the Fruits of Marriage, a Circumstance not much regarded by our Savages, therefore, one Male will be sufficient to serve four Females. That the remaining Hundred thousand may at a year Old be offered in Sale to the Persons of Quality and Fortune, through the Kingdom, always advising the Mother to let them Suck plentifully in the last Month, so as to render them Plump, and Fat for a good Table. A Child will make two Dishes at an Entertainment for Friends, and when the Family dines alone, the fore or hind Quarter will make a reasonable Dish, and seasoned with a little Pepper or Salt will be very good Boiled on the fourth Day, especially in Winter.

I have reckoned upon a Medium, that a Child just born will weigh 12 pounds, and in a solar Year, if tolerably nursed, encreaseth to 28 Pounds.

I grant this food will be somewhat dear, and therefore very proper for Landlords, who, as they have already devoured most of the Parents seem to have the best Title to the Children.**99**

JONATHAN SWIFT, *SATIRES AND PERSONAL WRITINGS*, PUB. OXFORD UNIVERSITY PRESS, LONDON, 1958

JAMES JOYCE'S IRELAND

A GENTLE APOCALYPSE

James Joyce (1882–1941) is one of the most important writers of our times. He revolutionized the form and structure of the novel and pushed language to extreme limits. Although he left Dublin in 1902, only returning sporadically thereafter, Ireland remained his major inspiration. "Dubliners" is a collection of short stories which did not appear until 1914 because the publishers were worried about potential libel actions. "Ulysses", first published in 1922, was immediately hailed as a work of genius.

66A few light taps upon the pane made him turn to the window. It had begun to snow again. He watched sleepily the flakes, silver and dark, falling obliquely against the lamplight. The time had come for him to set out on his journey westward. Yes, the newspapers were right: snow was general all over Ireland. It was falling on every part of the dark central plain, on the treeless hills, falling softly upon the Bog of Allen and, farther westward, softly falling into the dark mutinous Shannon waves. It was falling, too, upon every part of the lonely churchyard on the hill where Michael Furey lay buried. It lay thickly drifted on the crooked crosses and headstones, on the spears of the little gate, on the barren thorns. His soul swooned slowly as he heard the snow falling faintly through the universe and faintly falling, like the descent of their last end, upon all the living and the dead. **"**

JAMES JOYCE, *DUBLINERS*,
PUB. ALFRED A. KNOPF INC.,
NEW YORK, 1991

"I was thinking of so many things he didnt know of Mulvey and Mr Stanhope and Hester and father and old captain Groves and the sailors playing all birds fly and I say stoop and washing up dishes they called it on the pier and the sentry in front of the governors house with the thing round his white helmet poor devil half roasted and the Spanish girls laughing in their shawls and their tall combs and the auctions in the morning the Greeks and the jews and the Arabs and the devil knows who else from all the ends of Europe and Duke street and the fowl market all clucking outside Larby Sharons and the poor donkeys slipping half asleep and the vague fellows in the cloaks asleep in the shade on the steps and the big wheels of the carts of the bulls and the old cattle thousands of years old yes and those handsome Moors all in white and turbans like kings asking you to sit down in their little bit of a shop and Ronda with the old windows of the posadas glancing eyes a lattice hid for her lover to kiss the iron and the wineshops half open at night and the castanets and the night we missed the boat at Algeciras the watchman going about serene with his lamp and O that awful deepdown torrent O and the sea the sea crimson sometimes like fire and the glorious sunsets and the figtrees in the Alameda gardens yes and all the queer little streets and pink and blue and yellow houses and the rosegardens and the jessamine and geraniums and cactuses and Gibraltar as a girl where I was a Flower of the mountain yes when I put the rose in my hair like the Andalusian girls used or shall I wear a red yes and how he kissed me under the Moorish wall and I thought well as well him as another and then I asked him with my eyes to ask again yes and then he asked me would I yes to say yes my mountain flower and first I put my arms around his yes and drew him down to me so he could feel my breasts all perfume yes and his heart was going like mad and yes I said yes I will Yes. **"**

JAMES JOYCE, *ULYSSES*,
PUB. EVERYMAN'S LIBRARY,
LONDON, 1992

IRISH LANDSCAPES

THE LAKE ISLE OF INNISFREE

W.B. Yeats (1865–1939) was born and brought up in Dublin and remained an ardent Irish nationalist throughout his life. He was a senator of the Irish Free State from 1922–8, and in 1923 he was awarded the Nobel Prize for literature.

❝I will arise and go now, and go to Innisfree,
And a small cabin build there, of clay and wattles made:
Nine bean-rows will I have there, a hive for the honey-bee,
And live alone in the bee-loud glade.

And I shall have some peace there, for peace comes dropping slow,
Dropping from the veils of the morning to where the cricket sings;
There midnight's all a glimmer, and noon a purple glow,
And evening full of the linnet's wings.

I will arise and go now, for always night and day
I hear lake water lapping with low sounds by the shore;
While I stand on the roadway, or on the pavements grey,
I hear it in the deep heart's core.**❞**

W.B. YEATS, "THE LAKE ISLE OF INNISFREE"
FROM "THE ROSE", *THE POEMS*, PUB.
EVERYMAN'S LIBRARY, LONDON 1992

DRUMCLIFF CHURCHYARD

Although he died in the south of France, Yeats' body was brought back to Ireland for burial in Drumcliff. Heinrich Böll (1917–85) visited Ireland during the mid 1950's and went in search of his grave.

❝As the train entered Sligo it was still raining; kisses were exchanged under umbrellas, tears were wept under umbrellas; a taxi driver was asleep over his steering wheel, his head resting on his folded arms; I woke him up; he was one of those pleasant people who wake up with a smile.

'Where to?' he asked.

'To Drumcliff churchyard.'

'But nobody lives there.'

'Maybe,' I said, 'but I'd like to go there.'

'And back?'

'Yes.'

'All right.'

We drove through puddles, empty streets; in the twilight I looked through an open window at a piano; the music looked as if the dust on it must be an inch thick. A barber was standing in his doorway, snipping with his scissors as if he wanted to cut off threads of rain; at the entrance to a movie a girl was putting on fresh lipstick, children with prayer books under their arms ran through the rain, an old woman shouted across the street to an old man: 'Howya, Paddy?' and the old man shouted back: 'I'm all right – with the help of God and His most blessed Mother.'

'Are you quite sure,' the driver asked me, 'you really want to go to Drumcliff churchyard?'

'Quite sure,' I said.

The hills round about were covered with faded ferns like the wet hair of an aging red-haired woman, two grim rocks guarded the entrance to this little bay: 'Benbulbin and Knocknarea,' said the driver, as if he were introducing me to two distant relations he didn't much care about.

'There,' said the driver, pointing to where a church tower reared up in the mist; rooks were flying round the tower, clouds of rooks, and from a distance they looked like black snowflakes. 'I think,' said the driver, 'you must be looking for the old battlefield.'

'No,' I said, 'I've never heard of any battle.'

'In 561,' he began in a guide's mild tone of voice, 'a battle was fought here which was the only one every fought in all the world on account of a copyright.'

I shook my head as I looked at him.

'It's really true,' he said; 'the followers of St. Columba had copied a psalter belonging to St. Finian, and there was a battle between the followers of St. Finian and the followers of St. Columba. Three thousand dead – but the king decided the quarrel; he said: 'As the calf belongs to every cow, so the copy belongs to every book.' You're sure you don't want to see the battlefield?'

'No,' I said, 'I'm looking for a grave.'

'Oh yes,' he said. 'Yeats, that's right – then I expect you want to go to Innisfree too.'

'I don't know yet,' I said; 'wait here, please.'

Rooks flew up from the old gravestones, circled cawing around the old church tower. Yeats' grave was wet, the stone was cold, and the lines which Yeats had had inscribed on his gravestone were as cold as the ice needles that had been shot at me from Swift's tomb: 'Cast a cold eye on life, on death. Horseman, pass by!' I looked up; were the rooks enchanted swans? They cawed mockingly at me, fluttered around the church tower. The ferns lay flat on the surrounding hills, beaten down by the rain, rust-colored and withered. I felt cold.

'Drive on,' I said to the driver.

'On to Innisfree then?' 'No,' I said, 'back to the station.'

Rocks in the mist, the lonely church, encircled by fluttering rooks, and three thousand miles of water beyond Yeats' grave. Not a swan to be seen. 99

HEINRICH BÖLL, *IRISH JOURNAL*, TRANS. L VENNEUITZ,
PUB. SECKER & WARBURG, MCGRAW-HILL BOOK CO., NEW YORK, 1967

THE ARAN ISLANDS

John Millington Synge (1871–1909) went to the Aran Islands following a suggestion by Yeats, in order to write about the peasant lifestyle there. He visited annually from 1898 to 1902 and his book on the islands was first published in 1907.

66 The rain has cleared off, and I have had my first real introduction to the island and its people.

I went out through Killeany – the poorest village in Aranmor – to a long neck of sandhill that runs out into the sea towards the south-west. As I lay there on the grass the clouds lifted from the Connemara mountains and, for a moment, the green undulating foreground, backed in the distance by a mass of hills, reminded me of the country near Rome. Then the dun top-sail of a hooker swept above the edge of the sandhill and revealed the presence of the sea.

As I moved on a boy and a man came down from the next village to talk to me, and I found that here, at least, English was imperfectly understood. When I asked them if there were any trees in the island they held a hurried consultation in Gaelic, and then the man asked if 'tree' meant the same thing as 'bush', for if so there were a few in sheltered hollows to the east.

They walked on with me to the sound which separates this island from Inishmaan – the middle island of the group – and showed me the roll from the Atlantic running up between two walls of cliff.

They told me that several men had stayed on Inishmaan to learn Irish, and the boy pointed out a line of hovels where they had lodged, running like a belt of straw round the middle of the island. The place looked hardly fit for habitation. There was no green to be seen, and no sign of the people except these beehive-like roofs, and the outline of a dun that stood out above them against the edge of the sky.

. . . In spite of the charm of my teacher, the old blind man I met the day of my arrival, I have decided to move on to Inishmaan, where Gaelic is more generally used, and the life is perhaps the most primitive that is left in Europe.

I spent all this last day with my blind guide, looking at the antiquities that abound in the west or north-west of the island.

As we set out I noticed among the groups of girls who smiled at our fellowship – old Mourteen says we are like the cuckoo with its pipit – a beautiful oval face with the singularly spiritual expression that is so marked in one type of the West Ireland women. Later in the day, as the old man talked continually of the fairies and women they have taken, it seemed that there was a possible link between the wild mythology that is accepted on the islands and the strange beauty of the women.**

J.M. SYNGE, *THE ARAN ISLANDS*,
PUB. MAUNSEL & ROBERTS LTD,
DUBLIN AND LONDON, 1921

RELIGION

IRISH PROTESTANTISM

George Bernard Shaw (1856–1950) was a freethinker, whose unorthodox views mingled with his humor and love of paradox, made him an institution in his lifetime. He wrote over fifty plays and a number of essays and criticisms, and was awarded the Nobel Prize for literature in 1925.

❝I believe Ireland, as far as the Protestant gentry is concerned, to be the most irreligious country in the world. I was christened by my uncle; and as my godfather was intoxicated and did not turn up, the sexton was ordered to promise and vow in his place, precisely as my uncle might have ordered him to put more coals on the vestry fire. I was never confirmed; and I believe my parents never were either. Of the seriousness with which English families took this rite I had no conception; for Irish Protestantism was not then a religion: it was a side in political faction, a class prejudice, a conviction that Roman Catholics are socially inferior persons who will go to hell when they die and leave Heaven in the exclusive possession of Protestant ladies and gentlemen. In my childhood I was sent every Sunday to a Sunday-school where genteel little children repeated texts, and were rewarded with cards inscribed with them. After an hour of this we were marched into the adjoining church (the Molyneux in Upper Leeson Street), to sit round the altar rails and fidget there until our neighbors must have wished the service over as heartily as we did. I suffered this, not for my salvation, but because my father's respectability demanded it. When we went to live in Dalkey we broke with the observance and never resumed it.

What helped to make 'church' a hotbed of all the social vices was that no working folk ever came there. In England the clergy go among the poor, and sometimes do try desperately to get them to come to church. In Ireland the poor are Roman Catholics (Papists my Orange grandfather called them). The Protestant Church has nothing to do with them. I cannot say that in Ireland in my time there all the Protestants were the worse for what they called their religion. I can only answer for those I knew.❞

GEORGE BERNARD SHAW, *SIXTEEN SELF SKETCHES*,
CONSTABLE AND COMPANY LTD, LONDON, 1949

A WEDDING AND A FUNERAL

Edna O'Brien was born in Tuamgraney, County Clare, in 1932, and her novels are imbued with a nostalgic and lyrical image of her homeland. Her male characters are often treacherous but the abused heroines retain a warmth and sense of celebration that is intrinsically Irish.

❝There was much speculation about the wedding. No one from the village had been invited but then that was to be expected. Some said that it was to be in a Register Office in Dublin but others said that the bank clerk had assured the Parish Priest that he would be married in a Catholic church, and had guaranteed a huge sum of money in order to get his letter of freedom. It was even said that Miss Amy was going to take instruction so as to be converted but that was only wishful thinking. People were stunned the day the bank clerk suddenly left. He left the

125

bank at lunchtime, after a private talk with the Manager. Miss Amy drove him to the little railway station ten miles away, and they kissed several times before he jumped on to the moving train. The story was that he had gone ahead to make the plans and that the Connor girls and their father would travel shortly after. But the postman who was a Protestant said that the Major would not travel one inch to see his daughter marry a Papist. . . . **99**

66The funeral was to an island on the Shannon. Most of the people stayed on the quay, but we, the family, piled into two rowboats and followed the boat that carried the coffin. It was a jolty ride with big waves coming in over us and our feet getting drenched. The island itself was full of cows. The sudden arrivals made them bawl and race about, and I thought it was quite improper to see that happening, while the remains were being lowered and buried. It was totally desolate, and though my aunt sniffled a bit, and my grandmother let out ejaculations, there was no real grief and that was the saddest thing.

Next day they burned his working clothes and threw his muddy boots on to the manure heap. Then my aunt sewed black diamonds of cloth on her clothes, on my grandmother's and on Joe's. She wrote a long letter to her son in England, and enclosed black diamonds of cloth for him to stitch on to his effects. He worked in Liverpool in a motor car factory. Whenever they said Liverpool I thought of a whole mound of bloodied liver, but then I would look down at my watch and be happy again and pretend to tell the time. The house was gloomy. I went off with Joe who was moving hay and sat with him on the moving machine and fell slightly in love. Indoors was worst, what with my grandmother sighing, and recalling old times, such as when her husband tried to kill her with a carving knife, and then she would snivel and miss him and say 'The poor old creature, he wasn't prepared. . .'**99**

EDNA O'BRIEN, "THE CONNOR GIRLS" AND "MY MOTHER'S MOTHER" FROM *RETURNING*, PUB. PENGUIN BOOKS, LONDON, 1983

THE FEAST OF CORPUS CHRISTI
Born in County Monaghan, Patrick Kavanagh (1905–67) worked as a farmer for several years before he became established as a poet and journalist. His theme is often the discrepancy between the idealized view of the Irish peasant and the reality.

66The Catholic Church of Dargan was a building like a barn – a common rectangle, with a square belfry at the north gable; the church was scaling its mortar rough-casting and its pink wash was almost faded white. The roof span was wide and the roof timbers rotten so that only people with a strong faith in God's goodness-to-His-own would risk sitting in the centre aisle. The centre aisle was always packed, which proved that both faith and piety abided in the parish of Dargan. Standing on a rise in the middle of a weedy graveyard above the village with its shops and new dance hall the church looked shabby, but God would surely over-look this apparent disrespect in the blaze of the people's devotion. There were faith and piety and all the richness of human character that goes with a deep faith in the Hereafter. Father Daly said first Mass on the Feast of Corpus Christi. The chapel was crowded, for as well as being a Feast day of importance, on which the Faithful were exhorted to receive Holy Communion, this day was also the big summer fair day in the neighbouring town, and many of the congregation had business in the town and by coming to early Mass were able to serve both God and Mammon. The doors and windows were open, but still the place was stuffy with that morning closeness which comes before people are acclimatised to summer. Outside the door a group of men stood whispering while the less solemn parts of the Mass were being said. These men stared about them at the rolling country of little hills and commented on the crops, the weather, the tombstones or whatever came into their dreaming minds.

'Very weedy piece of spuds, them of Mick Finnegan's.'

'He doesn't put on the dung, Larry: the man that doesn't drive on the dung won't take out a crop.' A pause, 'nothing like the dung.'**

PATRICK KAVANAGH, *TARRY FLYNN*, PUB. THE PILOT PRESS LTD, LONDON, 1948

IRISH CHARACTERS

FAMILY

John McGahern was born in Dublin in 1934 and brought up in the west of Ireland.

**I came by train at the same time in July as I'd come every summer, the excitement I'd always felt tainted with melancholy that it'd probably be the last summer I would come. . . . All the meadows had been cut and saved, the bales stacked in groups of five or six and roofed with green grass. The Big Meadow beyond the beeches was completely clean, the bales having been taken in. Though I had come intending to make it my last summer at the hay, I now felt a keen outrage that it had been ended without me. Rose and my father were nowhere to be seen.

'What happened?' I asked when I found them at last, weeding the potato ridge one side of the orchard.

'The winter feeding got too much for us,' my father said. 'We decided to let the meadows. Gillespie took them. He cut early – two weeks ago.'

'Why didn't you tell me?'

My father and Rose exchanged looks, and my father spoke as if he was delivering a prepared statement.

'We didn't like to. And anyhow we thought you'd want to come, hay or no hay. It's more normal to come for a rest instead of just to kill yourself at the old hay. And indeed there's plenty else for you to do if you have a mind to do it. I've taken up the garden again myself.'

'Anyhow, I've brought these,' I handed Rose the box of chocolates and bottle of scent, and gave my father the watch.

'What's this for?' He had always disliked receiving presents.

'It's the watch I told you I'd get in place of the old watch.'

'I don't need a watch.'

'I got it anyhow. What do you think of it?'

'It's ugly,' he said, turning it over. . . .

I went idly toward the orchard, and as I passed the tar barrel I saw a thin fishing line hanging from a part of the low yew branch down into the barrel. I heard the ticking even before the wrist watch came up tied to the end of the line. What shocked me was that I felt neither surprise nor shock.

I felt the bag that we'd left to steep earlier in the water. The blue stone had all melted down. It was a barrel of pure poison, ready for spraying.

I listened to the ticking of the watch on the end of the line in silence before letting it drop back into the barrel. The poison had already eaten into the casing of the watch. The shining rim and back were no longer smooth. It could hardly run much past morning. **99**

> JOHN MCGAHERN, "THE GOLD WATCH"
> FROM *HIGH GROUND*, PUB. FABER AND
> FABER LTD, LONDON, 1985

MRS FITZGERALD

Virginia Woolf (1882–1941) stayed at the Dunraven Arms Hotel in Adare on May 3, 1934, and she described the character of the landlady in her diary, as follows:

66I wd like to describe the perfection of Irish conversation, which was Mrs FitzGerald's last night. She is exactly the great French lady – only living in a black jersey on an Irish bog. After dinner she came in, ostensibly to lend us a paper & offer advice, in fact to indulge her genius for talk. She talked till 11, & wd. willingly be talking now: about hotel keeping, about frigidaires, about her grandmother sitting on a chair in the kitchen & saying Thats done that wants another 2 minutes & so on, never stirring herself but somehow getting it done. We have the name of being good housekeepers. Then on about bogs, she has bought several fragments because now there may be money in it. However I can give no notion of the glowing, yet formed sentences, the richness & ease of the language; the lay out, dexterity & adroitness of the arrangement. There was the story of old Julia the cook, who had gone off home in a huff jealous of the young maids; had her daughter & the London husband on her, bought them gramophone records, & now wont own that she has wasted her savings. Mrs F. is one of those bluntnosed parted haired Irishwomen with luminous brown eyes & something sardonic and secretive in her expression. Talk is to her an intoxicant, but there is as Mr Rowlands said, something heartless about the I[Irish]: quite cold indifferent sarcastic, for all their melody, their fluency, their adorable ease & forthcomingness. She was very much on the spot, accurate, managing, shrewd, hard headed, analytic. Why arent these people the greatest novelists in the world? – with this facility, this balance, this fundamental . . . But why isn't Mrs F. a great novelist? Certainly the salon survives at Glenbeith, the lust for talk, & finishing one's sentence – only with complete naturalness. For instance, explaining the bogs, 'saturated, now whats the opposite word?' Dessiccated, L. suggested, & she adopted it with pleasure. She said one could never understand the Irish: one had to live as they did. They sit in their cottage talking about politics: they dont dance much; they have no amusements. They at once started to poach on her bog merely because she had bought it – otherwise it had been let alone for centuries. The bogs are full of trees, cant be self planted, so orderly, but now who has planted them? And they burn in a resinous way – go up – puf! – in a flash, like petrol. Suddenly she became severe and thought me a fool 'What does this good lady mean?' Her grandmother was an innkeeper; she herself went away for 25 years; Oh, as my grandmother said, one becomes able to read peoples characters before they step over the door, & ones never wrong one way or the other. Her quickness was amazing. This morning the talk began & L. very slightly put out his hand. ' Oh I know that means you wanting to be off' – & so we parted from the last representative of the French salon of the 18th Century, this strange mixture of county lady, peasant, & landlady. **99**

THE DIARY OF VIRGINIA WOOLF,
VOLUME FOUR 1931–1935,
ED. ANNE OLIVIER BELL, ASSISTED BY
ANDREW MCNEILLIE,
PUB. HARCOURT BRACE JOVANOVICH, NEW
YORK AND LONDON, 1982

MOTHER

Brian Friel, playwright and short-story writer, here has one of his characters, Eamon, describing their mother.

❝She was an actress. Did you know that? No, you didn't – that little detail was absorbed into the great silence. Yes; travelling round the country with the Charles Doran Company. Spotted by the judge in the lounge of the Railway Hotel and within five days decently wed and ensconced in the Hall here and bugger poor aul' Charles Doran who had to face the rest of rural Ireland without a Colleen Bawn! And a raving beauty by all accounts. No sooner did Yeats clap eyes on her than a sonnet burst from him – 'That I may know the beauty of that form' – Alice'll rattle it off for you there. Oh terrific stuff. And O'Casey – haven't they told you that one? – poor O'Casey out here one day ploughterin' after tennis balls and spoutin' about the workin'-man when she appeared in the doorway in there and the poor creatur' made such a ramstam to get to her that he tripped over the Pope or Plato or Shirley Temple or somebody an smashed his bloody glasses! The more you think of it – all those calamities – Chesterton's ribs, Hopkins's hand, O'Casey's aul' specs – the County Council should put up a sign outside that room – Accident Black Spot – shouldn't they? Between ourselves, it's a very dangerous house, Professor.**❞**

BRIAN FRIEL, *ARISTOCRATS*, PUB. GALLERY PRESS, 1983

JARS OF PORTER

Brian O'Nolan (1911–66), alias Flann O'Brien , worked for the Irish civil service in Dublin. "At Swim-Two-Birds", his first novel, published in 1939, mixes Irish folklore and farce with a realistic portrayal of lower-middle-class life.

❝It was only a few months before composing the foregoing that I had my first experience of intoxicating beverages and their strange intestinal chemistry. I was walking through the Stephen's Green on a summer evening and conducting a conversation with a man called Kelly, then a student, hitherto a member of the farming class and now a private in the armed forces of the King. He was addicted to unclean expressions in ordinary conversation and spat continually, always fouling the flowerbeds on his way through the Green with a mucous deposit dislodged with a low grunting from the interior of his windpipe. In some respects he was a coarse man but he was lacking in malice or ill-humour. He purported to be a medical student but he had failed at least once to satisfy a body of examiners charged with regulating admission to the faculty. He suggested that we should drink a number of *jars* or pints of plain porter in Grogan's public house. I derived considerable pleasure from the casual quality of his suggestion and observed that it would probably do us no harm, thus expressing my whole-hearted concurrence by a figure of speech.

Name of figure of speech: Litotes (or Meiosis).

He turned to me with a facetious wry expression and showed me a penny and a sixpence in his rough hand.

I'm thirsty, he said. I have sevenpence. Therefore I buy a pint.

I immediately recognized this as an intimation that I should pay for my own porter. The conclusion of your syllogism, I said lightly, is fallacious, being based on licensed premises.**

FLANN O'BRIEN, *AT SWIM-TWO-BIRDS*,
PUB. MACGIBBON & KEE, LONDON, 1966

THE THINKING IRISH

Brendan Behan (1923–64) is the controversial, nationalist enfant terrible of Irish literature. He was arrested in 1939 for his involvement with the IRA and describes his period in Borstal in "Borstal Boy" (1958). In the following speech, his character, Cronin, condemns English and American prejudice against the Irish.

**My wife tries to cheer me up by saying that girls like me – that she loves me. But then she is my wife. I mean, I don't mean that she just loves me because a wife is supposed to love her husband. Ah no! My wife is a very, very, exceptional person, and she is very kind to everyone, and particularly to me.

But I'll tell you something for nothing. There's a lot of nonsense given out by the English and Americans about our attitude to women. They say it just to flatter themselves. Some old Jesuit in America attacks the Irish for not screwing early and often enough. A hundred years ago screwing and having kids was out of fashion and Paddy was being lambasted because he got married too soon, and had too many kids. It's like saying all Jews are capitalists because Rothschild is a capitalist, and all Jews are Reds because Karl Marx was a Jew – if they don't get you one way they get you another. If they don't get you by the beard they get you by the balls.

The English and Americans dislike only *some* Irish – the same Irish that the Irish themselves detest, Irish writers – the ones that *think*. But then they hate their own people who think. I just like to think, and in this city I'm hated and despised. They give me beer, because I can say things that I remember from my thoughts – not everything, because, by Jesus, they'd crucify you, and you have to remember that when you're drunk, but some things, enough to flatter them.**

BRENDAN BEHAN, *RICHARD'S CORK LEG*,
PUB. EYRE METHUEN, LONDON, 1973

GRIEVING WOMEN

The plays of Sean O'Casey (1880–1964) deal with the dangers of Irish nationalism. When "The Plough and the Stars" was performed at the Abbey Theatre in 1926, it provoked riots. In the following speech from "Juno and the Paycock", his character has just heard of the shooting of her Republican son Johnny.

66Me home is gone now; he was me only child, an' to think that he was lyin' for a whole night stretched out on the side of a lonely counthry lane, with his head, his darlin' head, that I ofen kissed an' fondled, half hidden in the wather of a runnin' brook. An' I'm told he was the leadher of the ambush where me nex' door neighbour, Mrs. Mannin', lost her Free State soldier son. An' now here's the two of us oul' women, standin' one on each side of a scales o' sorra, balanced be the bodies of our two dead darlin' sons. (*Mrs. Madigan returns, and wraps a shawl around her.*) God bless you, Mrs. Madigan . . . . (*She moves slowly towards the door*) Mother o' God, Mother o' God, have pity on the pair of us! . . . O Blessed Virgin, where were you when me darlin' son was riddled with bullets, when me darlin' son was riddled with bullets! . . . Sacred Heart of the Crucified Jesus, take away our hearts o' stone . . . an' give us hearts o' flesh! . . . take away this murdherin' hate . . . an' give us Thine own eternal love!99

SEAN O'CASEY, *JUNO AND THE PAYCOCK*,
PUB. MACMILLAN LONDON LTD, LONDON, 1972

THE STRAND AT LOUGH BEG
Seamus Heaney was born in County Derry in 1939. His poems combine a strong physical sense of the environment with wider social and political concerns.

66Leaving the white glow of filling stations
And a few lonely streetlamps among fields
You climbed the hills towards Newtownhamilton
Past the Fews Forest, out beneath the stars –
Along that road, a high, bare pilgrim's track
Where Sweeney fled before the bloodied heads,
Goat-beards and dogs' eyes in a demon pack
Blazing out of the ground, snapping and squealing.
What blazed ahead of you? A faked road block?
The red lamp swung, the sudden brakes and stalling
Engine, voices, heads hooded and the cold-nosed gun?
Or in your driving mirror, tailing headlights
That pulled out suddenly and flagged you down
Where you weren't known and far from what you knew:
The lowland clays and waters of Lough Beg,
Church Island's spire, its soft treeline of yew.99

SEAMUS HEANEY, "THE STRAND AT LOUGH BEG" FROM *FIELD WORK*,
PUB. FABER AND FABER LTD, LONDON AND BOSTON, 1979

FIRST LOVE
Samuel Beckett (1906–89) was born at Foxrock, near Dublin, but spent most of his life in France. His plays and novels feature a distinctive, despairing tone with sharp use of black humor, and his work was enormously influential on English theater in particular.

66I met her on a bench, on the bank of the canal, one of the canals, for our town boasts two, though I never knew which was which. It was a well situated bench, backed by a mound of solid earth and garbage, so that my rear was covered. My flanks too, partially thanks to a pair of venerable trees, more than venerable, dead, at either end of the bench. It was no doubt these trees one fine day, aripple with all their foliage, that had sown the idea of a bench, in someone's fancy. To the fore, a few yards away, flowed the canal, if canals flow, don't ask me, so that from that quarter too the risk of surprise was small. And yet she surprised me. I lay stretched out, the night being warm, gazing up through the bare boughs interlocking high above me, where the trees hung together for support, and through the drifting cloud, at a patch of starry sky as it came and went. Shove up, she said. My first movement was to go, but my fatigue, and my having nowhere to go, dissuaded me from acting on it. So I drew back my feet a little way and she sat. Nothing more passed between us that evening and she soon took herself off, without another word. All she had done was sing, beneath her breath, as to herself, and without the words fortunately, some old folk songs, and so disjointedly, skipping from one to another and finishing none, that even I found it strange. The voice, though out of tune, was not unpleasant. It breathed of a soul too soon wearied ever to conclude, that perhaps least arse-aching soul of all. The bench itself was soon more than she could bear and as for me, one look had been enough for her. Whereas in reality she was a most tenacious woman. She came back the next day and the day after and all went off more or less as before. Perhaps a few words were exchanged. The next day it was raining and I felt in security. Wrong again. I asked her if she was resolved to disturb me every evening. I disturb you? she said. I felt her eyes on me. They can't have seen much, two eyelids at the most, with a hint of nose and brow, darkly, because of the dark. I thought we were easy, she said. You disturb me, I said, I can't stretch out with you there. The collar of my coat was over my mouth and yet she heard me. Must you stretch out? she said. The mistake one makes is to speak to people. **99**

SAMUEL BECKETT, *FIRST LOVE*, PUB. CALDER & BOYARS, LONDON AND NEW YORK, 1973

RUNNING AWAY
The novels of Roddy Doyle (b. 1958) are set in contemporary Dublin.

66I got my atlas out of my bag. We hadn't used it much, only for learning the counties of Ireland so far. Offaly was the easiest one to remember because it was the hardest. Dublin was okay just as long as you didn't mix it up with Louth. With Fermanagh and Tyrone it was hard to remember which was which. I stared at the map of Ireland from the top to the bottom. There was nowhere I wanted to run away to, except maybe some of the islands. I was still going to do it though. You couldn't run away to an island; you had to sail or swim part of the the way. It wasn't like a game though; there were no rules you had to stick to. An uncle of mine had run away to Australia. I opened the map of the world in the middle of the atlas. There were places right in the middle that I couldn't read properly because the pages wouldn't flatten fully for me.

There were plenty of other places though.

I was serious. **99**

RODDY DOYLE, *PADDY CLARKE HA HA HA*, PUB. SECKER & WARBURG, LONDON, 1993

Itineraries in Ireland

▲ A restaurant in Galway.　　▼ Greengrocer's in Athlone (Co. Westmeath).

▼ Housefront, Mallow (Co. Cork).

ML. DORE

DELI. CAFE

▲ Coffeeshop in Kilkenny. ▼ Butcher's shop in Galway

▼ *Dan Foley's* pub, Annascaul (Co. Kerry).

▲ Countryside, Co. Cork.　　　　　　▼ Traditional turf cutting.

▼ Connemara Lough (Co. Galway).

Tower house, Castlecove (Co. Kerry). ▼ Roundstone in the heart of Connemara (Co. Galway).

Wicklow Mountains (Co. Wicklow).

▲ Giant's Causeway (Co. Antrim).

▼ Glens of Antrim (Co. Ant

▼ Antrim Coast (Co. Antrim).

▲ LEINSTER 176

DUBLIN-WEXFORD ▲ 176
1 DUBLIN ▲ 142
2 POWERSCOURT
3 WICKLOW MOUNTAINS
4 GLENDALOUGH
5 WICKLOW
6 ENNISCORTHY
7 WEXFORD
8 ROSSLARE HARBOUR
9 JOHNSTOWN CASTLE
DUBLIN-WATERFORD ▲ 182
10 KILDARE
11 RUSSBOROUGH HOUSE
12 CARLOW
13 KILKENNY
14 JERPOINT AB
15 NEW R

DUBLIN

▲ LEINSTER
DUBLIN – HISTORY

1 PHOENIX PARK **2** HEUSTON STATION **3** GUINNESS BREWERY **4** FOUR COURTS **5** CHRIST CHURCH **6** ST. PATRICK'S CATHEDRAL **7** DUBLIN CASTLE **8** PARNELL SQUARE

◆ **G** C1

THE DUBLIN ARMS
The city was awarded
its coat of arms in
1607 by Daniel
Molyneux, Ulster
King of Arms and
principal herald of
all Ireland. The shield
is decorated with
three castles, symbol
of the city since the
Middle Ages, and
held on either side
by female figures
(Law on the left and
Justice on the right).
The flowers beneath
their feet symbolize
hope and joy.
The arms bear the
motto *Obedientia
Civium Urbis
Felicitas* ("Happy
the city whose
citizens obey").
A modified
version of the
Lord Mayor's
arms, including
the sword and
mace used
for official
ceremonies,
appears on
many Dublin
street lamps.

EARLIEST ORIGINS

The first mention of a town on the
present site of Dublin comes from Ptolemy in
the year 140, who knew of it as Eblana. It is generally
accepted, however, that today's city has its origins in the small
Viking encampment established on the spot in 841. The tiny
village from which Dublin has developed was set overlooking
a lake, near the confluence of the Liffey and Poddle rivers,
and the dark turf-colored waters gave the town its present
name (derived from the Gaelic *dubh linn*, or "black water").

ANGLO-NORMAN INVASION

In 1170 the Vikings relinquished control of the city. Dublin
was besieged by Dermot MacMurrough, King of Leinster, and
Richard FitzGilbert de Clare, Earl of Pembroke, known as
"Strongbow" ● *49*. Henry II confirmed his claim to
sovereignty, and for the next 750 years Dublin was to remain
under British rule, with the castle ▲ *167* as the seat of power
and symbol of the crown.

UNDER THE STUARTS

Dublin bloomed under
Stuart rule, following the
Restoration. The Protestant
aristocracy (Ascendancy
▲ *52*) began a development
of the city's industries, and
many ambitious building
projects were launched.

OBEDIENTIA·CIVIUM·URBIS·FELICITAS

RECENT HISTORY

The 18th century was Dublin's Golden Age. The Ascendancy ● *52* was at its height. English architect James Gandon designed many Georgian buildings and the city's elegant squares appeared. After the Act of Union ● *52* Dublin went into decline, although a century later it revived to become the center of a growing Nationalist movement and a literary renaissance ● *67*, which encouraged the awakening of consciousness to the idea of an independent nation. At the end of the Civil War ● *63* came the historic moment when Dublin was made the capital of the new independent Ireland.

DUBLIN, IN THE FOOTSTEPS OF JAMES JOYCE ✪
Two days are required to visit Dublin, the high-tech capital that has been successively a Viking landing post, a Scandinavian fort, a pirate kingdom, the spearhead of the Anglo-Norman invasion, the citadel of British power in Ireland, the fleeting pride of the Ascendancy and finally the melancholy capital of a deposed kingdom and an amputated republic. Strolling on foot is the best way to discover the city, with one eye on the sidewalk to spot the embedded plaques that mark the spots immortalized by Joyce in Ulysses.

143

THE O'CONNELL STREET MONUMENTS
The wide street contains many statues. Along with O'Connell himself there are also monuments to William Smith O'Brien (1804–64), leader of the Young Ireland movement ● *58*, the trade unionist James Larkin (1876–1947) ● *53*, and Father Matthew, 19th-century advocate of the temperance movement. Further on stands the astonishing statue of Anna Livia, Joyce's personification of the Liffey, known to Dubliners themselves as "the Floozie in the Jacuzzi" because of the foaming fountain that pours over her. She was erected in 1988 on the site of the Nelson Pillar (below) that was blown up in 1966. At the far end of the street is the monument dedicated to Charles Stewart Parnell (1846–91), upon which are carved his unforgettable words "No man has a right to fix the boundary to the march of a nation."

Dublin is capital of the Irish Republic and accounts for one third of its entire population. The city is prosperous, unpretentious and young in spirit. Pubs proliferate: there are said to be more than six hundred, including some frequented by James Joyce (and his heroes), as well as other eminent literary figures. The city is divided in two by the dark waters of the River Liffey. On the north side lay the ancient city, while to the south the charitable institutions, the barracks and the prisons were found. Along the banks of the river stand the impressive buildings of James Gandon.

CUSTOM HOUSE

The building was designed by James Gandon. It is a masterpiece of Georgian design (1781–91), extending 375 feet alongside the Liffey, not far from Butt Bridge and in the shadow of the metal railway bridge. The attic storey of Custom House is adorned with a number of statues based on allegorical themes (such as Navigation, Industry, and Wealth), while the copper dome is crowned with a statue of Commerce. The building was set on fire by Republicans in 1921 ● *62*, but has since been restored to its original splendor. Today it houses government offices.

ABBEY THEATRE. W.B. Yeats ● *122* and Lady Gregory ▲ *247* wanted to create an Irish national theater and in 1904 they founded the Abbey. Not all new works went down well: in 1907 the public gave a poor reception to the premiere of Synge's *Playboy of the Western World*, shocked by its realism and anti-heroic attitude. In 1951 the theater went up in flames. It was not rebuilt until the 1960's.

O'CONNELL STREET

O'CONNELL BRIDGE. The bridge was rebuilt in 1880 and is unusual in being almost as wide as it is long. When it was first erected, between 1794 and 1798, it made O'Connell Street (first named Gardiner Mall, then Sackville Street) the most important street in Dublin.

Dublin's tribute to James Joyce, her errant son, seems to stand guard at the entrance to Earl Street North as it crosses O'Connell Street.

O'CONNELL STREET. A STATUE OF DANIEL O'CONNELL stands at the entrance to the street, work of sculptor John Henry Foley and unveiled at the reopening of the bridge in 1882. Erin (Ireland) is handing O'Connell a copy of the 1829 Act of Emancipation. The four winged Victories (some with clearly visible bullet holes from the 1916 Rising) symbolize Courage, Fidelity, Eloquence and Patriotism, the virtues attributed to O'Connell "the Liberator". Further up the street is the GENERAL POST OFFICE (G.P.O.), the last major public building to be constructed by Francis Johnston, completed in 1818. During the Easter Rising of 1916 ● *60*, the G.P.O. was used as the rebel headquarters and was seriously damaged, although the Ionic portico remained intact. Inside is a statue dedicated to the victims of 1916 depicting the death of Cú Chulainn, hero of Irish legend. On the base is the text of the Proclamation of the Irish Republic ● *54*, first read from the steps outside. Not far from the G.P.O. is ST MARY'S PRO CATHEDRAL (1815, John Sweetman), a Greco-Doric structure.

PARNELL SQUARE

Parnell Square, originally named Rutland Square, lies at the

elegant former heart of Dublin; the city center later moved south of the river ▲ *160*. In the middle of the square is the Garden of Remembrance, dedicated to all those who gave their lives in the struggle for Irish independence ● *54*.

ROTUNDA HOSPITAL. The first maternity hospital in the entire British Isles was created through the generosity and determination of Doctor Mosse, who was distressed by the conditions in which poor women had to give birth in Dublin. The hospital was ready for its first patients only five years after works began in 1752. The ROTUNDA ROOM, from which the hospital took its name, dates from 1764. The PILLAR ROOM, which was once a sumptuous ballroom, has now been incorporated into the modern teaching department. The gem of the hospital is the CHAPEL ★, with a delightful Baroque interior in the Bavarian or Austrian style, making it one the most exceptional places of worship in all Dublin. This marvelous hospital building is admired throughout the world for the elegant restraint and harmony of its architectural design.

FIRST MATERNITY HOSPITAL
In 1745 Doctor Bartholomew Mosse, an obstetric surgeon horrified by the terrible conditions in which poor women were forced to give birth, founded a little hospital in an old theater in George's Lane, now Fade Street. A little later Mosse realized that more space was needed. He bought four acres of land north of the Liffey and entrusted Richard Castle with the building of a new hospital. The architect based his design on a modified version of the Leinster House ▲ *160* plans, and the first stone was laid in 1752.

The Writers' Museum.

PRELUDE TO THE CIVIL WAR
In 1922, when Republicans hostile to the 1921 Anglo-Irish Treaty occupied the Four Courts, Michael Collins ● 63, ▲ 224 resorted to

force. He shelled the building from the opposite bank. By the time the rebels retreated, the building was on fire and a quantity of documents were burnt.

DUBLIN WRITERS' MUSEUM. Opened in 1991 at nos. 18–19 Parnell Square this little museum houses a collection of letters, first editions, photographs and memorabilia of the capital's great authors.
MUNICIPAL ART GALLERY. The gallery, founded in 1908 by the wealthy art collector Sir Hugh Lane (nephew of Lady Gregory ▲ 247), is housed in the former home of the first earl of Charlemont (built in 1762 using the Scottish architect Sir William Chambers). Sir Hugh Lane went down with the *Lusitania*, the boat torpedoed by the Germans on May 7, 1915 off the Irish coast ▲ 224. He had left his collection, mainly of paintings by French Impressionists such as Manet, Monet, Renoir, Courbet and Corot, to the "nation". But which nation? Ireland had not yet gained independence. After decades of bitter wrangling, the two governments eventually reached agreement in 1960, dividing the paintings equally and exchanging them every five years. The Municipal Gallery has also extended its collection with the addition of works by more recent Irish painters such as Jack B. Yeats, Paul Henry and Louis Le Brocquy ● 116.
MOUNTJOY SQUARE. In 1770, a substantial building project was begun at North Great George's Street. The fine town houses of Mountjoy Square were erected between 1772 and 1818. These residential squares north of the Liffey are justly famous; their Georgian splendor is now faded and neglected, but they have lost nothing of their grandeur.

NORTHEAST OF THE RIVER

FOUR COURTS. From the south bank of the Liffey there is a marvelous view of James Gandon's second great work (1786–1802). As its name suggests, the building once housed four courts: Exchequer, Common Pleas, King's Bench and Chancery. Today the building is the seat of Ireland's High Court and Supreme Court.

ST MICHAN'S CHURCH (Church Street). The present church was built in the 17th century on the site of a Viking shrine (1095) and still retains a tower from the earlier building. There is a fascinating crypt and a lovely early 18th-century organ, still with its original gilding, upon which Handel played during his visit to Dublin.

THE FOUR COURTS

THE CRYPT OF ST MICHAN'S CHURCH
The walls of the crypt absorb humidity and as a result corpses within do not decompose. The skin turns brown but remains supple. Among the mummies that lie here are the Sheares brothers, executed for their part in the 1798 rebellion ● 52, ▲ 171.

WHISKEY CORNER. This area, once redolent of Jameson ● 79, has sadly lost its heart since the giant Bow Street distillery closed its doors in 1972. Since 1980, the old warehouse has been converted into the company headquarters. Behind the old warehouse there is a museum to visit, Whiskey Corner, where the different stages of manufacture of this famous national beverage ● 78 are described.

FRUIT AND VEGETABLE MARKET (7, St Michan's Street). The market building was erected in 1892 to replace the many grubby market stalls that then traded in courtyards all over the city. Spencer Harty was the architect of the handsome construction in red and yellow brick. Over the main entrance on Mary's Lane there is an immense Dublin coat of arms ▲ 142.

ST MARY'S ABBEY. Founded in the 12th century, St Mary's was one of the most important monasteries in the region. It also housed a number of different institutions in a city that always lacked adequate public buildings, including the State Treasury and the National Archives. In the 16th century it was the seat of royal authority in Ireland and it was here that the Crown's representative, "Silken Thomas" FitzGerald ● 50, denied royal authority and began his failed rebellion against Henry VIII. Today the chapterhouse is virtually all that remains of the old abbey.

HENRY STREET AND MARY STREET. The two pedestrian streets are at the lively heart of commercial north Dublin. On MOORE STREET the lilting accents of street vendors fill the air. Their fruits, vegetables and flowers are generally displayed on overladen prams.

KING'S INNS. Looking along HENRIETTA STREET, King's Inns, designed by Gandon in 1795, stands at the end of a marvelous perspective of Georgian façades. Built to house the Dublin inns of court, it was eventually completed in 1817 by Henry Aaron Baker and Francis Johnston.

MOORE STREET MARKET
This depiction of the market is characteristic of the "stained-glass" effect particular to Michael Joseph Healy (1873–1941), a painter specializing in street scenes. On his return to Dublin from Florence in 1901, he joined Sarah Purser's group An Túr Gloine ("the glass tower") and perfected this style of recreating everyday scenes with great warmth of color and feeling.

147

COLLEGE GREEN

The site of this important crossroads and key Dublin landmark was once a Viking meeting place and burial ground. Today statues of two outstanding figures in Irish history look down upon the place: Thomas Davis (1818–45), poet and founder of the Young Ireland movement ● *58*, and the famous parliamentarian Henry Grattan (1746–1820).

BANK OF IRELAND. This was once the seat of parliament and the center of government until the passing of the Act of Union ● *52*. Having lost its former purpose, the building was sold to the Bank of Ireland for the modest sum of £40,000. It was designed in the Palladian style by the young Edward Lovett Pearce and begun in 1729. The prostyle Ionic portico on the southeast façade faces a square courtyard flanked by two semicircular wings. When Westmoreland Street was created James Gandon added a new Corinthian portico to the eastern façade, attached to Pearce's building by a circular windowless structure. The oak-paneled Lords' Chamber is open to visitors; in it hang tapestries illustrating the Battle of the Boyne ▲ *194* and the Siege of Derry ▲ *318*.

TRINITY COLLEGE. In 1591 Queen Elizabeth I decided to found a university in order to "civilize" the Irish and to protect them from "papist" influence. The great Protestant families began to send their sons there, rather than to England. The stern visages of two former graduates, Edmund Burke (1729–97), statesman and philosopher, and Oliver Goldsmith (1728–74), poet and dramatist, look down upon the students of Trinity as they strive to emulate such and other illustrious predecessors, who include Jonathan Swift ● *119*, Wolfe Tone ● *52*, Bram Stoker (1847–1912), author of *Dracula*, J.M. Synge ● *123*, and Samuel Beckett ● *131*. The LIBRARY was built between 1712 and 1732 by Thomas Burgh, and was the first of a number of grand building projects undertaken in the 18th century. Originally the library had three floors, but in 1857, Benjamin Woodward had the ceiling removed from the middle floor in order to create the magnificent LONG ROOM, 209 feet in length, with a high barrel-vaulted ceiling, in which were placed the *Books of Durrow*, *Kells* and *Armagh*, the most precious treasures in Trinity ▲ *150*. This old library building also holds 200,000 of the total of 3,000,000 books now in the Trinity College

BRIAN BORU'S HARP
This instrument is on show in the Long Room at Trinity College and known as "Brian Boru's harp". In fact it was made in the 15th century, about four centuries after Boru's death (he was murdered shortly after the Battle of Clontarf in 1014 ● *49*). The harp appears on Irish coins and also on the national coat of arms.

Library, which has been a Copyright Library since 1801.
There are several important Greek and Latin manuscripts,
Egyptian papyri, Irish works dating from the 16th and 17th
centuries, and a Shakespeare first edition. The university
buildings are a good illustration of Dublin architecture over
the centuries: Burgh's library represents the 18th; from the
19th century there is Woodward's Museum Building (one of
the most inspired Victorian buildings in the country); and
recent additions are the New Library
(1964–7) and the Arts Block (which
houses the Douglas Hyde Modern Art
Gallery, one of the rare innovative
artistic centers in the city), designed by
Paul Koralek.

in the Long Room.
The room is
decorated with a
series of writers' busts
in marble, and the
names of the library's
benefactors engraved
in gold letters. The
book conservation
center is also in here.

THE HEART OF COMMERCE

GRAFTON STREET. Dear to Dubliners
and a popular symbol of the city is
Molly Malone, whose statue can be seen
wheeling its barrow with determined
stride along Grafton Street, one the
smartest and also the prettiest shopping streets in Dublin.
There is music to be heard at all hours of the day and night,
from old Irish airs to hard rock ● *73*. With changing
tastes, many of the old cafés have disappeared, while
others have been assimilated into the modern face of
Dublin. This is true of BEWLEY'S ORIENTAL CAFÉ,
which has stood the test of time. It was founded
by a family of Quakers respectful of the old
traditions of trade (correct measures,
reasonable prices and good quality), and in its
time has been frequented by many famous
writers (Yeats, Shaw, Beckett, O'Casey,
Wilde, Joyce and Behan ● *117*). Bewley's is
still a much-loved meeting place.

MOLLY MALONE
"She died of a fever,
No one could relieve
her." It is said that
the ghost of Molly
Malone, itinerant fish
seller, still haunts the
streets of Dublin.

POWERSCOURT TOWNHOUSE (South
William Street). An elegant and extremely
popular shopping center has recently been
created in the house once occupied by
the Viscount Powerscourt, and built in
1771 by Robert Mack.

The earliest Irish manuscripts that survive today date from around the year 600. During the 5th and 6th centuries, scribes in Ireland had created their own script and particular style, apparently inspired by examples from Gaul, Spain, Italy and even as far away as North Africa. The scriptorium, where the writing and decoration was done, was an important place within a monastery. Scribes were trained from an early age and first practiced their art on waxed tablets or slates. The finest scribes continued to work until they were very old, as long as their eyesight remained good enough.

WRITING MATERIALS The most important tool was the quill pen, taken from a goose, crow or swan, which would be cut with a chisel edge so that contrasting downstrokes and upstrokes could be made. The inkhorn held black ink, made from oak gall or from a solution of soot.

The pigments used for decoration were made from minerals and vegetable-matter crushed to powder and bound with resin or egg-white and water. Manuscripts were written on vellum made from prepared skins of sheep, cow or goat.

For the finest manuscripts, vellum made from calf-skin was used because it had the finest surface. The vellum sheet sometimes had holes, perhaps as a result of the animal being diseased or infested with warble-fly larvae, or the poor treatment of the skins, but scribes and illuminators knew how to make imaginative use of these imperfections. The layout of the page and the lines for text were traced with a ruler and a metal or bone stylus. Grids and circles were delicately marked out on the vellum to prepare for the decoration.

MARCUS

IRISH MAJUSCULE SCRIPT

The style known as "Irish majuscule" is basically a Latin half-uncial script incorporating shapes derived from Roman cursive script. The bold Irish majuscule is seen in the Gospel manuscripts, the *Book of Durrow* and the *Book of Kells*.

MINUSCULE

For works of lesser importance, which might be smaller in size or written in Gaelic, a minuscule script was used which made it possible to get more text onto each sheet. It is also used in the *Book of Armagh*, a masterpiece of calligraphy.

SAINT COLUMBA'S MANUSCRIPT ▲ *295*

The first example of a decorated manuscript is a Latin psalter generally attributed to Saint Columba of Ireland and Scotland, who died in 597. The ornamentation is quite rudimentary. There is no interlace design, but many of the elements that were to become typical of Irish illuminated manuscripts are already in evidence. There are large decorated initials followed by a diminuendo bringing the letters down to normal size. The initials are outlined with red dots, Coptic in origin, and there are triangles with curved sides, Celtic spirals, Germanic zoomorphic forms and the Christian motif of a fish or dolphin carrying a cross.

Most of the great illuminated manuscripts are Gospels, with ornamentation unequaled in color, complexity and sophistication up to that time. In general, each Gospel starts on a right-hand page and is particularly richly ornamented. Opposite is what has come to be called a carpet-page, completely covered with an amazing variety of interlace, spiral and foliate designs and fantastic zoomorphic creations.

THE "BOOK OF DURROW"
(second half of the 7th century)
The earliest of these Gospels does not have a lot of decoration. Of the 496 pages only 11 are illuminated, but the quality of the decoration is exceptional. Apart from black, the colors are limited to red, yellow, green and brown. These are combined to create an exuberant fantasy of spirals, knots, curved patterns descended from "La Tène" Celtic designs and, on one page only (f⁰ 192v), animals showing a Teutonic influence.

Giraldus Cambrensis, describing a manuscript of the Gospels
decorated by Irish monks, wondered whether
it were not the work of angels.

**8TH- AND 9TH-
CENTURY GOSPELS**
The range of
decorative motifs
expanded early in the
8th century, as can be
seen from the
Lindisfarne Gospels
(*c.* 700), the *Book of
Lichfield* and the
Echternach Gospels.
The largest of these is
the *Book of MacRegol*
(14 inches by
11 inches), made at
Birr ▲ *201* before the
year 822. There is a
certain roughness in
the decoration, but it
is marvelously bold,
both in its script and
in its colors: brilliant
red, golden yellow,

apple green and a
vivid purple. Apart
from these especially
elaborate Gospels
there were also
smaller, more
functional books such
as the *Saint Gall
Gospels* and the *Book
of Dimma,* which has
remarkable stylized
portraits of the
Evangelists. Even in
the *Stowe Missal*
(*c.* 800) and the *Book
of Armagh* (807),
books that are not
specifically collections
of the Gospels, it is
always the first pages
from the Gospels
that have been
decorated.

The *Book of Kells* is the most splendid of all these great manuscripts, perhaps the most beautiful of all medieval manuscripts in the Western world. It was probably begun on the Hebridean island of Iona in the second half of the 8th century, and brought to Kells by monks fleeing the Viking raids.

TEAMWORK
Four illuminators and at least three scribes worked on the book. The skins of 170 cattle were needed to provide the vellum for its pages. There are over two thousand decorated large initials, each one different, and about forty pages are entirely covered with illuminations. Here the artists indulged their skill and imagination to the full. The decoration is not entirely abstract. There are also fine and sensitive portraits of the Evangelists and characters from the Gospels, some of them reminiscent of Byzantine icons and mosaics. The artists of the *Book of Kells* did not confine themselves to the traditional design; they accompanied the text with numerous animals and scenes from everyday life, depicted in minute detail.

INTERLACE

This remained the most dominant theme in the design of the carpet-pages. Originally a stylized representation of running water, for the Chaldaeans it was a symbol of fertility. In a Christian context it signified purification. The interlace designs transform into foliage, into the bodies of serpents and the heads of men and birds. The interlace pattern itself is neither a geometrical shape nor a natural growing form, nor again does it have zoomorphic or anthropomorphic qualities. The effect is all the more remarkable as it is in fact created by mathematical means using squares and circles. But these are softened by the introduction of a number of asymmetrical elements which give the impression of freehand work. The transformation of living beings depicted in these illuminations seems to have links with the magical metamorphoses and the fantastic experiences of the heroes of the Irish sagas.

EXOTIC COLORS

"The painters of Kells used reds from red lead and kermes from the pregnant body of a Mediterranean insect (*Kermococcus vermilio*); yellow from orpiment (yellow arsenic sulphide, which served as a substitute for gold), ox gall and yellow ochre; purples, mauves and maroons from a Mediterranean plant (*Crozophora tinctoria*); white from white lead; bright green from verdigris . . . blue from either the oriental plant indigo or the north European plant woad, and most extravagantly several other shades of blue from lapis lazuli."

Bernard Meehan

155

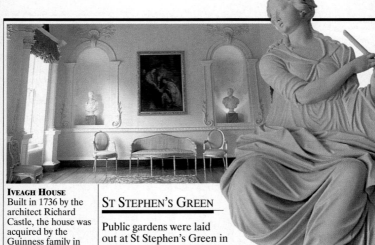

IVEAGH HOUSE
Built in 1736 by the architect Richard Castle, the house was acquired by the Guinness family in 1856. In 1919 the grandson of Arthur Guinness, who had become first Earl of Iveagh, renamed the house. He later gave it to the State.

Since then the foreign affairs department has been based in the house, which is closed to the public. Behind the austere façade are rooms decorated with stucco, wood bas-reliefs and sculptures. A Victorian ballroom was later added. The monumental staircase is an amalgam of 18th-, 19th- and 20th-century styles.

ST STEPHEN'S GREEN

Public gardens were laid out at St Stephen's Green in 1880, on what until 1663 was a piece of common land. Sir Arthur Guinness ▲ 170, the Dublin brewery owner, funded the project. The leafy paths make a delightful place to stroll or sit (see below), and it is much loved by all, from students to grandparents. Along the north side of the square ran what was known in the 18th century as "Beau Walk", an elegant place to stroll, see and be seen. Opposite stands the ever fashionable SHELBOURNE HOTEL (1867), the epitome of high-class gentility and still claiming to be "the best address in Dublin". It is worth peeping through the front doors for a glimpse of the delicate stucco decorations, some Rococo and others in the more classical Robert Adam style ● 106.

ROYAL COLLEGE OF SURGEONS. The building stands on the west side of the square. During the 1916 Easter Rising it was the headquarters of the Irish Citizens' Army, whose second-in-command was Constance Markievicz ▲ 286.

UNIVERSITY COLLEGE (NEWMAN HOUSE) (No. 86). The city's Catholic university has among its former graduates Pearse ● 61, De Valera ● 61 and Joyce ● 120. It was founded by Cardinal Newman to counterbalance the influence of Trinity College. The APOLLO ROOM is the most impressive: it is elaborately decorated with stuccos by the Lafranchini brothers, depicting Apollo and the nine muses (above). The UNIVERSITY CHURCH stands next to the College, an incredibly ornate Byzantine extravaganza, with an interior decorated in rich colored marble.

HARCOURT STREET AND DAWSON STREET

Two gracious Georgian thoroughfares lead from St Stephen's Green: Harcourt Street, which has a famous Gaelic bookshop at no. 6 (An Siopa Leabhar), and Dawson Street, where the best bookshops in Dublin are to be found.

MANSION HOUSE. The building was designed by Joshua Dawson (after whom the street was named) in 1710. It is decorated with massive Victorian cast-ironwork. Since 1715 the Mansion House has been the residence of the Lord Mayor. It was in the Round Room here, on January 21, 1919, that the Declaration of Irish Independence was ratified ● *62*.
ROYAL IRISH ACADEMY (19 Dawson Street). The academy was created in 1785 with the aim of encouraging science and learning. It is one of Europe's great scholarly institutions. The Ardagh Chalice, the Tara Brooch and the Cross of Cong were among the Academy's treasures, before they were donated to the National Museum ▲ *158*.

GEORGIAN DUBLIN

It was the English who gave Dublin the stately architectural flavor that it retains today. In the 18th century, they created the elegant squares and built graceful terraces of Georgian houses. The most fashionable districts developed to the south of the Liffey as a result of the influence of the Duke of Leinster.
KILDARE STREET CLUB. Benjamin Woodward built the premises between 1858 and 1861. For years the Club was the bastion of Dublin conservatism. Today a part of the building has been purchased by the State to house the Genealogical Office, conserving documents dating back to 1552 that were moved here in 1981 from Bedford Tower in Dublin Castle ▲ *167*. Here, too, is the State Heraldic Museum, where thousands of people come every year to trace their family origins.
NATIONAL LIBRARY. The library has a fine collection of first editions, old manuscripts, and works by Irish authors (Swift ● *119*, Goldsmith, Yeats ● *122*, Shaw ● *125*, Joyce ● *120* and Beckett ● *131*). There are also occasional exhibitions held here on native authors and their works.
NATIONAL MUSEUM ▲ *158*. Some of the greatest treasures of ancient Ireland are to be found here. The collection includes Celtic jewelry and Christian artefacts such as reliquaries and chalices. Two rooms are given over to a dramatic account of the events of 1916.

LEADEN BULLA
A heart-shaped lead bulla is conserved in the National Museum, one of five known in Ireland. Its origin and use remain a mystery, but it is known to date from the 8th century BC. It is a lump of lead, visible through scratches in its covering of gold leaf. Its design is a complex pattern of chevrons, triangles, crossed lines and concentric circles. Also in the museum is the Cross of Cong, an ancient and famous reliquary enclosing a fragment of the Holy Cross. The wooden center is covered with silver and gilt bronze engraved with animals, highlighted in gold.

The cross was kept at Cong until 1839, when it was brought to the museum.

157

The main attraction of the National Museum is its Irish antiquities, and in particular its collection of prehistoric gold jewelry (the finest in Europe of its kind) and early Christian treasures: chalices, brooches, crosses and reliquaries.

GOLD BOAT
(Broighter)
Discovered in Derry by a ploughman, it is part of a magnificent collection of treasure from the Celtic period. The boat is complete with all its equipment, and probably modeled on a large sailing vessel.

THE ARDAGH CHALICE
(early 8th century) The most famous treasure in the museum is one of the most exquisite examples of craftmanship to survive from the first millennium. The cup, the base and the handles are of beaten silver. The chalice has been embellished using the different metalworking techniques prevalent in Ireland at that time (filigree, enamel, engraving and embossing).

NECKLACE FROM GLENINSHEEN, County Clare, c. 800 BC.

"BREACH MAEDOG" (early 12th century) Three women saints are depicted on a tiny panel of this reliquary. Their appearance tells us much about the garments and hairstyles of the period.

THISTLE FIBULA (10th century)
The silver fibula takes its name from the resemblance of the decoration to thistle flowers. It is probably an example of a style of art developed to please the Vikings, who supplied the local artisans with metal.

LISMORE CROSIER (c. AD 1100)
The crosier-shrine is made from sections of gilded bronze covering a wooden cane. Pieces of blue glass decorated with red and white motifs are set into the bronze and there are also panels of zoomorphic interlace design, separated by inlays of millefiori glass. The ridge is formed by three fanged beasts.

THE TARA BROOCH (c. 8th century)
The brooch was found on the seashore at Bettystown, south of Drogheda. It is the most superb example of a penannular brooch: a large, richly decorated brooch worn on the shoulder with the pin pointing upward. It is of white bronze decorated with gold filigree and studded with amber and colored glass. On the face there are elaborate filigree interlace designs, with birds and beasts, while on the reverse there is intricate chasing, mainly of spiral patterns. Fixed to the side of the ring is a silver cord with a hinged and pivoting attachment decorated with the heads of wild beasts.

GOLD TORQUE (Broighter, 1st century BC)
The wide necklace is the finest example of the Irish goldsmiths' art, and a product of the "La Tène" period of Celtic civilization ▲ 151. It is unique in Europe, with a complex symmetrical design based on a floral motif. Similarities can be noted with the torque of the *Dying Gaul* in the Capitoline Museum in Rome.

A NEW FASHION
When James FitzGerald decided to build his house on the south side of the city he had many critics. But the Duke made a bold prediction that others would follow him. He was right: soon the aristocracy were all building their elegant Georgian residences in his preferred area.

They were to become the architectural pride of Dublin.

MERRION SQUARE
The square is lined with Georgian houses, and on one side stands the National Gallery. It is

now known as one of Dublin's finest squares, but it has not always enjoyed such a reputation. During the Famine ● 58 the central gardens were the site of one of Dublin's busiest soup kitchens.

LEINSTER HOUSE. In 1745 James FitzGerald, Earl of Kildare and future Duke of Leinster, asked the architect Richard Castle to build him the largest private residence in Dublin. The site he chose for his townhouse was on the southern outskirts of the city, virtually in the country. Today, Leinster House is the seat of the Dáil Éireann (Parliament) and of the Seanad Éireann (Senate).

NATURAL HISTORY MUSEUM. An amazing, old-fashioned museum containing fascinating skeletons of the Irish elk, a creature that became extinct ten thousand years ago.

NATIONAL GALLERY ▲ 162. The country's principal art collection has a wide range of works from the Irish school, giving a good overview. There are also a number of fine works by old masters (particularly Dutch and Italian). A new wing (1995) has now been added to the National Gallery, allowing many more works to be shown.

MERRION SQUARE. A colorful square, striking for its perfect architectural harmony. It is one of the finest groups of Georgian buildings in Dublin. The rich red brick, painted front doors, decorative fanlights and lacy wrought-ironwork have made it one of the sights of the city. Viscount Fitzwilliam of Meryon, eager to emulate the new fashion for elegant construction set by the Duke of Leinster with the building of his fine house, constructed a row of Georgian houses on Merrion Street. The charm of the district continued to attract newcomers, and over the years many well-known people have lived here: George Russell (no. 84), W.B. Yeats (nos. 52 and 82), Daniel O'Connell (no. 58), Sir William and Lady Wilde – the parents of Oscar – (no. 1: note the particularly delicate wrought-ironwork). Today the houses in the square have mainly been converted into offices.

EARLSFORT TERRACE. This building, begun in 1863, is in the classical style. Behind, in Coburg Gardens, is an amazing glass and metal structure originally intended as only temporary. It was built to house the Winter Garden opened for the International Exhibition of May 1865 where the latest scentific and artistic achievements of the age were on show. In 1908, after University College regained possession of the building, R.M. Butler altered it to give it its present appearance. When most of the university departments moved further south to Belfield, in 1974, the government decided to alter the interior to make a concert hall.

GEORGIAN SQUARES AND DOORS

In 1757 the Wide Streets Commission was set up, the first example of organized urban planning in Europe. Its role was to define practical and esthetic rules for building development. Other commissions were later given the responsibility for street paving and lighting. It was from this time that some of Dublin's grandest public buildings were erected, along with the stately Georgian squares. Close to Merrion Square, with its elegant fanlights and decorative door knockers, are Ely Place and Fitzwilliam Square (the smallest square in Dublin and, in 1825, the last to be built). They too have lovely Georgian architecture. Today the great families who once rivaled each other in the design and embellishment of their townhouses have moved out of the center of town. The Georgian houses were first divided into apartments and are now mostly converted into offices for the professions.

The fantastic success of the art exhibition mounted as part of the Irish Great Exhibition of 1853 was the catalyst for the creation of the National Gallery. At its opening in 1864 it had only 125 paintings. Today there are more than 13,000 works in all: 3,000 oil on canvas, 5,000 watercolors and drawings, and a great many prints, sculptures and other works of art. The range and quality of the collection of Old Masters, considering the meager funds available to the gallery, is proof of the generous donations that have been made. Sir Hugh Lane ▲ *146* (1875–1915) who was the director of the gallery until his death, bequeathed it works by Titian, El Greco, Chardin and Van Dyck. More recently the museum received a donation from Sir Alfred Beit of seventeen paintings by Gainsborough, Goya, Velazquez and Vermeer, and the Irish Jesuit Fathers donated a painting by Caravaggio (*The Arrest of Christ*). The National Gallery also has a vast collection of works by Irish artists (18th and 19th century).

PETER PAUL RUBENS
(1577–1640)
Paying Tribute
c. 1618
(**1**, detail) and (**5**)

CARAVAGGIO
(1573–1610)
The Arrest of Christ
c. 1602 (**2**)

PAOLO UCCELLO
(1397–1475)
Virgin and Child
c. 1440 (**3**)

FRANCISCO DE GOYA
(1746–1828)
Doña Antonia Zárata
c. 1805 (**4**)

| 1 |
| 2 |
| 3 | 4 | 5 |

REMBRANDT VAN RIJN
(1606–69)
*Rest on the Flight into
Egypt*
1647 (**1**, detail) and
(**4**)

JAMES BARRY
(1741–1806)
*Self-portrait as
Timanthes*
c. 1780 (**2**)

JOHANNES VERMEER
(1632–75)
Woman writing a letter
c. 1665 (**5**)

**THOMAS
GAINSBOROUGH**
(1727–88)
The Cottage Girl
1785 (**3**)

PROJECT ARTS CENTRE
(East Essex Street). This recently-opened center in the heart of Temple Bar favors work by contemporary artists and writers. It stages plays, concerts and exhibitions. Jim Sheridan, director of the films *My Left Foot* and *In the Name of the Father*, worked here.

TEMPLE BAR

HA'PENNY BRIDGE ★. A charming footbridge, and one of Dublin's popular landmarks. It was built in 1816 and given the official name of Liffey Bridge, but it soon gained its nickname from the halfpenny toll that had to be paid to cross it. The fine old metal structure has recently received the rather exaggerated embellishment of old-fashioned lamps.

TEMPLE BAR ★. The narrow street passing beneath Merchant's Arch leads into Temple Bar. This is now a fashionable district, but in the 1980's it was threatened with the ball and chain to make way for a vast bus terminal. Fortunately, the area has been improved instead, streets cobbled and the 18th-century houses saved. Temple Bar is now full of artists, designers and enthusiastic fledgling businesses, restaurants and cafés. The atmosphere is further enlivened by the colorful musicians, jugglers, acrobats and other street artists and entertainers who perform here.

THE MEDIEVAL CITY AND THE LIBERTIES

The Liberties are the oldest part of Dublin and are so named because they were built outside the city wall (a portion of which still remains). There are now granite stones set out to show the course of the old wall.

DAME STREET. The Dublin banking and business world has its center in this street of sturdy Victorian buildings. The only exception is Sam Stephenson's 1978 design for the Central Bank, which makes a striking contrast.

CITY HALL. The building was once the Royal Exchange and was the work of Thomas Cooley (1769). It is built in the Corinthian style, and is particularly impressive seen after dark, when it is illuminated. The twelve frescos that decorate the rotunda illustrate old legends of the city as well as episodes from the country's ancient history. The first Lord Mayor, Sir Daniel Bellingham, elected in 1665, gave Dublin the ceremonial mace and sword that are on show here.

DUBLIN CASTLE. The original castle was built by the Normans in the 13th century and for nearly seven and a half centuries it was the seat and symbol of English power in Ireland. Originally it stood on the southeast corner of the city's fortifications, surrounded by ramparts and a moat. This meant that the castle could be defended from an enemy attempting to take the town, as was the case with "Silken Thomas" in 1534

50. After two disastrous fires in 1670 and 1680 which destroyed a medieval hall on the west side of the courtyard, the castle was entirely rebuilt in the classical style between 1730 and 1800. As a result the UPPER YARD looks Georgian. Early in the 19th century the castle again underwent alterations, along with the BERMINGHAM TOWER on the southwest corner, this time in neo-Gothic style. The two north towers were only revealed during archeological excavations within the last decade, so they have fortunately remained unaltered. From the POWDER TOWER, which joined the castle to the city walls, it is now possible to visit earth fortifications from the Viking era. At the entrance to the castle stands the BEDFORD TOWER, its dome and sculptures being later embellishments by Van Nost. Today it leads into a conference center added in 1988. The south façade of the courtyard is mainly taken up by the state apartments, once the residence of the Viceroys, representatives of the British Crown in Ireland until independence ● 62. Groups are taken round the rooms, but they can be closed if important guests of state are being received. ST PATRICK'S HALL has a ceiling painted by the Italian Vincent Waldre. Other rooms are decorated in strong colors such as blue, yellow and green, and have a wealth of 18th-century stucco taken from Georgian houses in the city. The viceroy and the castle staff used to worship in the ROYAL CHAPEL (1807–14), which stands to the west of the RECORD TOWER. This is an elegant neo-Gothic construction designed by Francis Johnston. The exterior sculptures as well as most of the stucco inside were made by the Dubliner Edward Smith and his son John. At the main entrance to the castle stands a memorial to insurgents who died attacking the castle on Easter Monday 1916 ● 60.

TEMPLE BAR
The area considers itself to be at the forefront of cultural activity in Ireland today. *U2*, Ireland's internationally famous rock group, have bought up a number of buildings and turned them into theaters, concert halls, pubs and nightclubs.

"What counts for the visitor is the Dublin we bring to Dublin in our heads. We put that personal Dublin like a template over the real one and are more or less satisfied. . . . To hell with Dublin being Paris. Dublin has enough on its plate being the city of our imaginations."
      Thomas Keneally

STRONGBOW'S TOMB
Although said to
contain Strongbow,
leader of the Norman
knights who came to
conquer Ireland in
the 12th century, the
tomb dates from the
1340's.

ST WERBURGH'S CHURCH. This 18th-century church is closely bound up with the history of the FitzGerald family ● *50*: Lord Edward, who was wounded during his arrest for leading the 1798 rebellion ● *52*, is buried in the crypt. Ironically Major Henry Sirr, who defeated him, is buried in the churchyard of St Werbugh's.

CHRIST CHURCH CATHEDRAL. In 1038, Sitric Silkenbeard, the first Christianized Danish king to rule in Dublin, built a

simple wooden church within the city walls, calling it Christ Church of the Holy Trinity. With the arrival of the Normans, the building was replaced by a more substantial stone church. By the end of the 19th century the cathedral had fallen into such disrepair that drastic renovation work was needed. A large part of the medieval stonework had to be replaced, under the direction of George Edmund Street, and at the expense of the whiskey distiller Henry Roe. Further repairs were made in the 1980's. Fascinating details of the original Viking construction are still visible in the vaulted ceilings of the 12th- and 13th-century CRYPT (above). This is the most unusual and striking part of the building, unique in the entire British Isles for extending the length of the cathedral. There are a few remains of the Norman church, the city's most ancient stone building. Among them are the late Norman arches in the west bay of the chancel, resting on capitals carved with human figures and animals, and certain portions of the transept. In this cathedral the kings of Ireland came to pay homage to Richard II in 1394; James II stopped to hear mass here on his way to the Battle of the Boyne ▲ *194*, and William of Orange gave thanks afterward for having defeated him.

WOOD QUAY. The important archeological finds made in and around Christ Church make it clear that this was the heart of Viking and medieval Dublin. Sadly, despite bitter arguments, this did not prevent two tower blocks designed by Sam Stephenson being built here in 1986.

THE BRAZEN HEAD. The pub opened in 1688 and was the headquarters of Wolfe Tone's Society of United Irishmen ● *52* in the 1790's. Fifteen people were arrested here in one year. The desk of Robert Emmet, leader of the 1803 rising, is kept in the pub.

WOOD QUAY
No less than nine
quays have been
uncovered along the
stretch of river
between Wine Tavern
Street and Fishamble
Street. Some are very
primitive moorings,
but two are certainly
of Viking
construction, both
defensive. Also
discovered dating
from the same period
(around 1100) is part
of a stone wall that
probably encircled
the town. A
description of Dublin
given at the time of
the Norman invasion
of 1170 describes a
city wall with at least
two gates, a castle
and a keep. Finds
from excavations
made between 1962
and 1981 at Christ
Church Place, Wine
Tavern Street and
Wood Quay, are on
show in the National
Museum Annexe.
The sophistication of
these artefacts are
proof of a highly
civilized society:
boxes, combs carved
from bone and deer
antlers, scales with
sets of weights and
iron swords.

ST AUDOEN'S CHURCH. This medieval church has within its 12th-century tower the three oldest bells in Ireland (1423). There is a way into the church through the one remaining gate of the old city wall, on the corner of Cork Street.

TAILORS' GUILD HALL. The only guild hall left in Dublin was built in 1706. It has an assembly room with a musicians' gallery from which, in the 1790's, Wolfe Tone and Napper Tandy addressed the "Back Lane Parliament". Today Tailors' Hall is the headquarters of An Taisce, a national society dedicated to the preservation and restoration of old buildings.

ST PATRICK'S CATHEDRAL. Hostility toward the Christ Church authorities led Archbishop Henry de Londres to raise the nearby church of St Patrick's to the status of cathedral in 1213. In this rather unconventional way Dublin came to have two cathedrals. De Londres chose the Gothic style for the rebuilding of St Patrick's (1225–54). It is 330 feet in length, making it the longest medieval church in Ireland, and much of the stone carving was done by masons from the southwest of England. Part of their work can still be seen in the chancel. In the 19th century the building was in such a poor state that restoration was imperative; the money was provided by the brewer Sir Benjamin Guinness – inspiring Henry Roe to do the same for Christ Church. Guinness also commissioned his own statue to stand at the southwest porch. St Patrick's is now the cathedral of the Protestant Church of Ireland. It is famous also for having had Jonathan Swift (1667–1745) ● *119* as dean from 1713 to 1745. He is buried in the cathedral, at the foot of the second column on the right on entering the main doors, lying beside his beloved "Stella" (Esther Johnson).

MARSH'S LIBRARY ★. A delightful little library, still with three "cages" to enclose those who wished to study rare books. It was founded by Archbishop Narcissus Marsh, built in four years by Sir William Robinson, and opened in 1705 as the first public library in Ireland.

THE BRAZEN HEAD
The oldest pub in Dublin. It is claimed that a Viking inn once stood here.

BOYLE MONUMENT
(St Patrick's Cathedral) Richard Boyle, Earl of Cork, had the monument erected in 1632 to the memory of his wife, Catherine. It is decorated with painted figures, members of her family. Among the couple's children, bottom row, is the infant Robert Boyle (1627–91), physicist, later to formulate Boyle's Law on the pressure and volume of gases.

SIR ARTHUR GUINNESS (1725–1803)
On December 31, 1759, thirty-four-year-old Sir Arthur Guinness ● *156*, a confident young brewer, paid Mark Rainsford III £100, signed his name to a thousand-year lease at a rent of £45 a year and entered St James's Gate, his fate sealed. One of the world's great beers was about to be brewed for the first time.

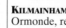

The brewery he had just leased consisted of a cooper's shop, a boiler, a mill, a malthouse, stabling for twelve horses and a loft for 200 tons of hay.

GUINNESS BREWERY
● **76.** The heavy, sweet smell of brewing has hung in the air around St James's Gate since 1759. It comes from the Guinness Brewery. Stout is one of the great Irish institutions, a smooth dark beer topped with a thick creamy band of foam. Its popularity never wains, and the brewery, one of the most famous in Europe, produces four million pints a day and exports more beer than any other brewery in the world. The factory covers 64 acres south of the Liffey and employs four thousand people. Adjoining it is a small museum where a film of the making of *Guinness* is shown, followed by the offer of a pint. Since it is said that *Guinness* doesn't travel well, this must be the best place in the world to drink it.

NATIONAL COLLEGE OF ART AND DESIGN. The college was founded nearly 250 years ago, but moved in the early 1980's from its old home in Kildare Street to John Power's abandoned distillery in Thomas Street. The buildings have been beautifully converted and the students have fitted in happily here, bringing some new life and enthusiasm to the district.

TOWARD PHOENIX PARK

KILMAINHAM HOSPITAL. Viceroy James Butler, Duke of Ormonde, representing King Charles II, initiated the building of the Kilmainham Royal Hospital in 1680. It was a military institution intended to take in wounded and veteran soldiers. It is an impressively simple and harmonious building fronted with colonnades around a central courtyard. Well restored between 1980 and 1984, in 1991 it was converted to house the Irish Museum of Modern Art.

The inner courtyard of Kilmainham prison.

Dray horses with their clopping hoofs, as well as wooden barrels and the coopers who made them, have all but disappeared from the city.

KILMAINHAM PRISON.

This prison is a powerful reminder of Ireland's struggle for independence. From 1796 onward it was frequently used to incarcerate political activists and many of the most famous figures of modern Irish history spent time here ● *52*. A great number were imprisoned after the 1798 rebellion of the United Irishmen, and it was from here that the Sheares brothers ▲ *147* were taken to be executed for their involvement.

Members of the Young Ireland movement were imprisoned here after the 1848 rebellion, as were the Fenians, after their unsuccessful attempt of 1867 and, in 1883, Land Leaguers (including Parnell and Davitt) filled the cells. Twenty-six of the Invincibles were imprisoned in Kilmainham in 1883; five of them were hanged and buried here. After the Easter Rising in 1916, the prison was packed with men and women who had taken part. Ninety-seven were court-martialled and condemned to death. In May 1916 sixteen men, among them the signatories of the Proclamation of the Irish Republic, were executed for treason (opposite page, bottom). In 1923 De Valera ● *63*, an opponent of the Treaty settlement ended up in Kilmainham with a number of his companions and was later liberated when the prison closed in 1924. After 1960 it was restored by volunteers, and is now open to visitors.

PHOENIX PARK. The park is nearly 2,000 acres in size and was once the grounds of a priory, taken to become royal hunting grounds in the 17th century, after the Reformation. The name Phoenix seems to be a corruption of the Gaelic *fionn uisce* ("clear water"). Among expanses of greenery stand the elegant residences of the Irish President, Aras an Uachtarain, formerly the Viceregal Lodge, and that of the American ambassador. To the south of the park, near the Parkgate Street entrance, is a garden of flowers called the People's Garden. Opposite stands a 200-foot obelisk, the Wellington Testimonial, erected in 1817. Not far from here are the Zoological Gardens, famed since 1857 for the birth of the first lion cubs to be bred in captivity.

LAST WISH
Robert Emmet (1778–1803) spent the night before his execution in Kilmainham prison. His words from the dock remained a challenge and reponsibility to those who followed him: "When my country takes her place among the nations of the earth, then and not till then let my epitaph be written."

MURDER IN PHOENIX PARK
In the spring of 1882, two key British politicians, Lord Cavendish and T.H. Burke, were assassinated there by an organization called the Invincibles. Although the struggles of the Land League to improve tenants' rights were at their height, this act of terrorism had little effect upon it.

Below left, Killiney Bay
(south of Dún Laoghaire).

THE SOUTHEAST

THE GRAND CANAL. Two canals were dug from Dublin in the late 18th century, the Royal Canal, which runs north of the city center, and the Grand Canal. The latter leads west to join the River Shannon ▲ *200* and south to join the River Barrow, so providing a means of transport for passengers and goods right across the country, to Limerick in the west and Waterford in the south. It was in commercial use until 1960. The Waterways Visitors' Centre, situated on the Grand Canal basin, recounts the history of the Irish inland water transport system.

CHESTER BEATTY LIBRARY (Shrewsbury Rd). The Oriental art and manuscripts in the library and gallery are among the finest in the world. It is, needless to say, one of the most important collections in Dublin. Alfred Chester Beatty (1875–1968) was an American who settled in the city in 1950, and was later made Ireland's first honorary citizen. He spent his large, self-made fortune on manuscripts, paintings, prints, scrolls, Korans and rare books (often with exquisite bindings) and furniture. His treasures came from Europe, India, the Middle East, China and Japan and the collection was left to the State. He also bequeathed some important canvases by painters of the Barbizon school, now hung in the National Gallery ▲ *162*.

CHESTER BEATTY LIBRARY
By 1905 Alfred Chester Beatty was already collecting 17th- and 18th-century Chinese snuff bottles. Today some nine hundred of them are on display in the Far Eastern section of the New Gallery, alongside jade books, rhinoceros-horn cups and two Chinese imperial robes. On the first floor is the Islamic collection,

including 270 Persian, Egyptian and Turkish Korans, some illuminated by great masters of calligraphy. The Garden Library, near the entrance, displays items from Western Europe, with prints by Dürer, Holbein and Piranesi, and also some precious illuminated works. Other items in the vast and varied collection are Babylonian clay tablets and Egyptian papyri.

DÚN LAOGHAIRE. The town (below), pronounced "Dunleary", is named after an ancient fortress built here in the 5th century by Laoghaire (Leary), King of Ireland. From a small fishing village it grew to become a busy port in the 18th century, through the growth of trade with England. From 1821 until 1920 it was called "Kingstown" in honor of George IV, who set sail from here in 1820. Today Dún Laoghaire is a popular residential district and seaside resort, as well as remaining an important terminal for ferries to Great Britain. As the main yachting center in Ireland, it has an attractive and lively harbor with plenty of stores and

restaurants. Behind the ROYAL MARINE GARDENS, in the
Moran Public Park, is the the former residence of the harbor
captain. From here, in 1898, Marconi transmitted one of his
earliest outdoor communications: a commentary on a
sporting event. The National Maritime Museum, in the old
Mariners' Church on Haigh Terrace, gives a good account of
Irish shipping history from its most primitive origins.

SANDYCOVE. Sandycove is probably best known for its
Martello tower ● *101* (1804). The English built a series of
these towers along the coast when fearing invasion by
Napoleon. The small, round fort with walls nearly 40 feet high
is also called JAMES JOYCE'S TOWER, because in 1904 the
writer spent a short time here and subsequently described it in
the first chapter of *Ulysses* ● *120*. In 1962 Sylvia Beach, who
had first published the novel in Paris, started the James Joyce
Museum here. Letters, documents, memorabilia, rare copies
and first editions are on show.

THE NORTHEAST

NATIONAL BOTANIC GARDENS. The property once belonged to
the family of the poet Thomas Tickell. The Royal Dublin
Society bought the estate and, in 1795, founded the Botanic
Gardens. Thomas Tickell's house is now the director's
residence. The celebrated essayist Thomas Addison may also
have lived in the area: certainly there is a yew walk called
"Addison's Walk". The Botanic Gardens cover some 50 acres
and contain a number of rare species of tree, shrub and other
plants. The Palm House was built by Richard Turner ▲ *302*, a
Dublin ironfounder who also made the greenhouses at Kew
Gardens. The property came into state ownership in the late
19th century, and the gardens are run by the Office of Public
Works.

"BLOOMSDAY"
On June 16 each year
Dublin celebrates
Bloomsday, Leopold
Bloom's day of
peregrination, as
described by James
Joyce in *Ulysses*
● *120*. On June 16,
1954, when Joyce was
still much
disapproved of in
Ireland, some writers
(among them Flann
O'Brien, Patrick
Kavanagh and Tom
Joyce) inaugurated
Bloomsday. Their
idea was to make a
sort of pilgrimage in
the footsteps of the
novel's characters.

The story goes that
they were in the end
unable to carry out
their good intentions
in full because a
number of the
obligatory stops were
Dublin pubs.
Bloomsday has
become a big event in
literary tourism, with
people dressed in
Edwardian costume
wandering the city,
bearing their copy of
Ulysses.

DUBLIN BAY PRAWNS
These are often enjoyed in a Dublin Bay prawn cocktail: cooked and peeled, they are steeped in white wine, covered in a well-peppered,

creamy sauce and surrounded by fresh, crisp lettuce.

MARINO CASINO ● *104*. An exquisite, miniature neoclassical villa (▲ *173*, top) designed by Sir William Chambers for the Earl of Charlemont, who laid the first stone in 1762. The attractive rooms within are beautifully proportioned. The gracious urns that decorate the roof are a disguise for chimneys. There are also some interesting underground passages. The influence of this building can be seen in the Customs House in Dublin ▲ *144* designed twenty years later by James Gandon, Chambers' pupil.

HOWTH. From Howth Head, at the end of the Howth Peninsula, there are views of Dublin and also the nearby village of Howth, with its steep streets and fine harbor. This is a popular place with Dubliners, and plenty of yachts lie alongside the busy fleet of fishing boats. A walk along the high cliff gives a breathtaking view of Dublin Bay and Lambay Island. The gardens of HOWTH CASTLE are particularly famous for their rhododendrons, which are a mass of purple flowers in May and June. Lady Emily St Lawrence, who planted them in 1850, had to have earth brought in to cover the slopes before putting them in. The species, *R. Ponticum*, is less popular now than other more colorful varieties, but it is one of the most hardy. Also in the gardens of the castle is an interesting TRANSPORT MUSEUM. A short walk further on is a CROMLECH, a Neolithic tomb dating from about 2000 BC. The huge stone slab is some 8 feet high and has been calculated to weigh 70 tons. Not surprisingly, it has gradually subsided over the ages.

IRELAND'S EYE. Just over a mile offshore from Howth Harbour (above right) lies a tiny rocky islet which has been made into a bird reserve. Excursions to Ireland's Eye leave from Dublin. On the islet can also be seen the restored remains of a 7th-century chapel (mentioned in a papal bull of 1179) and a Martello tower ● *101*.

MALAHIDE CASTLE (9 miles north of Dublin). In 1174 Henry II granted the land to the Talbot family and, apart from a few years of banishment at the time of Cromwell, they remained in residence until the

> "Delightful to be on the Hill of Howth, very sweet to be above its white sea; the perfect fertile hill, home of ships, the vinegrown pleasant warlike peak."

Anon. 14th-century, Irish poem trans. Kenneth Hurlstone Jackson

THE LEGENDS OF MALAHIDE CASTLE
Malahide Castle has the only medieval great hall still to exist in Ireland today. On the walls is an impressive collection of family portraits. It is said that fourteen Talbot cousins had breakfast here together before leaving for the Battle of the Boyne ▲ *194*. None of them returned. Another story concerns the carved Flemish panel of the *Coronation of the Virgin* in the Oak Room which supposedly disappeared when the Talbots were banished and mysteriously reappeared on their return to the castle.

mid 1970's. The Honorable Rose Talbot then had to sell the house, the 250 acres of land and most of the furniture and paintings that had been in her family for centuries. Fortunately, when Dublin County Council acquired the property they bought as much furniture as possible, to enable the visiting public to see the castle as it had been when the Talbots lived there. Over centuries of occupation the castle had been much altered. In the second half of the 18th century twin towers and a rampart were added. Today it is hard to tell that this was once a 15th-century defensive tower house. The interior, too, was redesigned in the 18th century, with Baroque-style plasterwork by Robert West and mantelpieces by the famous Italian craftsman Bossi. One of the rooms on the first floor, the Oak Room, still has its dark wood paneling dating from the 17th century, enlivened by some Dutch or Flemish pieces depicting the *Holy Virgin* and *Adam and Eve*. Irish paintings from the 18th century hang in the second-floor reception rooms, which have decoration from the Georgian period. Many of the works of art in the castle, particularly those in the medieval Great Hall, are portraits on loan from the National Gallery of Ireland ▲ *162*. There are thirty-one Talbot family members alone. The last Lord Talbot, Milo, left the property to his sister Rose. He was a diplomat but also a great gardener, and he brought many species of plant back from Tasmania where the family had another property. They can be seen in the gardens today.

FRY MODEL RAILWAY
A vast room has been constructed at Malahide Castle to accommodate the Fry Model Railway, a unique and detailed

NEWBRIDGE DEMESNE (North of Malahide, on the western edge of Donabate). The 320-acre estate has been a County Dublin regional park since 1986. The hillside pastures, gentle valleys, streams and woodland are delightful. NEWBRIDGE HOUSE itself is a fine neoclassical residence built in about 1737 for Rev. Charles Cobbe, who became archbishop of Dublin in 1746. The possession of such an agricultural estate in the 18th century would have permitted almost total self-suffiency. The Cobbe family archives going back to this period survive. They give a detailed picture of the day-to-day administration, incomings and outgoings of such an estate in Ireland at the time. There also survives a fascinating family Museum of Curiosities.

O-gauge layout (1:43). The miniature trains are reproductions of those dating from 1834 up to the present day, and there are also boats, trams and cars. They have taken Cecil Fry many years of dedicated enthusiasm to make.

PRETTY AS A PICTURE
Many films have been
shot in the stunning
and varied scenery
of this county so
convenient to Dublin.
The ruined tower
at Killincarraig
(between Delganny
and Greystones)
appears in the
opening scenes of
Stanley Kubrick's
Barry Lyndon. Part
of John Boorman's
Excalibur was filmed
around Bray,
Enniskerry and the
Wicklow Mountains
(Lough Tay); and
the combat between
Arthur and Lancelot
was shot at
Powerscourt waterfall.

The "Garden of
Ireland", County
Wicklow, is remarkable for the
beauty and variety of its landscape. The stark
outlines of the Wicklow Mountains contrast with rich,
abundant woodlands and lush green fields, at times ordered
into the geometrical shapes of a country-house garden. These
hidden valleys, wild gorges, dark lakes and dizzy waterfalls
have barely changed since Celtic and early Christian times.

SOUTH OF DUBLIN

BRAY. A Victorian seaside resort modeled on the English
town of Brighton. Handsome pastel-colored houses line the
seafront, which ends in the shadow of BRAY HEAD. From
the top there is a view over mountains, valley and sea. A
path leads along the cliff to Greystones, a similar resort.
POWERSCOURT DEMESNE ★. On the edge of the picturesque
village of Enniskerry lies this magnificent estate, named for
the Norman knight Eustace de la Poers. In 1609, James I
granted the property to Sir Richard Wingfield. A grand house
was built between 1731 and 1740, designed by Richard Castle
and modeled on the Palladian Villa Pisani near Venice.
Powerscourt is famed for its gardens, first laid out in the
18th century and probably designed by
Richard Castle. Their formality is
accentuated by the view over the

◆ **G** C1-C2-C3-B4

valley to the wild Great and Little Sugar Loaf mountains.
Daniel Robertson designed the upper terraces. In 1974 the
owners decided to open the house to the public and interior
renovations were carried out. During a lunch party to
celebrate these renovations a chimney caught fire; it was
thought the fire had been extinguished but later that night it
took hold and the owners narrowly escaped with their lives.
The entire top story was destroyed and only the walls remain.

WICKLOW MOUNTAINS

The massive granite outcrops, eroded over the centuries, are
wild and beautiful. J.M. Synge wrote: "I passed through a
narrow gap with high rocks on either side of it and fir trees
above them, and a handful of jagged sky filled with extraordinarily brilliant stars. In a few moments I passed out on
the brow of the hill . . . and smelt the fragrance of the bogs."
SALLY GAP. Passing through Glencree, join the old Military
Road leading past the deep lakes of Bray at the foot of Mount
Kippure to Sally Gap, a crossroads set between Djouce
Mountain to the east and Mullaghcleevaun to the southwest.
(There are now two possible routes to Glendalough.)
VIA ROUNDWOOD. Pass Lough Tay, where the valley sides
descend sharply to the deep waters, and the narrow Lough
Dan. The two are linked by the Cloghoge river. Roundwood
is the highest village in Ireland (768 feet). Stop at
Roundwood Inn before setting off up the Annamoe Valley.
VIA GLENMACNASS VALLEY. This carries along the Military
Road, alongside the spectacular Glenmacnass waterfall.

THE MILITARY ROAD
The English forged
this route into the
Dublin hinterland
to pursue rebels from
the 1798 rebellion,
who had taken refuge
in the Wicklow
Mountains. The
50 miles of road led
across the rugged hills
connecting a series
of military posts
whose ruins are still
visible (at Glencree,
Glenmalure, Laragh,
Drumgoff). It is a
good route by which
to explore Wicklow,
leading from the
outskirts of Dublin
to Aghavannagh.

St Kevin's Church.

THE TWO SAINTS OF GLENDALOUGH
Kevin (d. c. 618) was born into the royal House of Leinster but retired as a hermit to Glendalough. He had many disciples and he later founded what was to be an important monastery in the valley, becoming its abbot from 570. Despite being pillaged and burnt during the 9th and 10th centuries, the monastery remained a key religious and scholastic center. It was given a new lease of life in the 12th century by Laurence O'Toole (1128–80) who later became archbishop of Dublin, returning on occasion to Glendalough and the solitude of St Kevin's Bed. He was canonized in 1226.

Pilgrimage to Glendalough.

GLENDALOUGH ★

Set in a lonely valley beside two dark lakes, the monastic site of Glendalough (from the Irish, Gleann da Loch, meaning "Valley of the Two Lakes") was founded in the 6th century by Saint Kevin. Over nearly eight centuries the monastery was a flourishing religious center, surrounded by a large number of dependent dwellings, scriptoriums, an infirmary and a farm. Now only ruins remain, but Glendalough has lost none of its spiritual power. There is a Visitors' Centre which provides a good explanation of the site, and which also displays ancient crosses (including the 12th-century Market Cross) and tombstones that have been found there.

LOWER LAKE. The main buildings lie to the east of the Lower Lake, reached through a fortified gateway that was once two stories high (most unusual for its period). The ROUND TOWER, well over 100 feet high, probably dates from the 11th century. It is far taller than the other buildings and was a good landmark for approaching pilgrims as well as being a useful refuge in times of danger (as were the church and watch towers). The roof of the tower was reconstructed in 1876 using the original materials. ST MARY'S CHURCH and the CATHEDRAL are typical of early Irish churches: the former consists only of nave and chancel, the latter, which precedes it in date, has an unusual north doorway and a fine ornamental east window. The tiny PRIEST'S HOUSE has an exterior Romanesque arch and a carved lintel whose central figure is thought to be Saint Kevin. Priests were buried here during the suppression of Catholicism, hence its name. ST KEVIN'S CHURCH, also called St Kevin's Kitchen, has a steep corbeled stone roof and, making it unique in Ireland, a small round tower in addition. TRINITY CHURCH (near to the Laragh road) was once the same, but its tower collapsed in a storm in 1818.

There is another interesting Romanesque church among the trees, ST SAVIOUR'S (to the east, on Green Road), possibly built by Saint Laurence O'Toole. Note the decorations on the capitals of the chancel arch, including a serpent, a dragon and two crows holding a human head in their beaks.

UPPER LAKE. Along the walk between the car park and REEFERT CHURCH are five boundary crosses. The shrines around the Upper Lake were much revered, and a pilgrimage continued to be made here until 1862. The name Reefert comes from *rí fearta* ("tomb of the kings") because the kings of Leinster were buried here. Nearby are the remains of the Church of the Rock, or Teampull na Skellig, an ancient oratory mentioned in accounts of Saint Kevin's life.

TOWARD WICKLOW

DEVIL'S GLEN. The valley is steep and wooded. Through it the River Vartry rushes down a rocky bed to flow into the huge Devil's Punch Bowl. There are signed footpaths making it possible to admire the glen on foot.

MOUNT USHER GARDENS. Not far from Ashford is one of the finest parks in Ireland, Mount Usher Gardens (right). The gardens are famed for their immense variety of trees and exotic plants (more than four thousand species). On a nearby road stands Hunter's Hotel, one of the country's oldest coaching inns. Travelers have been welcomed here for over two hundred years.

WICKLOW. The county town is also a popular seaside resort overlooking a huge crescent-shaped bay. In Market Square stands a memorial honoring the Wicklow men who fought in the 1798 rebellion ● 52. On a cliff to the east of the town are the scant remains of BLACK CASTLE, dating back to the Norman invasion.

ACROSS THE VALLEYS

GLENMALURE. From Laragh, the Military Road leads to Glenmalure, the wildest valley in Wicklow and surrounded by mountains. Highest of all is Lugnaquillia, which at 3,039 feet is the tallest peak in the county. A nine-mile walk leads through the deep glen to Baravore.

VALE OF CLARA. Southwest of Glendalough a pretty road follows the Avonmore river to the village of Rathdrum, at the entrance to the Vale of Avoca.

GLENDALOUGH, AN ENCHANTED SPOT ✪
A Celtic retreat tucked away at the foot of the Wicklow Mountains, Glendalough overlooks the banks of two peaceful lakes. The forlorn ruins of its seven tiny churches lie scattered over the thick high grass that has enveloped the cemetery, eating away the tombstones and entwining the Celtic crosses and the round tower. A picnic by the edge of the lake is preferable to lunch in the packed hotel nearby.

TEMPTATION OF SAINT KEVIN
St Kevin's Bed is a deep ledge partly dug by hand into the rock face and set some 5 feet above the Upper Lake. It is said that the saint took refuge here to avoid the attentions of a young woman. One morning, finding her there beside him, he threw her into the lake.

"WICKLOW": THE ORIGIN OF THE NAME
"Wicklow" is derived from the Danish *Vikingalo* ("Viking field"), a strategically important 9th-century Viking encampment. The Irish name *Cill Mhantáin* refers to the church founded by Saint Mantan, who was said to be a disciple of Saint Patrick ● 56.

CHARLES STEWART PARNELL (1846–91)
Born to a Protestant family, in 1875 Parnell became Member of Parliament for County Meath giving his support to the cause of Home Rule. His leadership was most effective until the scandal broke of his liaison with Kitty O'Shea. Divorce proceedings instituted by her husband ruined Parnell's political career, and he died soon after, a broken man. Today he is celebrated as one of the heroes of Irish nationalism.

VALE OF AVOCA

AVONDALE HOUSE. The house is neoclassical in style and dates from the 18th century. It is filled with souvenirs of the politician Charles Stewart Parnell ● *53*, born here in 1846. The house is now a forestry school (set up by the English in 1904), and also contains Forestry Service offices. This would have pleased the former owner Samuel Hayes, who in 1794 wrote one of the first treatises on arboriculture and who planted the estate with trees native to Ireland. Today the forest has species from all over the world.

MEETING OF THE WATERS. The confluence of the the the Avonbeg and Avonmore, joining their waters in the River Avoca, has a magic that inspired the poet and composer of songs Thomas Moore to write the poem *The Meeting of the Waters* in 1807.

ARKLOW. The town was founded by the Vikings. It has lost its former importance as a port, and consequently its prosperity, but it retains its old reputation for yacht-building. There is a maritime museum, and visitors also come from Dublin to enjoy the beaches of Brittas Bay, to the north.

TOWARD WEXFORD

FERNS. The ruins of the imposing Anglo-Norman castle dating from the 12th and 13th centuries dominate the town, which was once the seat of the kings of Leinster. In one of the towers is a 13th-century chapel. Around the church of St Aidan are the remains of a 6th-century abbey.

ENNISCORTHY. The town has a history stretching back to the 6th century, when Saint Senan founded a church here. The 13th-century Norman castle, later rebuilt, overlooks the River Slaney. It houses the County Museum, a collection of photographs, documents and varied objects mainly relating to Enniscorthy's part in the 1798 rebellion and the 1916 Easter Rising ● *60*. The neo-Gothic cathedral of St Aidan was designed by Augustus Welby Pugin.

FERRYCARRIG ● *90*. The Irish National Heritage Park (left) gives an overview of nine thousand years of history through a number of reconstructions of ancient settlements and religious sites (*crannóg, rath*, monastery, Norman castle). A round tower was built here in 1857 in memory of those who died in the Crimean War.

WOODENBRIDGE GOLD RUSH
In the 18th century the village of Woodenbridge, five miles northwest of Arklow, was swamped by a rush for gold. Over a few months 2,600 ounces were found on Croghan Mountain. The largest nuggets are displayed in the National Museum, Dublin ▲ *158*.

WEXFORD. The capital of County Wexford stands on a site once occupied by a Belgian clan, and later by the Vikings (from the 9th to the 12th centuries) who founded the flourishing port of Waesfjord. The town was taken by Normans in 1169. Today it is known internationally for its Opera Festival, held annually in October. Near to Westgate Tower, the only one of five fortified gateways to remain, lie the ruins of SELSKAR ABBEY, scene of some important events: a treaty was signed here with the English in 1169; in 1172 Henry II did

> "Sweet vale of Avoca! How calm could I rest in thy bosom of shade, with the friends I love best, Where the storms that we feel in this cold world should cease, And our hearts, like thy waters, be mingled in peace."
>
> Thomas Moore

penance here after the murder of Thomas Becket; Strongbow's daughter married Raymond le Gros in Selskar in 1175. Cromwell destroyed the abbey in 1649 and massacred two hundred inhabitants of Wexford.

WEXFORD WILDFOWL RESERVE ■ *26.* For eight months of the year a large proportion of Greenland's white-fronted geese find peace on mud flats about 3 miles north of Wexford.

AROUND WEXFORD

JOHNSTOWN CASTLE. The estate belonged to the earls of Desmond in the 18th century. The vast 19th-century neo-Gothic building is now an agricultural college, and in the grounds is the Irish Agricultural Museum.

ROSSLARE. The town is a busy port, but also a popular seaside resort with a long and beautiful beach. There are ferries to Fishguard, Le Havre and Cherbourg.

TACUMSHIN. The village is encircled by Tacumshin Lake and Lady's Island Lake, lagoons surrounded by rich vegetation and renowned for their birdlife. There is a working windmill (below) dating from 1846.

KILMORE QUAY. A charming and genuine fishing village of thatched and white-walled cottages. *Guillemot*, an old lightship now moored along the quay, has been turned into a museum of the maritime history of Wexford.

SALTEE ISLANDS. The two uninhabited islands are Ireland's largest bird reserve, sheltering more than 220 of the 380 species known in the country. These include puffins, guillemots, razorbills, and gulls. The islands can be reached by boat from Kilmore Quay.

Scenes from the Irish Derby
run on the famous
Curragh racecourse

IRISH NATIONAL STUD
(Tully)
In 1943 the British

T he country roads that lead southwest from Dublin cross
the peaceful counties of Kildare, Carlow and Kilkenny,
passing huge dolmens, Norman castles, monasteries, celtic
crosses, medieval towns and fine country houses. Other
precious but little visited sites are to be found on the
borders of the three coastal counties of Wicklow, Wexford
and Waterford.

TOWARD KILDARE

CASTLETOWN HOUSE. At the foot of the Wicklow Mountains
▲ *177* stands the magnificent Castletown House, the first
Palladian villa to be built in Ireland. It was constructed
between 1722 and 1732 and designed
by the Florentine architect Alessandro
Galilei (1691–1737) and Englishman
Edward Lovett Pearce ▲ *148* for
"Speaker" William Conolly, Speaker
of the Irish House of Commons from
1715. In 1967 it was bought by Desmond
Guinness and later, in 1979, by the Irish
Georgian Society who undertook its
restoration and provided replacement
Irish furniture and paintings for any
originals that were missing. The central
block of the house is flanked by two
rounded and colonnaded wings. The
rooms are as they were in the 18th
century: the BROWN ROOM has pine
paneling and an unusual grooved
ceiling, and the LONG GALLERY ★ (left)
is decorated in a vivid blue Pompeian
style. The Rococo stucco on the staircase
walls was made by the much-admired
Lafranchini brothers ● *106*.

National Stud (once
the stud of Colonel
Hall Walker, and
given to the State in
1915) became the
Irish National Stud.
A museum traces the
history of the horse in
Ireland, and includes
among its display
items the skeleton
of Arkle, one of the
greatest racehorses
of the 20th century.
Hall Walker, later
Lord Wavertree, was
considered fairly
eccentric: he was not
interested in a foal
unless its star chart
was favorable.
Perhaps the nearby
Japanese gardens
that he had laid out
in 1904 were also
intended to have a
positive effect on
his youngstock.

NAAS. The town was once the capital of the kings of Leinster
and is at the center of a region famous for its horse-breeding.
Much horseracing takes place in the vicinity, in particular at
PUNCHESTOWN, 3 miles southwest of the town. Races here in
1868, graced by the presence of the Prince of Wales, drew a
crowd of 150,000 people. The meetings continue to be
popular.

KILDARE. The town grew up around a monastery founded
in the 5th century by Saint Brigid. It is said that she kept a
sacred fire burning in her church. It remained alight through
the Viking raids, but was extinguished at the beginning of
the 13th century on the orders of the archbishop of Dublin.
Shortly afterward the fire was relit, to burn until the
Reformation. ST BRIGID'S CATHEDRAL dates from the 13th
century but it was much restored in the 19th. There is an
interesting primitive font in the nave.

EMO COURT DEMESNE ● *104*. The estate belongs in part to
the Forest Service and has on it a house built in the classical
style (1790) by James Gandon for the Earl of Portarlington.
A magnificent avenue of sequoias, over one hundred years
old, runs through the gardens. There are also glorious cypress
trees, cedars, pines and spruces, some more than 100 feet in
height. Along the path leading to the lake four Greek statues
representing the Seasons stand on the lawns.

THE HORSE

In the pre-Christian era Ireland's Knights of the Red Branch already rode on horseback. The steeplechase was invented in Ireland in 1752, with the first race being run between two church steeples. For centuries the Irish have been justly proud of their horses. The two best-known breeds are the Connemara pony ▲ 266 and the Irish Draught, a heavy working horse. The latter is crossed with the thoroughbred to produce marvelous Irish Hunters, originally bred for the hunting field but, for many years now, successful as showjumping horses too. There are a number of local horse fairs in Ireland, always well attended, as are the numerous race meetings held on the country's twenty-seven racecourses. Each course has a unique atmosphere, but most famous is the Curragh, home of the Irish Derby.

Irish gang seize Vermeer and 15 other paintings in world's biggest art robbery

Old masters worth at least £8m were stolen last night in a seven-minute armed raid on a house near Dublin. It was the world's biggest art robbery. The gang, led by a woman with a French accent, who selected the paintings to be taken, tied up the owner, Sir Alfred Beit, and his wife. Among the stolen pictures were Jan Vermeer's " Love letter ", said by police to be worth £3m. As in the Kenwood robbery earlier this year, political motives are not being discounted

THE BEIT COLLECTION
This includes works by the Dutch and Flemish masters (Rubens, Jan Steen, Frans Hals), paintings

by Goya, Murillo and other Spanish artists, views by Guardi and portraits by Gainsborough and Raeburn.

TOWARD KILKENNY

RUSSBOROUGH HOUSE ● 105.
Brewer Joseph Leeson, later Earl of Milltown, employed the architect Richard Castle to build Russborough. He began the Palladian-style country house in 1741; it was finished ten years later by Francis Bindon. Inside is remarkable Rococo stuccowork by the Lafranchini brothers ● 106. The decoration of the staircase, probably by Irish pupils of the brothers, is so extravagant that one viewer ascribed it to a "raving lunatic". The property was bought in 1952 by Sir Alfred Beit, whose uncle, also Alfred Beit, made his fortune from the South-African diamond mines. He spent it on marvelous paintings, amassing his collection late in the 19th century. His nephew bought Russborough House to house the paintings but, in 1974, members of the IRA stole sixteen of them for ransom. They were caught and the paintings recovered. It did not prevent the Beits from opening the house to the public, while still in residence. In 1986 the best paintings were stolen once again in mysterious circumstances. Only one has since been recovered.

MOONE ▲ 206. On the site of a Franciscan abbey associated with Saint Columba ▲ 295 stands one of Ireland's most unusual Celtic crosses (9th century). It is relatively tall and slender, with carvings that, although still quite crude, have a remarkable depth of expression. The shaft is covered with scenes from the Bible, uncommon in that they run from top to bottom, and the base is decorated with a delightful series of very similar, wide-eyed figures of the twelve apostles.

BALTINGLASS. In the 12th century Dermot MacMurrough led the monks of Mellifont ▲ 198 to found a monastery called Vallis Salutis, the "Vale of Health". Although an important institution inspiring the creation of many others in the surrounding area, including Jerpoint ▲ 187, this Cistercian abbey is now reduced to just the ruins of the church, with remarkable capitals carved in typically Irish designs, and the cloister. The Baltinglass designs are an interesting fusion of Cistercian architecture ● 96 and Irish Romanesque ● 94.

CASTLEDERMOT. The two 9th-century granite High Crosses, the Romanesque doorway of a long-gone chapel, and the 10th-century round tower were all part of a monastery founded by Saint Dermot in 812. In the 14th century there was a Franciscan friary here, now also reduced to a few ruins. Once a walled town, Castledermot was also of great military significance. Edward Bruce was defeated here in 1316 by Sir Edmund Butler, and in 1499 a Parliament was held here.

CARLOW. The remains of William Marshal's CASTLE, along with the town's other ruins, are a forceful reminder of the battles endured by the inhabitants. Carlow was a prized position, set strategically on the confluence of the rivers Barrow and Burren. One of the bloodiest episodes in its history occurred in 1798. Six hundred Nationalist rebels tried to take the town and were massacred by the English. To the west of town, toward Graiguecullen, are the stone quarries where 417 of them lie buried. About 3 miles beyond stands Killeshin Church ★ where, despite the advancing brambles, a remarkable carved Romanesque doorway is to be admired, one of the most interesting in Ireland. Two miles northwest of Carlow, in the Browne's Hill demesne, is one of the largest dolmens in Europe. It is four thousand years old and the covering slab is calculated to weigh 100 tons.

KILKENNY ★

The county town of Kilkenny, set on the banks of the river Nore, is justly proud of both its castle and cathedral. It has some fine medieval buildings, handsome old houses, narrow streets and vaulted passageways. The delightful shopfronts add character and color to the town, while the sixty-eight licensed premises contribute much to its flavor.

HISTORY. The city developed around a monastery founded in the 6th century by Saint Canice, from which came the name "Cill Chainnigh". Strongbow built a fortress here late in the 12th century and, because of its strategic position, Kilkenny remained important in Anglo-Irish affairs. A number of parliaments were held here, and in 1366 the famous Statutes of Kilkenny were passed ● *50*. The town reached its peak of

importance between 1642 and 1648 after the founding of an independent parliament known as the Confederation of Kilkenny ● *51*. It then became weakened by internal dissent, and in 1650 Cromwell was able to take control after five days' siege. Kilkenny has long had a strong nationalist tradition and was active in the fight for independence early in this century. Sinn Féin member William Thomas Cosgrave was elected to Parliament for the city of Kilkenny, and in 1922 became the first president of the Irish Free State ▲ *54*.

THE KILLESHIN DOOR
This Romanesque doorway owes its unusual appearance to the different-colored stones used for the four arches of its archivolt. It was probably originally brightly painted, which would have made the capitals stand out. They are great carved heads with hair and beards entwined into Celtic

patterns in a manner that has been likened to Byzantine sculpture.

KILKENNY, THE MEDIEVAL CITY ✪
Once the capital of an Ireland fighting for its freedom and faith, Kilkenny has retained its medieval charm. On the banks of the Nore, the magnificent Butler-Ormonde Castle puts on contemporary art exhibitions in the Butler Art Gallery. Take advantage of the huge lawns in the gardens to stretch out in the sun, before weaving through the alleyways connecting Rothe House with St Canice's Cathedral, reminders of a rich and glorious past.

**TOMBS IN
ST CANICE'S**
The sepulchral
monuments that were
the main decoration
of the cathedral in the
16th century have
suffered the ravages
of time, not to
mention those
inflicted by
Cromwell's troops.
Some were
reconstructed from
fragments, not always
from the same tomb.
The largest
monument (right), in
the south transept,
has probably retained
its original
appearance. It is the
tomb of the eighth
Earl of Ormonde and
his wife Margaret
FitzGerald, dating
from 1539. In the
north transept are
some recumbent
figures with
hauntingly
memorable faces.

KILKENNY CASTLE. William Marshal built the castle late in the
12th century on the site of his father-in-law Strongbow's
original fort. In 1392 it came into the possession of the earls
of Ormonde, the Butler family. They made many alterations
to the castle over the centuries and it remained their
residence until 1935. In 1967 it was given to the State. The
veneer of French elegance given by 17th-century alterations
does not disguise the massive features of the medieval castle
(left), which overlooks the River Nore. Three sides of the
original quadrangle remain, with round towers and curtain
walls. The PICTURE GALLERY, built between 1858 and 1862 by
Benjamin Woodward, has an interesting collection of family
portraits, and an incongruous hammer-beam roof painted by
John Hungerford Pollen. The tea rooms benefit from a
charming setting in the old kitchen, still with massive cooking
ranges and gleaming copper pans: a good place to pause
before setting off to explore the grounds. The 18th-century
stables are converted into workshops for the KILKENNY
DESIGN CENTRE, a government-subsidized craft center
encouraging innovative work in traditional mediums (such as
weaving, pottery, jewelry-making).

ST CANICE'S CATHEDRAL ★. The lovely cathedral was built in
the 13th century. It stands on the site of St Canice's

monastery, founded in the
6th century, of which
nothing remains but a tall,
round tower. It is possible
to climb to the top for a
fine view of the town and
surrounding countryside.
The light and spacious
cathedral was built in a
pure Gothic style and has escaped almost entirely
from subsequent alterations. It contains a number of
Ireland's finest funerary monuments, some of them
extremely old, such as that of Henry de Pont de
Lyra's son (1285).

ROTHE HOUSE ★. The only Tudor merchant's house to survive in Ireland is a fascinating complex consisting of three buildings and two courtyards, erected in 1594 for the wealthy John Rothe Fitzpiers. It was once the headquarters of the Gaelic League ● 67, and today it houses the museum and library of the Kilkenny Archeological Society.

KYTELER'S INN (27 St Kieran Street). The inn occupies one of the oldest houses in Kilkenny, once the home of Dame Alice Kyteler, born in 1280. She was the widow of four rich husbands, and suspected also of their murder. When condemned to death for witchcraft, she escaped, leaving her servant Petronilla to be burnt at the stake in her place.

DUNMORE CAVES (5 miles north of Kilkenny). Those keen on speleology should visit these limestone caves with their impressive stalagmites and stalactites. The story goes that the monster Luchtigern, the "Lord of the Mice", was killed at the giant MARKET CROSS stalactite. These caves are one of three places of darkness and evil in Irish legend. The reputation may be based on fact: in 1967, the bones of over a thousand people were discovered here, victims of a Viking raid in 928.

TOWARD WATERFORD (VIA NEW ROSS)

In the 12th century the newly arrived Normans were drawn to County Kilkenny by its fertile and wooded countryside. This explains the number of medieval buildings in the county.

GOWRAN ★. The massive square tower and chancel of the original Collegiate Church of St Mary (1275) have been incorporated into the more recent Protestant church. It contains some fine sepulchral monuments and an effigy of the first earl of Ormonde in armor, on the floor of the nave.

JERPOINT ABBEY ● 96 ★. The abbey (above) is one of the most remarkable historic sites in County Kilkenny. It was founded around 1160, probably by Donal MacGillapatrick, Lord of Ossory, and it is laid out in the Cistercian cruciform plan with two square chapels in each transept. The south side of the nave has now disappeared, but there are some magnificent capitals on the north side, probably made by the same masons who worked at Baltinglass ▲ 184. The ancient barrel vault over the choir still remains, and above is the 15th-century tower with Irish battlements. There are tombs in both transepts and also in the choir, which had a dividing wall to separate monks and lay-brothers during services. The most striking monument here is the tomb of Felix O'Dullany (first abbot of Jerpoint and founder of Kilkenny cathedral), with a serpent gnawing the end of his crozier. What makes Jerpoint unique among Irish Cistercian abbeys is the cloister which, like the tower, was added in the 15th century. It is decorated with carved figures including Saint Margaret standing on a dragon, knights, and an intriguing monkey-like creature.

CELTIC CROSSES
Among the crosses in southern Kilkenny (Kilree, Kilkieran), the 8th-century High Crosses at Ahenny (above) have the most intricate carved patterns. Only on the base do human figures feature. Those on the more northerly cross would seem to be: *Adam and the animals* (east side), *Christ surrounded by six apostles* (west side) and *David leaving for battle on a chariot and returning with the head of Goliath, the giant's body being dragged by a horse* (the other two sides).

SMITHWICK'S BREWERY ● 77
The visit includes a chance to taste the famous "Kilkenny" beer, but also gives a history of local brewing. Monks at the now ruined St Francis' Abbey (1234) were making beer in the 14th century.

DUISKE ABBEY

The church, founded in 1204 by William Marshal, has suffered the ravages of time. Much of the nave has disappeared: the octagonal tower fell in 1774 with three of the supporting arches, burying many sculptured monuments under tons of stone. Over the centuries the floor level has risen owing to accumulated rubble from the crumbling structure. Despite this, the church is still a fine example of early English Gothic, with some beautifully carved capitals.

Graiguenamanagh Cross.

INISTIOGE. A tree-lined square and old stone bridge give great charm to this unpretentious village of pretty 18th- and 19th-century houses. Of the Augustinian priory founded in 1210 only the ruins of the nave, tower and chapel remain.

GRAIGUENAMANAGH, "THE GRANARY OF THE MONKS". An ancient religious center, now a prosperous market town set on the banks of the River Barrow, beneath Brandon Hill, and grown up around the ruins of the 13th-century Cistercian abbey of DUISKE. Despite the abbey's former importance, little of its history remains apart from details of its debts to Italian bankers in the late 13th century, or the last abbot's gift of a silver cross brought back from a pilgrimage to Santiago de Compostela in 1504 which disappeared at the monastery's dissolution, under Henry VIII. The exterior is now sadly changed, although the inside retains recognizable features.

ST MULLINS. The village has ruins of a 7th-century monastery founded by Saint Moling; its plan appears in *The Book of Moling*, an ancient manuscript conserved in Dublin. Close by, among ruins of several churches, stand a truncated round tower, a small oratory and a cross.

NEW ROSS. The town, which sprawls along the River Barrow, was founded by Isabella, daughter of Strongbow and wife of William Marshal. It was an important garrison and later became a thriving market town. In the cemetery are the ruined choir and transept of St Mary's Abbey (13th century), possibly the largest parish church in medieval Ireland. From here it is possible to visit the John F. Kennedy Memorial Park, 250 acres planted with six hundred species of trees. The late President's family came from County Wexford.

TOWARD WATERFORD (VIA CARRICK-ON-SUIR)

KELLS PRIORY. A circle of high walls and supporting towers surround the vast Augustinian priory founded in 1193. The church (14th and 15th century) looks tiny in the middle of this 5-acre enclosure, but it was considered quite large when it was built.

CARRICK-ON-SUIR. Nestling in the Suir Valley, the town straddles the border between County Tipperary ▲ *251* and County Waterford. It was founded by the Butler family. In the 16th century Thomas Butler, tenth Earl of Ormonde, known as "Black Tom", built the superb Elizabethan MANSION in expectation of a visit from Elizabeth I, who in fact never came. Two towers from the family's former castle still stand behind the manor.

WATERFORD AND WATERFORD HARBOUR

THE CITY. Waterford stretches along the south bank of the Suir. Behind the long riverfront quays are narrow streets that must have run there since medieval times. The town was a Norman stronghold established in the 12th century on the site of a Viking encampment. Commerce increased and by the 16th century Waterford had developed into a thriving port. There are some rare remains of the medieval town. The 12th- or 13th-century REGINALD'S TOWER (right), where Strongbow was married now houses the town museum. The central tower of BLACKFRIARS (1226), a Dominican priory, stands almost intact. There are also ruins of the FRENCH CHURCH (1240), so called because it was used by refugee Huguenots from France in 1695. But Waterford has a great many more Georgian buildings, some by John Roberts, including the Protestant CHRIST CHURCH (1770–9) and the Catholic HOLY TRINITY CATHEDRAL (1793–6). The latter possesses a collection of holy vestments discovered during the construction of Christ Church and presented by the Protestant bishop to his Catholic counterpart.

WATERFORD HARBOUR. There are a number of places of interest along the estuary that leads from Waterford to the sea. Cistercians founded DUNBRODY ABBEY in the 11th century on the east bank of the Barrow. The Gothic church was built in the 12th century and additions were made in the 15th century. The ruins have a graceful purity of style often found in Cistercian buildings. The walls of Duncannon Fort still stand proud upon their promontory, erected in 1588 to protect the region from attack by the Armada ▲ *316*. At the end of Hook Head stands HOOK TOWER, one of the oldest lighthouses in Europe. It was built by Raymond le Gros in the 12th century. Southwest of Garrycullen stand the ruins of TINTERN ABBEY, a Cistercian abbey founded by William Marshal after surviving a shipwreck on the coast in 1200.

An 18th-century view of Waterford.

WATERFORD CRYSTAL
The glassworks were founded in 1783 but, after reaching a peak of success, closed in the 19th century. Reopened in 1947, today Waterford's is the largest crystal factory in the world.

◆ **G** C1 **E** D6-E6-E5

WELLINGTON (1769–1852)
Arthur Wellesley, Duke of Wellington, took no pride in his native land. When once described as "Irish", he replied that had he been born in a stable, it wouldn't have made him a horse. He represented Trim in Parliament and was Chief Secretary for Ireland before becoming Prime Minister, but the "Iron Duke" gave in to O'Connell, passing the Act of Catholic Emancipation in 1829.

T he Valley of the Boyne, crossing the fertile plains of County Meath, was a land of pagan legend and Celtic kings, where later Saint Patrick was welcomed with his news of Christianity. All the more tragic, then, that it should have been the site of the great battle between Protestant William of Orange and Catholic James II. Some of the most important historic monuments in Ireland are to be found in the valley, illustrating its long and eventful history.

TRIM

The town of Trim stood on the outer edge of the Pale, the territory around Dublin under Anglo-Norman control.
KING JOHN'S CASTLE. The Norman baron Hugh de Lacy established the original fortress in 1173. It was destroyed by Roderick O'Connor, who was considered by some as the last of the Ard Rí ● *48*. The fortress was rebuilt around 1204, and came into the possession of John Lackland. It has continued to be called after the English king, although only five years later he returned it to the Lacy family. A moat was created by redirecting the waters of the Boyne, and an outer curtain wall built, defended by ten semicircular towers. By the mid-13th century, King John's Castle was one of the most important Anglo-Norman strongholds. In the 14th century it was returned to the possession of the English Crown; two hundred years later it was in ruins. The confederates repaired the castle but it was taken in 1649 by Cromwell's troops. Later it became the property of the Plunket family who sold it to the State in 1993: today it is Ireland's largest Anglo-Norman castle.
YELLOW STEEPLE (Across the river). The 14th-century tower was once part of the Augustinian Abbey of St Mary. It was severely damaged by Cromwell's army, as was the town's defensive wall, little of which remains apart from SHEEP GATE, where sheep brought in for the great fairs were taxed.
TALBOT CASTLE is an early 15th-century fortified manor built on the site of the abbey. In the 18th century it was converted into a school where Arthur Wellesley, later Duke of Wellington, was a pupil. ST PATRICK'S CHURCH was built on the site of a church founded by the saint in the 5th century.

> "The feis of Temur each third year,
> To preserve laws and rules
> Was then convened firmly
> By the illustrious kings of Erin." (poem dated 984)

BECTIVE ABBEY

On the left bank of the Boyne lie the
quiet ruins of one of County Meath's
most impressive abbeys. It was founded
for the Cistercian order in 1150 by
Murchad O'Meleghlin, King of Meath,
and grew rapidly in importance through
its influential abbot, who was a Lord of
Parliament. The main features of the
ruins are a fortified tower and an elegant
cloister (right) dating from the 15th

century when, like other abbeys, Bective was fortified ● 96.
The road along the river toward Drogheda, past Oldbridge,
leads to the site of the Battle of the Boyne ▲ 194.

HILL OF TARA

The immense importance of this low hill is not obvious to the
uninformed visitor. The grassy mounds are of little help to the
imagination in evoking its legendary past. The Interpretative
Centre offers good explanations and is a great aid to
understanding the extraordinary site and bringing it to life.
ANCIENT HISTORY. The oldest part of the site, the MOUND OF
THE HOSTAGES, is a Bronze Age passage grave. Later Tara
became an important place of pagan worship, and its very
name evokes memories of the great heroes of Celtic legend
such as High King Cormac MacAirt, whose daughter Gráinne
eloped with the warrior Diarmait ▲ 289 on the eve of a
wedding to another and High King Laoghaire who is said to
be buried upright in his armor, ready to confront his enemies.
TARA OF THE KINGS. Tara was the seat of the High Kings of
Ireland and the source of royal power. Every three years the
country's leaders would meet here to make laws and dispense
justice. It was thought that these *feis* were held in the part of
the site identified as the BANQUET HALL (right, a document
showing a seating plan). The two parallel earthworks are now
thought to have been a ceremonial entrance. The High Kings
were crowned on a stone called the CORONATION STONE (Lia
Fáil) which was said to sound if it approved the new leader.

**THE MEETING
OF TARA**
During the 1798
rebellion ● 52
thirty-two people
were killed on the hill
of Tara. In August
1843 O'Connell
deliberately chose the
ancient Gaelic site for
one of his great
meetings protesting
against the Act of
Union ● 52. Nearly
one million people
were there.

191

THE "BOOK OF KELLS" ▲ *154*
Most experts agree in dating the book from around 800. Opinions differ, however, as to where the astonishing illuminated manuscript was made. Some think it originated in Kells itself, others suggest Pict territory, in the east of Scotland, while the majority believe it to have been made at the monastery of Saint Columba on the Hebridean Isle of Iona. It was stolen from Kells in 1006, but found less than a year later, without the gold shrine that enclosed it. Since 1661 it has been kept in Trinity College, Dublin.

CHRISTIANITY ARRIVES. Tradition has it that Saint Patrick drove the Celtic druids from Tara. It is not known whether he actually converted the kings, but he won the population over to his faith, and the growing strength of Christianity ● *56* brought with it the decline of Tara's importance. The last pagan festival took place in the 6th century, and by the 8th century the kings no longer lived there. The site was finally abandoned c. 1022.

NAVAN

At the point where the green valleys of the Boyne and Blackwater rivers meet stands Navan, the capital of County Meath and, in far distant history, capital of Ulster for more than a thousand years. The most interesting monuments are outside the town. The noble LISCARTAN CASTLE, two square towers joined by a central hall, was held by William Talbot in 1633. DONAGHMORE CHURCH has a fine 12th-century round tower. Above its unusual doorway is a carving of *Christ on the Cross*, and there is a face carved on either side of the architrave. The church is said to stand on the site of Saint Patrick's first monastery.

KELLS (CEANANNUS MOR) ★

THE MONASTERY. Early in the 9th century the monks of Iona became so fearful of Viking attack that they fled to a monastery founded by Saint Columba ▲ *151*, *295* in the 6th century and set on the banks of the Blackwater. Whether they achieved their desired peace seems doubtful: Kells was invaded by Viking warriors five times between 807 and 1019.

THE "BOOK OF KELLS". The village of Kells is famed for an illuminated manuscript of the Gospels, stolen in 1006. The monastery was built on a circular plan (imitated later by the Norman defensive walls and, even today, preserved in the road pattern). At its center was the church from which the book was taken. The 19th-century building contains facsimiles and photographs of objects linked with the history of Kells. THE ROUND TOWER served as a watchtower and place of safekeeping. It is known to predate 1076, when the son of the king of Meath was assassinated there.

Slane Castle.

SOUTH CROSS. The cross probably dates from the 9th century, and owes its other name, the Cross of Saint Patrick and Saint Columba, to the scarcely legible Latin inscription that runs around the base. Among the many carvings on the cross are (east face) *Adam and Eve, Cain and Abel* and the *Sacrifice of Abraham*, and (west face) the *Crucifixion* and the *Last Judgement*.

WEST CROSS. Not far away is another cross, now broken. It was certainly one of the finest in Ireland. Water seems to be the predominant theme in the carvings, which include the apocryphal scene of the *Bathing of the Infant Jesus*, a possible representation of the *Wedding at Cana*, and, focusing on the sacrament of baptism itself, a depiction of the *Baptism of Christ*.

EAST CROSS. South of the church is an unfinished cross with a carving of the *Crucifixion*.

SAINT COLUMBA'S HOUSE ★. Just north of the churchyard is a steep-roofed stone oratory probably built to house the precious relics of Saint Columba brought from Iona. Possibly once linked to the graveyard by a tunnel, the only other entrance used to be high up, going into the upper floor where there are three small cells. These are now reached from within by a ladder. (Before heading for Slane by the N51, it is possible to take the road to Oldcastle, northwest of Kells, and visit Loughcrew.)

LOUGHCREW. A vast burial site lies on Slieve na Caillighe ("Hill of the Witch") in the Loughcrew Hills. Tumuli cover gallery tombs in which pieces of pottery dating from 2500 BC have been found. Note the many slabs with chevron and spiral designs.

SLANE

The hill above Slane offers a view up and down the valley that descends from Trim to Drogheda. There are remains of a famous monastery and church built in the 16th century on the site of a sanctuary founded by Saint Patrick. According to legend the saint lit a paschal fire here in 433, in defiance of the druids who were celebrating across the hilltops at Tara.

Below is SLANE CASTLE (1785–1821), the work of numerous architects including James Gandon and Francis Johnston.

The cross stands in the center of the village where the east door of the original monastery once was. In 1798 it was used as a gallows to hang local rebels. Among many interesting carvings there is a particularly fine *Hand of God* high up on one side of the shaft.

Saint Columba's House.

▲ THE BATTLE OF THE BOYNE

Louis XIV

Not so much a battle as a skirmish followed quickly by retreat, the Battle of the Boyne, whi took place a few miles from Drogheda, seems to have marked the end of James II's ambitions to regain the English throne that he had lost to his son-in-law William of Orange. This dynastic quarrel was also important in larger terms: James was supported by Louis XIV of France and William by the King of Spain, two major forces struggling for domination in Europe. The achievements of the relatively tolera William of Orange were later twisted by history. His 1691 Treaty Limerick was infringed, and he was taken as the figurehead of th fervently Protestant Orange movement, which spread the myth c the Battle of the Boyne as the triumph of Protestant over Papist.

JAMES II
He ascended to the English throne in 1685. His tyranny and fervent Catholicism alarmed his subjects. The birth of an heir in 1688 brought matters to a head, and a faction invited his son-in-law, William, Prince of Orange, to take the throne. James II went into exile, and in 1689 Parliament ruled that he had abdicated.

WILLIAM III
Son-in-law and nephew of James II, William, Prince of Orange, was welcomed into England with open arms. He an his wife Mary were ma king and queen. After bringing Scotland to h he landed in Ireland o June 11, 1690, and quickly defeated Jame II's followers there, an their allies. The Protestant nation had triumphed in Ireland.

THE FLIGHT OF JAMES II

James II fled the field of battle and set sail for France from Kinsale. Louis XIV gave him shelter, but he died a bitter man in exile. The Jacobites did not give up hope. Their activities continued with little success until well into the 18th century. The defeat of the "Young Pretender", Charles Edward Stewart, at Culloden, Scotland (1746) eventually put an end to their ambitions.

THE BATTLE

On July 1, 1690 (July 12 by the modern calendar), the 25,000 strong Jacobite army met William of Orange's 37,000 experienced soldiers at the River Boyne. The latter concentrated their attack at the hamlet of Oldbridge, where they crossed the river and forced the Irish back. James II, who did not use all his troops in the battle, fled. It was not a battle of great importance, but it gave William encouragement and eleven days later, at Aughrim, he gained the definitive victory.

THE TREATY STONE

It is said that the Treaty of Limerick was signed here on October 30, 1691, setting the seal on Protestant supremacy in Ireland.

THE ORANGE ORDER

Founded in 1795 "to maintain the laws and peace of the country and the Protestant constitution", it became increasingly influential in Northern Ireland.

NEWGRANGE AND THE
VALLEY OF THE
BOYNE, A PRODIGIOUS
TRIP THROUGH
HISTORY ✪
The imposing
prehistoric tumuli of
Dowth, Knowth and
Newgrange stand
between Drogheda
and Navan. The tightly
controlled access to
these sites does not
prevent congestion at
the height of the
tourist season. A few
miles to the north lies
Mellifont Abbey,
Ireland's first
Cistercian monastery,
and Monasterboice,
with three carved
crosses that are
authentic
masterpieces.

VALLEY OF THE BOYNE ★

Within the Valley of the Boyne can be found one of the most
extraordinary megalithic sites in the world, both for the number,
grandeur and state of preservation of the remains and for the
beauty of every detail. The huge mounds of Dowth, Newgrange
and Knowth, lying low in the valley, are proof not only of the
skill and vision of their builders, but also of their unshakeable
religious faith.

DOWTH. The Dowth tumulus has suffered damage on a number
of occasions, including a Viking raid and pillaging for stones
as late as 1857. The mound encloses a number of passage
graves and funeral chambers which are still being excavated.
The main passage grave is cruciform with two side chambers.
It is entered by a metal stairway and lined with stone uprights,
while massive lintels form the roof. Fallen blocks within the
chamber make viewing difficult. When reparations were made
in 1847, "Within the chamber, mixed with the clay and dust
which had accumulated, were found a quantity of bones
consisting of heaps as well as scattered fragments of burned
bones, many of which proved to be human".

NEWGRANGE ● 88. The enormous tumulus (295 feet in
diameter and over 40 feet high) is built partly with huge
stones from the river. It is encircled by standing stones possibly
more recent in origin, but only 12 of a probable 36 remain.
Around the bottom of the cairn are 97 kerb stones, some with
patterns. The famous threshold stone, just below the entrance,
is covered with spiral decorations. Carbon-dating shows
Newgrange to be a relatively late grave, from around 2500 BC.
It was not thoroughly restored until 1962. Some aspects of
the grave are unusual, especially the great wall of white
stone embossed with black pebbles at regular intervals. The
restoration was based on knowledge passed down by word of
mouth. The tumulus covers a 62-foot-long passage dolmen
formed by 43 pillars placed along its sides. The passage leads
to the central chamber, which is preceded by two side-
chambers. The roof is an extraordinary corbeled construction
made with 20-foot stone slabs. Three polished stone basins
were used for offerings. The axis of the passage symbolically
traces the direction of the rising sun at the winter solstice.

KNOWTH. The third of the valley's giant tumuli has been
undergoing painstaking reconstruction since 1960. Two big

passage graves have been found. The first, as at Newgrange, has a corridor that widens out into the main chamber. The carvings found at Knowth are particularly striking, both on the kerb stones around the outside of the mound (lozenges, squares and sun symbols), and in the chambers where there are lozenges, triangles and zigzags as well as concentric arcs (also found in Brittany). There are unusual stones with a dotted pattern similar to some discovered in Neolithic temples on Malta. Around Knowth are about twenty satellite tumuli, at least sixteen of which contain passage graves. From the remains of dwellings and tunnels that have been found, it is evident that the cairn had a variety of occupants over the centuries including Vikings and early Christians. (Before continuing to Drogheda, take the road to Dunleer, then to Ardcath, to visit the interesting passage grave on Fourknocks hill.)

FOURKNOCKS. On the hill is another huge grave (2200–1800 BC). A short passage leads to the main chamber, which was once uncovered, but is now surmounted by a dome that is pierced with holes giving ample light to study the extraordinary decorations. The chamber opens onto three niches with zigzag motifs on the lintels. Among the stones on the ground is one of particular interest, showing a strange carving of a human face.

● 51.

DROGHEDA TO DUNDALK

DROGHEDA. Of the many Parliaments that sat at Drogheda, the most famous is that of 1494, which brought in Poyning's Law. The town was once surrounded by a wall punctuated by ten gateways. The only one to remain is ST LAWRENCE'S GATE, an imposing 13th-century barbican with two round towers. Drogheda was the first town to suffer Cromwell's attack when he arrived in 1649 to subdue Ireland after the 1641 rebellion ● 51. MAGDELENE TOWER, all that remains of a Dominican monastery founded in 1224, still shows the scars of Cromwell's cannon, while the Protestant ST PETER'S CHURCH conserves a few fragments of a medieval church burnt by Cromwell to be rid of some one hundred men who had taken refuge in the tower. The Catholic ST PETER'S CHURCH has become a place

St. Lawrence's Gate, Drogheda.

THE SYMBOLISM OF NEWGRANGE
The Neolithic decorations of the outer stones at Newgrange, and those lining the chamber, are among the richest in Ireland. The chevrons, spirals, lozenges, zigzags and waves are similar to patterns found on ancient monuments in Brittany, France, but their symbolism continues to puzzle experts and remains little understood. It is possible that the spirals are a symbol of the labyrinthine path to the underworld. The concentric circles could be connected with sun worship. The arcs perhaps represent the great Earth Mother, protectress of the dead, and goddess of harvests and fruitfulness. The waves, snake patterns and zigzags may stand for the sea of the living world, an important force, but they may also evoke the celestial sea of religious meditation.

MUIREDACH'S CROSS
On east side are seen,
from bottom to top:
Adam and Eve and
Cain and Abel (on the
same panel), *David
and Goliath*, *Moses
striking water from
the rock* and the
Adoration of the Magi
(of whom there are
four); in the center
of the cross, the
Last Judgement with,
below, *Saint Michael
weighing souls*. On
the west side, from
bottom to top, are:
the *Taking of Christ*,
Christ arisen, and
*Christ giving Saint
Peter the keys and
Saint Paul the
Gospels*; in the center
is the *Crucifixion*,
with the *Resurrection*
on the right arm and,
below, the *Ascension*.
At the ends of the
arms are scenes from
the Passion: *Pilate
washing his hands*
(south arm), and
what may be the
Taking of Christ with,
below, *Saint Paul
and Saint Anthony
in the desert*.

of pilgrimage in reverence to the severed head of
archbishop and martyr Oliver Plunket ▲ *199* which is
embalmed and enshrined here.

MONASTERBOICE. The ruins
here are those of a
monastery founded in
the 5th century by
Saint Buithe,
disciple of Saint
Patrick ● *56*,
making it one of the
earliest in Ireland.
It was occupied for
a time by the
Danes until they
were chased out by the
king of Tara in 968.
The precious
manuscripts kept
in the tower had
disappeared,
probably destroyed by fire in
1097. The three crosses that stand
in the graveyard are of
greatest interest. Like
all crosses carved with
scriptural scenes, their
main purpose was to instruct the
faithful, showing episodes from both the Old and New
Testaments. MUIREDACH'S CROSS ▲ *206* (the nearest to the
entrance) takes its name from a 9th-century abbot (there is an
inscription low on the west side) and is topped by a carved
church. The WEST CROSS, or Tall Cross, the highest in Ireland
(21 feet), has suffered much damage from the elements, and
the carvings are harder to decipher. The NORTH CROSS, badly
damaged perhaps by Cromwell's troops, has a carving of the
Crucifixion on one side and an interlace design on the other.

MELLIFONT ● *97.* On his way to Rome, Saint Malachy, bishop
of Armagh ▲ *322*, stopped at Clairvaux in France in 1139 to
meet Saint Bernard, a founder of the Cistercian Order. On
his return to Ireland, Malachy began founding Cistercian
communities, starting with the Mellifont Abbey (Fons Mellis),
in 1142, and continuing with eight others, all following
Clairvaux's rule, including Bective ▲ *191* and Boyle ▲ *289*.
Little remains of the vast, stark and severe Mellifont Abbey

Details of carved capitals at Mellifont Abbey.

buildings, except the foundations, some of the cloister arches and part of the elegant octagonal lavabo (below), whose finely carved capitals were a foretaste of the Gothic style.

ARDEE. It is well worth stopping in the main street of this little village to see ARDEE CASTLE, a 13th-century fortified tower once used as a tribunal, and HATCH'S CASTLE (private), a rare example of a round-cornered tower. Two miles southwest lies KILDEMOCK with its curious little church, known as Jumping Church because of the startling angle at which one of its walls leans. It is said to have rocked forward to exclude an excommunicated man who had been buried within.

DUNDALK. The town's strategic position on the route from the north brought it under repeated attack over many centuries. The Scotsman Edward Bruce was among many who took Dundalk, having proclaimed himself King of Ireland from a nearby hill in 1316. Between 1560 and 1650 the town was besieged no fewer than six times. In the 18th century its fortifications were dismantled. Today Dundalk is a prosperous industrial town and capital of County Louth. Only two of the ancient monuments still remain: the bell tower of ST NICHOLAS' CHURCH which dates back to its foundation in 1207, and a 15th-century TOWER from a Franciscan monastery built in 1240. An old mill still stands in Seatown, and here too is KINCORA HOUSE where the arctic explorer Admiral Sir Francis Leopold McClintock (1819–1907) was born. Dundalk has two patron saints: Saint Brigid (also the patron saint of Ireland), who is said to have been born at Faughart (about 4 miles north) and who remains the object of veneration and pilgrimage, and Oliver Plunket, of whom there is a reliquary in the old church of Ballybarrack (2 miles south).

COOLEY PENINSULA

To visit Ballymascanlon and the famous PROLEEK DOLMEN ● 88 (over 11 feet high and with a capstone weighing more than 40 tons) is to venture into the land of the legendary epic of the *Táin Bó Cuailnge*. The Cooley Peninsula is a rocky finger of land between Dundalk Bay and Carlingford Lough, with magnificent views of the east coast and down onto the historic small town of Carlingford. This old port is set on the lough and faces the Mourne Mountains over the waters. The town is said to have once had thirty-two fortified castles. Among the few remains are the massive ruins of KING JOHN'S CASTLE, built on the king's orders at the lough's edge to defend the harbor.

King John's Castle, Carlingford.

THE SHANNON "CALLOWS"
Between Lough Ree and Lough Derg the river regularly overflows. This has created wetland pastures known as "callows" along the banks. They have never been of much use for cultivation and have therefore been little drained or treated; just a crop of hay is taken each summer. This old-fashioned and gentle farming has preserved a great variety of wild plants and has made the wetlands a sanctuary for nesting birds. However, with changing methods and intensifying production, the wildlife is now beginning to suffer.

The River Shannon rises on the slopes of Cuilcagh Mountain, County Cavan, in what is called Lug Na Sionainne, the "Shannon Pot". It makes its way 213 miles to the Atlantic Ocean, crossing several counties in between Leinster and Connacht. It is the longest river in the British Isles. The Shannon basin covers over 4,500 square miles, 20 percent of the surface area of Ireland. Edmund Spenser's "spacious Shannon spreading like a sea" is a gentle river descending gradually between marshy banks. It takes a lazy course that frequently opens out into large lakes, the first being Lough Allen. The river has long been a means of transport, providing a way into the thickly forested lands of central Ireland, but more important has been its role as a natural defense, as it is a particularly difficult river to cross. A project was begun in the 1840's to make the Shannon navigable and today more than 150 miles of the river are open. In addition, the recent reopening of the canal from Ballinamore to Ballyconnell has linked the Shannon to the network of the River Erne, in Northern Ireland.

PORTUMNA TO BALLINASLOE

PORTUMNA. The village of TERRYGLASS and the town of Portumna face each other across the northeast end of Lough Derg. Terryglass has many pretty houses, a delightful park on the banks of the water, a new marina, and a Norman castle. One of its two churches (1910) looks rather strange, surrounded by identical tombstones at the orders of its patron. Portumna is a pleasant town with a busy marina, bordered by a splendid park containing the ruins of a Dominican priory (13th–15th century). The PORTUMNA CASTLE estate ● 99 is now a wildlife reserve. The castle itself is the remains of a 17th-century fortified mansion, now being restored.

MEELICK. Although so apparently isolated, Meelick provided an important crossing point over the Shannon. Near to the 15th-century Franciscan priory is Victoria Lock, the biggest lock on the Shannon. A small fort was built here by the English, defended by nine cannons. It was intended to halt a French expeditionary force that was expected to advance to Dublin from the west coast ● *101*.

BIRR. The spacious layout and elegant houses of Birr make it one of Ireland's most beautiful provincial Georgian towns. It is best known, however, for its castle, which has been the seat of the earls of Rosse since the 17th century. The splendid GARDENS ★ (above) are open to visitors. Designed by the second earl, they now contain well over a thousand varieties of tree and shrub and they are a mass of blossom in the spring. The beech and maple trees make the autumn equally spectacular. In the formal gardens, the box hedges are reputed to be the highest in the world. Also in the gardens is the structure that housed the Rosse telescope, built in the 1840's by the third earl and used by the fourth to first measure the heat of the moon and to observe spiral nebulae. For seventy years the "Leviathan of Parsonstown" (Birr was formerly called Parsonstown) was the largest telescope in the world; it is now in the London Science Museum.

KINNITY, a few miles west, is a good place from which to explore the SLIEVE BLOOM MOUNTAINS, where forest paths lead up to stretches of turf bog ■ *32*.

BANAGHER ● *101*. Archeological finds have shown evidence of human habitation along this stretch of the river as far back as the Bronze Age, four thousand years ago. Bridges built across the water had to be defended, and along the banks lies a series of fortifications from different periods: Cromwell's Castle, Fort Falkland, Fort Elisa and a Martello tower. Together with Shannonbridge further north, Banagher was one of the most important strongholds on this part of the Shannon. The main street has buildings in various styles including the Georgian Crank House, which stands with its eye-catching pink façade in among traditional shopfronts and licensed premises (*Hough's, Lyons*). Anthony Trollope lived in Banagher when he was first sent as Post Office surveyor to Ireland, and Charlotte Brontë spent her honeymoon nearby.

SHANNON HARBOUR ★. The village was built in 1804, on the completion of the Grand Canal from Dublin, to service the river and canal traffic. Now the hotel is ruined and the bridge, the warehouses, the locks and basins, and the police station are silent. But the little harbor where the Shannon and the canal meet is full of colorful narrowboats and other craft.

CALLOWS BIRDLIFE
The callows are one of the rare spots in Ireland where species becoming increasingly rare elsewhere remain common. Among the waders, the most numerous are the grebes, marking their territory in the spring with a noisy call and airborne diving display. Other waders to breed here are the redshank, curlew and black-tailed godwit (below). Many species of duck make their nests here too, including the mallard, shoveler duck and teal. There are swans, dabchicks and great-crested grebes, coots and moorhens (above), all happy nesting in the thick reeds; and on warm, still evenings from late May until early July, the rasping sound of the corncrake can be heard, the rarest bird of all.

THE BATTLE OF AUGHRIM

A year after the Protestant victory at the Battle of the Boyne ▲ *194*, a second battle was fought, at Aughrim. French troops under General Saint-Ruth had been sent by Louis XIV to aid the Irish Jacobites. On July 21, 1691 the two armies met in Bloody Hollow at the foot of Aughrim Hill. Saint-Ruth was killed trying to block

William of Orange's troops on the road west. This, along with a determined cavalry charge led by Ruvigny, routed the Jacobite army. The Orangemen marched on into Galway that same day, and later that year the Catholic armies surrendered. In Aughrim, a cross commemorates the Irish and French dead.

CLONFERT CATHEDRAL ★, ● *95*. The monastery of Clonfert was founded in the 6th century by Saint Brendan the Navigator ▲ *239*, who, according to legend, sailed to America nearly one thousand years before Christopher Columbus. Around the year 1200 a beautiful and ornate doorway dedicated to the saint was inserted into an existing church wall. It is considered by many to be the finest Hiberno-Romanesque doorway of all. The capitals are highly sculptured, showing grotesque human and animal heads; the entire surface of the doorway shows an extraordinary combination of interlaced patterns, and a variety of carving executed with great skill and ingenuity. The columns, "instead of representing an element of calm and repose in the overall composition . . . are so covered with carving that their surface seems alive, almost sparkling, and the decorations continue irrepressibly on to the outer piers" (Françoise Henry). The cathedral is cruciform in shape, unusual for a Romanesque church in Ireland. The chancel, with a lovely window at the east end that should be viewed from both within and without, dates from around 1200. The slender tower and south transept, the latter now without a roof, were added in the 15th century. On the inner wall of the choir is the carving of a siren, a symbol of vanity, or it could be a creature met by Brendan on one of his famous voyages.

SHANNONBRIDGE ● *101*. The village gets its name from the lovely bridge, which is an extension of the main street at its western end across the Shannon. It was built around 1750, and in Napoleonic times fortifications were constructed on the west bank, remains of which are still prominently visible today.

CLONTUSKERT PRIORY ★. The priory was an Augustinian institution built on the site of a 9th-century monastery. Its doorway is decorated with the figures of Saint Michael, Saint Catherine and Saint John the Baptist, surrounded by mythical beasts.

BALLINASLOE. A horse fair has been held here every October since the 18th century. The village is linked to the Shannon by the River Suck, now made navigable and replacing a section of the Grand Canal which was in use from 1820 to 1960. In the village of Aughrim, west of Ballinasloe, there is an exhibition on the battle that took place in 1691, one of the bloodiest in the history of Ireland.

CLONMACNOIS ★

AN IMPORTANT CROSSROADS. Very near to Clonmacnois was the meeting place of two main routes of primitive Ireland. Here the east–west road, Eiscir Riada, met the north–south artery, the Shannon, making Clonmacnois a key crossing point. It is known that during the life of Saint Ciarán (512–45), and probably before, merchants from Gaul would travel up the river to sell wine. Three centuries later the Shannon brought less welcome visitors: Danes, led by their chief Turgesius, whose wife Ota would proclaim oracles at the high altar of the cathedral.

HISTORY OF THE MONASTERY. Ciarán founded his monastery here in 545, but unfortunately he did not live to see it prosper, dying later that same year. The saint continued to be revered, his grave became an object of pilgrimage, and the monastery flourished for many centuries. In the 16th century, however, English troops attacked and plundered the institution. It was never to be restored. Today the ruins of Clonmacnois monastery command a great sense of peace and serenity, and many still make them an object of pilgrimage.

CARVED STONES. A remarkable number of what may be ancient tombstones have been found at Clonmacnois (8th to 12th century), which can now be seen in the Visitors' Centre. They are carved with crosses of different designs, and often bear an inscription seeking prayers for the person whose name is on the stone. It has not been proved that these are tombstones, however, and a recent theory proposes that they marked the completion of a pilgrimage by the person whose name is inscribed.

CROSS OF THE SCRIPTURES

From an incomplete inscription at the bottom of the shaft it is known that the cross was carved by a man called Colman for the High King Flann Sinna (879–916). On the east face the only scene clearly recognizable is that of Christ, seated, handing the Keys to Saint Peter and the Gospels to Saint Paul. It has been suggested that the two panels below show either Joseph interpreting the pharaoh's dreams, or an Irish king helping Saint Ciarán to build his church. The *Last Judgement* is to be seen at the top. The west face of the cross depicts, from bottom to top, the *Watching over the Tomb*, the *Arrest*, the *Betrayal* and the *Crucifixion*. Although very worn, it is possible to follow the Passion on the lower part of the base, from Palm Sunday to Easter Sunday (above, Christ is seated with the Apostles). The Passion continues on the south face with the *Kiss of Judas*. The hunting scenes, also on the base, are difficult to explain, as are the panels on the narrow sides of the cross, apart from the one on the south side showing David playing his harp.

THE CROSSES. The three crosses of Clonmacnois have been recently moved into the Visitors' Centre. Copies of two of them show where they used to stand. The most important is the CROSS OF THE SCRIPTURES, which has fine elegant proportions, arms slanting slightly upward and the ring carved proud of the face. It is probably the cross mentioned in documents of 957, and later in 1060, at which time it marked the site of a shrine. The biblical scenes are hard to interpret. On the South Cross an inscription also found at the base of the shaft would seem to imply that it was carved at least seventeen years earlier for Maelsechnaill, father of Flann and son of Maelruanaid (846–62), the first true king of all Ireland. This cross is covered with panels with interesting geometric and zoomorphic motifs, but apart from a possible image of Adam and Eve on the base, the only biblical scene recognizable is the Crucifixion on the shaft. Only the shaft remains of the North Cross, with a strange cross-legged figure on its south side. Some think this may be the Gallic god Cernunnos.

THE TOWERS. Standing some distance from the other buildings is O'Rourke's Tower, partly rebuilt in the 12th century after being struck by lightning. The cone-shaped stone roof is missing, but must have resembled that of the smaller tower attached to the remains of a small Romanesque church, Teampull Finghin.

THE CATHEDRAL. Much of the structure probably dates back to the 10th century. However, the Romanesque west door was added later, as was the Gothic north door which was opened up in about 1460 by Dean Odo, with statues of Saint Francis, Saint Patrick, and Saint Dominic placed above. The vaulted ceiling in the eastern part of the building was added in the 15th century. This is the burial place of the last High Kings of Ireland ● *48*, Turloch Mór O'Conor and his son Rúairí.

> "And in Clonmacnois they laid the men of Teffia,
> And right many a lord of Breagh;
> Deep the sod above Clan Creide and Clan Conaill,
> Kind in hall and fierce in fray."
>
> T.W. Rolleston

THE SEVEN CHURCHES. The seven churches on the site may symbolize the seven hills of Rome and their churches, which would have been seen by Irish pilgrims. The smallest, TEAMPULL KIERAN, is also in its way the most important, since Saint Ciarán is thought to be buried there. It is known that in 1684 the church still had its roof and the faithful were still coming there to worship a relic of the saint's hand. To the west are the foundations of TEAMPULL KELLY. South of the cathedral are the two joined churches of TEAMPULL DOOLIN and TEAMPULL HURPAN (17th century); southwest stands a third, TEAMPULL RI (c. 1200), and to the north is TEAMPULL CONOR, which has been maintained and used by the Protestant Church of Ireland since 1780. TEAMPULL FINGHIN is at the north edge of the enclosure. The only structure to have been built at a distance from the walled monastery complex is the NUN'S CHURCH (c. 1166). It is about half a mile away to the east and can be reached along the old paved pilgrims' road. It is a typical Hiberno-Romanesque church, both in size and appearance. The roof is gone, but the doorway and the chancel arch retain fine decoration representative of the period ● 94.

THE CASTLE. On the riverside pastures to the west of the Visitors' Centre some ruins stand on a grassy mound. These are the remains of a Norman castle built early in the 13th century. They are a reminder that the Shannon was a natural frontier, across which the Normans fiercely defended the land that they had conquered. The collapsed state of the castle largely results from the action of Cromwell's troops in the 17th century, although it had probably long lost its strategic importance by then. The castle, built around the year 1210 at Athlone, 9 miles further north, which guarded a key crossing place on the Shannon at the lower end of Lough Ree, was to become the prominent stronghold. From here, the Normans began their conquest of Connacht in 1235.

CLONMACNOIS, THE PLACE OF SAGES AND SAINTS ✪
Whether approached by the river or by the roads from Athlone or Ballinasloe, the atmosphere of studious contemplation is immediately striking, as if the place were still aware of its position as one of the beacons of medieval spirituality and philosophy, renowned throughout western Christendom. To avoid the hordes of tourists, particularly in high season, it is advisable to explore this spiritual haven early in the morning (from 10am or even, from mid May to mid Sep., from 9am) or one hour before closing time (6pm, or 7pm from mid May to mid Sep.).

The stone crosses bound with a circular wheel that stand today as monuments to an intense Christian belief combined with a more general Celtic spirituality were erected by monks, by kings and by warriors. There are about one hundred crosses and High Crosses in all, but those at Ahenny, Clonmacnois and Cashel are particularly impressive because of the beauty and richness of their carvings. The High Crosses are a reminder of the religious spirit that has always remained strong in Ireland. Standing tall amid the ruins they are a precious treasure from the past and a powerful omen for the future.

1 **2** **3** **4**

STONE SLAB AT KILNASAGGART (1) On it is carved a Latin cross and the name of a priest, Ternoc, who died in 714.

NORTH CROSS AT AHENNY (2) belongs to the group of Ossory carved crosses dating from the 8th or 9th century.

THE CASHEL HIGH CROSS (4), 12th century, has a carving representing a crucifix with Christ in high-relief on one side.

THE CROSS AT MOONE is particularly interesting and unusual, with its clear detail and strong, simple figures. Like many Celtic crosses, it is carved with scenes from both the Old and New Testaments, as here: *Daniel in the Lions' Den*.

MUIREDACH'S CROSS (3) at Monasterboice is the best preserved of all the carved crosses. The panel of the *Taking of Christ*, just above the base, is in almost perfect condition.

THE BASE The Ahenny cross has a base carved with secular subjects: here a procession with a horse and dog. They are a contrast to religious subjects and abstract motifs.

Designs often include combinations of spirals, interlacing, animals' heads and Greek patterns.

CONSTRUCTION

The Celtic High Cross was set on a base that tapered toward the top. It was either carved from one block of stone or from several pieces fixed together with tenon and mortise joints. The basic Latin cross was bound by a wheel surrounding

the center, giving a more dramatic and decorative appearance. Ornamental carving was of interlace and serpentine designs, biblical scenes, or sometimes local stories. These crosses represent some of the finest medieval art to have been produced in Ireland.

THE CROSS OF THE SCRIPTURES AT CLONMACNOIS

The carvings are accomplished. The purity of their design shows the skill of the craftsmen who worked on these early carved crosses. Patterns and figures blend with a remarkable grace of line and form.

POWER OF THE CROSS

Celtic crosses have withstood the vicissitudes of history and the violence of successive invaders better than many other Irish religious monuments. The artistic power of these 8th- and 9th-century crosses has lost none of its fascination: their decoration, an inspired mixture of ornamental design and narrative drama, still expresses the potency of the mythical world that obsessed those who made them. Many subsequent works of art have been influenced by these complex and enthralling monuments of early Irish belief.

Detail from the *Last Judgement*, a scene carved on the Clonmacnois Cross of the Scriptures.

STYLIZED BEASTS

The incorporation of creatures from the Bible, often the serpent, into the carved interlacing is one of the most common decorative traditions on Irish medieval High Crosses.

THE SHRINE

The top of the cross, representing a shrine open to the sky, seems to symbolize Christ's ascension.

McGahern was born in Dublin in 1934 and has come to be respected as one of the leading writers of his generation. In the 1960's, however, the Irish authorities seized and banned his second novel, *The Dark* (1965), the story of a young man confronted by near-incestuous scenes with his father and homosexual advances from a priest. McGahern lost his job as a school-teacher and left the country. He spent time in London, Paris, Spain and the United States. He has now returned to live in Ireland. In his novellas (*Nightlines*, 1971, *High Ground*, 1985) and his novels (*The Barracks*, 1963; *The Leavetaking*, 1974; *The Pornographer*, 1978; *Among Women*, 1990) John McGahern reveals the abyss that lies thinly concealed behind the banal exterior of ordinary people's lives.

FROM ATHLONE TO CARRICK-ON-SHANNON

In 1183 Giraldus Cambrensis of Wales visited Ireland and in his survey he wrote that the Shannon "rightly holds the chief place among all of the rivers of Ireland, whether old or new, both on account of the magnificence of its size, its long meanderings, and its abundance of fish". The peaceful river is familiar to many Irish people and precious to all. The author John McGahern, who now lives in County Leitrim, has described how Republican prisoners would relieve their boredom and distress by describing imaginary walks along the banks of the river, each trying to remember details that the others missed out.

ATHLONE. JOHN'S CASTLE is Athlone's most impressive monument: a massive medieval structure, much changed and repaired, which has stood guard over the bridge at the southern end of Lough Ree for nearly eight

hundred years. Today the castle houses an Exhibition Centre and the Castle Museum; the present bridge dates from 1844. The old part of town lies around the castle, with some good old-fashioned pubs (*Higgins', The Palace, Séan's,* and *The Castle*). Just upstream is a fine railway bridge built in the 1850's. Athlone was the birthplace, in 1884, of the tenor John McCormack. A bronze bust in his memory stands in the town center. The CHURCH OF STS PETER AND PAUL is a modern building (1937) with some fine stained glass by Harry Clarke ▲ 214. The town was besieged twice during the war between James II and William of Orange. The military camp on the west bank, Custume Barracks, is named after a hero of the second siege in 1691.

RICHMOND HARBOUR. Richmond Harbour stands at the end of the Royal Canal, which was built to link the Liffey and the Shannon. It has been closed since 1961, but thanks to an energetic campaign it will be reopened in a few years.

CARRICK-ON-SHANNON. The largest town on the upper reaches of the Shannon is a busy and prosperous holiday boating resort, and also the county town of County Leitrim. In the

center is one of the world's smallest churches (roughly 15 feet by 12 feet). It is called the COSTELLO CHAPEL, and is the mausoleum of Edward Costello and his wife. Beyond Lake Drumharlow, northwest of the town, lies WOODBROOK HOUSE, the setting of David Thomson's novel *Woodbrook*. On the banks of Lough Key is LOUGH KEY FOREST PARK. Take a stroll through the forest with its bog gardens ■ 34, or simply enjoy the views.

Munster

CORK

◆ F D5

MACSWINEY
A hero of the Irish struggle for independence, Terence MacSwiney was arrested on August 12, 1920. He was sentenced to two years in prison, and taken to Wormwood Scrubs in London. He declared that he would be "out in a month, dead or alive", and went on hunger strike. Despite high-level attempts at intervention, as well as fervent prayers and masses, the British government would not relent.

Cork is set low down, centered on an island between two branches of the River Lee. In fact the name of the Irish Republic's second city comes from the wetland upon which it is built: the Irish *corcach* means "marsh". Some of the streets were actually built on tributaries of the river, and the high steps often seen in front of the city's houses are a reminder of a time when there was still a danger of floods in the center. Cork is a university town, and makes up for any paucity of architectural interest by its lively atmosphere and busy cultural life. It is a pleasant and stimulating city to spend time in, whether for good pubs or good art galleries (such as the Crawford Gallery, Triskel Art Centre and the Cork Arts Society Gallery).

HISTORY

EARLY TIMES. The city's history goes back to the 7th century, when Saint Finbarr ▲ *226* built a lonely monastery on the marshes where St Finbarr's Cathedral ▲ *214* stands today. The monastery prospered and the Vikings soon arrived, settling in Cork in the 10th century. The Normans came in their turn; in 1172 they took over from the Vikings. Henry II established a garrison and gave the city its first charter.

A REBELLIOUS CITY. Cork is a city that has always been quick to support a rebel cause. In 1491 the inhabitants welcomed the adventurer Perkin Warbeck, who claimed to be the son of Edward IV. In 1649 it supported the

Catholic Confederation, and was then taken by Cromwell. In 1690 Cork took the side of James II, then to be brought to order by John Churchill, later Duke of Marlborough. The Fenians ● *53* were active here in the 19th century. In 1920 the Lord Mayor of Cork, Thomas MacCurtain, was shot dead by the police; his successor, Terence MacSwiney, starved himself to death in an English prison, and the city center was burnt by the Black and Tans in reprisal for an ambush. In 1922, after the withdrawal of English troops, Cork was occupied by Republicans hostile to the Treaty and had to be brought to order by troops of the Irish Free State.

Terence MacSwiney died on October 25, 1920 after seventy-four days refusing nourishment. The sacrifice of the Lord Mayor of Cork made the headlines worldwide. It did serious damage to the reputation of England, losing the British much support.

THE CITY CENTER

Cork did not achieve much architectural distinction until the 19th century. The Pain brothers, pupils of John Nash of London, designed a number of handsome buildings, the finest of which are HOLY TRINITY CHURCH (Father Matthew Quay) and the COURT HOUSE (Washington Street). The heavy scent of brewing from the Beamish Brewery ● *77* hangs in the air around the elegant spire and classical portico of these imposing buildings.

GRAND PARADE AND PATRICK STREET. The two main shopping streets of Cork are lined with curved façades of fine late 18th-century houses. In the covered market, called the English Market, the stalls are filled with delicious and often unusual produce, including local specialties such as *cruibins* (pigs' feet), and *drisheen* (a glistening black pudding). Behind Patrick Street is the old Huguenot district which is now full of bookshops, art galleries, little cafés and restaurants, and shops selling specialty and luxury goods.

The increasing size of the English Market, where some traders have had their stalls for generations, is a sign of the growing agricultural prosperity of County Cork.

213

Frank O'Connor.

WRITERS
Two famous writers who come from Cork are Sean O'Faolain (1900–91) ◆ *330*, whose work suffered under the censor, and Frank O'Connor (1903–66), arguably as great a storyteller as Chekhov or Maupassant. Both Irishmen found inspiration in the work of Daniel Corkery (1878–1964), writer and Professor of English Literature at University College, Cork (*The Hidden Ireland*, 1925).

CRAWFORD MUNICIPAL ART GALLERY ★ (Emmet Place). The gallery has been housed since 1884 in an elegant building of warm orange brick designed by the well-known Cork architect Arthur Hill. It has a good collection of works by Irish painters of the 19th and 20th centuries (such as Daniel Maclise, Nathaniel Grogan and Walter Osborne); *Minerva* (1822) and other works by Hogan, a local sculptor; and also plaster copies of Roman statues done under the direction of Canova. Next to the Crawford stands the new OPERA HOUSE, built in the 1960's by Michael Scott to replace the former building (above), destoyed by fire in 1955.

SOUTH CORK

ST FINBARR'S CATHEDRAL. A three-spired cathedral built in early French pointed Gothic style between 1867 and 1879, on what is thought to be the site of the monastery founded by Saint Finbarr. It was designed, in typically flamboyant spirit, by the London architect William Burges. It is the Church of Ireland cathedral, and was funded by the city's Protestant families.

UNIVERSITY COLLEGE. Cork has been a seat of learning since Saint Finbarr founded his school here, and University College has as its motto "Where Finbarr taught, let Munster learn". The college was opened by Queen Victoria during a visit to Cork in 1849, and for a time it was called Queen's College. She knighted the architect, Thomas Deane, with whom Benjamin Woodward worked for a time. A statue was erected to the queen to commemorate the occasion (now tucked away in a corner). The HONAN COLLEGIATE CHAPEL (1915) is exquisite. It was designed by James F. Macmullen. The stained-glass windows were made by Sarah Purser and Harry Clarke in Art Nouveau style and include images of the eleven Irish saints in especially vivid colors. One of University College's earliest professors was the mathematician George Boole (1815–64), a pioneer of modern symbolic logic and the early theories leading to the development of computer technology.

CORK MUSEUM. A few hundred yards away, along Mardyke Walk, lies FITZGERALD PARK, the most pleasant and spacious of Cork's all-too-few parks and gardens. Housed in a Georgian mansion in the park is the PUBLIC MUSEUM, opened in 1945. On display are collections illustrating various aspects of the city and its history, encompassing geology, archeology and natural history, social and industrial history, and local crafts and traditions. Among the most interesting exhibits are Irish elk antlers dating back to the Iron Age, the little gold bird from Garryduff, pieces of silver and glassware made in Cork, and lace from Youghal ▲ *220*. In addition, there is a section on Cork in medieval times, and another on its role in the events of 1916 to 1922 ● *54, 60, 62*.

NORTH CORK

BUTTER EXCHANGE. Next to ST MARY'S CATHEDRAL (1808) is the Shandon Craft Centre. The building was formerly occupied by the Cork Butter Exchange, an institution founded in 1730 that organized sales and guaranteed the quality of Cork butter until 1925.

ST ANNE'S ANGLICAN CHURCH. The church of St Anne, Shandon, has a conspicuous pepper-pot steeple and is the most prominent building on the north side of the city. The Shandon district has become well known through paintings, songs and poems. Most famous is *The Bells of Shandon*, a poem by the 19th-century writer Francis Sylvester Mahony, under his pen-name Father Prout.

THE SURROUNDING AREA

ROYAL GUNPOWDER MILLS (Ballincollig). Charles Henry Leslie began manufacturing gunpowder here in 1794, in order to supply the British army. The mills finally closed in 1903, and today it is possible to visit them and see how the gunpowder was produced.

DUNKATHEL HOUSE (near to the village of Glanmire). The Georgian country house built in the 18th century by the wealthy businessman and Member of Parliament Abraham Morris is worthy of Palladio. It has a strikingly elegant staircase and there is also some interesting stuccowork along with superb watercolors by Beatrice Gubbins.

RIVERSTOWN HOUSE (5 miles northwest of Cork). The Protestant bishop of Cloyne ▲ *220*, Dr Jemmett Brown, built the magnificent Riverstown House in 1745. It is a perfect example of all that was fine and elegant in the Georgian period. There are splendid Rococo-style stucco panels by the Swiss brothers Paul and Philip Lafranchini ● *106*.

TOWN FESTIVALS
Cork has a large number of cultural events during the year. The Film Festival (October) has gained a reputation for its eclectic program and its encouragement of young Irish film makers. The Cork Festival (September) is a great gathering of lovers of traditional music, while there is also the Jazz Festival in October. The Cork Choral Festival is held in the spring, bringing together choirs from all backgrounds to compete in a city proud of its long musical tradition.

County Cork is a prosperous agricultural region. Traditionally it produced large quantities of butter which, up until World War One, was exported to Europe and America.

Rococo plasterwork in Riverstown House.

215

Blarney Castle was built in 1446 by Dermot Láidir MacCarthy. It stands on a rock high above the River Martin most probably on the site of a Norman fortress, its massive walls 18 feet thick and the tower 83 feet high. As the MacCarthy stronghold, it was besieged several times, taken by Cromwell, and finally lost to the troops of William of Orange. Blarney Castle is a magnificent building set in lovely grounds, and has breathtaking views from the top, but it is the Blarney Stone that has made it the most famous tourist site in the Cork region.

ORIGIN OF THE BLARNEY STONE

According to one story, Cormac MacCarthy received half of the Stone of Scone in gratitude for his support of Robert Bruce's troops at the Battle of Bannockburn in 1314. It was set into the castle keep just below the battlements and came to be called the Blarney Stone. There is no mention of its magical properties until early in the 19th century.

GIFT OF ELOQUENCE

It is said that anyone who kisses the Blarney Stone will receive the gift of eloquence. There is generally a queue to perform this feat, although to do so involves hanging head-first over the castle wall, the legs firmly held by two strong men. The origin of the legendary power of the stone is a mystery. One tale tells of a king of Munster who saved a witch from drowning. In return she promised that if he kissed the stone he would have such a persuasive tongue that his subjects would obey his every command.

A QUEEN VEXED BY THE BLARNEY

Cormac MacCarthy, Lord of Blarney in the reign of Queen Elizabeth I, claimed to be loyal to the Queen, but "with fair words and soft speech" avoided coming to agreement with her or her Lord Deputy over taking the tenure of his lands from the Crown. Exasperated, the Queen declared: "This is all Blarney! What he says he never means." And so, it is said, the phrase was coined.

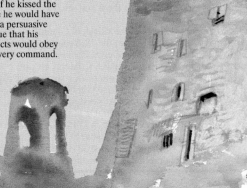

> "There is a stone that whoever kisses,
> O, he never misses to grow eloquent.
> 'Tis he may clamber to a lady's chamber,
> Or become a Member of Parliament."
>
> F.S. Mahony

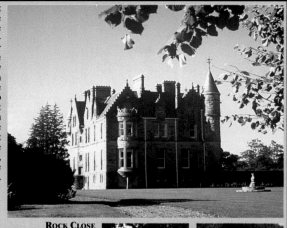

BLARNEY HOUSE
Attached to the massive keep are the remnants of a Gothic-style Georgian manor house built in the early 18th century by James St John Jefferyes. In the grounds there is also Blarney House, built in the Scottish baronial tradition late in the 19th century. It is lived in by the Colthurst family, descendants of the Jefferyes.

ROCK CLOSE
These gardens, planted around a number of standing stones said to mark a druidic site, have a magical atmosphere. There is a rock that looks like a witch, and steps that must be descended backward with the eyes shut for a wish to be granted. In the "Fairy Glade" the sun's first rays shine between the rocks onto the sacrificial stone; the ancient trees and massive stones blend to create a truly enchanted dell.

BLARNEY VILLAGE
At the end of the 18th century the village began to attract many visitors, among them Arthur Young, curious to see the prosperous and peaceful community created here by James Jefferyes. He had built a model village of ninety houses set around thirteen mills; each little house had its narrow garden behind. The industry went into decline, however, and the mills closed early in the 19th century. In 1824 Martin Mahony founded the Blarney Woollen Mills, bringing new life to the village and soon making it famous. Both the British and, later, the Irish soldiers of the two World Wars wore Blarney tweed.

The county of Waterford in the southeastern corner of Ireland is one of the mildest and wettest in the country. It is a popular holiday area with some pleasant seaside resorts. The road along the coast runs beside extensive sandy beaches, little harbors and pretty fishing villages, and offers some spectacular views over the wide and picturesque bays.

FOTA ISLAND

Once privately owned, Fota Island is set in the mouth of Cork Harbour and can now be visited. On it is a wildlife park. It is also possible to visit the arboretum attached to Fota House, filled with rare species imported by the Smith-Barry family in the 19th century that have flourished in the mild climate.

COBH ★

The port of Cobh.

QUEENSTOWN. Cobh is the Irish rendering of the Cove of Cork. In 1849, when Queen Victoria landed here, the sheltered port was renamed Queenstown. It remained so until resuming its original name in Gaelic form in 1922.

LAST PORT BEFORE AMERICA ● 59. The Queenstown Project, a permanent exhibition and heritage center, has been installed in the old Victorian railway station. It tells the story of the port from which so many set sail to start new stories of their own.

ANNIE MOORE
On January 1, 1892, her fifteenth birthday, Annie Moore was the first of seventeen million emigrants who were to pass through the Ellis Island immigration office on arrival at New York. There is a statue of her with her two brothers in front of the museum.

From 1845 to 1960, several million Irish people left Ireland from Cobh to sail to America, Australia and New Zealand. During the Famine the crafts on which the desperate refugees traveled came to be known as "coffin ships". Under better circumstances emigrants set sail aboard the many steamers that called at Cobh. After the success of the *Sirius*, the first steamship to cross the Atlantic, which left Cobh on April 14, 1838 and reached New York eighteen days later, many companies had begun to build bigger, faster and more comfortable boats to transport passengers, mail and freight. After World War Two transatlantic crossings called less and less frequently at Cobh, unable to compete with rapidly improving air services. The heritage center has a section on the *Titanic*, which made its last stop at Cobh on April 11, 1912, and on the sinking of the *Lusitania*, torpedoed by a German submarine on May 7, 1915, off Old Head, Kinsale ▲ *224*. Only eight hundred of the two thousand passengers survived, and many of the victims are buried near Cobh. A memorial to them stands in Casement Square.

THE VILLAGE. Cobh has a second museum, housed in an old Presbyterian church and concentrating on local history. The steep streets of the little town lead up toward its crowning glory, the French Gothic cathedral of ST COLMAN (1868–1919). From here there are views over Haulbowline Island, where there is a dockyard and naval headquarters, and Spike Island, once a prison from which many left for Botany Bay. In WEST VIEW a line of twenty-three identical houses has earned the nickname of "the pack of cards".

FAIRBARN'S PADDLEWHEEL
The massive iron wheel of the *Midleton* distillery (1852) remained in use until 1975. It is well over 20 feet in diameter and was used to produce energy for the works. When the water level was too low, steam engines were used to boost the power.

THE ROYAL CORK YACHT CLUB
The exclusive club, founded in 1720 as the Cork Harbour Water Club based on Haulbowline Island, claims to be the oldest yacht club in the world. It transferred its base to Cobh shortly afterward, and the name was changed in 1828. In 1854, the architect Anthony Salvin (1799–1881) was instructed to build a new headquarters for the club. His Italianate structure was built behind Westbourne Place, overlooking Cobh Harbour, which was used until 1969.

MIDLETON ★

Before going on as far as Midleton, the famous whiskey town ● *79*, there is an agreeable stop to be made at BARRYSCOURT CASTLE, near the village of Carriguohill. A pleasant little restaurant is just next to the castle.

A PRECIOUS HERITAGE. In 1825 the Murphy brothers bought some old wool-producing premises in Midleton and founded a distillery that was soon to be one of the most successful in the south of Ireland. In 1867 it merged with four Cork distilleries, and a century later this new company joined forces with the Dublin distillers John Jameson and John Power & Son. Today *Midleton* and *Bushmills* ▲ *314* are the two largest whiskey producers in Ireland. A part of the old distillery buildings now houses the Jameson Heritage Centre, where the long process of making whiskey is explained. There is a chance to taste the product afterward. (Take the R629 to Cloyne.)

GEORGE BERKELEY (1685–1753)
After studying at Trinity College ▲ 148, Berkeley took holy orders and taught Greek, Hebrew and theology. His study of John Locke inspired him to write his *Treatise Concerning the Principles of Human Knowledge* (1710), and his most famous doctrine was "Esse is percipi"

("to be is to be perceived"). He traveled in France, Spain and Italy, and returned in 1721, became Dean of Derry in 1724, but then spent time in America to pursue his project to found a Christian college in the Bermudas (which eventually failed). In the 1730's he became Bishop of Cloyne, and there is a monument to him in the cathedral. The city and university of Berkeley in California are named for him.

CLOYNE

Cloyne includes among its famous inhabitants the bishop and philosopher George Berkeley, who came here in 1742, and the more recent hero, Christy Ring, Cork star of hurling ● 83, who is honored with a statue in the town center. The CATHEDRAL dates from the 13th century, but lost much of its beauty during restoration. The west door still has some interesting primitive carvings of pagan symbols. Before continuing along the coast road to Youghal, lined with delightful little beaches and villages such as Ballycotton (above), it is worth stopping at Shanagarry to visit BALLYMALOE HOUSE, a restaurant and cookery school. The nearby ruined castle belonged to the Penn family and was the birthplace of the Quaker William Penn, founder of Pennsylvania.

YOUGHAL ★

Youghal (meaning "yew wood" and pronounced "Yawl") is set at the mouth of the River Blackwater, one of the country's most unspoilt rivers. Since the last century Youghal has been a popular seaside resort with a grand, sandy beach, but the happy holiday-makers distract attention from some unexpectedly interesting buildings.
MAIN STREET. The tall CLOCKGATE TOWER (1771) spans the street. The building was once a prison, where condemned men were hanged from the windows, but it now houses a museum. A little further on is the striking façade of the RED HOUSE, a large brick-built town house designed around 1710 by a Dutch architect for the Uniacke family. Opposite is TYNTE'S CASTLE, a 15th-century fortified tower, now in ruins (left). At the corner of Church Street are some 17th-century ALMSHOUSES.
COLLEGIATE CHURCH OF ST MARY. The church dates back to the 13th century, but was badly restored in the 19th. It still contains some magnificent and fascinating tombs and effigies including that of Richard Boyle in the south transept.

In 1619 he had a gigantic mausoleum built in the fashionable Italian style; but it was his brother John Boyle, the bishop of Cork, Cloyne and Ross, who was to be buried there a year later. In the graveyard lies the writer and journalist Claud Cockburn, who lived in Youghal and later Ardmore, where he died in 1981. Among other works he wrote an exuberant autobiography, *I, Claud*, as well as the novel from which the film *Beat the Devil* was made, starring James Cagney. Behind the church is a section of 13th-century town wall.

MYRTLE GROVE. This Elizabethan house is thought to date partly from the mid-15th century, and to be one of the oldest houses in Ireland. It was part of an estate confiscated from the FitzGerald family in the 1580's and presented to Sir Walter Raleigh, but there is no firm evidence that he spent time here.

LISMORE CASTLE. Before continuing along the coast, the road follows the wooded valley of the River Blackwater, famous for its salmon and trout, to reach Lismore. The castle, which overlooks the river, owes its present-day appearance to alterations made in the 1850's. It is a private house, but the gardens are open to the public and well worth a visit, with a yew-walk of trees almost a thousand years old. To get a feel of the wilder inland landscape, go and see the CISTERCIAN MONASTERY OF MOUNT MELLERAY (1832), over 600 feet up in the Knockmealdown Mountains. The views of the mountains and river valley are thrilling.

ARDMORE

Ardmore is another town popular with holiday-makers. It has one of the finest round towers in the country, still with its original conical stone roof, and decorative courses to mark the stories.

THE CATHEDRAL ★. Now a ruin known as St Declan's Church, the cathedral may stand on the site of the 6th-century monastery founded by Saint Declan. It is unique in Ireland for having a western façade covered with Romanesque reliefs. Inside are two ogham stones ● *66*. Next to the cathedral is the tiny ST DECLAN'S ORATORY, probably dating from the 8th century and restored in the 18th, in which the saint is thought to be buried.

ARDMORE CATHEDRAL ARCADING
Six of the thirteen bas-reliefs carved on the upper row of blind arcading date from the Romanesque period (late 12th century). They are similar in style and subject to scenes found on Celtic crosses ▲ *206*.

"MOBY DICK"
John Huston's film of Melville's novel was shot in Youghal in 1955. Some were unkind enough to criticize the masts that appeared over the roof tops for being so still when real masts would have moved with the wind and water. The waterfront pub, *Moby Dick's*, has pictures of the filming taking place.

221

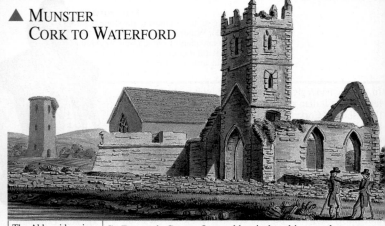

The Abbeyside ruins.

DYSERT CHURCH
Half a mile from the tower and cathedral in Ardmore are the ruins of a church probably built on the site of the *desertulum* ("little hermitage") of Saint Declan. Next to

it is St Declan's Well, where pilgrims used to bathe.

FAMINE VICTIMS
Not far from Dungarvan, on the road to Waterford, a sign marks a place where victims of the Great Famine ● *58*, particularly terrible in this area, lie buried. There is a cross in memory of the Irish who died during this dreadful time.

ST DECLAN'S STONE. Legend has it that this sacred stone carried the bell and garments of the saint over the waters from Wales, shortly after Declan visited Ardmore. The stone lies at the end of the long sandy beach and rests, rather like the stone slab of a dolmen, on two small rocks. It is said that both physical distress (rheumatism) and spiritual ills can be cured by sliding beneath the stone on July 24, St Declan's Day.

DUNGARVAN

KING JOHN'S CASTLE. The town of Dungarvan lies on the banks of the River Colligan, and is set prettily around a spacious central square. It looks across the wide bay to Helvick Head. The ruins of its castle, built by King John and much damaged by Cromwell in 1649, have now been partly converted into a restaurant.
ABBEYSIDE. On the east bank of the Colligan are the peaceful ruins of an Augustinian priory dating from the late 13th century. Take a walk from the graveyard toward the sea to enjoy a wonderful view over the bay of Dungarvan and Helvick Head.
AN RINN. A few miles from Dungarvan is a little village where Gaelic is still spoken and where eager students come to listen and learn. An Rinn lies at the heart of a Gaelic-speaking area ● *68*, and a number of traditional Irish-language singers have their roots here (Nicolas Toibin, Aine Ni Cheallaigh).

TRAMORE

The road to Tramore runs along a coast bordered with quiet sandy beaches and beautiful seaside landscapes such as Clonea Bay. It passes through the villages of Stradbally, Bunmahon and Annestown. In some places copper mines make it dangerous to go onto the cliffs. In contrast, Tramore itself has one of the busiest beaches in Ireland. Children who have had enough of sea and sand can learn about the great Irish myths and legends at the Celtworld theme park.
The main road (N52) leads on to Waterford, with recommended stops at KILMACTHOMAS (where the grandfather of Hollywood star Tyrone Power was born), and at KILMEADEN, a little town now known for the cheese that bears its name. After Waterford there is a ferry at Dunmore East to take cars over to County Wexford ▲ *180*.

Thackeray found it very hard to describe the beauty of Ireland. Words seemed to lack the delicate nuances required to convey the range of colors and variations of light playing over land and ocean. Elizabeth Bowen captures these extreme changes of mood: "On fine days the view was remarkable, of almost Italian brilliance, with that constant reflection up from the water that even now prolonged the too-long day. Now, in continuous evening rain, the winding wooded line of the further shore could be seen and, nearer the windows, a smothered island with the stump of a watch-

◆ F D5-D6-C6-B6-B5-A5

tower." Ireland is a challenge for painters too, especially the striking contrasts of landscape in the southwest.

THE COAST ROAD

KINSALE. Kinsale is jokingly referred to as the capital of the Irish Côte d'Azur, so it is no surprise to find it twinned with Antibes-Juan-les-Pins. The port is set around one of the most sheltered bays on the southern coast of the island, at the mouth of the River Bandon. It is a pretty town, well cared-for, buzzing with activity and happy to welcome its many visitors. It is a popular yachting center and also a favorite haunt of fishermen, especially those in pursuit of the blue shark ■ *20*. The town attracts almost equal numbers in search of good food: for an Irish town, Kinsale boasts an incredible number of restaurants. The annual Gourmet Festival has now been expanded to include an International Food Forum, bringing in food-lovers from far and wide. The narrow streets wind up from the harbor to reach the fields of Compass Hill. The church of ST MULTOSE dates from the 13th century and despite later alterations retains the feeling of great age. It is one of Kinsale's finest buildings, but there are a number of others to be seen. The early 18th-century Court House is now restored and houses the Kinsale Regional Museum. The Desmond Castle, a 15th-to-18th-century tower house, is also known as the French Prison (as it was so used). Many inmates died in a fire on January 27, 1747.

CHARLES FORT ● *100.* The star fort overlooking the sea beyond Summercove, 2 miles outside Kinsale, is a piece of military architecture in perfect Vauban style. It is the largest such construction from the 17th century to survive in Ireland.

THE BATTLE OF KINSALE
The Spanish fleet invaded in 1601 and held the town, aided by the Irish Earl of Tyrone. When the English regained Kinsale it was to mark the defeat of Gaelic Ireland; the "Flight of the Earls" to Europe was to follow. Kinsale became an English town, where the Irish were not allowed to live, until the late 18th century.

With the repeal of the Edict of Nantes in 1685, French Huguenots settled in the region and started a flourishing textile industry. In 1689 the French fleet landed the exiled King James II at Kinsale with a Franco-Irish expeditionary force: James wanted to regain his crown and Louis XIV wanted William of Orange out of the British Isles where he posed too much of a threat ▲ *194*.

Originally there was a small outpost on the site, destroyed when the Spanish fleet captured Kinsale in 1601. The English realized that such a strategically important harbor needed serious fortifications. They began by building James Fort (1602–4) whose ruins can still be seen on the opposite side of the inlet. The construction of Charles Fort was begun in 1678, in preparation for a Dutch seaborne attack. It was named for King Charles II. In 1681 the massive edifice was completed with fortifications on the landward side. In the 1690's John Goubet and Rudolph Corneille, Huguenot builders working for King William, made some modifications to the fort, and the main structure has remained virtually unaltered since. The barracks inside date from the 18th and early 19th century. The English evacuated Charles Fort in 1921. It was then occupied by Republicans hostile to the Treaty who were subsequently removed, with some damage to the fort, by the army of the Free State.

OLD HEAD OF KINSALE ★. On the craggy, wind-blown headland, surrounded by wild seas, stand the ruins of the De Courcy castle and a lighthouse. The *Lusitania* sank off Old Head in 1915 ▲ *219*.

TIMOLEAGUE. The village stands at the head of the Argideen estuary and incorporates the ruins of a 13th-century Franciscan abbey destroyed by Cromwell's troops in 1642.

CLONAKILTY. This part of West Cork saw much IRA guerilla action during the war for Irish independence. The events of this period are commemorated and recorded at a number of places, especially the WEST CORK REGIONAL MUSEUM in Clonakilty, and the MICHAEL COLLINS MEMORIAL CENTRE at Sam's Cross.

DROMBEG STONE CIRCLE. Between Rosscarberry and Glandore is one of Ireland's finest stone circles, consisting of seventeen regularly spaced standing stones (153 BC–AD 127). Dating from the same period, 200 feet away, are the remains of a kitchen hearth. There is a well and a trough where water was heated by throwing in hot stones that kept their warmth for about three hours.

CÉIM HILL MUSEUM ★. The little cottage in the middle of nowhere does not look at all like a museum. Yet the owner has packed three small rooms with an amazing mixture of exhibits, including prehistoric finds, memorabilia from the war of independence and various local artefacts.

CASTLETOWNSHEND. An old stronghold of the Ascendancy ● *52* that has been made famous by the

MICHAEL COLLINS (1890–1922) ● *63*
The leader of the Irish Liberation Movement became Minister of Finance in De Valera's Republican Ministry. He helped to get De Valera out of Lincoln prison, and organized Republican activity in the south. He was one of the negotiators of the Anglo-Irish Treaty, chairman of the Provisional Government, and commander of the IRA during the Civil War. The little farm of Woodfield where Collins was born on October 16, 1890, was burnt down in April 1921 by Black and Tans and he was murdered in an ambush nearby on August 20, 1922.

IRA volunteers during the war for independence.

Baltimore Lighthouse.

FASTNET
A yacht race has been held every other year since 1925, starting at Cowes on the Isle of Wight, passing the Fastnet Lighthouse and returning to Plymouth. The 1979 race was marked by terrible storms, claiming the lives of fifteen contestants.

writers Edith Somerville and Violet Martin (Martin Ross) ▲ *267*, who set their "Irish R.M." stories here. They are both buried in the ST BARRAHANE churchyard. There are many prehistoric remains in the area, but they can be quite hard to reach. KNOCKDRUM STONE FORT, an easily accessible one, stands on high ground in a field at the edge of the village. It has a round stone wall and some other remains.

BALTIMORE. A poem by Thomas Davis relates how in 1631 the little port of Baltimore was pillaged by Algerian pirates who took two hundred inhabitants into slavery. On the point stands a medieval lighthouse called LOT'S WIFE. Just offshore is SHERKIN ISLAND. Since 1975 it has been the site of the Marine Research Station, an institution responsible for keeping checks on the marine environment. There are a natural history museum and vivarium to visit. The east coast of the island, facing Baltimore, has deep waters where boats and yachts find good moorings. To the south can be seen the wild and rocky outline of CLEAR ISLAND, the most southerly in Ireland. Its bird observatory is well known for its study of migrating species, and the whole isle is a delight for birdlovers. In summer, puffins can be seen here on the cliffs, and out to sea there may be whales and dolphins ■ *20*. (Now proceed to Bantry by the N71, or continue to the southernmost tip of Ireland, Mizen Head.)

BANTRY ★. Bantry stands on an immense bay overlooking the Beara Peninsula. The bay was of great strategical importance in the past, and some dramatic events took place here, but today it is a vast and peaceful expanse of water, with a mild and sheltered climate that encourages lush vegetation. The town of Bantry has one of the finest houses in Ireland, BANTRY HOUSE, which overlooks the bay and the mountains beyond. The original long brick structure, three stories high, was built by the Hutchinson family around 1710. In the 18th century two wings were added, and in 1845 Richard White,

A FRUITLESS EXPEDITION
On December 15, 1796, a fleet of forty-three ships (16,000 troops) left Brest to come to the aid of the United Irishmen, whose leader Wolfe Tone ● *52* was on board. A storm blew many ships off course, including that of the commander, General Hoche, and only sixteen arrived in Bantry Bay. The second-in-command pressed on with the attack but it was prevented by gales, sleet and snow. Finally, the French ships returned home. It was a lucky escape for the English, since Bantry was very poorly defended. The wreck of the frigate *Surveillante* was raised in the 1980's.

ARCHEOLOGICAL REMAINS
The area around Bantry is full of ancient secrets. There is a circle of standing stones at Kealkil. At Kilnaruane the cross remains a puzzle to experts: the figures carved on the shaft seem to be of Saint Anthony and Saint Paul, while

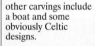

other carvings include a boat and some obviously Celtic designs.

second Earl of Bantry, had the house completely redesigned and surrounded by gardens in the Italian style. Bantry House contains a varied collection of fine works of art from all over Europe, and has been open to the public since 1945. Today the two wings of Bantry House have been refurbished to accommodate tourists. More than 48,000 visitors come each year to view the house and permanent exhibition: "1796 Armada Trust".

THE INLAND ROUTE

The River Bandon runs through unspoilt countryside, perfect for walking. Each bend in the river reveals another lovely view, and the ever-changing weather transforms the mood and atmosphere of the landscape from one hour to the next.

BANDON. The town was founded early in the 17th century by Richard Boyle, Earl of Cork. Kilbrogan Church, one of Ireland's first Protestant churches, was built here in 1610. At this time the town was populated with English and Scottish settlers, and Catholics were not permitted to live here. Bandon long continued to have a strong anti-Catholic reputation.

GOUGANE BARRA ★. Saint Finbarr, the founder of Cork ▲ *212*, was born in Gougane Barra. The legend goes that he lived in a hermitage here, at a place now marked by a cross (left), having rid the lake of Gougane Barra of a dreadful monster. The lake, surrounded by forests and mountains, has provided romantic inspiration for many writers and poets. The National Park nearby is very good for walking, with well-marked paths including one leading to the source of the River Lee.

BEARA PENINSULA

The climate is mild, the vegetation abundant and seals are often seen sunning themselves on the rocks at Glengarriff.

The Beara Peninsula is a wild and mountainous finger of land stretching out toward the Atlantic Ocean between the bays of Bantry and Kenmare. It remains a mysterious place, especially the little-visited inland areas. There are a number of small loughs, and in the center of the peninsula run the Caha and the Slieve Mickish mountains. The coast road,

bordered with lush vegetation, makes its way west around creeks and inlets, past beaches and bays and through tiny fishing villages. The inland road is extremely narrow and remote, leading between the sparsely covered mountain ridges.

GLENGARRIFF ★. The town stands at the entrance to the Beara Peninsula, and at the head of Bantry Bay. The Gulf Stream gives it a mild climate that has permitted an amazing number of Mediterranean plants to take root and flourish here in abundance, especially on south-facing slopes and beaches. In the bay just off Glengarriff lies GARINISH ISLAND ■ *38*, transformed into an exotic garden by its owner John Annan Bryce. For his

Gougane Barra.

ambitious project he brought tons of earth over from the mainland to cover the rocky land, and employed the well-known landscape gardener Harold Peto to design an Italian garden, certainly one of the most unusual and enchanting in Ireland. Before continuing to Kenmare over the HEALY PASS, a road cut through the Caha Mountains in the early 1930's, it is pleasant to spend some time on the Beara Peninsula discovering the traces of its ancient past. These include the tallest ogham stone in Ireland (17 feet), which stands overlooking the ocean at BALLYCROVANE.

CASTLETOWNBERE. On the outskirts of the village, surrounded by woods, is the ruined DUNBOY CASTLE, once the stronghold of O'Sullivan Bere and destroyed during a siege in 1602. Also to be found here are the remains of PUXLEY CASTLE (c.1866). This unusual building, half-French château, half-Italian villa, belonged to the Puxley family, who owned the Allihies copper mines. It was burned down by the IRA in 1921.

DURSEY ISLAND. The island is just off Crow Head, at the furthest end of the peninsula and emerges high and rocky from the sea, edged by steep cliffs. There is a cable-car trip to the island and many birdwatchers visit because it is a haven for seabirds ■ *20*. On the north side of the peninsula toward Kenmare, north of the village of Lauragh lies DERREEN HOUSE. Its gardens contain rhododendrons, azaleas, eucalyptus trees and New Zealand tree ferns.

BERE ISLAND. The long, narrow island lies sheltered along the south coast of the peninsula, just over a mile offshore from Castletownbere. In World War One it was a Royal Navy base but was relinquished by the British government in 1938. Today Bere Island is enjoyed by those who like fishing and sailing.

THE ALLIHIES COPPER MINES
Copper was discovered on the Beara Peninsula in 1810. Two years later it began to be exploited. At the height of their activity the Allihies mines employed 1,300 miners, some from Cornwall, and brought prosperity to the region. They also made the fortune of the Puxley family, on whose story Daphne Du Maurier based her novel *Hungry Hill*. The mining stopped for good in 1962.

◆ **F** B5-A5-A4-B4

**DANIEL O'CONNELL
(1775–1847)** ● 53
Son of a small
landowner, Daniel
O'Connell was
adopted by a rich
uncle and brought
up in France. He was
called to the Irish Bar
and campaigned for
the emancipation of
Catholics.

At fifty-three he
was elected Member
of Parliament for
County Clare ▲ 245.
O'Connell continued
to fight for the
Repeal of the Union,
making "Irish popular
opinion a force in
British politics for the
first time" (Robert
Kee).

County Kerry is renowned for its beauty, which is all the
more dramatic because it combines so many different
kinds of natural splendor. The coastline can vary from
enchantingly peaceful to wild and rugged, while inland the
landscape includes homely farms with walled fields and
small streams, as well as powerful, dark-watered rivers,
spectacular upland torrents, and craggy mountains, including
the tallest in Ireland, Mount Carantouhil (3,414 feet) on
the Iveragh Peninsula. The mild climate has also created
pockets of dense and lush vegetation, particularly south of
Killarney. There is a panoramic route leading around the
Iveragh Peninsula known as the Ring of Kerry. The winding
road passes through a succession of magnificent landscapes,
and has long been one of the favorite sightseeing tours of
Ireland.

KENMARE TO WATERVILLE

KENMARE. The small town (left) lies on
the Kenmare River estuary and was
founded in the 17th century by Sir
William Petty, an economist whom
Cromwell instructed to carry out a
general survey of Ireland. He amassed
the Lansdowne estate and, in 1775, his
descendant the Marquis of Lansdowne, came to live in the
town and started its first market and its first inn. Among many
ancient remains in the area is the mysterious circle of stones
called the DRUID'S CIRCLE, standing near the town center
beside the river.
PARKNASILLA. The house once belonged to the Bland family,
but was converted to become the Great Southern Hotel, with
George Bernard Shaw as its most famous guest. He is said to

> "Blue sky, roaring water, here black and yonder foaming of a dazzling white; rocks shining in the dark places, or frowning black against the light."
>
> William Makepeace Thackeray

have completed his play *Saint Joan* in what is now called the Shaw Library.

SNEEM. The village, through which the Ardsheelaun River rushes to the sea, is a popular stopping place. Winning a number of prizes for its tidy charm, it has made every effort to beautify itself for visitors; its pieces of modern sculpture in particular make it an interesting town. They include James Scanlon's curious pyramids, as well as the white *Peaceful Panda* (1986), symbolizing the peaceful relationship between Ireland and China; a metal tree given to the town in 1985 by the President of Israel; and Alan Hall's monument to commemorate General de Gaulle's stay nearby in 1969.

STAIGUE FORT ★. The fort lies less than 3 miles inland from Castlecove, in peaceful countryside. The massive circular dry-stone walls are 90 feet in diameter and remain in astonishingly good condition. They are 13 feet thick and up to 16 feet high, tapering toward the top. There is an intriguing system of diagonal runs of steps leading up to the top of the wall, which was probably surmounted by a palisade ● *91*. As usual there is a teasing legend to enliven the visit: it is said that the Iron Age fortress was built in a day and a night.

CAHERDANIEL. The town, whose name comes from CATHAIR DONAILL, a pre-Christian fort similar in construction to Staigue Fort, stands close to the lovely beach at Derrynane Bay. Just outside the village is DERRYNANE HOUSE, from 1825 the home of Daniel O'Connell (1775–1847), and now a museum. Sean O'Faolain gave this picture of O'Connell there: "He would breakfast on the hills, going quickly but intently through his letters, strewing the grass with The Times, The Universe, letters from France or America, reports from Dublin."

WATERVILLE. Once over the Coomakista Pass, which winds up to 700 feet, there is a magnificent drive down toward Waterville with views over Ballinskellig Bay and the Skellig Islands. Waterville itself sits between the bay and Lough Currane, famous for brown trout and salmon fishing. All around are lovely beaches and fine walks.

WATERVILLE TO VALENTIA ISLAND

CHURCH ISLAND. The island in Lough Currane has the ruins of a 6th-century oratory and a 7th-century church. Nearby

stand *clocháin* ▲ *236* (beehive huts), one of which is reputed to have been the cell of Saint Finan. In clear weather, when the water is still, it is possible to look down into the lake and see the submerged ruins of a castle.

BALLINSKELLIGS. The village of Ballinskelligs is set on a lovely beach where the first Celts are thought to have landed. This is a Gaelic-speaking community, and many come here to learn the language. Near to the water are the wind- and sea-worn ruins of an Augustinian monastery. There is also a ruined 16th-century castle built by the MacCarthys to rebuff attacks by pirates and other invaders. For those who enjoy mountain scenery there is a road to Portmagee, where the bridge crosses to

Valentia Island, over Coomanaspig Gap (1,080 feet). Otherwise, the coast road past ST FINAN'S BAY has equally spectacular views.

VALENTIA ISLAND. At the western end are the rocky cliffs around Bray Head, and to the northeast lies the little village of KNIGHTSTOWN, named after the Knights of Kerry, a branch of the Anglo-Norman FitzGerald family, whose ancestral seat is at Glanleam. Here too are the subtropical gardens of Lord Mounteagle, flourishing in the warmth of the Gulf Stream climate. Visitors can learn more about the life of the islanders

at the Valentia Heritage Centre. Many also enjoy the Skellig
Experience Visitor Centre which gives a history of the Skellig
Islands.

CAHIRCIVEEN TO KILLARNEY

CAHIRCIVEEN. Daniel O'Connell was
born here at CARHAN HOUSE, which
today is an ivy-covered ruin. The Catholic
church, the O'CONNELL MEMORIAL
CHURCH, is the only one in the world to
have been dedicated to a layman. Nearby
there are two interesting ring-forts.
LEACANABUAILE FORT is a massive
construction with a single entrance to the
east side. One of its three beehive huts

was occupied in the 9th and 10th centuries. CAHERGAL FORT
is similar to Staigue Fort. It has two dry-stone constructions
within, a beehive hut and a rectangular structure.
GLENBEIGH. The road leads back to the sea on Dingle Bay
and descends into the valley of the River Beigh. This ends to
the south with the circle of hills known as the Glenbeigh
Horse Shoe. The village is a popular resort because of the
nearby beach, lying along the sandy spit called Rossbeigh
Strand that reaches out into Dingle Bay. The mud flats
situated at the eastern spit of land offer some excellent
birdwatching. The fishing is also good, and the seafood
restaurants are notable. The road continues toward LOUGH
CARAGH, a long curved lake extending nearly 4 miles and well
known for its salmon and salmon trout.
KILLORGLIN. The town stands on the wide River Laune and
the salmon fishing is good nearby. But Killorglin is chiefly
famous for its Puck Fair, a three-day festival which takes
place the second weekend in August.

231

The craggy islands rise dramatically from the wild ocean, 10 miles off the western point of the Iveragh Peninsula. Little Skellig is now a bird reserve, while Skellig Michael (also called Great Skellig) is still a vivid reminder of the austerity of early monastic life in Ireland. The remote monastery on the Skelligs was the westernmost outpost of Christianity in the old world, and was once considered to be the end of the world itself. The rocky cliffs of the island rise 700 feet above the sea, steeper and more impregnable than any walls. Nevertheless, in the 9th century the Vikings dared to attack.

Puffin

A MAGNIFICENT SETTING
The tiny monastic settlement consists of two oratories, six beehive huts, a church and a graveyard, surrounded by a dry-stone wall. Over six hundred steps cut into the rocks by the monks lead up to it.

SKELLIG MICHAEL
Like so many holy sites perched on high rocks, the monastery is dedicated to the Archangel Michael, who is said to have helped Saint Patrick chase the snakes out of Ireland.

LITTLE SKELLIG
The isle is a nature reserve, and nearly twenty thousand gannets nest here each year. This flourishing colony was in great danger of dying out early in the century, but it is now protected. Landings on the island are strictly controlled.

THE MONASTERY
Saint Finan is said to have founded the monastery in the 6th century, and this is borne out by the style of construction. The monks left in the 12th century, taking refuge at Ballinskelligs ▲ 230.

PILGRIMAGE
Large numbers of the faithful have made the journey to Skellig Michael, one of the most holy spots in Ireland. After visiting the ruins, penitent pilgrims would make the hazardous climb up to the summit, Needle's Eye, to kiss the standing stone.

Manx shearwater

Razorbill

Gannet

Storm petrel

THE "CLOCHÁIN" ▲ *236*
Six cells in the form of beehive huts remain.
These *clocháin*, are dry-stone constructions,
rounded towards the top to create the roof,
which is finished with flat stones. They measure
15 to 25 feet in diameter. The exterior protruding
stones were probably for keying a covering of lime.

THE LAKES OF KILLARNEY, THE GATEWAY TO THE RING OF KERRY ✪
Killarney should be approached from Kenmare via the mountain passes, in order to explore its lakes, with their lush green islands. If the hike to the Upper Lake or Lough Leake seems too daunting, don't miss the drive up the narrow picturesque road that winds its way up to the Gap of Dunloe. Killarney is also the starting point of the Ring of Kerry, packed pubs where beer and whiskey provide convivial accompaniment to the ballads belted out by the citizens of Kerry.

HORSE-DRAWN VEHICLES
In Killarney and at the gates of Muckross House there are "jarveys" waiting with their "jaunting cars" ready to take tourists for a ride. Passengers sitting back-to-back can take a relatively safe horse-drawn tour of the hills and lakes.

Muckross House.

KILLARNEY AND SURROUNDING AREA

Coming from the bare, windswept Atlantic coast of Kerry, the richness of vegetation around Killarney is a surprise. There are immensely tall trees, impenetrable rhododendron groves, and a feeling of fertile, green profusion that can be almost sinister. This region gives real meaning to the name Emerald Isle.

KILLARNEY. The town has made efforts to gratify the tourist trade since its development in the 19th century, but it has little in the way of architectural splendor. St Mary's Catholic Cathedral, a neo-Gothic structure by A.W. Pugin built between 1842 and 1855, is the only building of interest in the town. Its interior was stripped to bare stone in the 1970's. The Church of Christ, Prince of Peace, was erected at Fossa, just outside Killarney, in 1977. A number of well-known Irish artists were involved in the project including John Behan, Patrick Pye and Imogen Stuart. The window behind the altar must have the finest view of any church in Ireland.

KILLARNEY NATIONAL PARK. Twenty-three square miles of lakes and forest around Muckross House, southwest of Killarney, are now a protected area. There are many walks, some more strenuous than others, along which to explore the magnificent, romantic landscape. Tourists also enjoy the park by bicycle and on horseback. The area is of particular interest to botanists because the many patches of virgin oak wood are typical of that which once covered most of Ireland. Many other species abound, including birch, holly, bilberry and the red-barked arbutus or strawberry tree. The mosses and lichens are vigorous and varied. From the Aghadoe Heights there is an extraordinary view over the mountains and the three lakes: Upper Lake, Middle Lake, and Lower Lake.

MUCKROSS ABBEY. Half-hidden amid oaks, sycamores and ash trees are the peaceful ruins of a Franciscan monastery. The abbey was destroyed by Cromwell's soldiers in 1652. The buildings are typical of the 15th century, particularly the Gothic windows with interlace pattern and the impressive square tower ● 96. Finest of all are the cloisters, with pointed and round-topped arches, set around a dark yew tree. This symbol of mourning seems to honor

The Gap of Dunloe is a shadowy and rocky pass between MacGillycuddy's Reeks and the Purple Mountain, past lakes to a wonderful view over the Upper Lake. Kate Kearney's Cottage (below), a place to stop for refreshment on the road to the Gap, has lost its terror now that Kate is no longer there to curse all who enter the establishment.

three Kerry poets buried in the abbey: Geoffrey O'Donoghue (d. 1677), Egan O'Rahilly (1670–1728), whose poems denounced the disappearance of the old Gaelic order crushed by colonization, and Owen Roe O'Sullivan (1748–84), whose lyrical accounts of ancient legends have been assimilated into Irish folklore. A fourth poet, the betrayed chieftain Piaras Ferriter, is said to be buried in the graveyard outside the abbey. He was hanged on the nearby Hill of Sheep in 1643.

MUCKROSS HOUSE. The neo-Gothic mansion, where Queen Victoria stayed in 1861, was built in 1843 by William Burn. Some of the beautifully furnished rooms can be visited, with views over well-tended gardens to the magnificent lake and hills beyond. In the grounds, the Kerry Country Life Experience has recreated a farm as it would have been early in the century.

ROSS CASTLE. On the banks of Lower Lake stands a castle dating from around 1500, and probably built by a local chieftain, O'Donoghue Ross. According to an ancient prophecy, it was to fall to a warrior come from over the sea. The story is told that, as a result, in 1649, when Cromwell's General Ludlow approached the castle, it was abandoned. In fact, Lord Muskerry's troops fled under fire from Ludlow's cannons.

INNISFALLEN ISLAND. There are over thirty islands in the Lower Lake. From a landing stage below Ross Castle boats leave for Innisfallen Island, described by Macaulay as "not a reflex of heaven, but a bit of heaven itself". Two little chapels remain from a 7th-century monastery where in the 13th century an important manuscript was produced called the *Annals of Innisfallen*. It is now kept in Oxford.

TORC WATERFALL. The road winds past the lakes. On the wooded slopes opposite, the Torc river drops in a dramatic 60-foot waterfall. Tennyson's poem, set to music by Britten, captures the haunting beauty of the place: "Blow, bugle, blow, set the wild echoes flying, Blow, bugle, answer, echoes dying, dying, dying." Further along the road is Ladies View ★, a vantage point from which to survey the lakes and the far-off Gap of Dunloe. The name has various explanations: one is that Queen Victoria's ladies-in-waiting were enraptured by the view in 1861.

Meanwhile, at Kate Kearney's Cottage in the Gap of Dunloe ...

They say you're a bit of witch, Kate?!

Don't anyone dare say that! I'll turn them into a toad! Heh! Heh!

ROMANTIC MUSE
Since the 18th century the special beauty of the landscape around Killarney has fascinated travelers, among them the philosopher George Berkeley ▲ 220, and many writers such as Scott, Tennyson, Thackeray and Shelley. There has long been a tourist industry catering to this image, but it has not managed to destroy the romantic magic of the place.

THE "CLOCHÁIN"
● *92*
It has proved difficult to date the beehive huts with any accuracy, and some are perhaps quite recent. But the oldest of the round, dry-stone structures were often monks' cells, and were later used by shepherds. There are a good number of huts on the Dingle Peninsula, resembling structures found in the Vaucluse, the Rhone Valley in France, and others elsewhere in Europe. Some of the Dingle huts are not officially indicated. When on private land they may be signposted at the farm or cottage gate. In such circumstances, although their date may be uncertain, they are particularly astonishing.

DINGLE, A LUSH PENINSULA ✪
A full day is required to explore Dingle from end to end, as there are so many sights that demand a closer look: cliffs, immaculate beaches and fields bordered by low stone walls that are the last remains of long-lost dolmens, cromlech tumuli, ogham stones, oratories, underground chambers with steps leading to the ocean shore and ruined fortresses, not forgetting what is left of the village specially reconstructed for the shooting of the internationally acclaimed film *Ryan's Daughter*.

To visit the Dingle Peninsula, the northernmost of County Kerry, is to venture into a world that is far removed from our everyday existence. The coast road, lined with red-flowering fuchsia hedges in summer, leads past an astonishing number of ancient remains, ogham stones, *clocháin* and early Christian shrines. The origins of many are still unknown, adding to the sense of mystery that pervades the place. It is known, however, that these holy places were visited by pilgrims, who would halt and congregate about them as they made their way toward Mount Brandon.

DINGLE TO DUNQUIN

BALLINTAGGART. Ogham stones ● *66* are the most remarkable remains of the pre-Christian era. There are nine of them in the circular cemetery at Ballintaggart (2 miles southeast of Dingle). Three of these standing stones have strange incisions on the edges which, together form an alphabet of twenty letters. Ogham script, used for funeral inscriptions, constitutes the earliest phase of the Gaelic language.

DINGLE. "Reached by miles of winding twists and turns, hellish descents and heavenward climbs" (Bernard Rio), Dingle is one of the westernmost towns in the whole of Europe. This port at the foot of Ballysitteragh (2,050 feet high) was once an important commercial center, with particularly strong trading links with Spain, but the troops of Elizabeth I and, later on, Cromwell destroyed the fortified walls and other ancient monuments. Today the county town of the Dingle peninsula has became a major tourist center, particularly in summer. It is particularly tempting to while away an afternoon in the charming Café Liteartha, with its small restaurant and bookshop (a veritable literary treasure trove). In recent years, however, the star of Dingle has been a dolphin called Fungi, often seen by swimmers. He has been the subject of poems and a television documentary, and has become a major tourist attraction. (Any visitors who wish to go straight back to Tralee can take the pretty road over Conor Pass, with its view of the three dark lakes of the Owenmore Valley.)

VENTRY. The narrow neck of land separating Dingle and Ventry harbors is traditionally said to have been the last territory occupied by the Danes in Ireland.

The town of Ventry is at the center of many of the area's legends. Here is the "White Strand" of the hero Finn MacCoul's battle with the "King of the World", a savage struggle lasting a year and a day. At this time, too, the beautiful Cael decided to give her hand to the man who composed the best poem in praise of her house. The fortunate winner, Crede, was not so lucky in combat. He died during the Battle of Ventry.

DÚN BEG FORT. The prehistoric fort stands on a narrow promontory at the very edge of the cliff. Its four outer stone walls contain the remains of a house and a beehive hut. An underground passage from the center of the fort to the outer defensive walls permitted escape in the event of a surprise attack.

FAHAN. Between Ventry and Slea Head, on the lower slopes of Mount Eagle, is an extended site of four hundred *clocháin* ● *92*. The best of them are at Fahan.

SLEA HEAD ★. The little road winds out toward Slea Head passing beneath Mount Eagle and leading at last to the headland. Over the blue waters to the south lie the Iveragh peninsula and the Skellig Islands, and to the west are the Blasket Islands.

DUNMORE HEAD. A little further east, beyond the tiny village of Coomeenoole and its pretty beach, lies Dunmore Head. At the highest point is an ogham stone with a long inscription.

DUNQUIN (DÚN CHAOIN). A pocket of Gaelic culture surrounds this land's end hamlet, and it has become another center of *Gaeltacht* ● *68*. Irish can be heard spoken everywhere, a thing rare in all but a few westcoast communities. Those who wish to learn the language can take summer courses at schools in Dingle, Ventry, Dunquin and Ballyferriter. Dunquin preserves a number of disappearing traditions, and *currachs* ▲ *276*, or *naomhógs*, beautifully made old boats, can be seen in the harbor. From Dunquin there are magnificent views of the Blasket Islands and the impressive cliffs to the north.

◆ F A4-B4-A3-B3

"RYAN'S DAUGHTER" (above).
In 1969, David Lean shot the exterior scenes of his epic film on Coomeenoole beach and in a reconstruction of an old village near Dunquin. The love story was set against the backdrop of the 1916 Rising ● *60*. It has considerably increased the number of summer visitors to Dingle.

The rusting wreck still to be seen on the Dingle coast is a reminder of the dangerous seas and rocks off Slea Head.

THE BLASKET ISLANDS

"This is a crag in the midst of the great sea, and again and again the blown surf drives right over it before the violence of the wind, so that you daren't put your head out any more than a rabbit that crouches low in his burrow in Inishvickillaun when the rain and salt and spume are flying. Often would we put to sea at the dawn of the day when the weather was decent enough, and by the end of the day our people on land would be keening us, so much had the weather changed for the worse." At the end of *The Islandman* Tomás Ó'Criomhthain tried to explain why the inhabitants finally left the island of GREAT BLASKET, many to try their luck in the United States ● *59*. Brought near to starvation by several disastrous seasons of fishing, the last twenty-two islanders were settled on the mainland by the government in 1953. Seen from the road to Slea Head, or from the top of Mount Eagle, the six islands hold a powerful fascination; not only the rocky silhouettes of the Blaskets themselves, however, but also the treacherous stretch of water, Blasket Sound, that separates them from the Dingle Peninsula. Two ships of the Armada sank here in a storm in 1588: the *San Juan de Ragusa* and the *Santa María de la Rosa* ▲ *316*. Today there are boats from Dunquin and Dingle to take visitors across. There is an Interpretative Centre near Dunquin providing an informative survey of the islands' archeological past and more recent social history.

BALLYFERRITER TO TRALEE

Oratory of Gallarus.

Before reaching Ballyferriter, the road runs along the cliffs of Clogher Head, with a fine view of the cliff ridge of SYBIL HEAD. Turning inland it goes through a pretty gorge below Croaghmarhin. Far off can be seen the outline of Mount Brandon.

BALLYFERRITER. A few miles from the village, at REASK, are some varied and interesting ancient remains. There are beehive huts alongside tombs and a ruined stone oratory, as well as a magnificent standing stone called the REASK PILLAR STONE, with remarkable circular carvings. Those keen on archeology will also want to visit the Heritage Centre at Ballyferriter, which has a collection of ogham stones ● *66*.

ORATORY OF GALLARUS ★ ● *92*. At Ballynana is a building erected using the same method as a for a beehive hut, but adapted to form a

> "She was fair as the rose of the summer,
> Yet 'twas not her beauty alone that won me;
> Oh no, 'twas the truth in her eye ever dawning,
> That made me love Mary, the Rose of Tralee."
>
> W. Mulchinock

rectangular structure. The Oratory of Gallarus is the only structure of its type to remain standing today, owing to the excellent skill of its drystone construction. There are no interior decorations to help with the dating of the oratory, but it is thought to have been built at some time between the 9th and the 12th centuries. Despite the number of visitors who come here, there is a feeling of spiritual calm around this perfect and utterly simple monument.

KILMALKEDAR ★. The 12th-century church of Kilmalkedar is on the pilgrim way to Santiago de Compostela, and is in the Romanesque style that is typical of the monuments along this holy route. The decoration on the doorway and chancel arch is true to the Hiberno-Romanesque style ● *94*. Note the strange creature on the door. There is a blind arcade on the interior wall of the nave, apparently copied from Cormac's chapel in Cashel ▲ *253*. The stone roof of the chancel is also typical of style and period (also seen at Glendalough ▲ *178*, Kells ▲ *192*, Cormac ▲ *253*).

ROSE OF TRALEE ★. The town of Tralee, well-positioned just inland from Tralee Bay and north of the Dingle Peninsula, is the capital of County Kerry. It is probably most famous for an annual competition held to celebrate the qualities of its womenfolk now scattered over the face of the planet. The contest honors the poet William Mulchinock (1820–64) and his lament written for a disdainful sweetheart. At the end of August each year, girls claiming Tralee origins come from near and far in the hope of being judged the most charming and beautiful: the Rose of Tralee. The festivities include a colorful carnival and other events to amuse the visitors, such as horse-races, Gaelic music, and poetry recitals. Pub life is also animated.

ARDFERT. Five miles northwest of Tralee is Ardfert, made an episcopal see by Saint Brendan and the site of one of his monasteries. Only part of the west façade of the original 12th-century Romanesque church remains. It was replaced in the 13th century by a cathedral, as it was probably too small to accommodate the large number of pilgrims. The ruined early Gothic cathedral with elegant lancet windows stands near two smaller churches, Teampull-na-Hoe and Teampull-na-Griffin.

239

For a long time County Clare saw few tourists compared to its better-known neighbors Kerry, to the south ▲ *228*, and Galway, to the north ▲ *258*. Today Clare's unspoiled natural beauty is highly prized, and its dramatic coastline entices many visitors. It has also been discovered by lovers of Irish music. The genuine traditions of singing and playing have remained widespread, both in pubs and during festivals.

KILRUSH AND SCATTERY ISLAND

The main street of KILRUSH, lined with Georgian houses, is where the coastal route begins, and leads on to the port of Cappa. From here it is possible to see the ISLAND OF SCATTERY, out beyond Hog Island. Legend has it that Saint Senan, who founded the first monastery on the island, in the 6th century, delivered Scattery of a monster that lived there. Successive monasteries were destroyed by invaders and the ruins of the five churches that can now be seen there date from the 12th and 13th centuries. The well-preserved round tower is unusual in that its door is at ground level rather than the more usual position between 12 and 15 feet above the ground ● *92*.

LOOP HEAD ★

CASTLE. On the edge of the village of Carrigaholt, overlooking the Shannon estuary, there is a fortified tower built by the MacMahons late in the 15th century. It was a stronghold of the O'Briens ▲ *245* and it was they who had the fireplace (1603) and most of the windows installed. The castle was occupied by the English and used as a garrison for Cromwell's troops. At the end of the 17th century Lord Clare, an O'Brien loyal to the Jacobite cause, raised and trained a regiment of the "Wild Geese" here, Irish Catholic Irish troops who fought in the service of France.

GALE-FORCE WINDS. The strength of the Atlantic winds have forced cottagers to devise a method of securing their thatched roofs with a grid of ropes ● *103*. The constant erosion of the coast by the wind and the sea can be seen at BRIDGE OF ROSS, a good place to set out on a walk along the cliffs. After you are exhausted by squalls and sea air, a visit to the church of Moneen proves restful. Here there is a portable altar used by Catholics for secret masses during times of prohibition ● *52*.

◆ **B** C3-B3-C2-C1-D1-D2-D3

DIARMAIT AND GRÁINNE'S ROCK
The rock sticking up out of the sea just off Loop Head was the refuge of the famous warrior Cú Chulainn, trying to escape the amorous pursuit of a witch called Mal.

When she joined him on the rock in one bound, he was so horrified that he leapt back to shore. She tried to follow once more, but fell at the foot of the cliffs, bleeding so profusely that the waves all along the coast were red with her blood. This tale explains the nearby place names of "Mal Bay" and "Hag Head".

Right, the church at Kilkee.

THE "WILD GEESE"
After defeat at the Battle of the Boyne
▲ *194*, the Irish Jacobite regiments joined
Louis XIV's army and formed the famous
Irish brigade of "Wild Geese" which was to
make a significant contribution to the French
victory at Fontenoy in 1745.

Another peaceful conclusion to an exploration of Loop Head is the seaside resort of KILKEE, with its sheltered, sandy beach on Moore Bay.

TO LISCANNOR BAY

QUILTY. The church, whose architecture was inspired by Celtic art, was funded by the crew of a wrecked French boat, saved by the villagers in 1907. The abundance of seaweed along the coast is a reminder that it was once an important resource, and vital during the Great Famine ● *58*.

MILLTOWN MALBAY. In July the population of the village triples for the annual William Clancy School of Music, named for one of County Clare's greatest pipers ● *72*. It is a week of intensive music-making, often continued late into the evening by unofficial "classes" held in pubs. Near to the village is a power station fueled by turf. To the southeast is the mountain of SLIEVE CALLAN (1,282 feet). On its slopes is a dolmen known as DIARMAIT AND GRÁINNE'S BED. Like other megaliths associated with the names of Diarmait and Gráinne ▲ *289* (an Irish legend similar to that of Tristan and Isolde), the stone is reputed to have aphrodisiac qualities and to cure sterility.

LISCANNOR BAY. The opening of the West Clare Railway in 1887 led to the development of the seaside town of Lahinch. ENNISTYMON, whose pretty and colorful main street is particularly lively on market and fair days, stands beside the gentle cascades of the River Cullenagh. LISCANNOR has a plaque in its harbor in recognition of the fact that it was the birthplace of John Philip Holland (1840–1914), inventor of the first submarine in America. On the edge of the village toward the coast stands the square 15th-century tower of LISCANNOR CASTLE. Not far from O'BRIEN'S MONUMENT, erected in 1853 by local landowner Cornelius O'Brien in his own honor, is ST BRIGID'S WELL, one of many springs in Ireland whose reputed powers of healing have their roots in ancient Celtic culture. A pilgrimage is made here on the last weekend of July.

St Brigid's Well.

WEST CLARE RAILWAY
A railway was built along the coast between Ennis and Milltown Malbay, and opened in 1887. In 1892, it was extended as far as Kilkee and Kilrush. It was a delightful way for visitors to travel (in carriages weighted to resist violent squalls), but the line was closed in 1961.

John Philip Holland.

THE INVINCIBLE ARMADA
Although Spanish Point is the only place name to recall the episode, the whole coast of County Clare witnessed the dramatic sinking of the Armada in 1588 ▲ *316*. Ships went down at Doonbeg, Tromra and Doolin, and survivors were for the most part executed. At Liscannor, the villagers gathered around the castle to prevent the crew of the galley *Zuñiga* landing and negotiating for supplies.

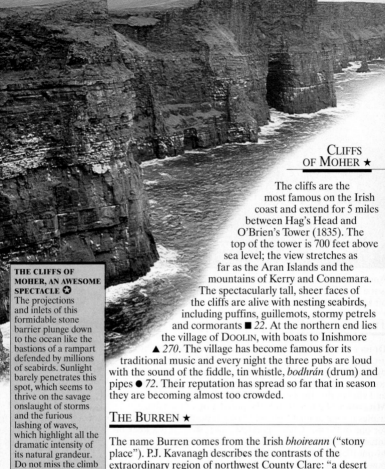

CLIFFS OF MOHER ★

The cliffs are the most famous on the Irish coast and extend for 5 miles between Hag's Head and O'Brien's Tower (1835). The top of the tower is 700 feet above sea level; the view stretches as far as the Aran Islands and the mountains of Kerry and Connemara. The spectacularly tall, sheer faces of the cliffs are alive with nesting seabirds, including puffins, guillemots, stormy petrels and cormorants ■ *22*. At the northern end lies the village of DOOLIN, with boats to Inishmore ▲ *270*. The village has become famous for its traditional music and every night the three pubs are loud with the sound of the fiddle, tin whistle, *bodhrán* (drum) and pipes ● *72*. Their reputation has spread so far that in season they are becoming almost too crowded.

THE BURREN ★

The name Burren comes from the Irish *bhoireann* ("stony place"). P.J. Kavanagh describes the contrasts of the extraordinary region of northwest County Clare: "a desert which is not a desert – cattle fatten on its limy grasses, and in spring Arctic flowers jostle with Mediterranean ones, sheltered in the cracks of its limestone slab". Yet Cromwell's surveyor complained of "a savage land, yielding neither water enough to drown a man, nor a tree to hang him, nor soil enough to bury".

LISDOONVARNA. The town was developed as a spa in the 19th century, and has become a popular seaside resort. It is now best known for its September Matchmaking Festival, when bachelors flood the town in search of a wife, along with many others who come just to enjoy the fun. Northwest of the village is BALLYNALACKAN CASTLE, a well-preserved example of a 15th-century fortified tower ● *99*. There is a road leading around the coast to Ballyvaughan past the beach at FANORE, BLACK HEAD and the 16th-century GLENINAGH CASTLE, overlooking the bay. It is also possible to take a closer look at the Burren on the Green Road footpath that

THE CLIFFS OF MOHER, AN AWESOME SPECTACLE ✪
The projections and inlets of this formidable stone barrier plunge down to the ocean like the bastions of a rampart defended by millions of seabirds. Sunlight barely penetrates this spot, which seems to thrive on the savage onslaught of storms and the furious lashing of waves, which highlight all the dramatic intensity of its natural grandeur. Do not miss the climb up O'Brien's Tower, now slightly curved from the gusts of raging winds and the flurries of rain mixed with sea spray! (Tower open daily from 9.30am to 5.30pm.)

RING-FORTS ● *91*
Thousands of these fortified circular structures remain in Ireland, including many in Clare. Some of the finest are at Cahermacnaghten and Cahercloggaun, northeast of Lisdoonvarna, Caher Balliny, on the Green Road toward Ballyvaughan and Cathair Scribin.

crosses barren stretches of the strange landscape and climbs the lower slopes of Slieve Elva (1,109 feet).

BALLYVAUGHAN. Most visitors come to the village because it is near the AILLWEE CAVE, the Burren cave that is the most easily accessible to the public. There are many megalithic sites in the surrounding area, although some are easily mistaken for piles of old stones. This is certainly not the case with the Neolithic POULNABRONE dolmen (on the road south to Corofin), whose striking, leaning silhouette has become the symbol of the Burren. South of Ballyvaughan is NEWTOWN CASTLE, an unusual round tower set back from the Corkscrew Road, the steep and winding road up to Corkscrew Hill. From the top there is a fine view over the region.

CORCOMROE ABBEY ★. The Cistercian abbey dating from the early 13th century is built to a cruciform plan. It is the most beautiful monument in the Burren. There are magnificent capitals in the choir and transept chapels, carved with human heads (right) and floral motifs of medicinal plants used by the monks (perhaps linked in some way with the Latin name of the monastery: St Mary of the Fertile Rock). There are some interesting tombs including that of Conor O'Brien, King of Thomond, who died in 1267. The eastern window embrasure still has traces of color and there are remains of drawings incised in the plaster of the choir (depicting an embarcation) and the south chapel (a lion). Northwest of the village of Burren is MOUNT VERNON LODGE, which belonged to Lady Gregory (1852–1932) ▲ 247, and where she entertained W.B. Yeats ▲ 122 and George Bernard Shaw ▲ 125.

Detail of capital at Corcomroe Abbey.

KINVARRA

DUNGUAIRE CASTLE overlooks the bay close to Kinvarra (County Galway). It is a 16th-century tower house ● 99, a fortified dwelling once belonging to the Martyn de Tulira family. Medieval banquets are now organized here.

CAVES IN CLARE
The largest network of caves is around Slieve Elva, including the Pollnagolum, Cullaun, Coolagh River and Doolin caves, and also, in the valley, Pol an Ionain with an incredible 23-foot stalactite. At Kilshanny there is a center where lessons in speleology are given, and equipment may be hired.

BUNRATTY

The banqueting hall in the keep is decorated with tapestries and furnished with medieval cupboards

and chests from France. In one of the window recesses is an example of a *sheela-na-gig*, a primitive carving of a naked woman in an immodest position. Nothing is known for sure of their significance, and numerous explanations have been offered. The hall and the chapel beside it have some rare examples of Irish stuccowork from the 17th century.

NORTH BANK OF THE SHANNON TO ENNIS

BUNRATTY. The castle was built by the MacNamaras in 1450 on a site that had been fortified since Viking times. A century later it fell into the hands of the O'Briens. In the 1960's Bunratty Castle was restored and the great hall is now used for medieval banquets enjoyed to the music of harps. These lighthearted occasions are a far remove from the bloody battles of the past. Beside the castle, the FOLK PARK recreates a rural Ireland of the 19th and early 20th centuries. There are additional features illustrating much earlier periods, such as the little 8th-century watermill. Fishermen's and workmen's cottages have been reconstructed accurately, based on those found in County Clare and Limerick in the 19th century. The peasant homesteads have tools, furniture and everyday household items of the time. Nearby is a typical late 19th-century Irish village with post office, grocer's shop, printer's, school and doctor's surgery.

CRAGGAUNOWEN. The original 15th- to 16th-century fortified tower was extended by the former owners, art historian John Hunt and his wife Gertrude, with the addition of a medieval-style hall to house their collection of works of art. Most of the collection (prehistoric objects, Greek antiquities, holy art from Ireland, including some lovely crucifixes) is now displayed in the Hunt Museum in Limerick ▲ 248. Hunt also initiated a number of projects to construct replicas of ancient Irish structures. In the grounds are a *rath* and a *crannóg* (above) ● 90, both based on archeological evidence combined with Hunt's own intuition. Since his death in 1975 the museum has grown and now has a *fulacht fiadh* (prehistoric oven) and the *currach* ▲ 276 that the young Tim Severin used to cross the Atlantic in order to prove that Brendan the Navigator ▲ 239 could have reached the New World before the Danes.

QUIN. One of the best-preserved examples of Franciscan architecture in Ireland is the abbey at Quin. It was built in 1433 within what remained of a Norman castle (there are still the ruins of some of its towers). The cloister is exceptional ● 96. St Finghin's Church (1278–85), with fine ogival windows, stands at the other side of the stream. The 16th-century Knappogue Castle is another venue for medieval banquets.

The Franciscan abbey at Quin.

"The stone-mason was awfully good at drip-stones…and when he came to do the St Francis he chose the nearest appropriate drip-stone head, and then attached a body to it. He wasn't too good at bodies."

Frank O'Connor visiting Ennis Friary

ENNIS

The capital of County Clare has benifited enormously in commercial terms by its proximity to Shannon airport, but Ennis has little to detain the visitor. Some eminent people were born here: Harriet Smithson (1800–54), Shakespearean actress and wife of Hector Berlioz, and William Mulready (1786–63), designer of the "Mulready envelope", the first postage stamp (1840).

POLITICS. Ennis has also played an important part in the political history of the nation. In 1828 the town voted by a huge majority for Daniel O'Connell ▲ *228* to become Member of Parliament for Clare. As a Catholic he was prevented from taking his seat at Westminster, but the Roman Catholic Relief act, passed by the British government in 1829 and granting Catholic emancipation, finally made him eligible. O'Connell is commemorated by a monument on the spot where he was first selected at a public meeting. He was succeeded in 1830 by Cornelius O'Brien who won the praise of Lord Palmerston for being the best Irish parliamentarian ever: "He hasn't opened his mouth for twenty years." Eamonn De Valera ● *54*, ▲ *224* future Prime Minister and then President of Ireland, was elected MP for County Clare in 1917, and continued to represent the seat until 1959.

FRIARY. The Franciscan monastery was founded in Ennis in 1242, but the buildings were subsequently much altered and most of the ruins are 14th century. There are some remarkable carvings, including a *St Francis with stigmata* in the nave, and the MacMahon tomb with fine panels depicting the Passion.

TOWARD THE BURREN

DYSERT O'DEA ★. There is a great feeling of tranquility around the ruins at Dysert O'Dea. The 8th-century Saint Tola (a hermit who has recently given his name to a local goats' cheese) founded the abbey and made it a place of prayer. However, in 1318 it was also the scene of a terrible battle when the Normans were forced out of Thomond. Beside a

O'BRIEN

COUNTY CLARE, LAND OF THE O'BRIENS
The O'Brien family goes back to King Brian Boru ● *49*. The three lions that decorated the standards and were worn by the soldiers at the Battle of Clontarf were those of the O'Brien armorial bearings. The family built or occupied most of the strongholds of the region and were key figures in its political history. Napoleon's general, Marshal MacMahon, belonged to one branch of the family.

ENNIS FRIARY
The abbey at Ennis survived the dissolution of the monasteries ● *50* thanks to its protection by Murrough O'Brien, but in 1651 Cromwell's troops ransacked it. The Franciscans made a brief return during the reign of Charles II before disappearing for good at the end of the 17th century. In 1969 it was once more handed back to the Franciscans.

RED MARY
In Leamaneh
Castle lived Mary
O'Brien, known as
Red Mary for the
color of her hair.
When her husband,
Conor O'Brien,
returned mortally
wounded from the
battle of Inchicronan
(1651), she is said to
have shouted from
the window "We
don't need dead men
here!" She nursed
him until his dying
breath. To protect
the estate, her son's
inheritance, she
offered to marry an
enemy officer, Cornet
J. Cooper. He had
no time to enjoy the

pleasures of his
marriage bed,
however. Mary was
so infuriated by his
insults about her
dead husband that
she threw him out of
a window of the
castle.

Kilmacduagh.

truncated 11th-century tower stands a
Romanesque church (much altered in the 17th
century). The doorway is decorated with carved
heads. Their striking Mongolian features may have
been copied from French Romanesque churches
seen by the Irish when making pilgrimages to
Compostela. In a field a little to the east of the
church is a HIGH CROSS dating from the 12th
century. It has interlaced, geometrical and
zoomorphic designs that can be traced in their
inspiration to Scandinavian art, although the
influence of the Danes was by this time
much reduced in Ireland. Narrative biblical
scenes, as found on 9th-century High
Crosses ▲ *204*, had not been entirely abandoned in the 12th
century. Here there are depictions of *Adam and Eve* and
Daniel in the Lions' Den on the lower panels of the
monument. On the cross itself are a *Crucifixion* and a figure
of a bishop or abbot thought to be Saint Tola. Not far away is
Dysert Castle, housing an ARCHEOLOGICAL MUSEUM.

COROFIN. The village is surrounded by lakes and is much
enjoyed by both walking and fishing enthusiasts. Overlooking
Lough Inchiquin, said to be the lake richest in fish, stands a
castle built by the O'Briens in 1459. An old legend warns that
if a swan on the lake is killed, a villager will die. The Clare
Heritage Centre gives an interesting picture of life in the west
of Ireland in the 19th century. It also provides a service to
help people investigate their genealogy.

KILLINABOY. There are two ruined churches in the village.
One, founded around 1200, has a double cross on its western
end and a *sheela-na-gig* ▲ *244* in the arch over the south
doorway, probably dating from the 15th century when the
church was much altered.

LEAMENEH. A castle looms on the horizon on the way to
Kilfenora. It consists of a 15th-century fortified tower with a
Tudor-style manor (1640) ● *99* built on to it. Over the
imposing door is the O'Brien coat of arms.

KILFENORA. The Burren Display Centre, created in 1975, has
exhibits and audiovisual presentations explaining the unique
geological and botanical features of the region. Behind stand
the ruins of a small CATHEDRAL (13th–15th century), part of it
now a parish church. In the old chancel, now without a roof,
there is a magnificent east window with carved pillars and two
ecclesiastical figures (one being Saint Fachtnan, who founded
a monastery here in the 6th century). Most impressive of all
are the 12th-century CROSSES standing around the ruins. The
DOORTY CROSS, west of the cathedral, has particularly
interesting carvings.

> "Here, traveller, scholar, poet, take your stand
> When all those rooms and passages are gone,
> When nettles wave upon a shapeless mound
> And saplings root among the broken stone."

W.B. Yeats

> "The trees are in their autumn beauty,
> The woodland paths are dry,
> Under the October twilight the water
> Mirrors a still sky;
> Under the brimming water among the stones
> Are nine-and-fifty swans."
>
> W.B. Yeats

KILMACDUAGH ★. On the road from County Clare to County Galway, going toward Gort, are the ruins at Kilmacduagh, founded as an episcopal see in the 7th century. The eye is drawn to the ROUND TOWER, probably pre-1200, which leans at a distinct angle. The CATHEDRAL has a remarkable doorway with an immense lintel-stone, typical of early Irish churches ● 92. This doorway was closed up in the 15th century when the building was much enlarged, and a new one was opened in the south wall. Nearby are the 13th-century bishop's residence, and O'HEYNE'S CHURCH, built of limestone with remarkable carved capitals, fine windows (1200) and a ruined cloister.

> "I, the poet William Yeats
> With old millboards and sea-green slates
> And smithy work from the Gort forge
> Restored this tower for my wife George.
> And may these characters remain
> When all is ruin once again."
>
> *Lines to be inscribed on a stone of Thoor Ballylee*

GORT

The town of Gort probably served as the model for Lady Gregory's town of Cloon, which features in a number of her works including *Hyacinth Halvey*, *The Full Moon* and *The Jackdaw*. The memory of so many of Ireland's great writers who spent time here, in a period of burgeoning literary revival, brings many to visit the area.

THOOR BALLYLEE ★. Yeats ● 122 discovered the dilapidated 17th-century tower (*thoor* in Gaelic) while staying with Lady Gregory at Coole House (above). He bought it in 1916, made it habitable, and spent time there in the 1920's, finding inspiration for a number of his works. It was restored in 1961 and opened to the public along with the museum in 1965, the hundredth anniversary of the poet's birth.

COOLE PARK. Lady Gregory's house was demolished (now just a stone outline remains), but the grounds are cared for and open for visitors to enjoy the woods and admire the lake. A moving reminder of Coole Park's literary past is the autograph tree, where Lady Gregory asked her friends to carve their initials (Shaw, Yeats, O'Casey, Synge ● 117). The road continues north past TULIRA CASTLE, home of the writer Edward Martyn (1859–1923).

◆ **F** D3-E3-E4

County Limerick is a fertile stretch of land bordering the south bank of the Shannon estuary. Life here is focused on the busy city of Limerick, a place that tourists have tended to avoid, nervous of its reputation as a rough, industrial center. Now its historical and architectural interests are being discovered. To the east lies Tipperary, Ireland's largest inland county. This is an agricultural region, which produces much of the country's milk. Most of the towns lie along the banks of the River Suir and its tributaries. They remain little known or visited. The most famous spot in the county by far is the Rock of Cashel ▲ *252*.

LIMERICK

HISTORY. Limerick was founded by the Danes in the 10th century, and later destroyed by the troops of Brian Boru after the Battle of Clontarf ● *49*. It became the residence of the kings of Munster after being rebuilt, but eventually fell into Anglo-Norman hands, and King John erected his castle in 1210. Now two towns developed side by side, an English and an Irish town. In 1651 Cromwell's troops under Ireton, his son-in-law, took the town from Hugh O'Neill after a six-month siege. Another long siege took place when the Jacobites, under Patrick Sarsfield, withdrew to Limerick after defeats by William of Orange and bravely defended the city. Eventually they capitulated and signed the Treaty of Limerick ▲ *195* which the English broke after a matter of months. The Catholics were once more savagely persecuted. A spirit of anger and rebellion seethed in the city right up until the early 20th century, manifested by the general workers' strike staged in protest at English rule. In historical terms the town center can be divided into three sectors: Irish Town, English Town and Newtown Perry.
IRISH TOWN. When Anglo-Norman domination was assured the native Irish were barred from the walled city, so from the 13th century a quarter began to develop outside the walls, across the Abbey River. The most interesting building in Irish Town today is the Georgian CUSTOMS HOUSE designed in 1769 by a Sardinian architect, Davis Ducart.

248

ENGLISH TOWN. The English Town lies on the site of what was originally the walled city. It is the oldest part of Limerick. ST MARY'S CATHEDRAL was founded at the end of the 12th century by the great church-builder Donal Mór O'Brien. Despite having been severely altered and restored, it retains the allure of a 13th-century Gothic church. There are some Romanesque features still in evidence, such as the west door, but also many 15th-century additions. KING JOHN'S CASTLE ● 98 was begun early in the 13th century and was the most formidable of all the Anglo-Norman citadels in the west of Ireland. It is a five-sided structure with round towers joined by curtain walls and a tower on either side of the main gateway. There are still signs of the bombardment by the troops of William of Orange in 1690. Archeological excavations have uncovered interesting remains of Viking dwellings which are now sheltered within the unlovely structure of the Interpretative Centre. On the other side of the River Shannon, at the western end of Thomond Bridge, the TREATY STONE stands on a plinth. On this stone the Treaty of Limerick was signed ▲ 195.

NEWTOWN PERRY. South of Irish Town lies a district dating from the 18th century, with lovely streets of red-brick Georgian houses. These were built as the plain but elegant and comfortable homes of well-to-do citizens.

HUNT MUSEUM (2 miles out of town, just off the Dublin Road). John Hunt's art collection ▲ 244 is well displayed in the premises of the National Institute of Higher Education. It features Irish and European antiquities from the Bronze Age to the Middle Ages, with many early Christian items.

THE SOUTH BANK OF THE SHANNON

ADARE. The village is often referred to as the prettiest in Ireland. Its charm was created by the Earl of Dunraven who had the thatched cottages built in the 19th century. The neo-Gothic ADARE MANOR (below) dates from the same period

The picturesque village of Adare typified what the 19th-century English imagined as the "rustic idyll". It was in fact created by the Earl of Dunraven (1812–71) as a part of his project to improve his estate. There is no denying the charm of the place, and today Adare has an architectural interest as an ensemble of neo-Gothic buildings.

and is now a hotel. The village has a much longer history, however. Beside the River Maigue stands DESMOND CASTLE, built by the Normans around 1200 and partially rebuilt in the 14th century. There is also a FRANCISCAN PRIORY (1464) with an interesting *sedilia* (the seat for the celebrants of the mass) and the remains of two abbeys: BLACK ABBEY (founded in 1325 by the Augustinians) and TRINITARIAN OR WHITE ABBEY, now the Catholic church.

CASTLE MATRIX. The castle dates from the 15th century and was once the property of Sir Walter Raleigh ▲ *221*. It has been sumptuously restored and is filled with fine furniture, old arms and other antiques.

GLIN CASTLE. The Knight of Glin, together with the White Knight and the Knight of Kerry, form the three different branches of the powerful FitzGerald House of Desmond, which dates back to the 12th century. Glin Castle is well worth visiting for its interior decoriation – the Adam-style front hall ceiling, the flying staircase lit by Venetian windows, the family portraits, landscape paintings, and also for the impressive collection of 18th- and 19th-century Irish Georgian furniture, which renders the castle a cradle of Irish art and crafts at its very best. The richness of the interior and the preservation of the whole building is no doubt due also to Desmond FitzGerald, present Knight of Glin, the 29th in direct succession, who is fervently involved in conservationism, and is an eminent writer on Irish architecture and the decorative arts.

LOUGH GUR

The horseshoe-shaped Lough Gur is surrounded by marshy land and guarded by two fortified towers, BOURCHIER'S CASTLE (15th century) and BLACK CASTLE (13th century). Excavations made around the lake have revealed the presence of a busy community here in Neolithic times. Beside the road from Limerick is a circle of thirteen standing stones. Axe heads, arrow heads and blades were discovered inside the circle, along with some vessels. The precise significance and function of these circles, which date back to 4000 BC, is still not certain. The slopes of Knockadoon Hill rise from the lough, the site of dwellings and circular enclosures from 3500 to 100 BC. There is an Interpretative Centre with models of the dwellings, giving some idea of life here during Stone Age times.

KILMALLOCK

The village of Kilmallock was once the third most important town in Ireland. It grew up around an abbey founded in the 7th century by Saint Mocheallóg. From the 14th to the 17th century it was the seat of the earls of Desmond. There are a number of fine Norman monuments to be seen in Kilmallock. KING'S CASTLE is a

SPENSER, GUEST AT CASTLE MATRIX
The poet Edmund Spenser (1522–99) stayed in the castle in 1580, as secretary of Lord Grey de Wilton. Grey was instructed to quell the Irish rebellions but used such brutal methods that he was recalled to England.

Spenser wrote his own *View of the State of Ireland* in 1598 (published in 1663). Even then he was searching for possible reasons to explain the state of agitation to be found there. His own solution was quite uncompromising: exterminate the population by an organized famine. There is a terrible irony in his proposition when remembering the behavior of Lord Mountjoy two centuries later.

15th-century fortified tower. The DOMINICAN PRIORY dating from the 13th and 14th centuries was partly destroyed when the town fell to Cromwell in 1640. There is a fine stone-built medieval house of the type erected by wealthy merchants and landowners. ST JOHN'S TOWER castle was once at the heart of the city's defences, and BLOSSOM GATE is all that remains of the old town wall.

TIPPERARY

Tipperary is comfortably set in the fertile Golden Vale. The town was founded by the Anglo-Normans and late in the 12th century it stood in the shadow of the castle built here by King John. Like Limerick, from early on Tipperary was known for its rebellious attitude to the English occupation, the growing resentment that would eventually lead the War of Independence ● 62. There was much involvement in the activities of the Land League in the 19th century. Visitors should note the gateway of a 13th-century Augustinian friary, the bronze statue of Charles Kickham (1826–82) the poet, novelist and patriot, and the memorial to the Manchester Martyrs, Allen, Larkin and O'Brien, Fenians executed at Manchester in 1867 ● 53.

Street scene in Kilmallock.

"IT'S A LONG WAY TO TIPPERARY"
The name of the town became famous when the song was taken up by thousands of troops marching to battle in World War One. The two men who composed the song in 1912, Jack Judge and Harry Williams, are said to have chosen the name just for its sonority. A scurrilous version has it that Tipperary was the name of a London brothel.

CAHIR

Along the road coming from Tipperary, following the River Suir, are ruins of an AUGUSTINIAN PRIORY (below) founded around 1220 by Galfrid de Camvill. Cahir is a pleasant town, on a major crossroads, with several Georgian houses and a lovely park. The dominating monument is Cahir Castle, best-preserved and most imposing of all the late medieval Irish castles to survive.

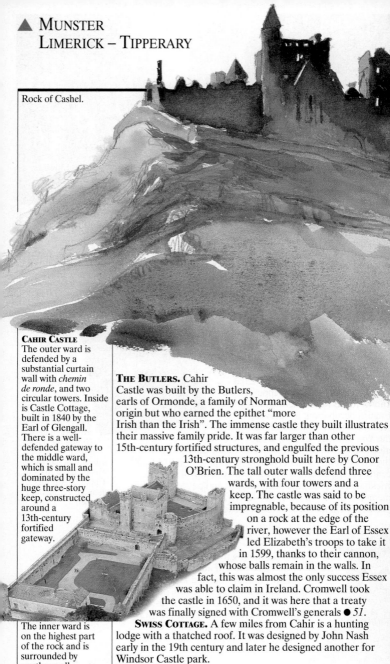

Rock of Cashel.

CAHIR CASTLE
The outer ward is defended by a substantial curtain wall with *chemin de ronde*, and two circular towers. Inside is Castle Cottage, built in 1840 by the Earl of Glengall. There is a well-defended gateway to the middle ward, which is small and dominated by the huge three-story keep, constructed around a 13th-century fortified gateway.

The inner ward is on the highest part of the rock and is surrounded by another wall, probably on 13th-century foundations. There are two square towers, of which the northeast has some remains of the 13th-century stronghold. Apart from the keep, it is the most imposing and strongly fortified of the castle.

THE BUTLERS. Cahir Castle was built by the Butlers, earls of Ormonde, a family of Norman origin but who earned the epithet "more Irish than the Irish". The immense castle they built illustrates their massive family pride. It was far larger than other 15th-century fortified structures, and engulfed the previous 13th-century stronghold built here by Conor O'Brien. The tall outer walls defend three wards, with four towers and a keep. The castle was said to be impregnable, because of its position on a rock at the edge of the river, however the Earl of Essex led Elizabeth's troops to take it in 1599, thanks to their cannon, whose balls remain in the walls. In fact, this was almost the only success Essex was able to claim in Ireland. Cromwell took the castle in 1650, and it was here that a treaty was finally signed with Cromwell's generals ● *51*.

SWISS COTTAGE. A few miles from Cahir is a hunting lodge with a thatched roof. It was designed by John Nash early in the 19th century and later he designed another for Windsor Castle park.

ROCK OF CASHEL

The tall and ancient buildings rise from the rocky spur of Cashel, overlooking the plains of the Golden Vale. They are the most spectacular group of medieval monuments in Ireland, and among the finest in Europe.

"CITY OF THE KINGS". As early as the 4th or 5th century Cashel was capital of the kingdom of the Eoghanacht, descendants of the hero Eoghan. One of them, Conall Corc, built the first fortress here. Brian Boru was crowned here in the 10th century and it remained the seat of the kings of Munster until 1101 when King Murtagh O'Brien gave the Rock to the Church.

DOMINION OF THE CHURCH. In 1127 Bishop Cormac MacCarthy, King of Desmond, began the building of the chapel that still bears his name. The first cathedral was built in 1169, but it has completely disappeared. In the 13th century work began on a new cathedral. The Hall of the Vicars Choral dates from between 1404 and 1440, as does probably the fortified Bishop's Palace. The shrine remained Catholic until 1729, when a first

Rock of CASHEL

Protestant service was held here. Twenty years later the cathedral roof was removed, and it was abandoned for good. Restoration work was carried out from 1874 to 1876, and again in 1975.

THE ROUND TOWER. The oldest building on the site is the 92-foot-high round tower, standing at a corner of the north transept of the cathedral. It dates from the 11th or early 12th century.

CORMAC'S CHAPEL. The most beautiful of all the buildings is Cormac's Chapel, which stands up against the cathedral on the south side. It is the most elaborately decorated of all surviving Irish Romanesque churches ● *94*, and has survived in miraculously good condition. Noticeable from the outside are the twin towers on either side of the nave and chancel, replacing a transept. These are unique. There is blind arcading on the exterior walls, and also within. Unlike other churches of its period, the door is not on the west. The ornate north doorway, now blocked by the cathedral, was the original entrance. Today the south doorway is used. Above each is a tympanum, possibly indicating Norman influence. The carving over the north door shows a beast being attacked by a centaur while holding another creature in its grip. The barrel vaulting of the nave supports the steep stone roof, as seen at Glendalough ▲ *178*. The ceiling of the chancel is almost Gothic in style, and is separated from the nave by a decorated arch. Above it are fragments of the only 12th-century frescos in Ireland. They appear to include a depiction of the Baptism of Christ, and a fortified town that might be the New Jerusalem. In the chapel is a sarcophagus, said to be King Cormac's. The 12th-century copper cross that once adorned it is now on display in the National Museum in Dublin ▲ *158*.

Tradition has it that Saint Patrick came to Cashel in the year 450 and converted King Angus and his family. Here too he is said to have compared the Holy Trinity to a shamrock leaf. ● *71*.

THE ROCK OF CASHEL, BASTION OF FAITH ✪
Cashel, the capital of Munster, possesses the most beautiful collection of runes in the whole of Ireland, assembled on a rocky hill overlooking the plain. It was in this cathedral-fortress, flanked by an enigmatic round tower, that the Plantagenet King Henry II first received the allegiance of the chiefs of the Celtic clans. At the start of the tour (which lasts about 1½ hours) the screening of a video, Bastion of Faith, provides useful background information. Staying the night at Cashel means that the Rock can be visited at 9am, before the crowds arrive.

253

ST PATRICK'S CROSS
▲ *204*
The 12th-century High Cross is unlike any other because it has vertical supports (only one of which remains) on either side of the main shaft. It may have been made on the model of an older wooden cross. Some believe the supports represent the crosses of the thieves crucified beside Christ. It is over 7 feet high and has a *Crucifixion* on one side and a picture of a bishop (probably Saint Patrick) on the other, with his feet resting on the head of an ox. The base is decorated with crosses, squares and interlaced designs.

Holycross Abbey was so named because a piece of the True Cross was kept here.

THE CATHEDRAL. The cathedral was built between 1235 and 1270. The lancet windows that light the interior are characteristic of Irish churches of the period. The massive square central tower was probably completed in the 14th century; there are spiral staircases up to the roof. On entering via the 15th-century doorway, there is a view of the nave, with fine capitals carved with heads and leaf patterns; the carved heads in the transept can also be seen and, most impressive of all, the tombs. There is a monument on the south side of the chancel to the perfidious Myler MacGrath (c.1621), who managed to be a Catholic and a Protestant archbishop simultaneously. In the north transept are 16th-century tombs decorated with saints, animals and geometric patterns. The massive fortified tower that is the 15th-century Bishop's Castle stands square across the end of the nave, curtailing the original plan.

THE MUSEUM. Access to the Rock of Cashel is now through the Hall of the Vicars Choral. This was built in the 15th century for the use of those in charge of cathedral music. Today the building is a museum. Its most interesting item is St Patrick's Cross. This was moved here from outside, and a copy placed on the original site.

HORE ABBEY. (Half a mile from the Rock.) First a Benedictine monastery, the abbey was later rebuilt by Cistercian monks from Mellifont ▲ *198*. The central tower was added in the 15th century.

ATHASSEL PRIORY ★. A few miles from the Rock are the ruins of a vast Augustinian priory founded in 1192. There is a magnificent doorway and tomb with an effigy of the founder.

HOLYCROSS ABBEY

The Cistercian abbey was founded in the 1180's by Donal Mór O'Brien, King of Thomond. It was almost entirely rebuilt in the 15th century thanks to the generosity of the many pilgrims who came to venerate its relic, a piece of the True Cross. In 1975 it was given a new roof and the cloister was restored. The church is cruciform, and is a fine example of late Gothic architecture, with particularly remarkable stonework, well preserved in the hard limestone of the region. The chancel has a magnificently carved triple-arcaded *sedilia*. In the transept is a mural of a hunting scene (such late medieval frescos are extremely rare in Ireland) and in one of the chapels can be found a curious structure with arches and twisted columns, which probably once displayed the holy relic.

Connacht

GALWAY

Scholars, idlers, tourists and men of business all feel at home in the relaxed atmosphere of Galway city. There are shops, pubs and restaurants for all tastes, and time flows by in an easy, cheerful manner.

Galway has grown faster than any other town in Europe in recent years, but it still has a medieval flavor that many other towns lost when they were developed in Georgian times. The old limestone buildings blend well with newer additions, and there is a whiff of the past around every corner.

HISTORY

Galway is a city on the water and its history is bound up with the sea, both in legend and in fact.

THE CITY'S FOUNDATION. The medieval city was founded on the east bank of the river where a fort built by the Anglo-Norman Richard de Burgo had stood. It was named for Galvia, a princess of the Firbolg tribe who was borne away by the waves. The city's university was founded in 1345. Galway was strategically placed on the estuary of the River Corrib, between Lough Corrib and the huge bay. It soon grew to become Ireland's third maritime port. The waters of the bay lapped against the city walls and, brought by favorable winds, Spanish ships arrived in ever greater numbers to discharge cargos of wine onto the stone quays. By the time Christopher Columbus arrived on a trade mission in 1477, Galway was on the way to becoming the linchpin of the Irish wine trade.

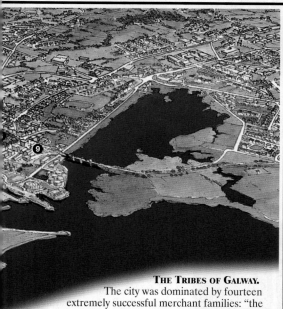

THE TRIBES OF GALWAY.
The city was dominated by fourteen extremely successful merchant families: "the fourteen tribes of Galway". In the 16th and 17th centuries their wealth and influence reached a peak and they built themselves fine dressed-stone mansions.
DECLINE. The prosperity did not survive the religious disputes of the Reformation. Galway was besieged twice, once by Cromwell's troops in 1652, and later by those of William of Orange in 1691. Maritime trade dwindled and the town went into decline.

EYRE SQUARE

Today Eyre Square is the heart of the city, the center of Galway life. The small park was once a practice ground for armed combat, set at the foot of the old town walls. Young men prepared for battle here until, in 1710, Edward Eyre gave the land to the city. Since then it has been a place for recreation. It is still known by its old name, although

GALWAY'S SONS
Two figures familiar to the inhabitants of Galway have been given their place in the park in Eyre Square, the writer Pádraig O'Conaire (1882–1928) and Liam Mellows, a prime mover in Galway's 1916 Rising ● *54*, subsequently killed in the Civil War ● *63*. O'Conaire, or Sean Phádraig ("Old Padraig"), is Galway's most famous writer in the Irish language (above). His carved figure is bent over a stone book, impervious to the busy throng around him. He wrote more than fifty novels and many short stories and articles before his death aged forty-six. He is buried in New Cemetery, half a mile away, along with William Joyce, better known as Lord Haw Haw, fervent admirer of Hitler and spokesman for Nazi ideas, who broadcast in English on Berlin radio. He was executed for collaboration following World War Two.

259

**"KENNY'S
BOOKSHOP"**
The bookshop and art
gallery is a world in
itself, and offers
hours of excitement
and discovery to its
customers. The
exploration can
continue through
several floors of old

books, prints, maps,
paintings and
sculpture. The Kenny
family has had the
bookshop since 1940,
and five of the six
children of Maureen
and the late Des
Kenny work here.

Above, Lynch's
Castle and the roofs
of the Collegiate
Church of
St Nicholas.

the garden is now
officially the John F.
Kennedy Memorial Park in
memory of the American president, who was made an
honorary citizen of Galway in 1963. In the center of the
square there is a fountain with an iron sculpture by Eamon
O'Doherty, evoking the sails of a Galway hooker ▲ *277* and
erected in 1984 for the city's five-hundredth anniversary.
The sculpture symbolizes the maritime history of Galway, a
city whose coat of arms shows a galleon, sails furled, with a
shield bearing a sleeping lion hanging
from the mast.

BROWNE DOORWAY. On the northwest
side of Eyre Square stands a magnificent
example of 17th-century craftmanship
and a proof of the wealth of the "Galway
tribes". It is the beautifully carved
doorway of the Browne family house,
which once stood in Lower Abbeygate
Street. The house itself is long gone. The
coats of arms are those of Martin Browne
and his wife, Marie Lynch, who had the
house built in 1627. The doorway was
erected in Eyre Square in 1905 and was
the entrance to the park until the fences
were removed.

TOWN WALL. Galway's medieval past has
been brought to the fore in the Eyre
Square shopping center, west of the
square. A section of the wall, built to
protect the inhabitants many centuries ago, has been restored
and incorporated into the busy modern commercial complex.
Two towers, Penrice and Shoemaker, also returned to their
former glory, are almost all that remain of fourteen towers
that once stood at intervals along the old ramparts.

THE MEDIEVAL CITY

LYNCH'S CASTLE ★. The medieval townhouse dating from the
late 15th or early 16th century is considered the finest in
Ireland. It stands at the crossroads of the two main streets of
old Galway, Shop Street and Abbeygate Street, and it was the
home of the Lynch family, the most powerful of all the
"tribes". There are carved gargoyles and other pieces of
decorative stonework, including the arms of King Henry VII
and those of the Lynch family on the Shop Street side, and on
the Abbeygate Street façade those of the Earl of Kildare,
victor at the Battle of Knockdoe in 1504. Lynch's Castle now
houses a branch of the Allied Irish Bank.
COLLEGIATE CHURCH OF ST NICHOLAS. The old parish church
of Galway is dedicated to Saint Nicholas of Myra, the patron

GALWAY'S MANY FESTIVALS
Galway hosts a number of festivals and events. The A.T. Cross Literature Festival takes place in April, the Arts Festival in

saint of sailors. The church was founded in 1320, during the period when the Normans were consolidating their westernmost positions in the province of Connacht. The church was altered, embellished and enlarged over the centuries, often with money from the wealthy merchant families. It is said that Christopher Columbus came here to pray in the Chapel of the Virgin in 1477. In 1484, the Church of St Nicholas was elevated to the status of a collegiate church. It was much damaged during the siege and occupation of Galway by Cromwell's troops in 1651–2, but in the 1950s the church was finally restored, and it has regained much of its former character. Such interest in the old church has also prompted further research into its history, revealing its importance in the story of Galway and its inhabitants. Eminent townspeople have been buried here since the 13th century. At the juncture of the choir and south transept is an early FRENCH TOMBSTONE with a floriated cross. There is also a lovely example of medieval craftsmanship in a capital depicting two young apprentices. The nave was widened in the 16th century and the transepts extended. This work was made possible by the generosity of local patrons whose tombstones are also much in evidence, carved with their armorial bearings and competing with one another in their magnificence. Other interesting features in the church are the LEPERS' GALLERY, with finely carved statues, the baptismal fonts, the holy water stoup, some late medieval tombstones marked with symbols of craft guilds, and some more recent war memorials.

LYNCH MEMORIAL WINDOW ★. The story is often told of the mayor of Galway, James Lynch, who condemned his own son to death in 1493 for the murder of a Spaniard with whom he had quarrelled over his lady. The mayor is said to have hanged the young man with his own hands from this medieval window in Market Street (right). During the 19th century a plaque was attached to the house to record the event, although no written record has ever been found to show that the story is true.

THE OLD MARKET. The only medieval remnant in modern Galway life is the market, still held every Saturday morning

July. The latter was started in 1978 and has achieved an international reputation, with plays, concerts, children's shows, and street theater. The *Film Fleadh* is held at the same time. Other events include the Galway Races (July) and the Galway Oyster Festival (September).

The seaside town of
Salthill in the 19th century.

"THE QUIET MAN"
It was O'Máille's
establishment, now
located in High
Street, that made
the costumes for
John Ford's film
The Quiet Man, shot
in the village of Cong

▲ *269*. The shop now
stocks an enormous
selection of Aran
sweaters.

Interior of Galway's
modern cathedral.

BLAKE'S CASTLE
Facing Spanish Arch
is Blake's Castle. Like
Lynch's Castle, it is a
fine example of the
tower houses ● *99*
built as residences
by the wealthy
merchant families
("tribes") during
the 15th and 16th
centuries. Blake's
Castle has been
recently restored
and has a remarkable
pointed doorway with
traditional corbeling
above: an entirely
Irish architectural
feature.

beside the Church of St Nicholas. Town and country folk,
residents and outsiders, gather to buy and sell a wide variety
of local foodstuffs and other products. During this lively and
picturesque occasion it is not uncommon to hear a voice
declaiming in Gaelic above the general hubbub.

NORA BARNACLE'S HOUSE. The smallest house in Bowling
Green dates from the 19th century and was for a time the
home of Nora Barnacle, wife and muse of the Irish literary

giant James Joyce ● *120*. It is known
that the writer and his son Giorgio
had already come here to visit Annie
Barnacle, mother of Nora, by 1909.
In 1912 the Joyce family spent part
of their vacation here, and Annie
Barnacle continued to live in the
house until her death in 1940.
Mary and Sheila Gallagher, who
have owned the house since 1987,
have restored it and opened it to
the public.

SALMON WEIR BRIDGE. The first stone of the handsome
bridge was laid on July 29, 1818 and it was finished sixteen
months later. This meant that sentenced men could once
again go from the Court House, built in 1815 on the east bank
of the Corrib, to the prison built in 1810 on the other side.
The site of the old prison is now that of the new Catholic
CATHEDRAL OF ST NICHOLAS, built in 1965. During
the spawning season it is possible to watch the
salmon leaping up a specially constructed staircase
over the flood barriers to make their way back
upriver.

SPANISH ARCH. A remnant of the old town wall
remains below the Claddagh Bridge. It dates from
1584 and was once part of the port's fortifications.
Now, however, a municipal museum is attached to it
containing a number of items linked with the city's past.
The façade and some of the stonework of the building came
from the Athy family house, dating from 1577.

CLADDAGH

On the west bank of the River Corrib stood a fishing village
of fewer than four hundred thatched cottages. It was far older
than Galway and had a strongly independent community.
In the 1930's the entire village was condemned as a health
hazard and demolished, although the villagers have retained
their close links and Claddagh is remembered in many of
their songs.

SALTHILL

Not long ago Ireland's busiest seaside resort was a quiet
suburb of Galway and a seaside spa. Only 3 miles from the
city, it is now surrounded by Galway's spreading housing
developments, but its center and long seafront promenade
retain a certain period charm. There are sandy beaches, a golf
course and pleasant public gardens, combining their
attractions with those of hotels, pubs, discotheques and
amusements to draw in the vacationers.

262

BLESSING OF THE BAY
In August every year a fleet of old boats such as hookers ▲ 277, leaves the old quays of Claddagh to take part in the traditional blessing performed by a Dominican priest. The boats form a circle on the water just as they used to when the fishermen prayed for clement weather and an abundance of herring.

THE CLADDAGH RING
The emblem of Claddagh is world-famous. The heart and the two hands symbolize Love, Faith and Honor. The ring is worn with the point of the heart toward the fingertip when engaged, and reversed when married.

◆ **D** B6-A6-A5-B5

CONNEMARA, BETWEEN DREAM AND REALITY ✪
Spiked with mountains, studded with lakes and peat bogs, this area demands more than a casual visit. It is the epitome of a land that must be explored by means of long walks and rambling detours. Experienced Connemara enthusiasts spurn the beaten track in favor of less well-known itineraries: the Brandy and Soda from Roundstone to Clifden, the Sky Road at the exit from Clifden or the scandalously overlooked western bank of Lough Mask.

Describing the landscape of Connemara, Kate O'Brien captured its unreal quality: "There is often an illusion that all is afloat, an uncertainty between hill and sky, an interchange of water and stone which the indescribably clear light seems paradoxically to exaggerate." Connemara remains the wildest, the most secretive and the most romantic place in Ireland. The original old Irish region of Conmhaicne Mara referred only to an area around Ballynahinch. Today the name covers almost all of County Galway, the section of land that juts out between Galway Bay, to the south, and Killary Bay. The west is bordered by the far Atlantic horizon, while Loughs Corrib and Mask form a natural frontier to the east. It is an area of mountains, loughs, heath and bog. Sun, rain and wind bring changing moods, patterns and colors. There are greens: the bright bracken against the dull, close-cropped turf; there are greys: lichen-patterned walls and steep rocky hillsides; there are rich browns in the turf bogs and rusty heathers, the lipstick-red of fuchsia hedges, and everywhere the gleaming silver lakes. The monuments, too, have a stern, proud beauty.

COASTAL ROUTE FROM GALWAY TO CLIFDEN

SPIDDAL (AN SPIDÉAL). Today artists, painters and craftsmen are particularly attracted by Spiddal, but its most lasting reputation has been as an important center of *Gaeltacht* ● *68*. When Martin O'Cadhain (1906–70) was born here, the village was already a place where people came to learn the language and traditions of old Ireland from the local countryfolk. He became one of the writers who did most to make Irish a living language once more.

COSTELLOE (CASLA). The road leads through Rossaveal (Ros an Mhíl), the biggest fishing village in the county and the departure point for boats to the Aran Islands ▲ *270*, to reach Costelloe, the village from which *Raidió na Gaeltachta* ● *67* broadcasts programs in Irish to an enthusiastic audience all over the west of Ireland. Down the rocky peninsula to the south is CARRAROE (An Cheathrú Rua), home of the great Irish painter Charles Lamb (1893–1964). He never tired of looking out over the reefs and tiny islets scattered along this coast, so ragged it resembles lace.

ROSMUCK. At Gortmore (An Gort Mór) a little road on the left leads to the Pearse Memorial Cottage. Here the writer and nationalist Patrick Pearse came to work, and refresh his energies. He was shot by a British firing squad for his part in the 1916 Easter Rising ● *60*.

CARNA. The road leads around Kilkieran Bay to reach Carna where there is a maritime research center and fishermen make a living from catching lobsters. On July 16 each year there is a pilgrimage to ST MACDARA'S ISLAND ● *92*, where there is a 12th-century oratory and a saint's cell which has been recently restored. On the tongue of land adjoining is the single tower of Ard Castle. Just over the water is MASON ISLAND where the *Concepción*, a galleon of the Spanish Armada, was sunk ▲ *316*.

CASHEL. On the far side of Bunnahown, leave the main road to explore the beautiful Bay of Cashel, which is named for a burial mound on the hill above.

ROUNDSTONE (CLOCH NA RON). Follow the BRANDY AND SODA ROAD, so named for the intoxicating purity of the air, along the shores of Gurteen Bay and Dog's Bay, lined with long white strands. At the foot of Mount Errisberg, from which there is an all-round panorama hard to match elsewhere in Ireland, lies the fishing village of Roundstone. The tiny port of white cottages was built by Alexander Nimmo early in the 19th century. In the pubs congregate a fascinating crowd of lobster fishermen, artists in search of inspiration, instrument makers and botanists drawn to the area to study the local flora. Out to sea on the island of Inishlackan there are the ruins of a Franciscan monastery.

IRISH HOLIDAY
After retiring from his duties as President of France in 1969, General de Gaulle spent a month in Ireland. He stayed for a few days at Cashel House, a secluded mansion surrounded by magnificent gardens on the Bay of Cashel. At the end of his holiday he declared: "At this difficult time in my life I have managed to do what I had to do here: come face to face with myself. Ireland made this possible in the most discreet and friendly manner."

BALLYCONNEELY. The village lies on the isthmus that separates Ballyconneely Bay and Mannin Bay. Its prosperity comes from the magnificent Connemara Golf Club whose eighteen holes are spread over the end of the peninsula that stretches west of the village into the ocean. There is a road leading off to the right to BUNOWEN. Here are the remains of a castle built by Richard Geoghegan, descendant of a Cromwellian who remained in Ireland, using material from an older building that had been the property of the pirate queen Grace O'Malley ▲ 278 and Donal O'Flaherty.

DERRYGIMLAGH BOG. The road toward Clifden runs alongside a stretch of bog where on June 15, 1919 John Alcock and Arthur Whitten-Brown were forced to land after making the first non-stop east–west transatlantic flight (below). It had taken them 16 hours and 12 minutes. On the spot, a monument of an airplane wing pointing skyward records their feat.

CLIFDEN. The market town, port and, now, busy holiday resort was founded in 1812 by John D'Arcy. It is the capital of Connemara, and the great annual event, the Connemara Pony Show, is held in mid-August. On the showground children in traditional costume dance jigs and reels, while the proud owners and breeders trot out their sturdy Connemaras in the different show classes. Plenty of buying and selling goes on, bringing in a mixed and noisy crowd of horse-dealers, along with many who just come to look over and admire the ponies. All about the town, up and down the streets of gaily painted houses (above), around the stalls that fill the pavements, and along the ropes of the show-ring can be heard languages from all over the world and accents from all four corners of Ireland.

THE CONNEMARA PONY

Intelligence and stamina are the great qualities of this hardy breed. The Connemara can be gray, bay, black, roan, or chestnut. It is an animal that is now appreciated and bred in many countries. The difficult terrain, rough climate and sparse vegetation have given the Connemara its attributes: the ponies are good jumpers and "good doers". The breed was originally evolved by crossing native ponies with pure-bred Arabs that arrived with the Armada and on the Spanish ships that came to the port of Galway with goods to trade ▲ 258. A Connemara can be up to 14.2 hands high. A pony of this height can be ridden out hunting by an adult, but its gentle and sensible nature will permit it to be ridden by a child too.

THE INLAND ROUTE

This route leads over mountains, along rivers and loughs, through forest and bog ■ 32 and across empty plains dotted with granite rocks. On leaving Galway it follows the River Corrib, passes through the village of MOYCULLEN and runs beside Ross Lake. On the bank stands Ross House where

Violet Martin was born. Better known by her pen-name Martin Ross, she wrote, together with her cousin Edith Somerville, two of the masterpieces of Anglo-Irish humor: *Stories of an Irish R.M.* and *The Real Charlotte* ▲ *224*.

EYRE CONNAUGHT. In this region lived the ferocious clan of the O'Flahertys. Their raids terrorized the population of Galway, who were known to pray: "From the ferocious O'Flahertys, Good Lord deliver us!" Two miles south of Oughterard is the impressive square keep of AUGHNANURE CASTLE, the 16th-century castle of the O'Flahertys. This was their most imposing fortress, which had a strong position over Lough Corrib.

OUGHTERARD. The lively market town of Oughterard is best known by fishermen who come here from far and wide when the fly-fishing season opens in May. Golfers have a good eighteen-hole course, and for walkers there is the Western Way footpath toward Curraun (opposite the Hill of Doon) which leads along Lough Corrib, dotted with islets of lush vegetation, and eventually reaches Leenane. The road runs on between lakes through a magnificent and deserted landscape. When the Comte d'Avèze visited Connemara in 1847 he wrote: "Not forty years ago Connemara, separated from the rest of Ireland by a natural barrier, was but little accustomed to the English rule of law; it was a huge ungoverned hideaway where bandits, smugglers and all kinds of outlaws could find refuge." The wrongdoers have been replaced by sheep, but it is easy to understand how this place remained so long beyond the rule of law.

MAAM CROSS (AN TEACH DOITE). The village nestles between lakes and mountains, at the foot of Mount Leckavrea. It is situated at the meeting of two of the major roads that traverse Connemara, from which it derives its name, and it also has a thriving animal fair.

BALLYNAHINCH. The road follows the wooded bank of Lough Ballynahinch. Reflected in its still waters are the heights of Benlettery, one of the group of mountains known as the Twelve Bens. From the summit there is a view over the whole of northern Connemara.

"THROUGH CONNEMARA IN A GOVERNESS-CART"
"[Oughterard] is the best village for its size this side of Galway,' said my cousin...And the place has improved so wonderfully. For instance there's the Widows' Almshouse. It isn't so very long ago that an old woman said to my grandmother,
'That's the Widdies Almshouse, and sorra widdy in it but one little owld man, and now it's simply bursting with widows – at least, I mean'."
  Somerville and Ross

Lough Ballynahinch.

GUGLIELMO MARCONI (1874–1937)
▲ *173, 311*
It was on the turf bog of Derrygimlagh that the Italian inventor (whose mother was Irish) set up his first station to transmit transatlantic telegraph messages.

BALLYNAHINCH CASTLE stands on the south bank of the lough, a lovely 18th-century mansion. It belonged to the Martin family and was the home of "Humanity Dick" Martin. In 1926 the house was bought by Ranji, Jam Sahib of Nawanagar, an Indian prince and well-known cricketer. Since 1945 it has been a high-class hotel patronized by fishermen.

FROM CLIFDEN TO CONG, VIA LEENANE AND MAAM

THE "SKY ROAD". Going north out of Clifden and taking the little "Sky Road", the desolate ruins of John d'Arcy's castle can be seen. There are magnificent views over the Atlantic Ocean from the little peninsula between Clifden Bay and Streamstown Bay.

CLEGGAN. The tiny fishing village with lively pubs is also the departure point for boats to the island of Inishbofin. On the island are some religious remains and a Cromwellian fort, a reminder that persecuted Catholic priests and monks were kept prisoner here.

LETTERFRACK. The main entrance and Visitor Centre for the Connemara National Park are in Letterfrack. The park covers 49,400 acres and includes part of the Twelve Bens, Diamond Hill (2,385 feet), and vast stretches of bog and heathland. Those who prefer literary pursuits may visit the RENVYLE Peninsula, and Renvyle House at its further end. Before becoming a hotel it was the home of the doctor, writer and humorist Oliver St John Gogarty, immortalized by James Joyce as Buck Mulligan in the first pages of *Ulysses* ● *120*.

Top, the fjord that separates Clifden and Streamstown bays. Above, Kylemore Abbey. It has a neo-Gothic church with an ornate, marble-floored interior.

KYLEMORE ABBEY. The abbey (left) stands beside a small lake surrounded by thick rhododendron groves and fuchsia hedges, wedged between the Twelve Bens and the Doughruagh Mountains, Altnagaighera and Garraun. It is an immense, Victorian, neo-Gothic castle built by a rich Liverpool businessman. French Benedictine nuns took over the establishment and opened a girls' boarding school at the

Detail from
Cong Abbey.

end of World War One. One mile from the abbey, a Victorian garden has been restored and is now open to the public (Abbey grounds, toward Clifden).

LEENANE (LIONAN CINN MHARA). The road follows a 10-mile-long fjord-like inlet that stretches from Killary Harbour to Leenane, a pretty fishing village. Leenane is featured in Jim Sheridan's film *The Field* (1989). (Take left fork toward Maam.)

JOYCE COUNTRY. The R336 crosses the picturesque Maam Valley and leads through the heart of Joyce Country. It follows the River Joyce winding between the Partry Mountains, on the left, and the Maamturk Mountains. The steep rocky sides are grazed by black-headed sheep, which make up a large part of the population of Connemara.

LOUGH CORRIB. The R345 to Cornamona runs along the narrow northwest end of Lough Corrib, the largest lough in the Republic of Ireland. It is 30 miles long and covers 44,000 acres, stretching from north of Galway ▲ *258* to the borders of County Mayo. It has 365 islands. On one, close to shore, is HEN'S CASTLE. According to legend it was built in one night by a witch and her hen, which, together with the castle she gave to O'Flaherty, would suffice to keep them alive if they were ever besieged. The pirate queen, Grace O'Malley ▲ *278*, wife of an O'Flaherty, also used the castle.

CONG (CONGA). The village stands on the border between Galway and Mayo. It is surrounded by magnificent woodland, with Lough Corrib to the south and Lough Mask to the north. The ruins of Cong Abbey are to be found here, including a very elegant cloister. The Augustinian abbey was founded by King Turlough O'Connor in 1137. The road out of the village leads past the towers of ASHFORD CASTLE (above), once owned by the Guinness family ▲ *170* and now converted into a luxurious country-house hotel. The gardens extending down to the lough are open to the public, and there is a boat to the little island of INCHAGOILL, which has some Romanesque ruins and other remains.

"THE QUIET MAN"
In 1951 John Ford (whose real name was Sean Aloysius O'Fearna) set up his cameras in the little village of Cong to make his much-loved film *The Quiet Man* (below). John Wayne, Maureen O'Hara, Victor McLaglen and Barry Fitzgerald played out their roles in a story-book Ireland, where the charms of rural life, the funny situations and the larger-than-life characters were all exploited to the full.

Some were less than pleased by this stereotyping of Ireland and the Irish. The critic Hilton Edwards stated in 1953 in *The Bell* that he saw no relation at all between the film and the Ireland he knew.

1 ROCK ISLAND **2** BRANNOCK ISLANDS **INIS MÓR** **3** DÚN AONGHASA **4** KILMURVEY **5** GORT NA gCAPALL **6** DÚN EOCHLA **7** CILL RÓNÁIN **8** KILLEANY **9** AIRPORT

THE ARAN ISLANDS, GRACE AMIDST BLEAKNESS ✪
Forgotten sentinels of the approach to Europe, the Aran Islands arch their dark backs, like monsters surging from the deep. If spending the night in Inishmore is not on the schedule, the best way to cover it is on a bicycle (which can be rented on all three of the islands), following the narrow roads leading to the strange outsize fortifications of Dún Aengus and even crossing over to the humble but unjustly neglected sister islands of Inishmaan and Inisheer. (There are sea links between the mainland and the islands throughout the year, and between the three islands in the summer.)

BIRTH OF TOURISM
With easier access provided by the new steamer in 1891, the Aran Islands became a place of pilgrimage for numerous learned men. Archeologists and sociologists, botanists, politicans and nationalists (above all Patrick Pearse ● *61*, who was determined that the English flag should not fly over Inis Meáin), painters, film-makers, linguistic experts and writers (Hyde, MacNeill, Synge) were all enraptured by the haunting beauty of these unspoilt islands.

The Aran Islands lie in the ocean like a school of whales surveying Galway Bay. Geologically they are a ridge of carboniferous limestone, an extension of the Burren ▲ *242*. The land is stony, scored with rocky valleys, and has almost no soil cover at all. Crops have had to be scratched from the dry, ungenerous surface of the islands, divided up into the tiny stone-walled fields known as "gardens". Nowadays the fourteen thousand inhabitants are able to improve their meager living with ever-growing tourism. This and fishing are their main sources of income. They remain Gaelic-speaking and immensely proud of their ancient island traditions. The impressive dry-stone forts (*dúns*) are the sturdiest, although perhaps not the earliest, testament to human life on the islands. The islanders are known to have been converted to Christianity early in the 6th century. Their courageous approach to the incredibly harsh island existence has inspired a number of writers, in particular John Millington Synge, who stayed here for long months at the turn of the 20th century. They were also inspiration for the American film director Robert Flaherty, maker of *Man of Aran*. A visit to the Aran Islands is a chance to see some unique and magnificent landscape, but also to step into a past world. The people seem hewn out of rock, wind and water: survivors from another age. In his poem "Lovers on Aran" Seamus Heaney expresses the ancient thrill of the islands: "Did sea define the land or land the sea . . . Each drew new meaning from the waves' collision. . . . Sea broke on land to full identity."

INIS MÓR (INISHMORE)

(From the jetty to the southern tip of the island.) Before coming to Cill Rónáin, there is a beach on the left called Tra na bhFrancach ("beach of the French"). A French ship sank here with all hands. A reminder of a happier event is the monument to mark the 1966 Atlantic crossing made in a rowing-boat by Ridgeway and Blythe.

CILL RÓNÁIN (KILRONAN). A Celtic cross has stood near the harbor since the late 19th century. It was carved by the father of Patrick Pearse ● *61* in honor of one of the island's curates, between 1881 and

◆ **D** A6-B6 **F** C1

1892, and
symbolizes the
modernization of the
fishing industry. It is said that
the curate wrote to the authorities in
Dublin on the islanders' behalf: his telegram
demanded either boats or coffins. The village has
another reminder of the past in the form of a police station,
now in ruins, once occupied by the British police. There is
still a police station on the island, but now the police wear a
different uniform. The
Protestant church is also
ruined, as no one has
worshipped there since the
1930's.

**TEAMPULL BHEANÁIN
(ST BENEN'S CHURCH).**
Standing on a headland in
Killeany Bay are the ruins of
CAISLEAN AIRCIN (Arkyn Castle). It replaced a 16th-century
fortification and was probably built by Cromwell's supporters
in 1652–3. Not far from Killeany, set on the side of a hill,
are the foundations of the only ROUND TOWER on the island.
On top of the hill is one of the smallest churches in Ireland,
TEAMPULL BHEANÁIN. It was named after Saint Benen, one of

STONE WALLS
The islands are a
like a checkerboard,
criss-crossed with dry-
stone walls enclosing
fields often not much
bigger than a pocket
handkerchief. In
order to grow any
crops at all, over
generations the
islanders put down
layers of rotted
seaweed to fill out
the almost non-
existent soil.

271

ARAN SWEATERS
The famous pullovers, knitted with homespun sheep's wool (*báinín*) have an amazing variety of intricate patterns. The significance of different stitches and designs relates to the life of the islanders. The cables are fishing

ropes and the diamonds are the nets. The honeycomb is in honor of the hardworking bee, the trellis represents the stone-walled fields, marriage lines are the ups and downs of married life and Trinity stitch brings in the strong Christian thread of island life.

Dún Eochla (Dún Oghil), a fort with two concentric walls, lies near to the village of Eochaill (Oghil), halfway between Kilronan and Kilmurvey.

Saint Patrick's youngest disciples. It has proved impossible to date the church accurately as there is no decoration, only a tombstone at the southeast corner inscribed with the letters "CAR". The church and round tower would have served as landmarks for the fishermen in their *currachs* ▲ *276*, boats which are still used by the islanders today. Other surrounding ancient buildings were raided for stone to build Arkyn Castle. They included a 15th-century FRANCISCAN MONASTERY.

ST ENDA'S CHURCH. It was with Saint Enda, who died in 530, that the islands made their first appearance in history. The saint first entered a monastery in Scotland before coming to Inis Mór, where he was the first to teach the Irish the rules of monastic life. The island became "the capital of the Ireland of the saints". Disciples left to found other monasteries, centers of learning that were to kindle the flame of Irish literature and art. Killeany means "church of Saint Enda" and there is a shrine called Teaghlach Einne ("House of Saint Enda") near to the water's edge, on what was once the site of the monastery. This is the most holy and venerated place on the Aran Islands. There are 125 saints, including Enda, said to be buried here. In the church are the remains of one or two High Crosses from the 12th century, incorrectly restored, with interlaced carving, and the figures of Christ, a cleric and a horseman. (Going northward on Inis Mór.)

MONASTER KIERAN (ST KIERAN'S CHURCH). The church is named for Saint Ciarán, thought to be the founder of the monastery at Clonmacnois ▲ *203*. It is built of the same austere, bare limestone as other churches on the island, but the windows suggest that the church dates from about 1200. Around it are some interesting pillars decorated with crosses, some ancient tombs and the remains of what must have been a sundial.

GORT NA GCAPPAL. Liam O'Flaherty (1896–1984), author of *The Informer* and *Skerrett*, was born in this village. Literary talent ran in the family, as his nephew Breandán Ó hEithir (1930–90), also a native Aran islander, is known for his writings in both Gaelic and Irish. Máirtín Ó Direáin (1911–88), who came from Inis Mór, is considered by many to be one of the finest contemporary poets in the Gaelic language.

KILMURVEY HOUSE. The house was the residence of the island's biggest landowner. He was famous for his cruelty and unjust evictions. Máirtín Ó Direáin wrote a poem about him, *O Morna,* and Liam O'Flaherty made the events the subject of his novel *Land*. It tells how, during the time of the Land League agrarian revolt, the islanders took their revenge on the landowner by leading his cattle blindfold over the cliffs.

TEAMPULL MACDUAGH. The church is dedicated to Colman MacDuagh, founder of Kilmacduagh. It was originally a plain rectangular building with antae (square pilasters forming the corners of the building). The choir, undecorated, was probably added at the end of the 12th century, with a crenelated parapet (a 15th-century embellishment).

DÚN AONGHASA (DÚN AENGUS) ★ ● *91.* The 19th-century archeologist George Petrie described Dún Aengus as "the most magnificent barbaric monument now extant in Europe". The vast and rugged semicircular stone fort, set right on the edge of a sheer cliff that drops 300 feet to the ocean, is the most extraordinary site on the Aran Islands. There are three concentric walls. The well-preserved inner wall has flights of steps and conceals various chambers. Outside the middle wall is a circle of *chevaux de frise*, a mass of pointed rocks bristling from the ground, to deter attackers from the seaward side. There is a natural raised platform of stone at the center of the fort. This may indicate that it was a place where public sacrifices were held. Recent excavations in the thin soil that covers the rock here have not helped determine the purpose of Dún Aengus any further. They did permit a more accurate dating of the site, however, estimating it to have been occupied at the end of the Bronze Age, around 900 BC, or earlier. (Return to Kilmurvey.)

DUN EOGHANACHTA. The small circular fort has marvelously preserved walls, very similar in construction to Dún Aengus, with sets of steps on the inside running up to the parapets. It stands on a natural shelf overlooking one of the most lovely monuments on Inis Mór, Teampull Bhreacáin.

THE MYSTERY OF THE ARAN FORTS
Local folklore is surprisingly unhelpful in explaining these forts. Many others have been ready to speculate, however. The latest theory, the most fantastic of all, is that they were built by refugees from Atlantis! It is also believed that the defenses were built by the chiefs of the Firbolgs, ancient inhabitants of Aran. As to how the Firbolgs came to be on Aran, it used to be

told that this tribe, assimilated to the Belgae, were subjugated by Julius Caesar, and escaped to the Aran Islands to avoid Roman taxes.

"MAN OF ARAN"
The American film
director Robert
Flaherty, who was
of Irish origin, made
the remarkable
documentary *Man
of Aran* in the 1930's
after spending two
years on the Aran
Islands. It was
awarded the Venice
Film Festival Grand
Prix in 1934. Flaherty
dramatizes the

desperate struggle of
the islanders against
storm and sea. He is
one of many to find
artistic inspiration
in life on the Aran
Islands (in particular
J.M. Synge and Liam
O'Flaherty). Those
who have seen the
film and were moved
by the spectacular
storm scenes will
want to visit the spot
where they were
filmed, between
Inis Mór and the
Brannock Islands.
Easier to reach is a
little cottage built for
the film, now open
as a restaurant. Any
who have not seen
Man of Aran can
attend a showing in
Cill Rónáin during
the tourist season.

Above, a *currach* on
the beach.

**TEAMPULL BHREACÁIN
(ST BRECÁN'S CHURCH).** Curiously,
one of the most important religious buildings
on the island stands at its westernmost and least
accessible end. Saint Bhreacáin was the grandson of the first
Christian prince of Thomond. The richly carved shaft of a
cross, standing west of the church, marks his grave.
It was opened in the 19th century by George Petrie
to reveal a skull. The little church has a choir and
nave, divided by a semicircular arch, all much
rebuilt and restored. A number of tombstones
surround the building, inscribed with exhortations
to the passer-by to pray for the deceased.
Fragments of some large 12th-century crosses
include one with a primitive carving of the
Crucifixion. Another piece of cross lies fenced-off in a field
northeast of the church. A stone slab with the inscription VII
ROMANI could refer to seven Irishmen who went on a
pilgrimage to Rome, although it was long interpreted as proof
that Romans made the pilgrimage to Aran. The Aran Islands,
where Saint Brendan the Navigator ▲ *239* had so often
landed, were of great religious importance in the 12th century
and large numbers of people made pilgrimages here. It is
known that late medieval buildings on the site were used to
shelter pilgrims who came here to venerate the saint. Many of
the plundered churches of the Aran Islands, few of them
earlier than 12th-century, were used (as was Teampull
Bhreacáin) as chapels for pilgrimages. During the 15th and
16th centuries the islands again became an important center
of Christianity. The remains of numerous little churches are
proof of a long and fervent history of worship.

INIS MEÁIN (INISHMAAN)

The narrow strait that separates Inis Mór from Inis Meáin
(Middle Island) is called Sunda Ghriora ("Gregory's Sound")
after Saint Gregory. Despite his desire to be buried on Aran,
Gregory was interred in Rome. According to legend, his
coffin rose up in rebellion from Roman earth and set off for
the islands. J.M. Synge's stay on Inis Meáin made a great
impression on its inhabitants. He stayed every summer from
1898 to 1902 in the MacDonnchas' house. It has been known
ever since as SYNGE'S COTTAGE, and even jokingly as Ollscoil
na Gaeilge, "the Gaelic University", because of the number of
intellectuals who gathered under its roof. Even today you can
sit on Cathaoir Synge, "Synge's Chair", the cliffside place
where the writer liked to gaze out over the sound.

DÚN CHONCHÚIR (DÚN CONOR). The large oval fort is set on
the side of a narrow valley, facing west. According to myth,
Conor was the brother of Aengus, the legendary chief of the
Firbolgs.

DÚN FEARBHAI (OR DÚN MOHER). The smaller D-shaped fort
stands to the east of the island on a low mound, looking out
over the village of Baile an Mhothair.

CILL CHEANANNACH. The stone oratory, or "canons' church"
dates from the 11th or 12th century. It has walls 2 feet thick
(one stone block measuring 18 feet long) and a massive lintel.
O'Donovan, the 19th-century Irish collector, thought it
Ireland's most perfect primitive church.

INIS OÍRR (INISHEER)

TEAMPULL CHAOMHÁIN (ST CAVAN'S CHURCH). Next to the
landing strip, in the midst of the dunes, lie the ruins of a little
church dedicated to
Saint Kevin, the
island's patron
saint. It dates from
around 1200, or
possibly later.
Each year the
ruins are gradually
covered by the sands, to be

cleared in time for the annual pilgrimage, June 14, when the
islanders pay homage to Saint Kevin, probably a brother Saint
Kevin of Glendalough ▲ *178*.

O'BRIENS' CASTLE. The O'Flahertys of Connacht and the
O'Briens of Munster vied for control of the Aran Islands in
medieval times, but the O'Briens dominated Inis Oírr (East
Island). The ruins of the 14th-century castle are testament to
their power, built from the stones of a prehistoric fort Dún
Formna, but destroyed by Cromwell's troops in 1652.

CILL GHOBNAIT (ST GOBNET'S CHURCH). The little 11th- or
12th-century church is dedicated to Saint Gobnet, patron
saint of apiculture.

The first inhabitants of Ireland may have reached the island from Britain in boats of stretched hide, not unlike the *currachs* of today. Boat-making began in the Bronze Age, with the hollowing-out of tree trunks. These were clumsy craft, however, and could not put to sea in all weathers. Then the technique of making boats from tanned animal skins developed. Such craft are still in use in a few areas elsewhere in the world (China, Greenland and Alaska).

THE FIRST "CURRACH"
Improvements were gradually made to the simple Irish *currach*. The first coracle was very small, made with animal skins stretched over a wicker frame. Oars replaced paddles and the first masted and sailed *currachs* probably made their appearance in the early days of Christianity.

THE MODERN "CURRACH"
Today a *currach* is built from a frame of wooden laths, onto which are stretched strips of tarred canvas. It has no keel, and slides over the waves rather than ploughs through them. The boats are very light and can land without need of a sheltered harbor. There are several types of *currach*, adapted to the climatic conditions of different regions. The Aran *currach* is about 17 feet long and can have up to three oarsmen.

THE HOOKER
The hooker seems to have first appeared in County Cork in around 1700, although there is still doubt as to whether it originated in Spain or in the Low Countries. The Galway hooker is stronger than that of Kinsale, the craft most commonly used until 1900. Originally the hooker was a fishing boat, but by the 19th century it was being used to transport goods and passengers from island to island and along the coast.

THE CAPACITY OF THE "CURRACHS"
It is estimated that the Galway *currachs* were able to transport two cows and twenty-one sheep; and that the first *currachs* with oars, in early Christian times, could travel over 90 miles per day with nine or ten people on board, in fair weather. About 140 years ago, a man and his wife put their furniture and horse into a small paddle *currach* to go from Aranmore to Burtonport, nearly 2 miles away on the coast of Donegal.

◆ D A5-A4-B4-A3-B3-
C3-C4

THE SOURCE
Ballintober Abbey
▲ *282*, south of
Westport, was the
starting point of the
pilgrimage to Croagh
Patrick (bottom).
It had its roots in
a pagan festival
honoring the Celtic
god Lug. Ballintober
was dedicated to the
Irish patron saint, and

Cathal Grovdearg,
king of Connacht,
had an abbey built
there in 1216 for the
Augustinians. The
church is cruciform,
but the nave has no
aisles. Much of the
nave is Gothic,
while there is fine
Romanesque
decoration at the
base of many capitals
and around the three
blocked windows
over the altar. At
the junction of nave
and transept is an
elaborate altar-tomb.
On the pediment five
remarkable figures
remain, most likely
part of a row of
ecclesiastics. Within
the sacristy, added in
the 17th century, is
the mausoleum of the
viscounts of Mayo.

County Mayo is the jutting northwest corner of the
province of Connacht. Lough Corrib and the Killary fjord
form its southern boundaries, while to the west and north is
the Atlantic Ocean, rounding the points of Erris Head and
Benwee Head and pushing inland into the Bay of Killala.
Leading south from here the county's eastern border roughly
traces the route of General Humbert and his small French
army who landed in 1798 and gave the county its nickname,
"French Mayo".

THE MURRISK PENINSULA AND CLEW BAY

KILLARY HARBOUR. Leaving Leenane ▲ *269* the route leads
past the rushing waterfall at Aasleagh where the River Erriff
tumbles into the waters of Killary Harbour. Turning left off
the main road, follow the steep northern bank of the fjord-
inlet before bearing right and heading inland to the DELPHI
fishing lodge. The Delphi Valley was given its name by Lord
Sligo, because its peace reminded him of Apollo's shrine in
Greece. Passing along the silent banks of dark DOO LOUGH,
the road climbs up to a pass leading out of the valley. Here
stands a stone recording that this lake and mountain
wilderness was one of the "congested districts" of Ireland in
the 19th century. (Before reaching Louisburgh there is a road
on the left to Roonah Quay where boats cross to Clare Island.)
CLARE ISLAND. The largest island in Clew Bay was the family
seat of the pirate-queen Grace O'Malley. She is thought to be
buried in the ruined Carmelite abbey founded by her family in
1224. Queen Elizabeth I offered to confer honors on her, but
Grace O'Malley refused them disdainfully, declaring that she
was a queen in her own right: Queen of the West. Her island
fortress is a massive square tower, overlooked by Mount
Knockmore and protected to the northwest by spectacular
cliffs scattered with warrior and monastic remains. It is an
extraordinarily wild and beautiful place.
LOUISBURGH. The village stands on the moors, built in the
18th century on the banks of the Bunowen river. It has a small
museum with displays relating both to Grace O'Malley and to
the ancient sites of the surrounding area. These include ring-
forts, the megalithic stone alignment at ASKILLAUN, the early
church at THALLAGHBAWN, and KILGEEVER ABBEY.
LECKANVEY. In the village itself
there is a MEMORIAL CROSS,
recording the
emancipation of

"Saint Patrick stood bell in hand, and every time he rang it he flung it away from him…and every time it thus hastily was rung, thousands of toads, adders, and noisome things went down, tumbling neck and heels one after the other."

Thomas Otway

829, when Catholics in Ireland were at last accorded the status, in theory at east, of full British citizens. Not far rom the village is a long stretch of beach packed by dunes, into which thousands of rabbits have burrowed their warrens.

CROAGH PATRICK. The road toward Westport runs along the base of Croagh Patrick: the "rick" of Saint Patrick (2,513 eet). The saint fasted here for forty days and nights, beseeching God to take care of the Irish. Here, too, he destroyed all he snakes and toads in the land, ringing is bell and flinging it into the abyss. His aithful follower Calvus Totus is buried on the hill. On the last Sunday in July housands of barefoot pilgrims climb the tony slopes of Mayo's holy mountain ▶ *336*, starting from the remains of the 5th-century Murrisk Abbey and making heir way up to the chapel on top. The iew from the summit is extremely good f the day is clear. Fields, villages and bogs stretch away to the horizon, and slands stand like sentinels along the ocean's edge.

WESTPORT. Westport is a pleasant town designed by James Wyatt, one of the great architects of the Georgian era. THE MALL has an aristocratic air, shaded by ime trees whose branches are reflected n the serene waters of the Carrowbeg iver. WESTPORT HOUSE, the Marquess of Sligo's family seat, is a mansion designed n 1730 by Richard Castle, embellished by Thomas Ivory, and completed by James Wyatt around 1778. Both Thomas De Quincey, author of *Confessions of an English Opium-Eater*, and William Makepeace Thackeray spent time here.

NEWPORT. The village is renowned for its good fishing, both in Clew Bay and in the oughs that lie inland on either side. Two miles northwest of Newport are the ruins of BURRISHOOLE ABBEY, all that remain of a Dominican priory founded by Richard Burke in 1469. A little further on s the sturdy, square tower of CARRIGAHOOLEY, also called ROCKFLEET CASTLE, where Grace O'Malley fought off an English attack in 1574.

MULRANY. Sitting on the isthmus between Clew Bay and Blacksod Bay, Mulrany has a microclimate that has fostered the growth of rhododendrons and giant fuchsias. The superb beaches of fine sand and lovely views over the wild landscape of the Curraun Peninsula make this a popular holiday region with the Irish.

Heinrich Böll had a cottage at Dugort and often came to stay between 1954 and 1983.

ACHILL ISLAND

The island covers 55 square miles and is the largest off the coast of Ireland. It was joined to the mainland in 1888 by the Michael Davitt swivel bridge. This crosses from the Curraun Peninsula to reach the village of Achill Sound. Achill Island is a magical and unspoilt region, covered with moorland and heather. There are impressive mountain peaks reaching well over 2,000 feet in height, some descending to sheer sea-cliffs and others sloping down to end in fine sandy beaches. The inhabitants of Achill have always had an extremely hard existence, often depending on the generosity of departed family members to survive.

THE NORTH COAST. The little village of Dugort, at the foot of Mount Slievemore, withstood the siege of a Protestant mission which began on August 1, 1834, when the Church Missionary Society leased the island. The Reverend Edward Nangle arrived to found "The Settlement", near Dugort, and tried to win the islanders away from their Catholic faith. He started free schools, an orphanage and a newspaper, and provided cottages and allotments at low rents, as well as a soup kitchen for the needy in hard times. Although he ended up owning a large part of the island, the mission was a failure. Nangle left Achill in 1852. The climb up Mount Slievemore provides an opportunity to see a number of ancient remains, and also a sad, deserted village. It is probably the one described by Heinrich Böll: "The skeleton of a village, cruelly distinct in its structure, neatly laid out on the sombre slope, as if for an anatomy lesson. . . . The main street, a little crooked like the spine of a labourer." From the beach at POULAVADDY there are boat trips to see amazing seal caves in the cliffs. A magnificent view can be had over the tall cliffs from Saddle Head, the tip of the promontory on the extreme northwest end of the island.

Bennee Head.

THE SOUTH COAST. The village of Dooagh, set on a bay renowned for its abundant fish, had a famous resident at CORRYMORE HOUSE: Captain Boycott ▲ *283*. From the next village east, KEEL, the smooth sands of Trawmore beach extend for 2 miles to end abruptly with the Menawn Cliffs. They rise to tower nearly 800 feet above the sea. The picturesque road that leads round Achill Island, called Atlantic Drive, continues from DOOEGA and winds around the southern tip of land to end at Achill Sound. It passes another stronghold of Grace O'Malley, the 15th-century KILDOWNET CASTLE. There are fine views over to the mainland. Not far away are the restored remains of a small 15th-century church, with Gaelic Stations of the Cross.

Fishermen at Inishglora, on the Belmullet Peninsula.

BELMULLET PENINSULA

A little further north is Belmullet Peninsula, or the Mullet, roughly 15 miles long and 9 miles wide. It is an area of outstanding beauty, famous for its bird life, with a large number of interesting ancient remains including cairns, megalithic tombs, stone huts, pillar stones, churches and ruined forts.

ERRIS HEAD. The headland juts out at the western end of Broad Haven, the bay north of the Mullet. Spectacular rocky cliffs extend for nearly 14 miles along this stretch of coast. The promontory fort at DOONAMO has a circle of *chevaux de frise* very similar to that seen at Dún Aengus on the Aran Islands ▲ *273*.

INISHGLORA. The bare island nearly 3 miles off the west coast from Binghamstown is of significance in Ireland's Pagan and Christian past. In Celtic legend the children of Lir were buried here, having become mortals again after being changed into swans for thrice three hundred years ▲ *311*. There are also an interesting chapel and monastery founded here by Saint Brendan, who died in 577 ▲ *239*.

BLACKSOD BAY. The bay lies protected by the Belmullet Peninsula, south of the isthmus that separates it from the mainland. Here, on September 7, 1588 the *Rata* sank. She was the largest galleon of the Spanish Armada, commanded by Don Alonso de Levya. From Belmullet to Belderrig the road runs along vast and desolate areas of bog. This coast, battered by Atlantic winds, seems forsaken by both God and man.

SHARK FISHING
Of all the seventy-three species of fish that live off the Irish coast, the shark remains the most glorious catch for any fisherman. The Irish used to brave storms in their fragile *currachs* ▲ *276* to harpoon basking shark, harmless fish that can weigh several tons. Today deep-sea fishing, between June and September, still requires stamina and courage, but the boats now measure from 25 to 60 feet and are motor-powered.

THE FRENCH LANDING
On August 22, 1798 three frigates dropped anchor off Kilcummin Head. Under the command of General Humbert, 1,067 French soldiers landed and took the town of Killala, shortly followed by Ballina. Local men loyal to Wolfe Tone's United Irishmen came to swell the ranks of the French, but the nationwide movement soon fell apart, as they had no real support. At Castlebar, on August 5, the tiny army managed to rout an English force of five thousand infantry and one thousand cavalry. But Lord Cornwallis and General Lake moved their best troops west to surround them at Ballynamuck, County Longford. Outnumbered, Humbert was forced to surrender.

INLAND THROUGH COUNTY MAYO

KILLALA. Killala, taken by the French in 1798, is a pleasant seaside and cathedral town. Saint Patrick founded the episcopal see here, and the town is named after his original church, which he entrusted to Saint Muiredach. Killala has the finest round tower in County Mayo (left), as well as a Protestant cathedral built in 1670 on the ruins of a Catholic one. The French are said to have held the bishop and his family, and treated them with courtesy throughout. There is a monument to the landing on Kilcummin Head.

FOXFORD. The town is set among delightful scenery, on the River Moy, near to the loughs of Conn and Cullin. Foxford is proud to have among its sons Admiral William Brown, "father of the Argentinian navy". In 1892, the Reverend Mother Agnes Morrogh Bernard created the Providence Woollen Mills here, to stem the flow of local people abroad. They remain in business today, and can be visited.

STRAID. Michael Davitt is buried here in the village where he was born to a peasant family. He was the founder of the Land League, in 1879, and worked with Parnell. Thanks to him tenants saw the first reforms in the Irish land system.

CASTLEBAR. The county town of Mayo is the site of the battle of 1798 (below) in which the French put the English into headlong flight (the "Castlebar Races"). There is a monument to the 1798 Rebellion in the shady, tree-lined Mall, beside the tomb of John Moore, president of the short-lived Republic of Connacht. On nearby FRENCH HILL there is a memorial to the French who fell at Castlebar and in the town church a tablet to the dead of the Fraser Fencibles, the best English regiment present at the debacle.

BALLINTOBER ▲ *278*. About 8 miles along the road leading to Ballinrobe lies BALLINTOBER ABBEY, thoroughly restored between 1964 and 1966. It is the only abbey in Ireland where Mass has been celebrated without interruption since its foundation in 1216. Near to CARROWNACON, on the east bank

Cliffs at Downpatrick.

of Lough Carra, are the lonely ruins of Moorehall, John Moore's mansion and birthplace of Irish novelist George Moore (1852–1933). He spent time in Paris, where he became a close friend of Manet; he was also one of the leading lights of the Irish literary revival, and was involved in the founding of the Abbey Theatre ▲ *144*.

LOUGH MASK HOUSE. Southwest of Ballinrobe, Lough Mask House was the home of Captain Charles Boycott, land agent for Lord Erne. His poor treatment of the tenantry made him, in 1880, the first victim of Parnell's sending to "Moral Coventry" by supporters of the Land League. He was "left severely alone" and forced to use Orange farm workers from the north, protected by English soldiers. His name has become part of the English language.

KNOCK. On the plains 7 miles east of Claremorris stands Knock, one of the most important centers of Catholic pilgrimage today. On August 21, 1879, the Blessed Virgin, Saint Joseph and Saint John appeared, with a lamb, on the gable wall of the Church of St John the Baptist. The visions recurred, and an enquiry was held which concluded that they were genuine. Since then Knock has been the destination for hundreds of thousands of pilgrims every year. The pilgrims gather to pray at the church dating from 1828. Nearby a basilica has been built, consecrated in 1976 to the Blessed Virgin. Capable of holding twenty thousand people, it has a circular ambulatory supported by thirty-two pillars, one for each county in Ireland. On September 30, 1979 Pope John Paul II came to Knock during the first papal visit to Ireland. An international airport was opened just outside Charlestown in 1986.

CÉIDE FIELDS
(On the north coast, west of Ballycastle, Downpatrick Head.) Recent excavations in the turf bogs of northern County Mayo have revealed long stretches of stone wall, set wide apart. They seem proof of a highly advanced state of social cohesion and community organization. Discovery has also been made, under layers of turf, of megalithic tombs and dwellings dating from the Stone and Bronze ages. All information on the excavations is available in the little pyramid-shaped museum at Céide Fields, the name that has been given to the site.

So often were the green and wooded valleys, the lofty mountains and the sandy beaches of County Sligo evoked in the poetry of W.B. Yeats and in the paintings of his brother Jack, that a part of the county has come to be known as Yeats Country. The outlines of megalithic monuments guarding their ancient secrets stand out starkly from the vast expanses of bog, heather and broom.

SLIGO

The town stands on the Garavogue, the river linking Lough Gill to the Atlantic. The name "Sligo" comes from the Gaelic *sligeach*, meaning "shelly river". It grew up around a Dominican abbey founded in 1252, when the Anglo-Norman knights were taking over the northern territory of Connacht. Its fortunes oscillated until the second half of the 18th century, when Sligo prospered with the growth of trade with England and the New World. The ornate façades of the banks in Grattan Street and Stephen Street are proof of the resulting prosperity.

SLIGO ABBEY. The oldest building in Sligo is the abbey. It was badly damaged by fire in 1414, and rebuilt only to be ransacked during the Ulster rebellion in 1642. The eight pointed windows in the choir, widely splayed on the inside, are original. The window in the east wall and the high altar date from the 15th century, as do the three sides of the cloister that remain. Along the south wall of the choir is the richly carved MONUMENT TO O'CONOR SLIGO and his wife, and in the north wall of the nave is the TOMB OF CORMAC O'CREAN (1506), member

WILLIAM BUTLER YEATS (1865–1939)
As a child, he and his brother Jack ● *113* spent many holidays with their maternal grandparents at Ballisodare and Sligo. His first poems were inspired by folk-tales and Gaelic legends. Winner of the Nobel prize in 1923, in his work Yeats remained faithful to the land that nurtured his vocation.

of a wealthy merchant family. The Dominicans left the abbey early in the 18th century, when penal laws were made forbidding the Catholic clergy to practice in Ireland ● *52*.
MUNICIPAL ART GALLERY AND COUNTY MUSEUM. Along with collections of local interest and the fiddle of Michael Coleman, one of Ireland's greatest folk players, a section is devoted to the Yeats brothers. There are paintings and drawings by Jack, and William's letters, along with first editions and other memorabilia.

LOUGH GILL ★

PARKE'S CASTLE. The tranquility of Lough Gill inspired Yeats, although in the past its calm must have been disturbed over

◆ E A4-A3-B3-A5-A6

several centuries by life at the two castles that succeeded each other on its north bank. Excavations made within the walls of the present-day Parke's Castle have revealed that the high outer walls once surrounded a fortified tower built in the 15th or 16th century. It is suggested that this may have been Brian O'Rourke's fortress, possibly where he gave refuge to Captain Francisco de Cuellar of the Spanish Armada ▲ *316*. De Cuellar managed to get back to his homeland safe and sound, and left a thrilling account of his adventures. It appears that when Robert Parke built his castle in the 1620's, he dismantled the tower and reused the stones. Parke was an "entrepreneur", arriving in Ireland when the "plantation" of English and Scottish settlers was arranged early in the 17th century ● *51*. They brought with them their language, their culture and their architecture. Parke's Castle is one of the few "planters' castles" in Ireland.
HAZELWOOD DESMESNE. Richard Castle designed the Palladian mansion in 1731. Today it is the headquarters of a Korean company. Nearby is Half Moon Bay, where a large park is laid out with modern sculpture by Irish and foreign artists.
DEERPARK. The monument has the Gaelic name of "Leact Chon Mhic Ruis", and has also been called the "Irish Stonehenge" because of its pillars traversed by lintels that recall the famous monument on Salisbury Plain. It is in fact a fine example of a court tomb ● *89*, with a 50-foot-long oval court flanked by standing stones. Below the main site are ruins of other graves and a small fortified enclosure with an underground passage.

PARKE'S CASTLE
In contrast to the tall O'Rourke Tower that stood within the walls before, Parke's Castle is a long, single-story edifice adjoining the ramparts. The interior has been restored recently and exhibitions are held here. A visit to the castle includes an audio-visual presentation. The outer defensive wall is well-preserved, and now encloses stables and a forge rebuilt on their original site.

"THE ISLE OF INNISFREE"
In 1890 William Butler Yeats, "exiled" in London, wrote the nostalgic poem dreaming of his native land, Lough Gill, and the "lake isle of Innisfree" on its southern bank. "I will arise and go now, for always night and day, I hear lake water lapping with low sounds by the shore; While I stand on the roadway, or on the pavements grey, I hear it in the deep heart's core."

COUNTESS MARKIEVICZ (1868–1927)
Constance Gore-Booth met the Polish Count Casimir DuninMarkievicz, her future husband, when she was a student at the Beaux Arts in Paris. She was condemned to death for her part in the 1916 Easter Rising, but her sentence was commuted to life imprisonment in June 1917. In December 1918 she was elected for Dublin as the first woman member of the British House of Commons, but did not take her seat. Liberated in 1919, she was later made a minister in the first government of the Irish Republic.

DROMAHAIRE. This was the ancient capital of the O'Rourkes, kings of Breffni. On the banks of the Bonet River are remains of the royal castle. Adjoining are the ruins of "Old Hall", a manor built in the 17th century by the English settler Edward Villiers, who had been granted the lands confiscated from the O'Rourkes. On a hill across the river from Dromahaire is CREEVELEA ABBEY, a Franciscan monastery founded in 1508. The remains are in a reasonable state of repair, and there are some plain but very lovely carved reliefs of Saint Francis.

TOWARD DONEGAL

DRUMCLIFF. Yeats died in the south of France in 1939, but it was not until 1948 that he was finally buried, near the Protestant church at Drumcliff, where his grandfather had been rector. He wrote his own epitaph: "Cast a cold eye, On life, on death. Horseman, pass by!" In the 6th century Saint Columba founded a MONASTERY here, but there is little left apart from the foundations of a round tower. On the walls of the Catholic cemetery are an 11th-century High Cross carved with scenes from the Old and New Testaments.

LISSADELL HOUSE. The estate and house, built in 1834 in an austere neoclassical style, belonged to the Gore-Booth family. Yeats was pleased to be a guest at Lissadell and much admired Constance and her sister Eva, the poetess. "Two girls in silk kimonos, both Beautiful, one a gazelle." Between Carney and Lissadell there is a nature reserve where barnacle geese from Greenland spend the winter.

STREEDAGH POINT. Three ships of the Spanish Armada went down here in 1588. The story only survives in the account of the Captain Francisco de Cuellar. Those who managed to get ashore were massacred by the local inhabitants.

CREEVYKEEL. Just east of the village of Cliffony is a court tomb ● *89*, dating back to 2500 BC. The site at Creevykeel has been recently restored and is one of the finest examples of this type of ancient grave in Ireland. It has a large oval court, with the entrance on the eastern side. This leads to a chamber traversed by a central wall. There are two smaller dolmens in the sides of the mound, perhaps of a later date. The monument is surrounded by stone slabs. In the Middle Ages the court was used by a blacksmith who installed a forge.

INISHMURRAY. The Island of Inishmurray lies 4 miles off the coast of Sligo and can be reached by boat from the little port of Mullaghmore. On it are remarkable monastic remains, with the main buildings grouped inside a *cashel* reminiscent of some forts on the Aran Islands ▲ 273. It is not known if these fortifications are contemporary with, or pre-date, the monastery founded by Saint Molaise (bottom right) in the 6th or 7th century. The oval enclosure is in almost perfect condition and divided into three sections. The structures within include an 11th- or 12th-century church, a late medieval "Church of Fire", "Saint Molaise's house" (a stone-roofed oratory that may also be the tomb of the founder), and a beehive hut, known as Tory Bhrenell in honor of Saint Brendan ▲ 239. There are also three carved pillar stones and three altars, the largest of which has curious stones on its surface. The stones are used, according to ancient custom, for cursing. Until early in the 20th century an annual pilgrimage used to be made to Innishmurray. The faithful would make

CURSING STONES
According to an old custom, he who turns a stone can put a curse on anyone who has done him harm. However, if the grievance is not justified, the curse will turn back on him. It is told that an Englishwoman came here especially to turn a stone against Adolf Hitler.

their way around the island from east to west, following the Stations of the Cross, which can still be seen. (Return to Cliffony and continue to Grange where the road left, heading inland, will lead to the scenic Glenliff Horseshoe.)

GLENLIFF HORSESHOE LOOP DRIVE ★. The little road leads through magnificent landscapes, with views of Benwiskin, King's Mountain and Truskmore. The area is sparsely populated, although there is some pastureland.

GLENCAR LOUGH. A little further to the south is a small lough famous for its trout and salmon fishing ■ 44. At the eastern end is a waterfall which cascades down 1,000 feet from the plateau above, to a final 50-foot drop into the lough. It has been described by Yeats in his poem *The Stolen Child*: "Where the wandering water gushes From the hills above Glen Car". In Gaelic the cascade is called *Sruth-i-naghaidhan-áird* ("torrent going back upward") because gusts of wind often blow the water in sprays back to the top of the cliff.

Carrowmore
and Carrowkeel.

KNOCKNAREA. West of Sligo rises Knocknarea ("hill of executions"), crowned by an enormous tumulus. It has been claimed that this is the tomb of Maeve, the legendary queen of Connacht. In fact the cairn probably covers a passage grave, as yet untouched, and Maeve is believed to lie at Rathcroghan.

CARROWMORE. The huge burial site, on a low hill near to Knocknarea, still has about fifty megalithic remains in all, despite much destruction by quarrying. A number of dolmens are in a good state of preservation. The earliest graves date from about 5000 BC, and many were surrounded by stone circles. Piles of charred bones found here are likely testimony to the mass cremations that probably took place at Carrowmore.

COLLOONEY. The road leading to this village passes through BALLYSADARE, known for its salmon fisheries ■ *44*. At the entrance to Collooney stands a statue raised late in the 19th century to Captain Bartholomew Teeling. He fought side-by-side with the French general Humbert to force back Colonel Vereker's Limerick militia on September 5, 1798 ● *52*.

South of the village is MARKREE CASTLE, built in the 18th century but with 19th-century additions and alterations in neo-Gothic style. The crenelated gateway at the entrance to the estate was designed by the London architect Francis Goodwin in 1830. Markree is now a hotel.

BALLYMOTE. Before reaching Ballymote, the road leads through KESHCORRAN where there are hillside caves. One legend has it that Cormac MacAirt, Ard Rí of Ireland ● *48*, was raised here by a she-wolf. Richard de Burgo built a massive castle at Ballymote in 1300, at a period when the Anglo-Normans were consolidating their hold over north Connacht. Although the fortress, abandoned in the 17th century, has not been greatly restored, the vast ruins leave no doubt as to its massive strength. *The Book of Ballymote* (left), an important codex giving a key to the ogham alphabet ● *66*, was compiled in the 15th century in the Franciscan friary at Ballymote, whose ruins also remain.

CARROWKEEL ● *88*. The slopes of the Bricklieve Mountains, overlooking lovely Lough Arrow, are covered in wild heathland and bog, in places dangerous to cross. This is the site of a superb group of passage graves. Some of the cruciform graves have corbeled vaults. There are also wedge dolmens ● *89*. Neolithic pottery has been discovered here dating from 2500 to 2000 BC. Carrowkeel was also used as a site for individual burials during the Bronze Age, until 1500 BC. A number of the dolmens are in a dangerous condition, but one of the roofed tombs has been made safe for the public to visit. On the northern slopes are the remains of a prehistoric village.

CURLEW MOUNTAINS. The Curlew Mountains, a striking and unspoiled range of hills, separate the counties of Sligo and Roscommon. From the southern slopes there is a view over the pastures of Roscommon and Lough Key. At the foot of the hills, entering the town of Boyle, are the remains of a 12th-century Cistercian monastery.

BOYLE ABBEY ★. The MacDermots founded the abbey around 1160 and the church is an interesting illustration of the development of building techniques and architectural styles from the time of its foundation to 1220. The choir and transepts are the oldest part, with recessed chapels in both north and south transepts. On the south side of the nave are solid rounded arches in the English Norman style, with scalloped capitals (c. 1180); while on the north are three early pointed Gothic arches with exquisite moldings forming the corbels of the vaulting arches (c. 1200). At the intersection of the tower there are three segmental arches, and above is a

tower added in the 13th century along with the three lancet windows in the west gable. The cloister was seriously damaged in the 17th century when the monastery was used as a barracks. The porter's lodge and other buildings on the southern side of the monastery are from the 17th century.

LOUGH KEY. The huge wooded Lough Key National Park was once part of the estate of Rockingham House, property of the

DIARMAIT AND GRÁINNE
Keshcorran is also associated with the legend of Diarmait and Gráinne. The daughter of Cormac MacAirt agreed to marry Finn MacCoul, chief of a mythical army called the Fianna. But Finn was much older than Gráinne and she fell in love with Diarmait, one of Finn's soldiers. She eloped with him, and Finn pursued them across Ireland in vain. Diarmait was eventually to die on the slopes of Benbulben after being wounded by a wild boar, but for several years he and Gráinne spent happy times at Rath Ghrainne, near Keshcorran, where they had four sons and a daughter.

**SCOTTISH
MERCENARIES**
The warriors in long
coats of chainmail,
grasping their swords,
are two of the eight
figures on the tomb

of Felim O'Conor in
the nave of
Roscommon Abbey.
Such professional
soldiers came from
Scotland in the 15th
century. They were
hired as bodyguards
by local barons, or
taken into the best
army regiments.

Church of the
Sacred Heart,
Roscommon.

King Harman family. The house has gone, but interesting
features are a bog-garden ■ *34*, temple and ice-house.

RATHCROGHAN. The significance of this ring-barrow,
northwest of Tulsk, can easily elude the visitor. It is hard to
believe that it has such importance in Irish literature.
Rathcroghan, or Cruachain, was where the kings of Connacht
were crowned. It is mentioned in the Gaelic legends as the
capital of Ailill MacMata, husband of Maeve. Maeve herself
is thought to be buried here. The site had great religious
significance, for among the cairns is Oweynagat, "Cave of the
Cats", the gateway to the Other World. The lintel
stones at its entrance have inscriptions in ogham
● *66*.

CLONALIS HOUSE. Before coming to Roscommon a
visit can be made to the home of the O'Connor
Dons, descendants of Roderick O'Connor, the last
Ard Rí of Gaelic Ireland ● *48*. The house was built
at the end of the 19th century and contains family
furniture and objects linked to their past.

STROKESTOWN HOUSE. At the eastern end of the
elegantly planned Strokestown stands the house of
the Mahon family. In the 1730's, Richard Castle
seems to have redesigned the residence in Palladian
style at the request of Thomas Mahon. The two-
story central block contained the family
apartments; the more modest wings were
outbuildings. The mansion has been carefully restored and
furnished with pieces of the period. It also contains a museum
on the subject of the Great Famine ● *58*.

ROSCOMMON. The town's name, "Coman's Wood", comes
from that of Saint Coman who founded a monastery here in
the 6th century. The monastical remains, however, are from a
later 13th-century DOMINICAN PRIORY. They lie near the
Abbey Hotel (N63). The tomb of its founder, Felim O'Conor,
King of Connacht, is carved with his effigy (14th
century) and watched over by eight armed
figures (late 15th century). On the west
side of town are the ruins of a CASTLE
built in 1269 by the Royal Justiciar of
Ireland, Roger d'Ufford. The building
was badly damaged by Cromwell's
men in 1652, but the four round
towers still stand at its outer walls,
as does the fortified gateway to
the east, and the postern gate to
the west. The mullioned
windows were added
in 1578.

Ulster

▲ ULSTER

DONEGAL ▲ *294*
1 DONEGAL
2 SLIEVE LEAGUE
3 GLENCOLUMBKILLE
4 GLENTIES
5 DUNGLOE
6 ARANMORE ISLAND
7 GWEEDORE
8 TORY ISLAND
9 HORN HEAD
10 ROSGUILL
11 FANAD
12 RATHMULLAN
13 LETTERKENNY
14 GLENVEAGH
15 INISHOWEN
16 GRIANAN
OF AILEACH

DERRY TO ARMAGH ▲
35 DERRY
36 DUNGIVEN
37 BANAGHER
38 STRABANE
39 ULSTER AMERICAN
FOLK PARK
40 SPERRIN MOUNTAINS
41 NAVAN FORT
42 ARMAGH
43 ARDRESS HOUSE
44 LOUGH NEAGH

BELFAST

▲ ULSTER
DONEGAL

◆ **E** B3-B2-A1-B1-
C1-C2-D1

Donegal remains far less familiar to tourists than other areas. It has remained unspoilt and little explored. Some consider it the most beautiful county in Ireland, with varied landscapes and a long and magnificent coastline that boasts more beaches than any other Irish county. The many ancient remains are an added fascination. As early as the 5th century the northern part of Donegal was occupied by the O'Neills. The south was under the domination of the Conaill and the Eoghain families (Cenel Conaill and Cenel Eoghain), and two main regions are named after them: Inis Eoghain (the Eoghain Peninsula) and Tír Chonaill (Conaill Country).

DONEGAL TO GLENTIES

Doe Castle,
County Donegal.

The dizzy heights
of the Slieve
League cliffs.

DONEGAL. Donegal lies in the deep recesses of Donegal Bay, at the mouth of the River Eske. It is a pleasant and lively town, at the crossroads of three main routes. One road leads round the west coast, another goes east toward Derry ▲ *318*, and the third south to Sligo ▲ *284*. Donegal was founded by the Vikings, and its name means "fortress of the foreigners" (Dún na nGall), but it rose to importance as the stronghold of the O'Donnell clan. The two major monuments, DONEGAL ABBEY and DONEGAL CASTLE, were built in 1475, by Nuala O'Brien, and in 1505 by her husband, Red Hugh O'Donnell. In 1595, however, Hugh O'Donnell, the last prince of Tyrconnell, set fire to the castle rather than leave it to the English. It was a futile gesture, and the city fell to his enemies after the "Flight of the Earls"(1607) ● *50*, and was restored as part of the plantation scheme ● *51*. Captain Basil Brooke, in charge of replanning Donegal, built a stately, fortified Jacobean manor ● *99* into the remains of the castle. **SLIEVE LEAGUE ★.** Along the coast to the east is the port of

KILLYBEGS, boasting just over fifteen hundred inhabitants. It is surprising to learn that this is one of the most important fishing ports in the country, along with Greencastle ▲ *299* and Inishowen ▲ *298*. From here to the little village of KILCAR the road descends with spectacular views. Kilcar is famous for its tweed, as is CARRICK nearby. Carrick marks the start of a Gaelic-speaking area, and it is also the starting point for boat excursions to see the formidable Slieve League cliffs, the highest in Europe (nearly 2,000 feet). They are best seen from the sea or from BUNGLASS POINT.

GLENCOLUMBKILLE. The Glen Valley, bordered on one side by mountains and on the other by a wild and rocky coast, was a place of retreat and prayer for Saint Columba (also known as Saint Columcille, *c.* 521–97) and his disciples. Each year on June 9 a pilgrimage is held in honor of the saint, locally called the Turas ("journey"). The barefoot pilgrims make their way past some fifteen Stations of the Cross spread over 3 miles. Along the way are stone crosses and the cell oratory, the bed, the well and the chair of Saint Columba. The village of Glencolumbkille, set in the Glen Valley, is where Father James McDyer decided to "save the West". He formed a market-gardening co-operative with the aim of relieving the poverty of his parishioners. The FOLK MUSEUM ◆ *387* was another of his ideas: three thatched cottages illustrate the life of peasants in Ireland at different periods of history. (The steep road crosses uninhabited hills and leads over the wild Pass of Glengesh, before descending to Ardara.)

GLENTIES. Playwright Brian Friel comes from this pleasant town, and used it as the setting for his play *Dancing at Lughnasa*. There is a handsome 19th-century COURT HOUSE, and nearby is ST CONNELL'S MUSEUM, with a collection of local items. ST CONAL'S CHURCH is modern, designed by Liam McCormick. Around the coast to the west are more good beaches, well worth exploration.

DUNGLOE TO RAMELTON

THE ROSSES. The soil in this area is so poor that it is virtually impossible to grow anything. Until late in the last century 75 percent of the population of The Rosses spoke Irish ● *68*; now the proportions are reversed, which still makes it one of today's strongest areas of *Gaeltacht*. The region is welcoming more and more visitors, however. Dungloe is usually their base for exploration of the wild, windbeaten landscape to the north and west, scattered with tiny lakes and studded with granite rocks. (From Burtonport, there is a regular ferry service to Aranmore Island.)

ARANMORE ISLAND. Although the island has an aura of calm, the 750-foot cliffs on the west coast are battered by powerful

SAINT COLUMBA AND THE "BATTLE OF THE BOOK" ▲ *151*
Saint Finian claimed possession of the copy Columba had made of his illuminated Latin psalter, called the *Cathach* ("battler"). The High King of Tara pronounced judgement: "as to every cow belongs its calf, so to every book belongs its copy". Columba, whose other Christian name, it should be

remembered, was Crimthan ("wolf"), provoked a bloody battle at Cooladrummon, in 561, between his followers and those of Finian and the High King. Three thousand men were killed, and Columba was banished to Scotland to expiate his sins.

Above, carts in the Glencolumbkille Folk Museum.

295

Atlantic
waves. The
lighthouse was the first
to be built in Donegal
(1798), and it sweeps the seas
with the most powerful beam of any along the Irish coast.
Aranmore is inhabited all year round, but only comes to life
in summer, when fishing and tourism are at their height.
ERRIGAL MOUNTAIN. Toward Errigal Mountain the landscape
becomes wilder and more rocky. The cone-shaped quartzite
peak, whose outline is strangely reminiscent of Mount Fuji, is
the highest in Donegal (2,466 feet). From the top, on a clear
day, one can see as far as Scotland and the peaks of
Connacht. At the foot of Errigal Mountain lies the village of
DUNLEWY, on Lough Lacung. Its Church of the Sacred
Heart (1877) has splendidly colorful marble decoration. The
nearby village of GWEEDORE, also set against the mountain
backdrop, became known for its hotel (now closed). The far-
sighted and philanthropic landlord Lord George Hill started
the establishment to draw tourists
and help relieve the poverty of the
local people.
TORY ISLAND. Tory
Island can be seen
8 miles offshore from BLOODY
FORELAND (so-named after the
gory colors of the sunsets that

can be seen from the point). According to legend the island was given to Saint Columba, and the ancient remains at the village of West Town may be those of a monastery he founded here. They consist of a ROUND TOWER, the 6-foot-high cross, a rare TAU CROSS of Saint Anthony (bottom left), and a church, TEAMPULL NA MUIRISEAR ("Church of the Seven"), named after seven pilgrims that Columba resuscitated in order to administer last rites. To the east of the island are the remains

Donegal seen from the island of Aranmore.

The harbor at Bunbeg.

of a fort, DÚN BHALOIR, a reminder that in legend the island was a stronghold of the Fomoriens, a race of giant pirates. Their chief, "Balor of the Evil Eye", had a single eye in the middle of his forehead. There are boats to the island from Magheraroarty and Bunbeg (above right). About 130 people live on Tory Island, making their living mainly from fishing. Derek Hill, an English painter, spent time here and inspired the start of the island's school of primitive painting.

HORN HEAD. The scenery is magnificent along the road west, which leads between the foothills of Muckish Mountain and the sea. It passes through Falcarragh, the last outpost of *Gaeltacht* ● 68. From the 800-foot cliffs of Horn Head, a favorite place for many varieties of sea bird, it possible to see how the Atlantic Ocean has torn away at the coast, leaving a few islands (Inishbofin, Inishdooey, Inish Beg and Tory) and a confusion of narrow sea channels and ragged bays.

ROSGUILL PENINSULA. A road known as Atlantic Drive leads around the peninsula, passing Carrigart and the nearby seaside resorts of Rosapenna and Downings. It runs above sea level until it reaches Tranarossan Bay, after which it descends to follow the wooded shores of a narrow estuary called Mulroy Bay, with sandy coves and tiny islets along its edge. Milford stands at the southern end of the bay, a good base for fishing on the River Lennon and Lough Fern.

FANAD PENINSULA. There are two routes signposted around the peninsula, but only the Fanad Peninsula Scenic Tour goes as far as Fanad Head, the curved headland at the entrance to Lough Swilly. The lough is in fact a sea inlet separating the Fanad Peninsula from the Inishowen. The name Swilly may come from a legendary former inhabitant of the bay, Suileach. This was a monster with one hundred eyes, killed by Saint Columba. The other route, the Knockalla Coast Road, follows the schist and heather-covered hills of Knockalla Mountain.

RATHMULLAN. The PRIORY in the center of the town was built for the Carmelites in 1516 by Owen Roe MacSweeney. In the tower of the stone fort standing on the sea front is a permanent exhibition on the region's history, and in particular the departure of the earls of Ulster for France in 1607, the crucial event known as the "Flight of the Earls" ● 50.

DOE CASTLE
The stronghold is well positioned, deep within the bay of Sheep Haven that separates Horn Head from the Rosguill Peninsula. Doe Castle was built early in the 16th century by the MacSweeney family. It was attacked many times by rival northern clans, and used to be protected by a moat hewn out of the rock and crossed by a drawbridge. In the graveyard beside the castle, where there was a Franciscan monastery founded by the MacSweeneys, many chiefs of the Donegal clans lie buried. There is a tombstone in the wall carved with a fine cross, the family coat of arms and mythological figures.

LETTERKENNY TO GLENVEAGH

LETTERKENNY. This rapidly growing town is now the largest in Donegal. It has the COUNTY MUSEUM, which is worth visiting for its broad collection of objects. ST EUNAN'S CATHEDRAL was built at the turn of the century. It is decorated with Celtic designs and stained glass. The carved throne is the work of a Dublin company owned by the father of the poet and hero of 1916, Patrick Pearse ● 61.

COLMCILLE HERITAGE CENTRE. Gartan, birthplace of Saint Columba, or Saint Columcille, is now the site of the Colmcille Heritage Centre. It stands not far from various sites linked with the saint: the stone on which Saint Columba's mother is said to have given birth, ST COLMCILLE'S ORATORY, the monastery founded by the saint (of which only two crosses and a ruined church remain) and, to the northeast, Kilmacrenan, where he was brought up and built his first church. The museum tells the story of the missionary saint and has a section on early illuminated manuscripts ▲ 150.

GLENVEAGH. The NATIONAL PARK covers 36 square miles of countryside around Lough Beagh, and includes GLENVEAGH CASTLE and gardens. This Victorian castle was built in 1870 by the American John Adair and his wife Cornelia to designs by J.T. Trench. The granite building with its battlements and towers is set against a dramatic backdrop of rugged mountains. The narrow, barrel-vaulted entrance hall has a black and white Victorian tiled floor. The main drawing room is filled with Irish Chippendale furniture.

GLEBE HOUSE AND GALLERY
A 19th-century vicarage in the quiet parish of Gartan (near to the Colmcille Heritage Centre) was purchased in 1953 by the English painter and theater designer Derek Hill. Donegal was important to Hill: discovering it had filled him with new inspiration, and he eventually gave Glebe House to the State in 1981. The house illustrates the energy, and wide tastes and interests of its owner. Drawings by William Morris are to be seen alongside prints brought back from Japan and embroidery from Boukhara. There is an eclectic collection of paintings (Pasmore, Hokusai, Picasso, Kokoschka, and Tory Island primitives).

The round tower contains a music room lined in green tartan and decorated with antlers. In 1938 the property was bought by Henry McIlhenny, President of the Philadelphia Museum of Art. He transformed the grounds, creating a spectacular garden first with the help of Jim Russell and then Lanning Roper. The magnificent Gothic Revival conservatory was designed by Philippe Jullian. Glenveagh is now owned by the state and open to the public.

INISHOWEN PENINSULA ★

The peninsula lies between the deep sea-loughs Lough Swilly and Lough Foyle, and is bounded by the Atlantic to the north. The land is rocky and mountainous, rising to the central peak of Slieve Snaght, 2,019 feet high. The peninsula forms a rough triangle, the three points being Inishowen Head, Dunree Head, and Malin Head, the most northerly place in Ireland (above). There are some sites of architectural interest on the peninsula (O'Dochertys' Keep at BUNCRANA, DUNREE FORT and GREENCASTLE FORT, and the resorts of MOVILLE and BALLYLIFFIN), but it is really for the superb scenery and archeological sites that visitors come here.

GRIANAN OF AILEACH ★. The most impressive ancient monument in the county. The massive circular fort stands on a hill 800 feet above sea level, with views over loughs Swilly and Foyle. The walls are 17 feet high and 13 feet thick at the base, and they surround a space 79 feet in diameter. Around the main fort are three earth ramparts, now only partly discernible. Like Staigue Fort ▲ *229*, the site is probably pre-Christian. It was the seat of the O'Neill dynasty, kings of Ulster, from the 5th to the 12th century, and it was twice destroyed, in 676 and in 1101. The Grianan of Aileach was restored in the 1870's. At the foot of the hill is ST AENGUS CHURCH, built in 1967 by Liam McCormick and Una Madden.

CROSS OF CARDONAGH. A remarkable cross (below) stands against the wall of the Protestant church, dating from the 8th or perhaps 7th century. It is carved with human figures and interlace designs. Most unusual are the two smaller stones standing on either side, also decorated. There is another standing stone in the graveyard showing a *flabellum* (a fan-shaped liturgical object) which must have been copied from one of the relics of Saint Columba.

CLONCA. The church probably dates from the 17th century and was built on the site of a monastery founded by Saint Buodan. Inside is the tombstone of Magnus MacOrristin, a Scot, on which are carved a sword and a hurley ● *83* along with an inscription in Scottish Gaelic ● *66*. In a field to the west is a Celtic cross. On the east face is the *Miracle of the Loaves and Fishes* and, on the other side, a depiction of two men, who could be Saint Paul and Saint Anthony in the desert.

COOLEY. Inland from Moville is Cooley where Saint Finian is said to be buried in the GRAVEYARD. There are also the remains of two churches and a burial place called the SKULL HOUSE. On the other side of Lough Foyle from the Inishowen Peninsula lies Northern Ireland. The nearest town over the border is Derry ▲ *318*.

GRIANAN OF AILEACH
The word *grianan* means "house of the sun". Neither the name nor the fort's original purpose have yet been fully explained. The walls curve in slightly towards the top, and within they are terraced. On each side of the entrance gate are passages inside the thickness of the wall extending half way round the fort. Their entrances are at the northern and southern ends. When Murtogh O'Brien, King of Munster, defeated the O'Neills here in 1101, he ordered the fort to be dismantled and many stones were carried away.

The tall cranes of the *Harland & Wolff* shipyards, founded in 1862, builders of the doomed Titanic.

The city of Belfast lies on low land between green hills, at the mouth of the River Lagan where it flows into Belfast Lough. Its name comes from "Béal Feirste" ("sàndy ford"). Around it are mountains that continue along the northwest bank of the lough, a long, wide inlet from the North Channel. Belfast is the second largest city in Ireland and grew rapidly in the 18th and 19th centuries because of its busy port, shipbuilding yards, and linen industry. It is the industrial capital of Northern Ireland. Many of the old quarters of Belfast were bombed in the Blitz, and others pulled down by planners in the 1960's. However, the city has friendly pubs, some remarkably ornate churches and a number of impressive buildings erected during its heyday. The Anglo-Irish novelist and short-story writer William Trevor wrote: "When the sun shines on this city, and when its people smile, there is a warmth that does you good to be close to."

◆ E F3-F4-E5

SHIPBUILDING, BELFAST'S PRIDE
The industry developed from 1791 onward and still represents an important factor in the local economy thanks to *Harland & Wolff*, one of the largest shipbuilding and repair yards in the United Kingdom, and *Short Brothers*, the second largest company in Belfast in terms of employees.

AN ARCHITECT'S TOWN

Most of the waterside property in the city once belonged to the earls of Donegal. The family had accumulated such colossal debts that the second earl was forced to sell all his land. As a result speculators were able to acquire the green and undeveloped banks of the Lagan. The greater the instability of financial institutions became in the 19th century, the more important it was to have an impressive building exuding wealth and dependability. They employed architects to give them this ring of confidence.

Of the fifty banks registered in Belfast at the end of the century, not one remained forty years later. The 19th-century architects who put their mark on Belfast were Sir Charles Lanyon (1813–89), W.H. Lynn (1829–1915) and William J. Barre (1830–67).

LANYON, FATHER AND SON. The Englishman Charles Lanyon was a ruthless property speculator, an engineer, an architect, a Conservative politician and a "ladies man" who married the boss's daughter and became Mayor of Belfast. He brought with him an architectural language new to the people of Belfast, who previously had little conception of what a building could be. Under his influence, banks became castles protecting the wealth of the linen manufacturers: examples can still be seen, such as the NORTHERN BANK (Waring St) and the FIRST TRUST BANK (Victoria St). The apparently indestructible NEW HOUSE OF CORRECTION (now the Crumlin Road prison) was a fearful warning to wrongdoers, and the COURT HOUSE, to which it is linked by an underground corridor, was an equally intimidating symbol of law and order. And the churches soared skyward to evoke yet higher powers. Among those that Lanyon built is the SINCLAIR SEAMAN'S CHURCH (near the docks), of all the most spectacular. The throne is made of a bowsprit and the figurehead from the prow of the *Mitzpah*; the organ is decorated with port and starboard lights; there is the gleaming copper bell of the World War Two vessel *HMS Hood*, and the collection is taken in miniature model lifeboats. The University quarter (south Belfast) is also strongly marked by the work of Charles Lanyon. The mock-Tudor ● *99* buildings of QUEEN'S UNIVERSITY (University Rd) are of a warm red brick that blends admirably with the style. Nearby are the famous BOTANIC GARDENS. The Tuscan Doric ASSEMBLY'S COLLEGE (east of the university) was for a short time the seat of parliament, and today houses the

Union Theological College. CUSTOMS HOUSE (Queen's Sq.), containing a collection of paintings on a maritime theme, is also by Lanyon. His son designed the imposing medieval-style JENNYMOUNT MILL (North Derby St), and also BELFAST CASTLE (Antrim Rd) which imitates the Scottish baronial tradition. The latter was built for the Earl of Donegal before all the money was gone.

W.H. LYNN, "AN ECLECTIC AMONG ECLECTICS". Lanyon's partner W. H. Lynn gave Belfast some varied and original buildings. On Donegall Square North stands the LINEN MERCHANTS' WAREHOUSE that he built in 1869, now converted to house a branch of Marks & Spencer. It is on a street near a much older building, the LINEN HALL LIBRARY (1781), named after the hall that used to stand in the center of the square. It is an excellent library, open to the public, containing a collection of documents on the recent political troubles ● 64. As access to this section is limited, lots are drawn to decide who can enter. There is a second building by W.H. Lynn at nos. 4–10 May Street. It is built in a mixture of Venetian and Gothic styles and is decorated with an eye-catching design of red, white and blue bricks. This once housed the YOUNG MENS' SOCIETY of the Church of Ireland. Another example of his work is the HARBOUR OFFICE (Corporation St).

WILLIAM J. BARRE, COMPETITION WINNER. Although Barre's designs were often chosen over those of Lanyon in architectural competitions, he did not have the same friends in high places. His lack of useful contacts meant that he was seldom able to raise the funds necessary for his projects. A number did come to fruition, however. They are the ULSTER HALL (Bedford St), built in 1860, now used for concerts by the Ulster Orchestra, the ALBERT MEMORIAL CLOCK TOWER (Queen's Sq.), which is not impressive enough to make it a real tourist attraction, the METHODIST CHURCH (University Rd), built in 1864 in the Lombardo-Venetian style, the FIRST TRUST BANK (Royal Ave), built in the same year, and a small hospital (116, Great Victoria St).

A TOWN OF PUBS AND CHURCHES

THE PUBLIC HOUSES. Near the Europa Hotel, which has the uneasy reputation of being the European hotel most exposed to the danger of bombs, there is an amusing piece of sculpture dedicated to the women of easy virtue who used to people the streets of Belfast after nightfall. There is even a story, almost certainly invented, that a passage led under Great Victoria Street to take the girls from the Opera House directly to another no less baroque establishment: the thoroughly Victorian, tiled and mirrored, CROWN LIQUOR SALOON ★, even today lit by gas, where they could enjoy Guinness and oysters with their young men in the snugs.

"CROWN LIQUOR SALOON"
This is the haunt of actors, journalists, art students and tourists. The building was once the Ulster Railway Hotel (where Sarah Bernhardt spent the night), and was opened by Patrick Flanigan in 1885, who was inspired by the many railway hotels in which he had stayed while traveling in

Spain and Italy. The interior is Victorian and highly ornate, with brightly colored glass and tiles that are reflected in the polished mirrors behind the long counter. Over the entrances of the individual wood-paneled snugs are carved heraldic beasts.

ROADSIDE PORTRAIT GALLERY
When passing no. 10 Donegall Square South, look up. Some famous men are staring down at you: Humboldt, Jacquard, Washington, Galileo, Columbus, Newton, Stevenson, Moore, Watt, Michelangelo, Homer, Shakespeare and Schiller. The busts that cover two stories of the façade are the work of Charles Lanyon.

BELFAST AND THE STAGE
Of all the theaters in the city the Grand Opera House (Great Victoria St) is the favorite of both artists and public alike. It offers an impressive program of opera, ballet, drama and variety. Part of its charm is the theater interior itself, sumptuously decorated with velvet, extravagant gilded molding, and the odd Renaissance-style touch. The Lyric Theatre (Ridgeway St) specializes in Irish drama and the classics, while the Arts Theatre (Botanic Ave) puts on musical comedies and modern plays. The Group Theatre (Bedford St) specializes in plays from Ulster.

ROBINSON'S, almost next door, is a pleasing reproduction which imitates the great Irish institution of the "spirit grocer", a grocer's shop that also provides customers with drinks at a small bar. Spirit grocers are still found in some country areas. MORRISON'S (Bedford St) is similar. The MORNING STAR (Pottinger's Entry) is one of Belfast's famous old oyster houses. In the city's oldest pub, KELLY'S CELLARS (Bank St), there is still something of the conspiratorial atmosphere that must have reigned at the time of the United Irishmen ● *52*, when Henry Joy McCracken was forced to hide behind the bar to escape the pursuit of English soldiers. DU BARRY'S, named after Louis XV's favorite, and where the painter Stanley Spencer's brother used to play the piano, is now closed. It was a shady place of secret assignations. The KITCHEN BAR and BITTLE'S BAR do their best to cheer up gloomy Victoria Square, once the heart of theatrical life in the city. They are among the rare traditional pubs to have survived in the center. Further south, toward the university, and marooned amid cafés and fast-food restaurants, is LAVERY'S GIN PALACE, a flourishing establishment in the 19th century which now retains a distinctly 1960's atmosphere. On the road to the docks is the ROTTERDAM BAR. It stands on the spot where orphaned and destitute girls were once handcuffed for transportation to Van Diemen's Land (now Tasmania). Today, the bar is known for good music from such far-flung places as Eastern Europe and South America, as well as from Ireland.

THE CHURCHES. ST GEORGE'S CHURCH (High St) offers more measured enjoyment. The sobre building is Corinthian in

style. It was built in 1811 on the former site of the CHAPEL OF THE FORD (1306), an important monument in Belfast's history, since the first written mention of the founding of the city is linked to the chapel. It stood on a tributary of the River Lagan called the Farset, which now runs underground. Until early in the 19th century choirboys from the chapel came to fish for salmon. However, archeologists have discovered flint arrowheads dating from the Stone Ages, affording the site an altogether more ancient history. The perfect lines of the First Presbyterian Church (Rosemary's St) are the work of Roger Mulholland. It dates back to 1781, making it not only the first Presbyterian church in the city but also the oldest. The Catholic ST MALACHY'S CHURCH (Alfred St) is interesting inside because of the construction of the vaults. The Protestant ST ANNE'S CATHEDRAL was designed by Sir Thomas Drew in 1899 to the plan of a basilica in a style imitating Hiberno-Romanesque architecture. The cathedral underwent alterations in 1981. Inside there are a number of beautiful mosaics by Gertrude and Margaret Martin, and carving by Morris Harding.

ROBINSON'S

The divine Sarah Bernhardt and the inimitable Anna Pavlova both played at the Grand Opera House.

OTHER PLACES OF INTEREST

CITY HALL (Donegall Square). The huge City Hall (below) was completed in 1906 to the design of Sir Brumwell Thomas, its dome inspired by St Paul's Cathedral. It stands on the site of the 18th-century White Linen Hall. The Renaissance-style building has a WHISPERING GALLERY in the dome and on the main landing is a mural (1951) by John Luke, which today appears somewhat naive. It is a romanticized portrayal of the great old industries of Belfast (rope-making, linen and shipbuilding), trades which may have brought wealth to some but offered many others little more than a hard life spent in poor, overcrowded sectarian ghettos. Outside the City Hall a STATUE OF QUEEN VICTORIA overlooks Royal Avenue. To the east side of Donegall Square note the line of GEORGIAN HOUSES in Chichester Street (nos. 7–11). Better still are those in Joy Street (nos. 14–26), built twenty-six years later: the finest example of Georgian architecture in the city.

STATUE OF VICTORIA In the gardens of Donegall Square, Queen Victoria stands on a pedestal. At her feet are bronze figures symbolizing weaving and shipbuilding.

ULSTER MUSEUM (Botanic Gardens). On display here are the incredible treasures salvaged from the wreck of the Spanish galleon *Girona*, the pride of the Armada, sunk in October 1588 along the rocky northern coast of the province ▲ *315*. The jewels, of inestimable value, and other objects were found by the Belgian archeologist Robert Sténuit and acquired by the museum in 1972. Dazzled visitors will come across the odd curiosity, such as a thin gold ring belonging to a Spanish officer that has *"No tengo mas que dar te"* ("I have nothing more to give you") engraved inside. A room on the third floor gives detailed information on the country's flora and fauna. On the fourth floor are paintings by many artists from Ireland and from elsewhere in Europe. Among the most striking in the collection are the images of the Giant's Causeway ▲ *312* by Andrew Nicol and Susannah Drury, some brilliant post-Impressionist works by George Campbell and Gerard Dillon, and William Conor's portrayal of the Belfast poor.

Bronze plaque with enamelwork and millefiori (Armagh, 8th century BC).

STORMONT (About 4 miles east of Belfast). The grand building in the classical style by A. Thornely was built in the early 1930's at the expense of the British government to be the Parliament and seat of government for Northern Ireland. So it remained until 1972. Today it houses the Northern Ireland Office.

Southwest of Belfast lie the woods and pastures of the Lagan Valley Regional Park, where the Giant's Ring dolmen stands. Surrounding what

was probably a place of worship is a circular earth rampart nearly 600 feet in diameter, 12 feet high and with a base 60 feet wide. The original dry-stone structure has long been overgrown, and has disappeared beneath earth and grass. At the center is the dolmen, under which a burial site has been discovered.

SAINT PATRICK
The Saint Patrick Center was opened in February 2001 and uses the latest developments in technology to evoke the figure and heritage of Ireland's patron saint.

COUNTY DOWN

ARDS PENINSULA. East of Belfast, a long arm of land extends southward, separating Strangford Lough (below) from the Irish Sea. The narrow, winding road leading along the banks of the lough is of more interest than the eastern side of the peninsula. It leads through quiet countryside, between fuchsia hedges, passing waterside villages, castles and ruined abbeys. Before setting off, there are a number of things worth seeing. The fascinating ULSTER FOLK AND TRANSPORT MUSEUM is at Cultra. Bangor has a marina, Donaghadee is a charming seaside resort, and BALLYCOPELAND has one of only two working windmills left in Ireland, dating from 1780. From NEWTOWNARDS, a market town known for its town hall and for the ruins of a Dominican priory, go west to the SCRABO COUNTRY PARK. This was designed by Charles Lanyon in 1857 for the Mountsteward family from Londonderry. On a hill is Scrabo Tower, with a climb of 125 steps to one of the finest views in the region. Crossing by causeway to Mahee Island, the remains of NENDRUM MONASTERY ● *92*, founded in the 5th century, lie within three concentric wards. There are the ruins of a church and a round tower from the 10th or 11th century, as well as a grand sundial. At the southern end of Strangford Lough is CASTLE WARD HOUSE (1762), built for Mr Bernard and Lady Anne Ward. The house is a masterpiece of architectural compromise. The front façade is classical, according to the tastes of Mr Bernard, and the rear is neo-Gothic, the choice of his wife Anne. The rooms also follow the two styles; the architect is unknown. The house and grounds (now a nature reserve) have been preserved and are administered by the National Trust. There are also farm buildings, a slaughterhouse, grain mill and laundry to visit. Concerts and recitals are held here during the summer. From the village of STRANGFORD there are boats to PORTAFERRY, a delightful harborside village which now has the Exploris Sea Aquarium. On the east bank of the lough lie the vast of GREYABBEY (1193) ● *96*. The church, in Early English style, consists only of a simple nave with no aisles. MOUNT STEWART HOUSE ★ was the Irish family seat of the Marquess of Londonderry; Viscount Castlereagh, the early 19th-century politician was born here. He is said to have brought the twenty-two chairs (now in the dining room) used at the Congress of Vienna; each is embroidered with the coat of arms of the delegate and the country he represented (Wellington, Metternich, Talleyrand . . .). The house was built in two stages during the first half of the 19th century, on the site of a former family residence. London architect George Dance designed the west façade (1804–5), but the main part of the building was built to the neoclassical design of William Vitruvius Morrison, for the third marquess of Londonderry. The interior was redecorated by Edith, wife of the seventh marquess, who also created the gardens.

St Patrick's Country. In the graveyard of DOWNPATRICK CATHEDRAL, at the end of elegant English Street, a stone marks the possible burial place of Saint Patrick. On the other side of the River Quoile lie the ruins of INCH ABBEY, founded by John de Courcy in 1180 for a Cistercian order. At the center of the ruins the three breathtaking pointed windows of the chancel rise up. Further south, toward Ardglass, known for its herring fisheries and its "seven castles", the road crosses the source of the STRUELL, whose waters are said to possess strange powers. At Saintfield, to the northeast, lie the gardens of ROWALLANE, famous for their azaleas. Southwest is DUNDRUM CASTLE, a link in the powerful chain of defense created by the Norman John de Courcy. From the hill the imposing castle with circular keep overlooks the port of Dundrum, its defenses reinforced by a moat cut into the rock.

Mourne Mountains (below right). The prettiest landscape in County Down is provided by the Mourne Mountains, sloping gently toward the sea and the town of NEWCASTLE, on Dundrum Bay. Newcastle was a fashionable seaside resort but it now owes its reputation to the fame of its golf course. The Royal County Down Golf Club is considered to be one of the ten best courses in the world. This region of mountain and forests is marvelous for walking. Near to the summit of Slieve Croob, the highest of a range of mountains near Dromara, is the LEGANANNY TRIPOD-DOLMEN (above), the most remarkable in Ulster. Between Banbridge and Rathfriland is an area known as BRONTË COUNTRY, where Patrick, father of the writers, was born, worked and preached.

A MUCH-COVETED STRONGHOLD
Over a period of five hundred years Carrickfergus Castle was taken a number of times. First, John Lackland's siege subjugated his unruly barons. A little over a century later the Scottish soldiers of Edward Bruce spent a year wearing down the English defenses. Late in the Middle Ages the fortress was being used more for administrative purposes and fell into disrepair, until Schomberg took it for William III. It was from here that William began his campaign of 1690 ▲ 194. The last action seen at the castle was in 1760 when it fell to Captain Thurot, leader of a French

expeditionary force, after a desperate resistance during which the defenders even resorted to tearing off their trouser buttons to use as amunition. A final episode in the history of Carrickfergus came in 1778, when it witnessed the engagement between John Paul Jones, founder of the American navy, with the British ship HMS *Drake*.

The long coast road offers spectacular views over the Irish Sea. It is bordered by red sandstone rocks worn by the sea, and white chalk cliffs, rich in fossils. Rising above are the Antrim Mountains, wind-blown and heather-covered moorland heights where grouse live in fear of buzzard and crow. To the north is the moonscape of the Giant's Causeway, stepping from the sea up to the cliffs, and the ancient territories of Sorley Boy MacDonnell with his romantic castle of Dunluce defying the seas and the elements that work daily to crumble the cliffs beneath its walls.

CARRICKFERGUS CASTLE

ON THE ROCK OF FERGUS. Carrickfergus Castle stands on a rocky base that juts out from the north bank of Belfast Lough. It is the best-defended castle in Ulster and, along with Trim Castle ▲ 190, one of the best-preserved Norman strongholds in Ireland. For centuries it has controlled traffic in and out of the lough, and it was of prime importance in the Norman conquest of Ulster led by John de Courcy, who first fortified the site between 1178 and 1204.

BEHIND THE RAMPARTS. De Courcy built the keep, which has its entrance on the first floor. The Great Chamber, on the second floor, has a fireplace, and was for the use of those of highest rank or station, while de Courcy probably occupied the third floor, which has a roof dating from the 16th century. The keep stood surrounded by wards and protected by high walls. The defenses were improved in the 13th century by the addition of a further rampart flanked by two solid towers on the northern side.

CHURCH OF ST NICHOLAS. In peacetime the soldiers would leave the castle to attend the Church of St Nicholas, in the town. Built from the 12th to the 16th century, the different phases of construction can be easily distinguished.

◆ E F3-F2-F1-E1

GLENS OF ANTRIM

THE GLENS. Nine glens (long narrow valleys) lead up from the sea toward the ancient Antrim Mountains. The glens have rivers and waterfalls, and are full of birds and wild flowers. Until the middle of the 19th century each glen remained isolated from the next. William Bald and Charles Lanyon ▲ *302* had the limestone cliffs blasted to create the coastal road permitting communication between them.

LARNE. Ferries arrive from Scotland at Larne, which stands at the mouth of a lough that bears its name. The lough islets are a delight for ornithologists. Following the road to Ballylumford, a dolmen four thousand years old (below) stands in a tiny cottage garden.

BALLYGALLEY. In the village are the ruins of a brigands' stronghold, a lovely beach and a castle. The latter is a Scottish baronial residence built in 1625 by James Shaw of Greenock and typical of the style favored by the Scots who came over to colonize the province in the early 17th-century "plantations". It is now a hotel, with a bar in the ancient keep (haunted, of course).

THE NINE GLENS
Each glen has a name that tells something about it: Glenarm, valley of the army; Glencloy, valley of the hedges; Glenariff, valley of the laborer; Glenaan, valley of the rushes; Glenballyeamon, Eamon's valley; Glencorp, valley of the slaughterer; Glendun, brown valley; Glenshesk, valley of the sedges; and Glentaisie, Taisie's valley (seductress of Rathlin Island, fought over by Vikings and natives).

Waterfall in Glenariff.

GLENARM. Despite its coastal setting, dust fills the air of Glenarm, the oldest village in the glen. This comes from the adjacent limestone quarries. Glenarm Castle was the seat of the earls of Antrim. It is a peculiar and not very successful mixture of many styles, which can be entered by a bridge and mock-medieval gateway that was built in 1825.

CARNLOUGH. A charming little port at the lower end of Glencloy with an old posting inn inherited by Winston Churchill, the LONDONDERRY ARMS. Over the road is a white stone bridge built for the railway that until the 1960's transported limestone from the quarries above down to the port. A little further north stands GARRON TOWER, a castellated mansion built in 1848, which would look more at home on the Rhine. It is the venue for a week-long summer seminar devoted to the literary traditions of the North.

GLENARIFF ★. In Glenariff Forest Park, which is bisected by the A43, is the enchanting woodland waterfall known as Ess na Larach.

RED BAY ★. The long bay curves round beyond Garron Point. It owes its name to the water that rushes down into it, which is colored by the surrounding sandstone hills. The distinctive outline of LURIGETHAN (1,150 feet), with steep sides and a flat top, can be seen in the distance.

CUSHENDALL. A delightful village at the bottom of three glens that has charmed many travelers. Thackeray noted that he dined well here on fish and beer. There is a red sandstone tower (1809) built to be "a place of confinement for idlers and rioters", and to the west, further up Glenaan, are ancient stone remains that have been wrongly called Ossian's Grave. Ossian was the warrior bard, son of Finn MacCoul ▲ *312*. Certainly, the contemporary poet John Hewitt (1907–87), who loved Cushendall best of all, wished it to be his burial place.

CUSHENDUN. Clough William-Ellis, architect of the Welsh seaside village of Portmerion (where the television series *The Prisoner* was filmed), designed a large part of Cushendun. The village is now listed and protected. The English poet John Masefield courted and married a young girl of Huguenot descent whose family owned CUSHENDUN'S CAVE HOUSE, which can be entered through a cave 200 feet long.

MURLOUGH BAY ★. The view over sloping green meadows down to the waters of Murlough Bay is idyllic, and the little white cottage that nestles beside the water must be the dream

THE FLAVORS OF BALLYCASTLE
Dulse (an edible seaweed, to be chewed once it has been dried) and "yellow man" (a hard toffee) are two of the gastronomic treats to be sampled during the *Ould Lammas Fair* in Ballycastle.

of everyone who sees it. Halfway down to the bay, amid the grass and buttercups, is a memorial to Sir Roger Casement, a man decorated for his humanitarian work, but eventually stripped of all honors and hanged for treason.

FAIR HEAD. The spectacular promontory, known for the good trout fishing offered by its loughs, is at the extreme northeast of Ireland, ending in 600-foot-high cliffs looking out to the Scottish islands. There are traces of prehistoric dwellings (in particular a *crannóg* ● *90*), around Fair Head. The cliffs can be reached either by a narrow road winding between fuchsia hedges, or else by Grey Man's Path, which leads walkers over broken rocky surfaces that seem to have been shattered by a giant's footsteps.

BONAMARGY. The ruins of a friary, founded in the year 1500 and once thatched, lie to the east of Ballycastle. In a vault in the church are buried Sorley Boy MacDonnell and his descendants, the earls of Antrim.

BALLYCASTLE. The two valleys of Glenshesk and Glentaisie meet at Ballycastle, an agreeable port with boats to Rathlin Island. Marconi's assistants received the first radio messages here from the lighthouse on Rathlin Island, later to be used to inform insurance companies of the safe passage of ships. In June every year Ballycastle hosts the *Fleadh Amhráin Agus Rince*, three days of traditional music and dancing, and at the end of August the *Ould Lammas Fair* takes place, the oldest fair in Ireland.

RATHLIN ISLAND. One hundred people live on the L-shaped island. Puffins and guillemots crowd onto the ledges of its high cliff, near the lighthouse at the western end, to nest and breed. The reedy loughs offer plenty of brown trout, and wild flowers sparkle in the pastures. There is a guest house, a restaurant, a pub and a social center ready to welcome and entertain visitors, whether their arrival is intended or forced upon them by stormy seas. Robert Bruce (1274–1329), crowned King of Scotland in 1306, exiled himself to Rathlin Island after his defeat at the hands of the English at Methven. It was here that a determined spider, trying again and again to make her web on the slippery wet walls of his cave inspired him to find courage to take up arms again.

CHILDREN OF LIR
A legend recounts how the four children of Lir, the sea god, were changed into swans by their stepmother. In one

version they were forced to swim in the rough waters of the sea of Moyle, between the Irish coast and Rathlin Island.

SIR ROGER CASEMENT
Casement grew up in the region, and was knighted for his humanitarian work in the Belgian Congo and Putumayo, Peru. He was arrested on the Kerry coast during World War One, after landing in a German submarine. He had hoped to bring the Kaiser's support to Sinn Féin and the Nationalist cause. His diaries, which also describe homosexual practices, were long suppressed, and their authenticity is still in question.

It comes as no surprise to learn that the Giant's Causeway has been included in a list of World Heritage Sites since 1987: it is one of the wonders of the natural world. According to legend, it was made by a giant; it is now known that sixty million years ago underground volcanic explosions sent up molten basalt that solidified into these polygonal columns of rock.

THE GIANT'S CAUSEWAY, CITADEL OF LEGEND ✪
The fantasy of this Cyclopean setting seems to be dictated by a mysterious but astute architect. The 40,000 columns seem to conjure up the beginnings of time. Approach it on foot from the Giant's Causeway Center, along the majestic amphitheaters and rock formations with evocative names, before climbing up the "Berger steps" to the top of the cliff and thus returning to the point of departure.

STORIES OF GIANT PROPORTIONS
One well-known legend has it that Finn MacCoul built the causeway to bring over his love, a giantess, from the Hebrides. In another version the giant was involved in a long-distance quarrel with a Scottish giant by the name of Fingal. Unable to settle their differences, the two were preparing for battle, but had not yet met. They began by emitting hostile roars at one another over the Irish Sea. Finn constructed the causeway, certain that his enemy had begun his on the other side (there are, in fact, similar rock formations on the Hebridean islands of Iona, Staffa and Mull). He ventured forward but when he heard the heavy tread of Fingal's approach, he retreated in fright to Antrim. His wife, Oonagh, helped him to construct a huge cot in which he disguised himself as a baby. Fingal arrived and saw the size of what he thought was Finn MacCoul's child and, imagining how big the father must be, he quickly left and made his way back home across the causeway. Finn grasped a sod of earth, leaving a crater that formed Lough Neagh ▲ 324, and threw it after his retreating opponent. The clod missed Fingal, fell into the sea, and remained there as the Isle of Man.

A GEOLOGICAL PHENOMENON
There are about forty thousand columns of basalt fitting together so perfectly that only the thinnest cracks remain visible between them. They form cliffs and irregular surfaces, and the molten basalt continues beneath the sea. It was on these reefs that the Spanish galleon *Girona* sank in 1588 ▲ *315*.

TOURISM
Naturally enough the causeway has always held a fascination for local people, but it was not until the 18th century that large numbers of travelers as well as scientists began to visit, among them Sir Walter Scott and Thackeray. In 1883 the new railway from Belfast increased tourism further still.

NAMES
The causeway's different geological formations have come to be known by special names, usually linked with legend: "Giant's Organ", "Giant's Well", "Giant's Cannon", "Chimney Point", "Wishing Chair", "Giant's Gateway", "Lord Antrim's Parlour" and "Lady's Fan".

Although he didn't like being hounded as a tourist when he visited the causeway, Thackeray was still impressed: "When the world was moulded and fashioned out of formless chaos, this must have been the *bit over* – a remnant of chaos." (*The Irish Sketchbook*, 1843)

BETWEEN SEA AND SKY
West of Dunineny Castle, the coast road passes a path leading to the Carrick-a-Rede rope bridge, which crosses a gap of 65 feet over an 80-foot chasm between the cliff and a basalt pillar. It is in place between April and September and is used by salmon fishermen for their nets.

Sir John Perrot, reputed to be the son of Henry VIII.

DUNINENY CASTLE. Remains of the castle where Sorley Boy MacDonnell lived until his death in 1590 are scattered over the cliffs west of Ballycastle. His brother Colla's stronghold, the castle of Kinbane ("white head"), set high above the sea, is a more picturesque and impressive ruin.

BALLINTOY. The road to Ballintoy, a bright and breezy little port, passes a most eccentric house built by an artist determined to have unrivaled views. At PORTBRADDAN is the tiny church of St Gobhan (not alone in its claim to be the smallest in Ireland). It sits huddled at the cliff base, west of the crescent of sand that borders White Park Bay.

DUNSEVERICK CASTLE. Ireland's oldest love story is about Deirdre who ran away with Naoise, the bodyguard of King Conor, her betrothed. She was tricked into returning to Dunseverick; her lover was betrayed and assassinated, and she killed herself. The present-day ruins, which can also be reached by footpath from the Giant's Causeway, date only from the 16th century.

BUSHMILLS ● *79.* West of the causeway is the small village of Bushmills. Through it runs the River Bush, known for its good fishing. The village itself has established a reputation for its marvelous peat-flavored whiskey, and the air is sweet with its fumes.

The first license to distill whiskey was accorded in 1608 to Sir Thomas Phillips, but the earliest records of distilling go back to 1276.

DUNLUCE CASTLE ★. The romantic ruins of Dunluce Castle cling to the top of a rocky promontory, above cliffs that drop 100 feet to the water below. The castle is cut off from land by a vast cave that runs beneath the promontory, making access only possible by bridge. The cave can be visited by boat. It may have been the MacQuillan family who first took advantage of the natural defensive position and fortified it. In the 16th century it fell into the hands of the MacDonnells, a clan of Scottish origin who had obtained large amounts of land in the region. In 1584, during Sorley Boy MacDonnell's occupation, the castle was taken by Sir John Perrot after a lengthy siege, but the crafty Sorley Boy got one of his men to infiltrate the castle staff and used baskets to get his soldiers onto the cliffs where they were able to take control of the fortress once again. The earls of Antrim, descendants of MacDonnell who had subsequently made peace with the English, abandoned the castle in 1690 after the Battle of the Boyne, because they had donated their fortune to the cause of James II. The security of its position encouraged the building of an elaborate and relatively luxurious castle. It once had four ROUND TOWERS joined by an outer wall, two of which have survived. The one that looks out over the sea (Maeve's Tower) is said to have sheltered a fairy. The style of the towers and gables of the fortified gateway to the southeast leave no doubt as to the Scottish origins of the MacDonnells. The fortifications facing toward land made it possible to scrutinize visitors before permitting them to enter over what was then a drawbridge. A Renaissance-style LOGGIA is an unusual feature, and the only one in Ireland of this type of structure. At the right-hand corner is a Great Hall with three mullioned windows in the west wall that appear to date from the 17th century.

PORTBALLINTRAE. At this seaside resort, and also in its more crowded and noisier neighbor Portrush, one of the most exciting expeditions available is a deep-sea fishing trip in a hired boat, or else a tour of the caves around the Giant's Causeway, Portcoon and Runkerry.

PORTSTEWART. The peaceful resort lying on the eastern bank of the Bann estuary is an alternative to the brashness of Portrush.

DOWNHILL. Buildings along the cliff were erected by Frederick Augustus Hervey, whose estate was here. This Anglican Bishop of Derry ▲ 319, who became Earl of Bristol, was immensely wealthy. On the edge of the cliff is MUSSENDEN TEMPLE, built by Hervey in 1785 in honor of his cousin Mrs Mussenden: it became her memorial. The eccentric bishop allowed the local Catholic priest to say mass in it weekly. It is possible to walk along the sand dunes all the way to MAGILLIGAN POINT where there is a Martello tower ● 101.

The three *Bushmills* whiskey labels.

DISASTER
On the seaward side of the promontory on which Dunluce Castle stands is a court surrounded on three sides by buildings once occupied by servants. Apparently, in 1639, the northern end of the promontory crumbled into the sea, taking the kitchens and seven servants with it.

DANGEROUS ROCKS
Having rounded Ramore Head, the captain of the Spanish galleon *Girona*, escaping after the humiliating defeat of the Armada, mistook the chimneys of the Giant's Causeway ▲ 313 for those of Dunluce Castle, where he hoped to find refuge. The ship sank off Port na Spanniagh late in the summer of 1588. The Belgian archeologist Robert Sténuit held underwater searches for the wreck and succeeded in bringing up its treasure and other remains, now on display in the Ulster Museum, Belfast ▲ 305.

315

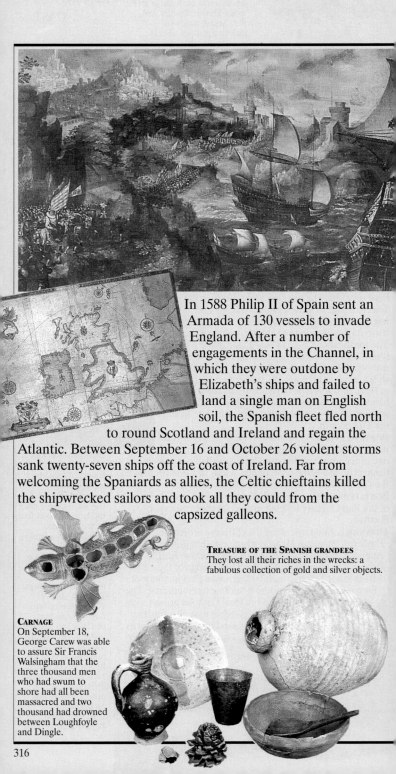

●THE INVINCIBLE ARMADA

In 1588 Philip II of Spain sent an Armada of 130 vessels to invade England. After a number of engagements in the Channel, in which they were outdone by Elizabeth's ships and failed to land a single man on English soil, the Spanish fleet fled north to round Scotland and Ireland and regain the Atlantic. Between September 16 and October 26 violent storms sank twenty-seven ships off the coast of Ireland. Far from welcoming the Spaniards as allies, the Celtic chieftains killed the shipwrecked sailors and took all they could from the capsized galleons.

TREASURE OF THE SPANISH GRANDEES
They lost all their riches in the wrecks: a fabulous collection of gold and silver objects.

CARNAGE
On September 18, George Carew was able to assure Sir Francis Walsingham that the three thousand men who had swum to shore had all been massacred and two thousand had drowned between Loughfoyle and Dingle.

The galleons were powered by sail and oars, and had a formidable battery of arms.

SPAIN HUMILIATED
What Philip II of Spain (below) had envisaged as a second Lepanto ended in utter disaster. On learning of the sinking of his ships he is said to have remarked that he had sent them to do battle with the English, not the elements.

BITTER RIVALRY
The emnity between the two countries involved both religion and politics. The Catholic Philip II of Spain and the Protestant Elizabeth I of England (above) were struggling for control of the Atlantic, which was of strategic importance to both countries. Spain wanted to protect the routes to its colonies, while England wanted to remove all obstacles to its flourishing maritime trade.

"RULE BRITANNIA"
The defeat of the Armada resulted in an enormous expansion in the English economy, to Ireland's cost.

◆ E D2-D3-D4

THE MAP OF DERRY
In the old center of
Derry the streets are
laid out on a grid, a
common feature of
twenty-three other
towns in the province

which goes back to
the "plantations".
Roads radiate from
a central square
called the Diamond,
crossing each other
at right-angles and
leading to four gates
in the city walls.
Philadelphia was also
laid out on this plan,
which was originally
inspired by the
French town of
Vitry-le-François.

THE SIEGE OF DERRY
In 1689, behind the
unbreached walls
of the town, seven
thousand people
died of hunger in
the longest siege in
Irish history. The
Protestant inhabitants
managed to resist
the Jacobite army
until a boat carrying
provisions, the
Mountjoy, managed
to break through
the blockade on the
River Foyle, thereby
saving the town. The
memory of the siege
is perpetuated in the
Loyalist political
slogan "No surrender",
which was used then
for the first time.

D erry lies on the gentle slopes that
descend to the banks of the River
Foyle. It still has well-preserved 17th-
century town walls, but is deeply marked
by a turbulent past. The city was founded
in the 6th century, and is today the second
largest in Northern Ireland.

HISTORY

CELTIC AND CHRISTIAN ROOTS. In legend,
the tribe of the Tuatha Dé Dannan, so fair that they
could not bear the sight of their own reflection, took
refuge in the bowels of the earth. The entrance
was at the mouth of the River Foyle, where
Derry stands today. What is known for certain is
that Saint Columba ▲ *295* came in around 546 and
founded a monastery at the heart of the *diore*, the
oak wood that covered the hillside. The wood gave the town
its name, and Columba is its patron saint. The monastery
flourished for two hundred years, until the arrival of the
Vikings.
THE "PLANTATIONS" ● *51.* James I came to the throne in 1603
and gave new impetus to the colonization of Ulster with the
"plantations". Not averse to using either flattery or force, he
persuaded members of the London craft guilds (such as
drapers and vintners) to set up business in Derry along with
their workers. This is why in 1613 it was rebaptized
Londonderry.
THE SIEGE. After holding out against Royalist troops for
twenty weeks in 1649, the city was relieved. In 1688 Derry, a
garrison town, was threatened with a regiment of Catholic

troops. The town
did not dare declare
open opposition to
King James II, but
in the December
a handful of
apprentice boys
closed the city
gates. In March of
the following year
James II's troops besieged Derry and did not retreat until
July, after 105 days of siege.
THE "TROUBLES" ● *64.* In 1968 Derry was witnessing a
growing civil rights movement, demanding equal treatment,
both political and social, for the Catholics in a city where the
Protestants were dominant. The first demonstration march
was felt by the authorities to be provocation, so they refused
permission for it to take place within the city walls. As a result
the outlying district of the BOGSIDE, Catholic and working-
class, was the setting for what deteriorated into a riot. The
Bogside became a "no-go area" and was barricaded from
1969 to 1972 as a reaction to assaults on police and Loyalists.
But January 30, 1972, Bloody Sunday, is the day most deeply
engraved on the memory of the Catholic community of Derry
(center, top). Murals at the bottom of Westland Street honor
the memory of the thirteen people who died, killed by British
paratroopers. On a housefront in the Bogside the words

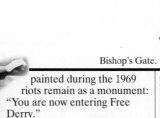

Bishop's Gate.

painted during the 1969 riots remain as a monument: "You are now entering Free Derry."

VISITING THE TOWN

ST COLUMBA'S LONG TOWER CHURCH. (Outside the walls.) This was the first Catholic church to be built after the Reformation and the "plantations", and has superb neo-Renaissance decoration. It was built on the site of the great Teampull Mor ("big church") which dated from 1164 and was mostly destroyed in the 17th century. Only its tall tower stood for longer, from which this church takes its name.

THE WALLS ● 100. Derry was the last fortified town to be built in Ireland and it has the best-preserved old walls of any town in Europe. A walk around them provides lovely views of the city, the River Foyle estuary, and the surrounding countryside. The way up is at SHIPQUAY GATE, a dour three-arched gateway, and from there the wall can be walked as far as FERRYQUAY GATE, which is decorated with the carved busts of heroes of the siege. On the other side of Artillery Street and St Columba 's Cathedral is BISHOP'S GATE. This was rebuilt as a triumphal arch in honor of William of Orange in 1789.

BISHOP'S STREET. On this street stand the COURT HOUSE (1817) and the MASONIC HALL. The latter was once the Bishop's Palace, rebuilt by Bishop Frederick Augustus Hervey, fourth earl of Bristol, and a man so rich and enamored of travel that across the whole of Europe businessmen renamed their hotels *Bristol* in the hope of increasing their clientele ▲ 315.

ORANGE PARADES
The Battle of the Boyne ▲ 194 intensified religious antagonism in Ireland, and all the weight of collective memory can be felt during the annual Orange marches held on July 12, "The Twelfth" ● 70, commemorating the Battle of the Boyne, and August 12, the Apprentice Boys' March. Over recent years the two events have been the

occasion of some violent and dreadful demonstrations, and there is no doubt that tensions between the Catholic and Loyalist communities are always heightened at these times. Murals in the mainly Protestant Waterside district show the victory of King Billy (William of Orange).

The gentle curves of the Sperrin Mountains (formed of schist and gneiss) that lie southwest of Derry. The highest peak is Mount Sawel (2,240 feet).

The tower of the Protestant cathedral of St Columba has a spire that was added in the 19th century.

"Singing pub" in Strabane.

"DANNY BOY"
The notes of the "Londonderry Air" were taken down by Miss Jane Ross when she heard it played by a traveling violinist at Limavady, 16 miles east of Derry. It is not known why Irish emigrants to the United States took up this song in particular, which was a special favorite at funerals.

ST COLUMBA'S CATHEDRAL. Behind the Court House stands the first specifically Protestant cathedral to have been erected in Ireland after the Reformation (1633). The pure, well-balanced style of which it is an excellent example came to be known as "Planter's Gothic". It has remarkable stained-glass windows and the locks and keys of the original town gates are kept here, as well as souvenirs of the siege.

SHIPQUAY STREET. On the far side of the Diamond, the central square, Shipquay Street climbs steeply uphill. Off it are some of the loveliest streets within the walls, and in one is the DERRY CRAFT VILLAGE. There are Georgian housefronts to admire and, near to the top of the hill, the BELFAST TELEGRAPH BUILDING, which was once the Wesleyan Chapel.

THE TOWER MUSEUM. The little museum has audiovisual displays explaining the history of Derry. A new center, "The Fifth Province", opened in 1995, explores the role of the Celtic peoples in the history of civilization.

THE GUILDHALL. The neo-Gothic building (1912) stands alongside the river and was once the town hall. The stained-glass windows telling the history of Derry are worth studying.

AROUND DERRY

AMELIA EARHEART COTTAGE. Three miles from the town is a little cottage with a museum dedicated to the woman known as Lady Lindbergh, the first woman to make a solo flight across the Atlantic (1932). (Take the A6.)

DUNGIVEN PRIORY ★. The 12th-century Augustinian priory has an intricately carved tomb against the south wall of the church. On it can be seen an armed man (probably one of the O'Cahan chiefs, Cooey-na-Gall, who died in 1385) along with six Scottish mercenaries in kilts. (Take the B74.)

BANAGHER ★. There is a remarkable ancient carving on a small stone burial vault in the graveyard, depicting an ecclesiastic holding a cross and raising his other hand in blessing.

DERRY TO ARMAGH

STRABANE. The town has long been a center of printing and publishing and was extremely active in the 18th century. It was here that John Dunlap learnt his trade (Gray's Printing Press); he went on to be the first man to print the American Declaration of Independence. Strabane is also the

birthplace
of the writer and
journalist Flann O'Brien ▲ *129*.

ULSTER HISTORY PARK (Culion). Like Craggaunowen ▲ *244* and Ferrycarrig ▲ *180*, the park offers a number of life-size reconstructions of different structural types to have been erected in Ireland over the last six thousand years or more. They include a Stone Age camp, late Stone Age megalithic tombs, a *rath* ● *91*, a *crannóg* ● *90*, a Christian monastery from the late Middle Ages ● *92*, Norman defenses and Planter houses.

ULSTER AMERICAN FOLK PARK. Over the last two centuries the port of Derry has witnessed the departure of many thousands of emigrants. The second major exodus, when Catholics were forced to leave during the Great Famine, is probably the most famous ● *58*. But it should not be forgotten that in the 18th century there were many Presbyterians whom King James had encouraged to leave Scotland for the north of Ireland and who then emigrated once more: 250,000 of them crossed the Atlantic. The Ulster American Folk Park tells the story of all these emigrants, beginning with the cottage of Thomas Mellon, who left for America in the 1820's (it is one of his descendants, Andrew Mellon, who created the park). It has many reconstructed sites: typical Irish country dwellings of the 19th century and the kind of homes they would have lived in once they had arrived in America. One thought-provoking creation is an Irish quayside rebuilt just as it was, from which visitors can board a boat and disembark from the other side onto an American quay of the same period. (Take the A505 at Omagh.)

BEAGHMORE. On moorland at the edge of the Sperrin Mountains, in County Tyrone, are some enigmatic circles of standing stones. From the way they are laid out, it seems possible that they were for some kind of fertility rite. (Return to the A5.)

IRISH AT THE WHITE HOUSE
Once their feet were on American soil, the Irish emigrants quickly adapted to their new life. Some of them, such as Ulysses S. Grant, hero of the American Civil War (above), went on to reach the highest echelons of power: the north of Ireland provided the United States with a dozen presidents. Other emigrants such as Robert Ross chose more original ways to achieve their ambitions: he rode into the White House on horseback and set fire to the Capitol during the night of August 24, 1814.

NEAR THIS SPOT
ON THE NORTH SIDE OF THE GREAT CHURCH
WAS LAID THE BODY OF
BRIAN BOROIMHE
SLAIN AT CLONTARF. A.D. MXIV.

THE STORY OF MACHA
Cruinnuig, the owner of much land in Ulster, forced his wife Macha, who could run as fast as the wind, to race against the horse of Conor, King of Ulster, during the annual gathering of Ulates. Macha was about to give birth and asked the king for a postponement, but he refused. She won the race and then gave birth to twins (*emain* in Gaelic). Before dying she cursed all the men of Ulster to

NAVAN FORT. This was the ancient capital of Ulster, seat of its kings. "Emain Macha" ("Macha's twins") was, according to legend, founded by Macha as her palace and refuge. It was here that the legendary King Conor MacNessa presided over the court of the Knights of the Red Branch, guarded by the young warrior Cú Chulainn. It is here, as well, that Deirdre, who killed herself at Dunseverick, near the Giant's Causeway, first saw her lover Naoise ▲ *314*. This place also provided the framework for the tales of the great deeds of the warriors told in the *Tain*. What can be seen today is a mound on top of a hill, surrounded by an earth rampart and a ditch. Such a configuration suggests that the site is of ritual rather than defensive importance. The mound that tops the hill has been excavated, and successive occupations going back to 700 BC have been traced. The remains of five concentric circles of large wooden posts were found set around a central mast. In about 100 BC this odd structure seems to have been roofed over. It was subsequently filled with stones and the posts burned, probably in a huge ritual fire. What remained became covered with earth and grass, and forms the mound visible today. In the Interpretative Centre nearby, the eventful past of Navan Fort is brought alive with imaginative modern techniques. Other monuments and discoveries in the surrounding area indicate that Navan Fort was a place of religious significance. This might explain its diminishing importance once Saint Patrick brought his new religion to Armagh.

suffer the pains of childbirth, exempting only children, youths and Cú Chulainn.

ARMAGH

The name Armagh comes from the Irish "Ard Macha" ("hill of Macha"). It is the ecclesiastical capital of all Ireland. Like Dublin, it has handsome Georgian buildings. The architect Francis Johnston (1760–1829), a native of the city, left his mark on both places. Armagh is dominated by the two cathedrals, Catholic and Protestant, facing each other from adjacent hills.

THE MALL. The oval tree-lined green at the center of Armagh was once used as a racecourse. Prisoners also used to walk across it, from the Court House at one end to the prison at the

> "There is a through-otherness about Armagh
> Of tower and steeple, Up on the hill are the arguing
> graves of the kings And below are the people."
>
> W.R. Rodgers

other (now closed). These days, on summer evenings, people play cricket here. The Mall is bordered by some Georgian houses with fine façades, among them one housing the ARMAGH COUNTY MUSEUM (east side) and another, MUSEUM OF THE ROYAL IRISH FUSILIERS (north side), both full of town history. From the northern end of the square, College Hill leads to the OBSERVATORY founded in 1790 by Archbishop Robinson, who was also responsible for general improvements to the town's layout and appearance. There is also a Planetarium where interesting exhibitions are mounted.

ST PATRICK'S CATHOLIC CATHEDRAL.

The cathedral (below right), with its two symmetrical towers, was built between 1840 and 1873. Inside, it is entirely covered with mosaic decoration, giving it a Byzantine air. In the sacristy is a clock still awaiting collection by the winner of a lottery held to raise funds for completion of the building work after the Great Famine ● 58.

ST PATRICK'S PROTESTANT CATHEDRAL.

Much restoration work was done to the medieval Church of Ireland cathedral late in the 19th century. It stands near to the spot where Saint Patrick founded his church in 447. Armagh was his first episcopal see. The chapterhouse contains some interesting pre-Christian carved figures, including one that is called *St Patrick* and another representing Queen Macha, her breasts bare. High up on the cathedral walls are grotesque carved heads. An exterior wall bears a tablet recording that Brian Boru ● 49 was buried nearby. The CATHEDRAL LIBRARY (1771) in Abbey Street has some interesting rare editions, among them a copy of *Gulliver's Travels* annotated by Swift himself, but it no longer has the *Book of Armagh* ▲ 151, pawned for £5 in the 17th century.

ST PATRICK'S TRIAN. The Interpretative Centre gives an account of Armagh's history and also has a children's display recreating Jonathan Swift's land of Lilliput. Swift spent time at Gosford Castle, about 6 miles to the southeast.

ARCHBISHOP'S PALACE. The palace itself now houses the District Council Offices. In the grounds are the ruins of a Franciscan friary (1263) and the Palace Stables Heritage Centre which consists of the tackroom, carriage house and hayloft, with an audiovisual presentation.

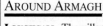

"ROAD BOWLING" The game, also called "bullet", originally came from Holland. It was once popular in many areas but is now only played in

Cork and Armagh. It takes place on a road with plenty of bends. An iron ball weighing nearly two pounds is thrown along one-and-a-half miles of turns and curves. Whoever completes the course with the fewest throws is the winner. The bowler is preceded by a tactician who stands at the corners, legs apart, and points out where the ball should be aimed in order to get round the bend. Games are held on summer Sundays. The championships take place in August.

LOUGHGALL. The village lies at the heart of Ireland's main fruit-growing region, best explored in May when the apple trees are in bloom. In Loughgall is a small museum dealing with the creation of the Orange Order here in 1795 ▲ *195*.

ARGORY AND ARDRESS HOUSES. About 3 miles northeast of Armagh, among the apple orchards (left), are two fine houses: ARGORY (1824), which is still lit by acetylene gas, and ARDRESS HOUSE, a small 17th-century country house enlarged in the 18th century and decorated with stuccowork by Michael Stapleton representing the four seasons ● *106*.

LOUGH NEAGH. The counties of Armagh, Antrim, Derry and Tyrone all border Lough Neagh, the largest lake in the British Isles. It is approximately 18 miles long and 11 miles wide. Ten rivers flow into it and one, the Bann, flows out northward. The banks cannot be walked, but to the south is PEATLANDS PARK, a peat-bog nature reserve which can be visited on a small railway and offers information on the ecological, economic and social significance of turf in Ireland ■ *36*. Lough Neagh has enormous numbers of wild fowl, especially duck in winter, and ARBOE is one of the best points from which to observe the birds. For those more interested in ancient remains, there is also a tall CELTIC HIGH CROSS at Arboe. Near Portadown is OXFORD ISLAND. This has the Lough Neagh Discovery Centre for those wishing to explore further. At Toomebridge, to the north, are the largest eel fisheries in Europe.

MOY. The ruins of the Charlemont star fort, built in 1602 by Mountjoy, Queen Elizabeth's Lord Deputy, overlook the River Blackwater. On the other side is the village of Moy where one of the biggest horse fairs in Ireland used to be held, attended by bloodstock agents from all over Europe.

BENBURB. In 1615 Sir Richard Wingfield built a castle here, and it still stands overlooking the Benburb Valley Park, which lies along the banks of the River Blackwater. The Benburb Valley Heritage Centre is housed in a 19th-century linen-weaving workshop and concentrates on the industrial and social history of the area.

The loughs, islands and wooded scenery of the Lake District of County Fermanagh make it a romantic and mysterious place. The waters are a challenge to the fisherman's skill, but promise a rewarding catch. For others they simply provide enchanting scenery. County Cavan, which touches the southern end of Upper Lough Erne, is also famous for its lakes and woodland.

ENNISKILLEN

The county town of Fermanagh is the town of Enniskillen, set strategically on an island in a narrowing of Lough Erne.
MAIN STREET. The principal thoroughfare winds its way through the town under several different names, as though it were imitating the course of the River Erne. Along it stand large business buildings (note the pointed forged-iron pickets that stick out along the lower windows to persuade cattle and loafers to keep their distance on busy fair days), also the COURT HOUSE, the PRESBYTERIAN church and the offices of the local paper, *The Impartial Reporter.*
THE HILLS. On one hill stands the Town Hall, which has niches displaying statues to represent the town's two British regiments:

◆ E C4-C3-B3

KEY POSITION
A statue of Major General Galbraith Lowry Cole (1772–1840), erected in 1857, surveys the isle of Enniskillen.

the Inniskilling Dragoons and the Royal Inniskilling Fusiliers. On another hill stand the Catholic CHURCH OF ST MICHAEL, with a window dedicated to Saint Molaise, and the Methodist church. On Church Street is the Protestant CATHEDRAL OF ST MACCARTIN, much of it 17th century.
BUTTER MARKET. Down the hill on the north shore of the island is the old BUTTER MARKET, now occupied by craft workshops. Among the more unusual items offered are flies for trout fishing, casts of sculptures and religious artefacts, both pagan and Christian.
ENNISKILLEN CASTLE. Near to Castle Bridge is the Watergate. It was built in 1612 by Sir William Cole, to whom the town had been given after the Tyrone rebellion. He used the castle of the Maguires (local Irish chiefs renowned for their excesses) as the basis for his own building. In the keep is the MUSEUM OF THE ROYAL INNISKILLING FUSILIERS. The COUNTY MUSEUM, with which it is associated, along with the Heritage Centre, shop and café, is housed in the same complex. The casts of stone heads as well as other pieces of sculpture discovered along the banks and on the islands of this lakeland county are an inspiration to visitors to go and see the originals.

From high on his Doric column set in the middle of Fort Hill gardens, he overlooks the meandering River Erne. There are 107 steps to climb, winding up the inside of the column, before one reaches the stone general brandishing his sword.

Siege of Enniskillen in 1594.

Set on a hill to the west of the town, over West Bridge, is Ireland's oldest Protestant Public School (1608). Oscar Wilde and Samuel Beckett were pupils here (as was James White, the man who in 1787 gave King George III his first kangaroo). PORTORA CASTLE, behind the school, was the subject of an explosion in 1859 resulting from the boys' careless handling of explosives.

CASTLE COOLE. The neoclassical mansion lies southeast of the town. It was designed in the 18th century by the brilliant English architect James Wyatt for Armar Lowry-Corry, Earl of Belmore, and has furniture from the period and marvelous plasterwork.

Castle Coole is the most splendid example of a neoclassical country house in Ireland. Completed in 1798, the house is built from pure Portland stone. It was given to the National Trust in 1951, and they have recently completed an expensive course of restoration and redecoration.

EARTHLY PARADISE
In May the islands on Lough Erne are covered in bluebells and celandines. At this time, trout fishermen arrive to spend patient days on their boats casting with real mayflies, blown by the wind onto the water, to tempt their prey. This kind of fly-fishing is called "dapping".

LOWER LOUGH ERNE

DEVENISH ISLAND ★. Lower Lough Erne, north of Enniskillen, has a number of holy islands. Devenish Island, green and deserted, lies at a widening of the lough near its southern end. On it is one of the finest monastic sites in Northern Ireland. As with most monastic settlements, there is a ROUND TOWER (12th century), used as a lookout. It has interesting windows and a remarkable cornice decorated with a frieze. In the 1970's the foundation of a second round tower was discovered, probably of earlier date. Nearby are the walls of the ORATORY OF ST MOLAISE, which no doubt once held the remains of the saint who established the monastery in the 6th century. Judging from its decoration, it is 12th century, and it once had a stone roof which collapsed about two hundred years ago. Unlike some monasteries, this one flourished in the Middle Ages, despite Viking raids. Down the hill, toward the landing stage, is TEAMPULL MOR ("big church") which has a lovely window clearly dating it from the 13th century, although it was enlarged about one hundred years later. On the island's highest point sits the ABBEY CHURCH OF ST MARY. A priory was built here for Augustinians in the 15th century, with a tower and cloister to the north. A CROSS with intricate carving, possibly also 15th century, stands nearby, outlined against the sky. Lastly there is a small MUSEUM, with a display of Roman coins and a detailed history of the monastery.

TULLY CASTLE. Just after Inishmacsaint ("plain of sorrel island") the colonial fortified dwelling comes into view. It was built in 1613 and is one of a number of residences built by English and Scottish colonials drawn to the area for its rich and fertile soil. Tully and Monea (take the B81 toward Enniskillen) were links in a defensive chain that included Crom, Portora, Enniskillen, Archdale, Crevenish and Caldwell. Unfortunately most of these fortified dwellings were burned down in devastating fires. (Beyond Monea on the B81, turn left after Derrygonnelly onto the road to Lough Navar.)

CLIFFS OF MAGHO. The 1,000-foot cliffs in the Navar Forest Park offer a magnificent view over Lough Erne as far as the Atlantic, taking in both Boa Island and Castle Caldwell.

BELLEEK. The village is situated on the Erne at the point where it becomes a river once again. Since 1857 a special porcelain has been made here. It is a fine and delicate lustreware.

CASTLE CALDWELL. Visitors may be lucky enough to see terns nesting in the nature reserve. Less elusive is the stone violin carved at the gateway to the ruined castle in memory of a drunken violinist who was drowned nearby, and is accompanied, not surprisingly, with a verse warning of the incompatibility of boating and boozing.

BOA ISLAND. The road runs through Boa Island at the northern end of Lough Erne over bridges at either side. In Caldragh cemetery, hidden among untended greenery, is the extraordinary two-faced statue known as the Janus Figure (right). Next to it is a smaller statue called "Lusty Man".

WHITE ISLAND. Further north, on the east bank (boat from Castle Archdale), White Island is known for seven enigmatic and unsettling statues and a mask dating from between the 8th and 10th centuries. They were found in 1928 and are displayed on the wall of an ancient church. Most of the figures are Christian but one is a *sheela-na-gig* ▲ 244.

BELLEEK PORCELAIN
John Caldwell Bloomfield created a particular type of pottery made in Belleek that has earned an

international reputation for its fine decoration and delicate glaze. Caldwell Bloomfield decided to go into the ceramics business in 1857, when he realized that all the necessary raw materials were available locally (felspar, kaolin, flint, clay, schist and turf). A visit to the workshops can be arranged.

"I let the boat drift
... past the
boathouse at the
mouth, and out into
the lake. It was only
the slow growing
distance from the ring
of reeds round the
shore that told that
the boat moved at all
on the lake. More
slowly still, the light
was going from the
August evening."
John McGahern,
High Ground

A visit to the Marble
Arch Caves includes
a boat trip on an
underground lake.

UPPER LOUGH ERNE

Upstream from Enniskillen lies the shallower Upper Lough
Erne, a labyrinth of water and wooded islands whose
appearance varies with the changing skies. Herons stand like
statues amid the waterside irises. Great crested grebe bob on
water disturbed by passing boats and dive beneath the surface
where rudd and bream ■ *44* are lurking. The meanderings of
the upper lough also conceal unusual statues (Innishkeen and
Cleenish graveyards) as well as ancient tombstones carved
with chilling motifs: coffin, hourglass and skull (Galoon
Island). The old Ballyconnell–Ballinamore canal has been
reopened so that boats can now get from Lough Erne to the
Shannon ▲ *200*.

LISNASKEA. The 1,000-acre estate of NEW CROM CASTLE
(1838) is open to visitors. In the village is CASTLE BALFOUR, a
fortified dwelling dating from 1618, and also a CELTIC CROSS.
To south and west the Lake District continues. The serene
and enchanting countryside extends into County Cavan
(Lough Oughter, left) and further west to County Leitrim
(Lough Allen).

WESTERN COUNTY FERMANAGH

FLORENCE COURT. The three-story country house was built in
the 18th century by Lord Mount Florence, and the wings of
handsome arcades were added later. The interior is very fine,
especially the rococo stuccowork. In the park is a magnificent
yew tree, from which the species Irish Yew, also called the
Florence Court Yew, was propagated.

MARBLE ARCH. The awe-inspiring series
of caves are encrusted with magnificent
stalagmites and stalactites. Experienced
speleologists can also explore other more
difficult caves, of which there are many in
County Fermanagh.

LOUGHS MACNEAN. The upper and lower
loughs are places to catch pike and crayfish.
Further north, LOUGH MELVIN is famous
for its plentiful salmon and no less than five
varieties of trout: brown, sea, *sonaghan*,
gillaroo (Irish trout) and *Salmo trutta ferox*
■ *44*.

formation

ADDRESSES

→ IN THE UK

■ **Embassy of the Republic of Ireland**
17 Grosvenor Place
London SW1X 7HR
Tel. 0207 235 2171
Fax 0207 235 2851
e-mail: ir.embassy@
lineone.net

■ **Bord Fáilte (Irish Tourist Board)**
150 New Bond St
London W1Y 0AQ
Tel. 800-039 7000
Fax 0207 493 9065
www.ireland.travel.ie
www.irelandtourism.
net
www.irelandtravel.
co.uk

■ **Northern Ireland Tourist Board**
24 Haymarket
London SW1 4DG
Tel. 08701 555 250
Fax 0207 766 9929
e-mail:
infogb@nitb.com
www.discovernorthern
irelandtourism.com

→ IN THE US

■ **Embassy of the Republic of Ireland**
2234 Massachusetts Ave., Washington D.C. 20008
Tel. (202) 462 3939
Fax (202) 232 5993
www.irelandemb.org

■ **Irish Consulates**
– 44 Montgomery St
3830, San Francisco
CA 94104
Tel. (415) 392 4214
Fax (415) 392 0885
e-mail: IrishCGSF@
aol.com
– Ireland House
345 Park Ave.,
17th Floor
New York,
NY 10154-0037
Tel. (212) 319 2555
Fax (202) 980 9475
e-mail: congenny@
aol.com

■ **Embassy of the United Kingdom**
3100 Massachusetts Ave., Washington D.C. 20008
Tel. 202 588 65 00
Fax 202 588 65 68
www.britain-info.org

■ **British Consulates**
–11766 Wilshire
Blvd., Suite 400
Los Angeles
CA 90025

Tel. (310) 477 3322
Fax (310) 575 1450
– 345 Third Ave.
New York
NY 10022
Tel. (212) 745 020
Fax (212) 754 3062

■ **Bord Fáilte (Irish Tourist Board)**
345 Park Avenue
New York
NY 10154
Tel. 800 223 6470
Fax (212) 371 9052
e-mail: info@irish
touristboard.com
www.irelandvacations.
com

■ **Northern Ireland Tourist Board**
551 Fifth Avenue
New York, NY 10176
Tel. (212) 922 0101
Fax (212) 922 0099
e-mail: infousa@nitb.
com
www.discovernorthernі
relandtourism.com

CLIMATE

■ **Temperature**
January and February are the coldest months, with average temperatures of 30°F to 45°F. July and August are the warmest months with average temperatures of 57°F to 61°F

■ **Sunlight**
May and June tend to be the sunniest months with an average of 5 to 6½ hours of sunlight a day.

■ **Rain**
April is generally the driest month, although in the south of Ireland June tends to be the driest of all. December and January are usually the wettest months. Dublin and the surrounding area is the least rainy part of Ireland (an average of 30 inches per year), and the west of Ireland tends to be the wettest, with a yearly average rainfall of of 40 to 50 inches.

■ **Snow**
Snowfalls are rare, except in the mountainous areas.

■ **Wind**
Between June and September the winds are at their least forceful, with strong winds blowing from November to March. The wind is strongest on the south, west and north coasts.

■ **Water temperature**
Water temperatures vary from coast to coast, from 45°F in the northeast to 50°F in the southwest in winter, and from 55°F to 59°F in summer for those respective areas. Taking into consideration the latitude of Ireland, these temperatures are fairly high.

ELECTRICITY

220 volts. Three-pin plugs are used, except for electric shaver in hotels. (Bring an electrical adaptor if you are traveling from the US.)

FORMALITIES

■ **Identity card/ passport**
US citizens need a valid passport. No documentation is required for either Northern Ireland or the Republic of Ireland for UK nationals.

■ **Minors**
Authorization for underage persons traveling without their parents.

■ **Driving license**
Driving license (or international driving license if you are not a UK citizen). If you are traveling in your own vehicle, check whether you need to take out extra insurance cover for the areas (standard UK policies usually

cover travel in Northern Ireland, but not the Republic). You will also need to display a country of origin plaque on the rear of the vehicle.

■ **Form E111**
Form E111 (if you are a UK resident) entitles you to medical treatment under the NHS; this is available from post offices. Other nationals are advised to take out personal medical insurance.

MONEY

→ REPUBLIC OF IRELAND
Eire's official currency is the Euro, which, at the time of this update, had not officially been lanched. Prices are therefore approximate. Please check with your bank or travel agent before departure

→ NORTHERN IRELAND
The monetary unit is the pound sterling (£), as in the rest of the United Kingdom.
£1 = approx. $1.5

TOUR OPERATORS

Many tour operators offer flexible holiday packages in Ireland. Some include accommodation as a paying guest with an Irish family. Detailed information is available each year through the Irish Tourist Board (Bord Fáilte) or the Northern Ireland Tourist Board.

→ SPECIALIST TOUR OPERATORS
Aer Lingus holidays
Tel. 0151 231 1480
Cie Tours Int'l
Tel. 0208 667 0011
Cliff Smarts Angling
Tel. 01536 724 226

Da Study Tours
Tel. 01383 882 200
Drive Ireland
Tel. 0151 231 1480
Irish Ferries Holidays
Tel. 08705 17 17 17
Leisure Angling
Tel. 0151 734 2344

→ STUDENT TRAVEL
■ **Campus Travel**
52 Grosvenor Gdns
London SW1W 0AG
Tel. 08702 401 010

TRAVEL BY AIR
→ FROM THE UK
Flights to Dublin,
Shannon, Cork,
Knock and
Waterford are
available from many
airports throughout
the UK. British
Airways and British
Midland operates
hourly flights to
Belfast from London.
■ **Aer Lingus**
Tel. 0208 899 4747
(London)
Tel. 0845 973 7747
(other areas)
www.aerlingus.ie
www.flyaerlingus.com
■ **British Airways**
Tel. (0345) 222 111
www.britishairways.
com
■ **British Midland**
Tel. 08706 070 555
www.flybmi.com
■ **Manx Airlines**
Isle of Man
08457 256 256
www.manx-airlines.
com
■ **Ryan Air**
Tel. 08703 331 231
www.ryanair.com

→ FROM THE US
Flights are available
from New York and
Boston direct to
Shannon and
Dublin airports. Aer
Lingus is the only
airline offering
flights to the
Republic of Ireland.
Alternatively, it is
possible to fly to the
UK and then take a
connection
to Ireland.
■ **Aer Lingus**
Tel. 800 474 4247
www.aerlingus.ie
www.flyaerlingus.
com

TRAVEL BY CAR AND FERRY
→ REGULAR CAR FERRIES
Ireland is linked to
Britain by a variety
of ferry routes,
and prices vary
depending on the
time of year. Ferry
companies
frequently offer
promotional
faresaver packages
alongside their
standard tariffs.
Length of crossing
varies from about 2
hours for the fastest
crossing from
Holyhead to Dún
Laoghaire to
11 hours from
Liverpool to Belfast.
Consult the general
website for ferries
to Ireland
www.iol.ie
or contact the

following
companies:
■ **Hoverspeed**
Tel. 08702 40 80 70
Fax 01304 865 203
www.hoverspeed.co.uk
■ **Irish Ferries**
Tel. 08705 17 17 17
www.irishferries.com
www.irishferries.ie
■ **P&O Irish Sea Ferries**
Tel. 08702 424 777
■ **P&O European Ferries**
Tel. 0800 409 049
■ **Stena Line**
Tel. 08705 70 70 70
■ **Swansea-Cork Ferries**
Tel. 01792 456 116
www.swansea–cork.ie

TRAVEL BY COACH AND FERRY
Coach services are
available between
the UK and Ireland.

These are organized
by various private
operators and also
by the national Irish
bus company Bus
Éireann. Services
run from various
towns throughout
the UK, including
Birmingham, Bristol,
London, Cardiff,
Reading, Fishguard
and Newport to
Athlone, Ballina,
Cork, Donegal,
Ennis, Galway,
Killarney,
Letterkenny,
Limerick, Rosslare,
Skibbereen, Sligo,
Tralee, Waterford,
Westport and
Wexford. For details
of services and fares,
contact:
■ **Bus Eirann**
Irish Bus Booking
Office, Busáras
Store Street

Dublin 1
Tel. (01) 836 6111
or (01) 830 2222
www.buseirann.ie
■ **Euroline (UK) Ltd**
Tel. 08705 143 219
www.eurolines.com
■ **National Express**
Tel. 08705 808080
www.national
express.co.uk

TRAVEL BY TRAIN AND FERRY
Traveling by a
combination of train
and ferry is a
relatively fast,
comfortable and
economic way to
travel to Ireland. A
rail service connects
all parts of Britain to
all ports for
shipping services to
Ireland. This then
connects with the
Irish Rail service to
stations throughout

Ireland.
■ **National Rail Enquiries**
Tel. 0845 7484950
www.nationalrail.co.uk
For train times and
fare information.
■ **The Train Line**
www.thetrainline.com
For train times and
fare information.
Online booking
service.
■ **Irish Rail**
www.irishrail.co.ie

TELEPHONE
■ **To call the Republic of Ireland**
International access
code + 353 + area
code (omitting the
initial 0) + number.
■ **To call Northern Ireland**
International access
code + 44 + area
code (omitting the
initial 0) + number.

TIME DIFFERENCE
Ireland has the same
time as the United
Kingdom, and is
5 hours ahead of
New York.

TOURIST BROCHURES
The Irish Tourist
Boards are very
efficient and publish
a wide range of
brochures which
include specialist
interests such as
angling, walking,
literature, golf, etc.

WEBSITES
www.ireland.travel.ie
www.irlgov.ie
www.ukonline.gov.ie
www.heritageireland.ie
(Irish heritage).
www.angling.travel.ie
www.golf.travel.ie

WHEN TO GO?
Take advantage of
the better wather in
May and June. In
summer airlines and
ferry companies
charge much higher
prices, and you have
to reserve a long
time in advance. The
same is true of hotel
prices, which may
double in summer.

◆ LOCAL TRANSPORT FROM A TO Z

PRICES GIVEN ARE APPROXIMATE.

AIR TRAVEL

→ DOMESTIC FLIGHTS
■ **Aer Lingus**
Tel. (01) 17 05 67 05
Regular flights
between Dublin,
Shannon, Cork,
Sligo, Galway and
Farranfore (Kerry).
■ **Aer Arann**
Tel. (91) 59 30 34
Flights between
Dublin and
Carrickfinn
(Donegal), and
Galway and the
Aran Islands.

→ AIRPORTS–CITY CENTERS
■ **Dublin bus**
Shuttle service
(Airlink) between
Dublin airport and
the central bus
station, and
between the airport
and Connally and
Heuston railway
stations. Runs every
10 to 20 mins from
5.45am to 11.30pm.
Cost: around €4.50.
■ **Bus Eireann**
Offers a regular
service between
Cork airport and the
city center (€3.20),
and between
Shannon airport and
Limerick (€4.50).
■ **Taxis**
In Dublin, Cork,
Galway and
Limerick, taxis have
meters. There is a
basic pick-up charge
of around €2.50.
Elsewhere the fare is
to be agreed with
the driver before
the journey.
Cost: Dublin airport
to the city center
(around €19),
Shannon airport to
Limerick (around
€20), and Cork
airport to the city
center (around €15).

BICYCLE

→ BICYCLE TOURS
Exploring Ireland
by bicycle is very
pleasant due to the
size of the island,
but bear in mind
the relentless winds
and frequent hills.
Many organizations

offer tours.
■ **Information**
Walking Cycling
Ireland
www.kerna.ie
wci@kerna.ie

→ BICYCLE RENTAL
■ **Rates**
Around €13 per day
and €57 per week
for a mountain bike
(you will be
expected to leave a
deposit of one
week's hire plus a
surcharge should
you wish to return
the bike to a
different branch).
■ **Dublin bike tours**
The Harding Hotel
Fishamble Street
Dublin 8
Tel. 01 679 08 99

CAR
The road system
has been upgraded,
but the majority of
roads are difficult,
narrow country
roads (except in
Northern Ireland) so
traveling from one
place to another
may take longer
than anticipated.

→ MAPS
■ **Road map**
available from the
Irish Tourist Boards
■ **Michelin map of
Ireland no. 405**
(1:400,000)
■ **Ordnance Survey
and Bartholomew**
series of maps
(1:25,000) are
available in five
sections covering
the whole of Ireland
See also Map
section at the end of
this book ◆ 385

→ DRIVING CODE
Driving is on the
left-hand side with
priority to the right.

■ **Speed limits**
Built-up areas
30 mph (48 kph),
main roads 60 mph
(97 kph), and
highways 70 mph
(113 kph).

> **In case of accidents**
> Tel. 999
> and Irish Visiting
> Motorists' Bureau
> 39 Molesworth St.
> Dublin 2
> Tel. 01 676 99 44
> Fax 01 676 11 08

→ ROAD SIGNS
You will find all
sorts of signposts
side by side: older
ones are white with
the place names in
black and written in
Gaelic or Gaelic and
English and with
distances in miles or
in miles and
kilometers. More
recent signposts
(white lettering
on a green
background for
main roads and
white lettering on
a blue background
for freeways) are
written in Gaelic
and English and
the distances
in kilometers. In
Northern Ireland
road signs are
only written in
English with
distances indicated
in miles.

→ CAR RENTAL
■ **Agencies**
Major international
car-rental companies
have branches
in Ireland, with
reservation desks
in various airports
throughout the
Republic and
Northern Ireland.
Local companies
include:

COUNTY CAR RENTALS
Rochestown Avenue
Dun Laoghaire
Dublin
Tel. (01) 235 20 30
Fax (01) 285 70 16
www.countycar.com
rent@countycar.ie
IRISH CAR RENTALS
Tel. 00 800 474742 27
(free phone)
www.irishcarrentals.ie
■ **Rates**
Expect to pay
the following
prices per day
when renting a
medium-sized car
with third-party
insurance and
unlimited mileage:
HIGH SEASON
Around €370
LOW SEASON
Around €225
Warning
*Should you intend
to travel between
the Republic and
Northern Ireland
you must inform the
rental company
when making the
booking.*

COACH

→ REPUBLIC OF IRELAND
■ **Bus Éireann**
The national
company offers
regular express
services between
all cities and most
major towns.
SINGLE TICKET:
Dublin–Cork:
around €16
Dublin–Galway:
around €32
Dublin–Limerick:
around €13
Dublin–Rosslare:
around €13
INFORMATION
Central Bus Station
Store Street
Dublin 1
Tel. (01) 830 22 22
www.buseireann.ie
■ **Dublin bus**
Tourist routes
around Dublin and
the surrounding
area.
INFORMATION
Dublin Bus Office
59 O'Connell
Street
Dublin 1
Tel. (01) 873 42 22

DISTANCES BY ROAD AND AVERAGE LENGTH OF JOURNEY		
Dublin–Galway	135 miles	4 hrs
Dublin–Belfast	102 miles	3 hrs
Dublin–Donegal	137 miles	4 hrs
Rosslare–Sligo	201 miles	5¾ hrs
Dublin–Killarney	191 miles	5½ hrs
Dublin–Cork	159 miles	4½ hrs
Cork–Galway	129 miles	3¾ hrs
Cork–Athlone	114 miles	3½ hrs

→ NORTHERN IRELAND
There are many reliable buses linking cities in Northern Ireland.
■ **Ulsterbus**
Great Victoria St. Belfast
Tel. (028) 90333000

COMBINED COACH AND TRAIN TICKETS
■ **Irish Explorer Ticket**
Offered by Irish Rail and Bus Éireann (not valid on Dublin city bus services). This ticket can be purchased from any station in Ireland.
■ 5 days' travel by train in a 15-day period (consecutive days).
Adults: €85
Children (for the under 16's): €42
■ 8 days' travel by coach and train in a 15-day period (consecutive days).
Adults: €127
Children (for the under 16's): €63.50
■ **Irish Rambler Ticket**
3 days' travel by coach in an 8-day period (consecutive days).
Adults: €35.50
Children: €18
■ **Irish Rover Ticket**
5 days' travel by train in a 15-day period (consecutive days).
Adults: €83
Children: €52
■ **Emerald Card**
15 days' travel by coach and train in a 30-day period (consecutive days).
Adults: €254
Children: €127
■ **Travelsave Stamps**
A student travel pass (you must show your International Student Identity Card) that offers reductions on long-distance journeys by coach and train. Available from all USIT agencies in Ireland.

FERRIES
Very convenient as they make journeys considerably shorter by crossing river estuaries.

→ MAIN FERRIES
■ The crossing of the Shannon estuary between Tarbert in the south and Killimer in the north takes about 20 mins.
■ The crossing of the Waterford estuary between Ballyhack in the east and Passage East in the west takes 10 mins.
■ The crossing from Glenbrook, near Douglas, to Carrigaloe, near Cobh, takes 5 mins.

TRAIN
→ REPUBLIC OF IRELAND
Traveling by train from Dublin to other major cities in the Republic is quick and easy.
■ **Cost of a single ticket**
Dublin–Cork: €44.50
Dublin–Galway: €20
Dublin–Limerick: €34
Dublin–Rosslare: €14
Dublin–Killarney: €47
■ **Irish Rail/ Iarnród Éireann**
Connolly Station Dublin 1
Tel. (01) 836 62 22
www.irishrail.ie

→ NORTHERN IRELAND
The railway network in Northern Ireland is limited to three lines. An unlimited travel card combining coach and train is available:
1 day: £11
3 days: £27.50
7 days: £40
■ **Northern Ireland Railways**
Central Station Belfast
Tel. (028) 90 89 94 11

◆ GETTING AROUND FROM A TO Z

PRICES GIVEN ARE APPROXIMATE.

ACCOMMODATION

There are many types of accommodation available, but reservations are essential if you are planning to visit Ireland in summer.

Warning
Depending on the establishment, prices are given per double room or per person sharing a double room.

■ **Republic of Ireland**
There are more than 150 tourist offices in the Republic, some of which are open all year round and some which operate only during the summer months. Most tourist offices have the facility to rent you self-catering accommodation or a cottage (approved by the Irish Tourist Board) for a fee of €1.30–2.50.
Any establishment booked through the tourist office is approved by them and is listed in the Tourist Office's *Accommodation Guide*. This means that they comply with certain hygiene and safety standards. All these establishments display a green cloverleaf and an "Approved" sign. Hotels and guesthouses are classified by the Irish Tourist Boards

as "Quality Hotels" and follow a certain system of classification.
■ **Northern Ireland**
The Northern Ireland Tourist Board has a similar guide entitled *Where to stay*. There are approximately fifty tourist offices in Northern Ireland, which have the same opening hours and offer the same facilities as those in the Republic.

→ **HOTELS**
Five categories from luxury ***** to basic *.
■ **Prices**
Prices are given for a double room in the high season for a medium-category hotel: around €115 (breakfast included), and €80 in the low season.

→ **GUESTHOUSES**
Generally smaller than hotels and often run by the owners. They are classified from 1-star (*) to 4-star (****).
■ **Prices**
Around €95 for a double room (breakfast included) in the high season, and €70 in the low season.
■ **Irish Guesthouse Owners Association**
Kathleen's Country House, Killarney, Co. Kerry
Tel. (64) 32810
Fax (64) 32340
■ **Premier Guesthouses of Ireland**
4 Whitefriars
Aungier Street
Dublin 2
Tel. (01) 475 18 13
Fax (01) 475 53 21
info@premier-guesthouses.com

→ **MANOR HOUSES**
Many beautiful country manors or castles (some still occupied by their owners) have been turned into hotels and guesthouses,

providing a fine welcome and comfortable rooms.
■ **Prices**
Around €135 for a double room (breakfast included) in the high season and €80 in the low season.
■ **Elegant Ireland**
PO Box 6080
Dublin 8
Tel. (01) 475 16 65
Fax (01) 475 10 12
■ **Hidden Ireland**
PO Box 31
Westport, Co. Mayo
Tel. (01) 662 71 66
Fax (01) 986 66 51
www.hidden-ireland.com
info@hidden-ireland.com
■ **The Blue Book (Irish Country Houses and Restaurants Association)**
Ardbraccan, Glebe, Navan, Co. Meath
Tel. (46) 23416
Fax (46) 23292
www.irelands-blue-book.ie

→ **PAYING GUESTS**
■ **Bed and Breakfast**
Irish hospitality at its best. Ranging from huge old houses to tiny cottages, basic comfort and a friendly welcome guaranteed.
■ **On farms**
Do not expect too much from the actual buildings, which tend to be utilitarian, modern houses set separately from the farm. Some, however, can be quite charming.
■ **Prices**
From €20 per person sharing a double room (breakfast included).
The Irish Farm Holidays/B&B
2 Michael Street
Limerick
Tel. (61) 40 07 00
Fax (61) 40 07 71
farmhols@iol.ie
Friendly Homes of Ireland
71 Waterloo Road
Dublin 4

Tel. (01) 668 64 63
Fax (01) 668 65 78

→ **SELF-CATERING HOUSES OR APARTMENTS**
Accommodation ranging from small, genuine cottages to castles.
■ **Prices**
Prices vary as much as the actual places on offer. Around €480 per week for a comfortable, 4- or 5-people house in the high season, and €280 in the low season. Reservations are essential in the high season.
■ **Irish Cottage Holiday Homes Association**
c/o Mr John Waldron
4 Whitefriars
Aungier St
Dublin 2
Tel. (01) 475 19 32
Fax (01) 475 53 21

→ **YOUTH HOSTELS**
Open most of the year. Reservations are essential in summer.
■ **Prices**
From €6.50 per night.
■ **An Oige–Irish Youth Hostel Association**
61 Mountjoy Street
Dublin 7
Tel. (01) 830 45 55
Fax (01) 830 58 08
mailbox@anoige.ie
■ **Independent Holidays Hostels**
57 Lower Gardiner Street, Dublin 1
Tel. (01) 836 47 00
Fax (01) 836 47 10
www.hostels-ireland.com
ihh@iol.ie
■ **Usit Accommodation Centres**
Tel. (01) 706 10 71
Fax (01) 706 11 29
accom@usit.ie

EMBASSIES

→ **UK**
29 Merrion Road
Dublin 4
Tel. (01) 676 72 54 or
(01) 676 72 55
Fax (01) 676 88 92

→ US
42 Elgin Road
Ballsbridge
Dublin 4
Tel. (01) 668 87 77
Fax (01) 668 99 46

EMERGENCIES

Both in the Republic
of Ireland and
Northern Ireland,
there is a single
number for the police,
fire brigade, and
ambulances: 999.

FOOD

→ LOCAL CUISINE
The food in Ireland
is wholesome and
served in generous
portions, and as
high-quality products
are readily available
Irish cooking can be
delicious. Beef and
lamb are particularly
tasty as the animals
are often raised on
open grassland. Fish
is easily available, as
is seafood in general
(try the Dublin
prawns and Atlantic
lobsters) and
shellfish (Galway
oysters, with their
slightly sour taste,
go extremely well
with a pint of
Guinness). Meals are
usually served with
potato (traditionally
the staple food of
Ireland) and a
selection of other
vegetables. Dairy
produce is an
important part of
the Irish diet: butter,
salted and creamy,
appears on the table
at most meals; a
variety of cheeses,
some of them fairly
strong: Milleens,
St Killian, Cashel
Blue, Ardrahan…
also highly
recommended
are desserts or
puddings such as
apple tart,
gooseberry or
rhubarb crumble,
served with custard
or cream. Another
Irish specialty worth
looking out for is
carrigeen moss
(seaweed).

→ MEALS
The usual custom in
Ireland is to eat
three substantial
meals a day, the
most copious being
breakfast and dinner.
■ Breakfast usually
consists of fruit
juice, fruit, cereal
or porridge
followed by a fried
breakfast of eggs,
bacon, tomatoes,
mushroom,
sausages, white and
black pudding, or
sometimes kippers,
and accompanied
with tea or coffee
and toast or soda
bread ● 85, with
butter and
marmalade or jam.
Certainly enough to
keep you going
until dinner time.
■ Traditionally the
main meal is served
at midday but
frequently lunch is
just a light snack.
■ Dinner is usually

eaten between 7pm
and 8.30pm, but
does not follow any
specific tradition.

→ WHERE TO EAT?
There are numerous
classic Irish
restaurants and
many hotels have
restaurants which are
open to the general
public. Expect to pay
from around € 50 for
a basic dinner for
two with house wine.
■ Tourist menu
More than 360
restaurants offer a
set menu consisting
of three courses for
€9, €11.50 or €15
depending on which
main course you
choose (the set

menu is often
restricted to
lunchtime and early
evening). For a list
of these restaurants
see *Dining in Ireland*,
available from most
tourist offices. They
are indicated with a
small chef's head
and toque.
■ Pubs
Many pubs offer pub
lunches and serve
basic food (dish of
the day, soup and
bread, salad) for very
reasonable prices
(around €6.50).
■ Coffee shops
Coffee shops
usually serve food
all day (and prices
are generally lower
than in traditional
restaurants).
■ Farmhouses
Farmhouses often
serve dinner, but only
for overnight guests
and it will need to be
ordered in advance
(from about €15.50).

→ TIPS
Service is not
generally included
(except in the
more expensive
hotels and
restaurants) and
it is customary to
leave a 10 percent tip.

→ NORTHERN IRELAND
The cost of eating
out in Northern
Ireland is much
lower than in the
Republic. A guide
to restaurants,
Where to Eat,
is available from
tourist offices.
Look for the label
A Taste of Ulster, to
guarantee good-
quality traditional
food.

LEISURE

→ CABIN CRUISERS
Variable in size
cabin cruisers can
accommodate 2 to
8 people and
are equipped as
genuine, small,
floating houses that
offer every comfort.
No license is required
and boats are rented
on a weekly basis
or at weekends,
according to
availability. Around
€900 per week in
peak season for
4 to 6 people.
Book early.
**Athlone Cruisers
companies**
◆ F F1 E B6
Jolly Mariner Marina
Athlone
Co. Westmeath
Tel. (0902) 72892
Fax (0902) 74386
Ireland Line Cruisers
◆ F E2
(based in Killaloe,
Co. Clare)
Tel. (061) 37 50 11
Fax (061) 37 53 31
Emerald Star Line
◆ E B5
The Marina, Carrick-
on-Shannon,
Co. Leitrim (based
also in Portumna
and in Belturbet)
Tel. (078) 20234
Fax (078) 21433
Shannon Castle Line
◆ F E2
Williamstown Harbour
Whitegate, Co. Clare
Tel. (061) 92 74 75
Fax (061) 92 74 26
Silver Line
◆ F F6
The Marina
Banagher, Co. Offaly
Tel. (0509) 51112
Fax (0509) 51632
Waveline Cruisers
◆ F F6 E B6
Killinure Point,
Glassan, Athlone,
Co. Westmeath
Tel. (0902) 85711
Fax (0902) 85716
www.waveline.ie

→ GOLF
■ Golf courses
The links courses
have established a
good reputation for
golf in Ireland.
They are coastal,

extremely windy, and subject to quirks of nature such as dunes and sand holes which, made worse by the wind, make the game more challenging and put golfers' nerves to the test. Links courses are playable all year round since any rainfall drains away through the sand. There is a steadily increasing number of parkland courses, particularly in the center and the east, though even these, set among the gentle rolling hills, have their own particular difficulties. Here you can detect the signature of the great international golfers (Jack Nicklaus, Nick Hawtree or Arnold Palmer).

■ **Golf lessons**
Hundreds of professional and ex-professional golfers, all belonging to the Irish Professional Golfers Association and affiliated to the various different clubs, offer coaching at all levels. Reservations are essential. Expect to pay €25 for a 30-minute lesson.

■ **A round of golf**
Booking is required although, in most cases, a telephone call a day or two in advance will suffice. A round of golf on any of the internationally acclaimed courses will need to be booked well in advance as these are extremely busy, particularly at weekends.

→ FISHING
■ **Angling**
Salmon and trout fishing requires a permit. Pike fishing is subject to strict regulations and the number of catches is limited.

■ **Permits**
The cost varies according to duration and number of districts required. A license costing €32 would cover all areas for the full season, while a single district, full-season license costs €3.80, and a temporary license valid for 21 days and all districts costs €13. These can be purchased from fishery boards, tackle stores and some hotels.
– CENTRAL FISHERIES BOARD
Balnagowan House Mobhi Boreen Glasnevin, Dublin 9 Tel. (01) 837 92 06 Fax (01) 836 00 60 www.cfb.ie
Several regional branches.

■ **Coastal fishing**
There are a number of coastal centers in Ireland offering various options. The type of fish you may catch depends on the area in which you are fishing and the depth of the sea. Pollack, cod, eel, dogfish, conger, ling and whiting are found in the deep fishing waters; bass (special regulations between May 15 and June 15), turbot, gray mullet, gurnard and ray are more common in the shallower areas. Venture on the high seas on well-equipped boats (around €50 per person, reel and outing) for ray and shark-fishing trips. A fishing license is not required.
– CASTLEPARK MARINA CENTRE

Kinsale
Tel. (021) 477 49 59
Fax (021) 477 49 58
maritime@indigo.ie

→ RAMBLING AND HIKING
A wide range of designated Irish footpaths and walks offer various levels of difficulty.
Information
Walking Cycling Ireland
www.kerna.ie
wci@kerna.ie
Western Way
◆ **D** B5-B6-**D** C3
120 miles (highest point 1,300 feet). Starting at Oughterard, Co. Galway it leads to Ballina, Co. Mayo via the Connemara mountains and Newport on trhe coast.

The Cavan Way and the Leitrim Way
◆ **E** B3-B4
Approximately 60 miles (highest point 1,230 feet). Dowra (Co. Leitrim) is at the center of a star with arms leading toward Drumshambo (Co. Leitrim), Bellcoo (Co. Fermanagh), Manorhamilton (Co. Leitrim) with the option of taking the Ulster Way.
Táin Trail and the Ulster Way
◆ **E** E5-F5-F4-F3-F2-F1-E1-D2-C3-B3-C4-D4-E4
The Tain Trail, approximately 20 miles long (highest point,1,200 feet) leads to the pretty and relatively unknown Cooley Peninsula, to the north of Dublin. The Ulster Way, 430 miles long, goes right around the north of Ireland via the Mourne Mountains, the Antrim coast, the Giant's Causeway, and the lake country of Fermanagh.
Kildare Way
◆ **G** B2
(Grand Canal Towpath, Barrow Towpath Royal Canal Towpath) 130 miles spreading from Kildare, mainly along canal tow paths, through lush pastures. (Highest point 301 feet).
Slieve Bloom Way
◆ **F** F2 **G** A2
38 miles long (highest point 1,300 feet). A complete circuit starting from Glenmonick Forest car park. In a mountainous area, in the middle of Ireland, between Birr and Mountmellick. Attractive and unspoiled, wooded and boggy in places. A path leads to the

monastic site
of Clonmacnois
▲ *203*.

Wicklow Way
◆ **G** B2-C2-B3-C3
82 miles (highest
point 1,850 feet).
south of Dublin,
through the Wicklow
Mountains, continues
from glen to glen
following old turf
paths and roads
once used to move
livestock, as far as
Aghavannagh, from
where one can see
Glendalough ▲ *178*,
and finally arrives in
the green lower
ground of Clonegal,
Co. Carlow. The
route is uneven and
varied. On a clear
day, you can even
see the Welsh
Mountains on the
other side of the
English Channel.
The most attractive
waterfall in Ireland,
the Powerscourt
Falls, is passed en
route.
Caution
The weather, which
because of the
altitude is very
changeable, can
make walking
conditions difficult
and even dangerous.
Kerry Way
◆ **F** B4-A4-A5-B5
134 miles (highest
point 1,808 feet).
Loop around Killary
via Glencar,
Glenbeigh, with a
possible detour to
Valentia Island or
to Waterview, then
Sneem, Kenmare.
The lushness of
the scenery around
the lakes contrasts
dramatically with
the austere rocky
mountains, with the
the vast Atlantic in
the background.
Dingle Way
◆ **F** B3-B4-A4
95 miles (highest
point, 1,800 feet).
Goes from Tralee
to Castlegregory
via Dingle and
Cloghan.
Rich Finistere
scenery.

Burren Way
◆ **F** D1-C1-C2
27 miles (highest
point 850 feet),
leads from
Ballyvaughan
to Liscannor via
Doolin and the
spectacular
Cliffs of Moher
▲ *242*.The delicate
flora (gentian,
cranesbills, dryas)
contrasts with
the rugged
gray reliefs of the
karstic mountains.
Stone route
markers.

Aran Islands Way
◆ **F** C1 **A** B1-C1
These three islands
▲ *270* still maintain a
traditional Celtic way
of life. See the stone
forts, remains of early
Christian tombs,
ruined churches and,
of course, the sea.

→ **RIDING**
There are 250 riding
centers approved by
the Association of
Riding Establishments
(AIRE). Any of these
will be able to
supply you with
good horses.
■ **AIRE (Association**
of Riding
Establishments)
11 Moore Park
Newbridge
Co. Kildare

Tel. (045) 43 15 84
Fax (045) 43 51 03
and through the
Irish Tourist Board.
These approved
centers are
recommended
because they are
guaranteed to be
of a certain
standard. The
animals are usually
a mixture of horses
and Connemara
ponies which,
though small, can
be ridden by adults.
■ **Prices**
A one-hour lesson
for either beginners
or more experienced
riders costs around
€20.
A two-and-a-
half hour hack costs
in the region of
€30, and depending
on the area may
include a gallop
along deserted
beaches.
■ **Brennanstown**
Riding School
Hollybrook
Kilmacanogue
Bray
Co. Wicklow
Tel. (01) 286 37 78
Fax (01) 282 95 90
■ **Clonshire**
Equestrian Centre
Adare
Co. Limerick
Tel. (061) 39 67 70
Fax (061) 39 67 26

■ **Devil's Glen**
Holiday and
Equestrian Village
Ashford
Co. Wicklow
Tel. (0404) 40637
Fax (0404) 40638
■ **Ladestown House**
Riding and Trekking
Mullingar
Co. Westmeath
Tel. (044) 48218
Fax (044) 43367

MONEY
→ **EXCHANGE**
You can change
money at banks
and airports.
■ **Autotellers**
There are many
autotellers, and
they accept all
major bankers cards.

→ **BANKS**
■ **Republic of Ireland**
Open Mon.–Wed,
Fri. 10am–4pm and
Thur. 10am–5pm.
■ **Northern Ireland**
Open Mon.–Wed, Fri.
10am–4pm and
Thur. 10am–5pm.
Banks close between
12.30pm and
1.30pm in medium-
size and small towns.

POST OFFICE
→ **REPUBLIC OF**
IRELAND
Letter: around
€0.40.
Stamps are sold
at post offices and
post office agents
located in small
country pubs.

→ **NORTHERN IRELAND**
Letters up to 20 g
or postcard: £0.25
Stamps are sold at
post offices
or at establishments
bearing the red sign
"We sell postage
stamps".

PUBLIC HOLIDAYS
→ **REPUBLIC OF**
IRELAND
■ January 1
■ March 17
(St Patrick's Day:
national day)
■ Good Friday
Not a bank holiday,
although most
banks and

businesses choose to close that day.
- Easter Monday
- May 1
- 1st Monday in June
- 1st Monday in August
- Last Monday in October
- December 25 and 26

→ **NORTHERN IRELAND**
- January 1 and 2
- March 17
- Easter Monday
- May 1
- Last Monday in May
- July 12 (Orange Day: national day)
- Last Monday in August
- December 25, 26 and 27

PUBS
A whole variety of beverages are available, but the local brews come highly recommended. These invariably include two key ingredients, both 100-percent Irish: mineral water from a nearby source and locally grown barley. Once the barley grain has sprouted, it is dried and turned into malt. Local malts are then used in the production of a range of whiskeys and beers.

→ **BEER** ● 76
Three types of draught beer are available by the pint or the "glass" (half pint). Foreign beers are more expensive (around €3.80 a pint) than Irish beers (all around €3.55 a pint in Dublin, less in the rest of the country). **Lager** (Harp leads the market); **bitter** slightly sweetened (Smithwick's, brewed in Kilkenny ▲ 187 is the most popular); **stout**, a dark, rich brew (Guinness is probably the most

famous, with its carefully drawn dark body and head of white foam).

→ **WHISKEYS** ● 78
Forty percent proof, pure malt whiskey, made from grain dried in closed barns, triple distilled and allowed to age for a minimum of three years produces a light, smooth-tasting whiskey. Served at room temperature, without ice or water, a whiskey usually

costs €3 per glass. There are various different brands and everyone has their own favorite. Many of them are sold under the Irish Distillers label: Jameson, Paddy, Powers, Tullamore, Bushmills (distilled in the village of the same name, in Ulster ▲ 315).

→ **VISITS TO BREWERIES AND DISTILLERIES**
■ **Guinness Hopstore** St. James' Gate Dublin 8 Tel. (01) 4084800 Fax (01) 4084965 www.guinessstore house.com

Open Mon.–Sat. 9.30am–6pm, Sun. 10.30am–6pm (winter Mon.–Sat. 9.30am–6pm).
■ **Jameson Heritage Distillery** Midleton Co. Cork Tel. (021) 4613594 Open daily 10am–6pm.
■ **The Old Jameson Distillery** Bow Street Smithfield Dublin 7 Tel. (01) 8072355 Fax (01) 807269 Guided tours every

GUINNESS IS GOOD FOR YOU

40–45 mins
www.irish-whiskey-trail.com
■ **Old Bushmills Distillery** Bushmills, Co. Antrim, Northern Ireland Tel. (028) 2073 1521 Open Apr.–Oct.: Mon.–Sat.

9.30am–5.30pm, Sun. noon–5.30pm; Nov.–Mar: Mon.–Fri. 5 guided tours a day.

→ **PUB OPENING TIMES**
■ **Republic of Ireland** Open Mon.–Sat. 10.30am–11.30pm (Sep.–May 10.30am–11pm), Sun. 12.30–2pm and 4–11pm.
■ **Northern Ireland** Open Mon.–Sat. 11.30am–11pm, Sun. 12.30–2pm and 7–10pm.

SHOPPING
→ **STORE OPENING TIMES**
■ **Republic of Ireland** Open Mon.–Sat. 9am–5.30pm or 6pm. In Dublin stores remain open until 9pm on Thursdays. In small towns, stores close in the afternoon on Wednesdays. Commercial centers have late-night opening on Thursdays and Fridays. Grocery stores and newsagents are open on Sunday morning.
■ **Northern Ireland** Open Mon.–Sat. 9am–5.30pm in Belfast. Elsewhere closing times may vary (usually one afternoon per week, or at lunchtime).

→ **SOUVENIRS**
■ **Tweed** Tweed is one of the traditional products of Ireland, and some of the best tweed is woven in Donegal.

SIZES			
Women's clothing			
Ireland/UK 10	12	14	16
US 8	10	12	14
Men's clothing			
Ireland/UK and US men's jacket, trouser and shirt sizes are the same.			
Women's shoes			
Ireland/UK 4	5	6	7
US 7½	8½	9½	10½
Men's shoes			
Ireland/UK 7	8	9	10
US 7½	8½	9½	10½

– MAGEE & CO.
The Diamond
Donegal Town
Tel. (073) 21 00 50
Open Mon.–Sat.
9.45am–6pm (until
9pm in summer).
The most prestigious
of the classic Irish
tweeds is that which
bears the Magee
label. Produced by
the same family for
many generations
and made using
the colors of the Irish
countryside, these
tweeds frequently
appear in the
collections of many
of Ireland's top
couturiers. The
factory is in the
center of Donegal
and is open to the
public. Tweed is sold
from around €25.40
a yard (91.44 cm).
– MCNUTTS OF
DONEGAL
Downings,
Co. Donegal
Tel. (074) 55643
Open 9am–6pm.
Closed Sat. am
and Sun.
Donegal is also
home to another,
smaller, tweed
manufacturer,
McNutts, which
produces beautiful
tweed available by
the length (from
around €15.30
a yard) or as ready-
to-wear clothes
(around €127 for
a lovely jacket).
– FOXFORD
WOOLLEN MILLS
Foxford, Co. Mayo
Tel. (094) 56104
Open Mon.–Sat.
10am–6pm,
Sun. 2–6pm.
Located in the same
building is a Visitor
Centre which relates
the history of the
Foxford Woollen
Mills that were
founded by a Sister
of Charity at the end
of the 19th century
to provide work for
poor young girls in
the area.

■ **Craft stores**
Tweed articles such
as caps, scarves and
fishermen's hats can
be found in craft
stores throughout
Ireland, along with
all kinds of Irish
crafts: crystal from
Waterford, Galway
or Tyrone; porcelain
china from Arklow
or Belleck, damask
linen, Connemara
marble, Celtic
jewelry, straw
crosses of Saint
Brigid, pottery, etc.
– BLARNEY
WOOLLEN MILLS
21–23 Nassau Street
Dublin 2
Tel. (01) 671 00 68
– BLARNEY
WOOLLEN MILLS
Blarney
Co. Cork
Tel. (021) 438 52 80
– DUBLIN WOOLLEN
COMPANY
41 Lower Ormond
Quay
Dublin 1
Tel. (01) 677 50 14
– QUILLS WOOLLEN
MARKET
The Square
Killarney
Co. Kerry
Tel. (064) 32277
Other stores in
Kenmare and
Sneem, Co. Kerry.
– CARRAIG DONN
Lodge Rd.
Westport
Co. Mayo Tel. (098)
25566
Also in Cork,
Kilkenny, Sligo, etc.
– CRAFTWORKS SHOP
Bedford St.
Belfast BT27FB
Tel. (02890) 24 44 65
■ **Kapp & Peterson
pipes**
For more than 200
years these curved
pipes, favored by
connoisseurs, have
had the reputation
of being the most
elegant and best
quality of their kind
In their Sherlock
Holmes range the
latest addition is the
"Milverton".
Prices: from €30
to €300.
– KAPP & PETERSON
117 Grafton Street
Dublin 2
Tel. (01) 6714652

■ **Nicolas Mosse
pottery**
This rustic-style
ware is handpainted
with "naive" floral
or animal patterns
using a 19th-century
sponging technique.
**Nicolas Mosse
Pottery**
Bennettsbridge
Co. Kilkenny
Tel. (056) 27105
Fax (056) 27491

TELEPHONE
**→ TO CALL THE UK/US
FROM THE REPUBLIC OF
IRELAND**
00 + 44 + number
omitting the 0 for
the UK.
00 + 1 + state code
followed by the
number for the US.

**→ TO CALL THE US
FROM NORTHERN
IRELAND**
00 + 1 + state code
followed by the
number.

TOURIST OFFICES
Do take advantage
of the efficient
services offered by
the Irish tourist
offices who provide
invaluable
information and a
vast number of
brochures.

**→ REPUBLIC OF
IRELAND**
■ **Dublin**
Suffolk Street
Dublin 2
www.visitdublin.com
information@
dublintourism.ie
■ **Southeastern
region**
(Counties Carlow,
Kilkenny, South-
Tipperary, Wexford
and Waterford)
41 The Quay
Waterford
Tel. (51) 87 58 23
Fax (51) 87 67 20
■ **Southwestern
region**
(Counties Cork
and Sud-Kerry)
Tourist House-
Grand Parade, Cork
Tel. (21) 427 32 51
Fax (21) 427 35 04
user@cktourism.ie

■ **Shannon region**
(Counties Clare,
Limerick, Nord-
Kerry, North-
Tipperary
and South-Offaly)
Arthur's Quay
Limerick
Tel. (61)31 75 22
Fax (61) 31 79 39
■ **Western region
and Connemera**
(Counties Galway,
Mayo and
Roscommon)
Aras Fáilte
Forster Street
Galway
Tel. (91) 53 77 33
Fax (91) 53 77 00
info@irelandwest.ie
■ **Northwestern
region**
(Counties Cavan,
Donegal, Leitrim,
Monaghan and
Sligo)
Aras Reddan
Temple Street, Sligo
Tel. (71) 61201
Fax (71) 60360
■ **Lake District
(Central)**
(Counties Kildare,
Laois, Longford,
Louth, Meath
Nord-Offaly
Westmeath
and Wicklow)
Dublin Road
Mullingar
Tel. (44) 48650
Fax (71) 40413

→ NORTHERN IRELAND
■ **Belfast**
– NORTHERN IRELAND
TOURIST BOARD
59 North Street
Belfast BT1INB
Tel. (028) 90231221
Fax (028) 90240960
– BELFAST
WELCOME CENTER
47 Donegal Square
Belfast BT17AD
Tel. 02890 246609
■ **Derry
Tourist Board**
44 Foyle St.
Derry
Tel. (028) 71 26 72 84

WEIGHTS AND
MEASURES
1 mile = 1.6 km
1 pound = 0.450 kg
1 gallon = 4.55 liters
1 pint = 0.57 liters
1 acre = 0.4 ha
1 yard = 0.91 m

◆ FAIRS, FESTIVALS AND EVENTS

REPUBLIC OF IRELAND

Time	Place	Event
FEB.	ENNIS ◆ F D2	IRISH DANCING NATIONAL CHAMPIONSHIP
	DUBLIN ◆ G C1	SIX-NATION TOURNAMENT (Rugby)
MAR.	ARKLOW ◆ G C3	MUSIC FESTIVAL
	CORK ◆ F D5	FLAME FESTIVAL OF CELTIC MUSIC
	LIMERICK ◆ F D3	INTERNATIONAL BRASS BAND FESTIVAL
MAR. 17	IRELAND	ST. PATRICK'S DAY (Irish national holiday)
APR.	KILLARNEY ◆ F B4	GOLF COMPETITION FOR YOUNG PEOPLE
	FAIRYHOUSE ◆ G B1	IRISH GRAND NATIONAL (Horseracing)
	IRELAND	PAN CELTIC FESTIVAL (Celtic musicians, singers and dancers from all over the world)
APR.–MAY	KINSALE ◆ F D6	HEINEKEN KINSALE SEVEN BY SEA (7-player rugby)
MAY	BANTRY ◆ F B5	MURPHY'S INTERNATIONAL MUSSEL FAIR
	GALWAY ◆ F D1	MUSIC FESTIVAL (12th- to 17th-century dances and costumes)
	KILLARNEY ◆ F B4	BRIDGE TOURNAMENT
	NEW ROSS ◆ G A4	CHOIR COMPETITION
JUNE	LISTOWEL ◆ F C3	WRITERS' WEEK
	CARRICK ◆ E A2	THE CARR MEMORIAL WEEKEND (Traditional music weekend)
	EDENBURRY ◆ G B1	EDENDERRY ESAB 3 DAYS CANAL ANGLING FESTIVAL
	KINSALE ◆ F D6	KINSALE POINT-TO-POINT FESTIVAL (Horseracing)
	WESTPORT ◆ D B4	HORSE FAIR
JUNE 16	DUBLIN ◆ G C1	BLOOMSDAY, CELEBRATION OF JAMES JOYCE'S WORK, *ULYSSES*, IN THE STREETS OF DUBLIN
JUNE–JUL.	(PLACE MAY VARY)	IRISH OPEN (golf)
	KILLARNEY ◆ F B4	IRISH-AMERICAN MUSIC FESTIVAL
JUL.	MILTOWN MALBAY ◆ F C2	WILLIE CLANCY SUMMER SCHOOL (Gathering of traditional Irish musicians and dancers from all over the world)
	GALWAY ◆ F D1	GALWAY ARTS FESTIVAL
JUL.–AUG.	MITCHELSTOWN ◆ F E4	MUSIC FESTIVAL
	WICKLOW ◆ G C3	REGATTA FESTIVAL
	SLIGO ◆ G C3	WB YEATS INTERNATIONAL SUMMER SCHOOL
AUG.	DUBLIN ◆ G C1	DUBLIN HORSE SHOW (Horseracing)
	KILLORGLIN ◆ F B4	PUCK FAIR
	KILKENNY ◆ G A3	KILKENNY ARTS FESTIVAL
	ENNISCORTHY ◆ G B4	FLEADH CHEOIL NA ÉIREANN (Yearly gathering to celebrate Irish music)
	CLIFDEN ◆ D A5	CONNEMARA PONEYS FAIR
	TRALEE ◆ F B3-B4	ROSE OF TRALEE INTERNATIONAL FESTIVAL
SEP.	CAPE CLEAR ISLAND ◆ D B6	STORY-TELLERS FESTIVAL
	CLARENBRIDGE ◆ D C6	OYSTER FESTIVAL
SEP.–OCT.	LISDOONVARNA ◆ F C1	MATCHMAKING FESTIVAL (The largest gathering of single people in Europe)
	WATERFORD ◆ G A5	LIGHT OPERA FESTIVAL
	DUBLIN ◆ G C1	ANTIQUE FAIR IN BALLSBRIDGE, DUBLIN 4
	BALLINASLOE ◆ E A6	HORSE FAIR
OCT.	DUBLIN ◆ G C1	THEATER FESTIVAL
		DUBLIN CITY MARATHON
	CORK ◆ F D5	FILM FESTIVAL
		GUINNESS JAZZ FESTIVAL
	WEXFORD ◆ G B5	OPERA FESTIVAL
NOV.	KILL ◆ G B2	THOROUGHBREDS SALE
	DUN LAOGHAIRE ◆ G C2	TOY COLLECTORS' FAIR

NORTHERN IRELAND

MAR. 17	NORTHERN IRELAND	PILGRIMAGES TO ARMAGH, BALLYMENA, DOWNPATRICK AND NEWRY ON ST PATRICK'S DAY
MAR.	DERRY ◆ E D2	NORTHESTERN STORY TELLERS FESTIVAL
MAY	BELFAST ◆ E F3	BELFAST CIVIC FESTIVAL AND LORDMAYOR'S SHOW (Street theater, shows and parades)
	DERRY ◆ E D2	INTERNATIONAL JAZZ AND BLUES FESTIVAL
JUL.		ORANGEMAN'S DAY (Commemoration of the Battle of the Boyne)
AUG.	BALLYCASTLE ◆ E F1	OUL' LAMMAS FAIR (The oldest fair in Ireland, seafood festival)
	SPERRIN MOUNTAINS ◆ E D2	SPERRIN MOUNTAINS WALKING FESTIVAL
OCT. 31	BELFAST AND DERRY ◆ E	HALLOWEEN PARADES
NOV.	BELFAST ◆ E F3	BELFAST FESTIVAL (Queen's University)

PRICES GIVEN ARE APPROXIMATE.

→ Addresses are grouped under four provinces. Within each province cities and towns are listed in alphabetical order and are followed by the names of their respective counties (Co.).

Leinster	341
Munster	344
Connacht	348
Ulster	350

→ Establishments located in Northern Ireland are indicated by the letters N.I. in brackets (N.I.) following the county's name.
→ The coordinates (e.g. ◆ A A1) refer to the map section on page 385.
→ A full list of symbols is given on page 329.
→ Restaurant prices are given for a complete meal, excluding wine; hotel prices are for two people sharing a double room.

LEINSTER

BANAGHER, CO. OFFALY

◆ F F1

→ **PUB-RESTAURANT**
Flynns Bar and Restaurant
Main St.
Tel. (0509) 51312
Restaurant open daily 12.30–2.30pm and 5–9pm
Live music on Fri. and Sun.
▢◉♫◉

→ **ACCOMMODATION**
Crank House
Tel. and fax
(0902) 57561
This youth hostel relocated into a fine Georgian house with a pink façade stands proudly on Banagher High Street. Coffee shop next door.
€10 *for a dormitory or double room (breakfast not included)*
◉◉

BIRR, CO. OFFALY

◆ F F2

→ **ACCOMMODATION**
Dooley's Hotel
Emmet Sq.
Tel. (0509) 20032
Fax (0509) 21332
dooleyshotel
@esatclear.ie
Closed Dec. 25.
Former post house. Comfortable and full of charm.
▢◉✗♫◉

CARLINGFORD, CO. LOUTH

◆ E E5

→ **ACCOMMODATION**
Mc Kevitt's Village Hotel
Market Sq.
Tel. (042) 937 31 16
Fax (042) 937 31 44
www.mckevittshotel.com
Warm welcome and comfortable rooms in the town center.
▢◉✗♫◉

Viewpoint
Omeath Rd.
Tel. and fax
(042) 937 31 49
www.omeath.net/viewpoint.htm
Great position on a hilltop between the sea and the mountains. Veranda and large bay windows to enjoy the wonderful views while having breakfast.
▢✗♨️P◉

DUBLIN, CO. DUBLIN

◆ G C1, B

→ **PUBS AND CAFÉS**
Bewley's Oriental Cafe
◆ B E5
78–79 Grafton's St.
Dublin 2
Tel. (01) 677 67 61
Open Mon.–Thur. 7.30am–1pm,
Fri.–Sat. 7.30am–6pm, Sun. 8am–1pm
Famous for its decoration by Harry Clarke and its stained-glass windows, Bewley's now opens for dinner.
▢◉◉

Brazen Head
◆ B C4
20 Lower Bridge St.
Dublin 2
Tel. (01) 679 51 86
Open Mon.–Wed. 11am–11pm,
Thur.–Sat. 11am–12.30am,
Sun. noon–11.30pm
Hot buffet from 12.30–2pm
Known as the oldest pub in Dublin, Brazen Head is always quite lively. Traditional Irish music from Mon. to Fri., blues on Sat., and contemporary Irish groups on Sun.
▢◉♡♫◉

Davy Byrne's
◆ B E5
21 Duke St.
Dublin 2
Tel. (01) 677 52 17
Open Sun.–Wed. 10.30am–11.30pm,
Thur.–Sat. 10.30am-12.30am
Immortalized as Leoplold Bloom's lunch spot in James Joyce's Ulysses, this pub serves food from noon until 9pm (Mon.–Thur.), until 6pm on Fri. and until 7pm on Sat. and Sun. Speciality: oysters.
▢◉◉

Eamonn Dorams
◆ B E4
Crown Alley
Temple Bar
Dublin 2
Tel. (01) 679 91 14
Open daily 11.30am–2.30am
Meeting place for traditional music and dance enthusiasts every Fri. from 7–10pm (also on Sat. and Sun. in summer). Traditional Irish cuisine with international influences.
▢◉♡♫◉

International Bar
◆ B E4
Wicklow St.
Dublin 2
Tel. (01) 677 92 50
A small traditional pub in the heart of Dublin. Upstairs, a Comedy Club puts on shows on Mondays, Wednesdays and Thursdays (featuring comedians, live music, etc.)
♫

Mc Daid's
◆ B E5
3 Harry St.
Dublin 2
Tel. (01) 679 43 95
Open Sun.–Wed. 11am–11.30pm,
Thur.–Sat. 11am–12.30am
Traditional Irish pub on the literary Dublin route.
▢

O'Donoghues
◆ B E5
15 Merrion Row,
Dublin 2
Tel. (01) 676 28 07
Open Sun.–Wed. 11am–11.30pm,
Thur.–Sat 11am–12.30am
Authentic pub that comes alive with live Irish music every night from 9.30pm.
▢♡♫

→ **RESTAURANTS**
The Commons Restaurant
◆ B E5
85–86 St. Stephen's Green
Dublin 2
Tel. (01) 475 25 97
Open Mon.–Fri. 12.30–2.15pm and 7–10.15pm
Historic setting and sumptuous cuisine tastefully created. Highly sophisticated service.
▢◉♡♣

Cooke's Café
◆ B E5
14 South William St.
Dublin 2
Tel. (01) 679 05 36
Open Tue.–Sat. noon–5pm

and 6–11pm
First opened at the beginning of the 1990s, Cooke's Café has lost none of its charm. Still very popular, it offers Italian- and New York-style dishes.
⬚⬚⬚⬚

Dobbins
◆ **B** F5
15 Stephen's Lane
Dublin 2
Tel. (01) 676 46 70
Open Mon.–Fri.
12.30–2.30pm,
Tue.–Sat.
7.30–10.30pm
*The food, made with the freshest ingredients and prepared as it is ordered, as well as the impeccable service make Dobbins an absolute must.
Piano-bar Thursdays to Sundays 9.30pm–midnight.*
⬚⬚⬚⬚

Les Frères Jacques
◆ **B** D4
74 Dame St.
Dublin 2
Tel. (01) 679 45 55
Open Mon.–Fri.
12.30–2.30pm
and 19.15–10.30pm,
Sat. 7–11pm
This renowned restaurant serves seafood and game (when in season) specialties. The interesting wine list offers over a hundred different vintages. Piano-bar weekends.
⬚⬚⬚⬚

Kilkenny Café and Restaurant
◆ **B** E4
6 Nassau St.
Dublin 2
(2nd floor of the Kilkenny Design Centre)
Tel. (01) 677 70 66
Open Mon.–Wed.,
Fri. 8.30am–5pm,
Thur. 8.30am–7pm,
Sat. 9am–5pm,
Sun. 11am–5pm
Unusual but pleasant and

relaxed place. The Food Hall on the ground floor displays the fresh produce served by the upstairs restaurant, or at the café for visitors in a rush. Quiches, salades, stews, home-made cakes and bread.
⬚ ⬚

La Med
◆ **B** D4
22 East Essex St.,
Temple Bar
Dublin 2
Tel. (01) 670 73 58
Open daily noon–
5pm and 6–10pm

Fine winebar serving Mediterranean-style dishes. You can enjoy an unhurried brunch on Sundays. (around €10).
⬚⬚⬚

Restaurant Patrick Guilbaud
◆ **B** F5
21 Merrion St.
Dublin 2
Tel. (01) 676 41 92
Open Tue.–Sat.
12.30–2.15pm
and 7.30–10.15pm
This restaurant is an institution in Dublin. Top-quality French cuisine.
⬚⬚

Roly's Bistro
◆ **G** C1
7 Ballsbridge
Terrace, Dublin 4
Tel. (01) 668 26 11
Open daily
noon–3pm
and 6–10pm
Fine Irish-European cuisine, and a wonderful "grand café" atmosphere.
⬚⬚

Ryan's
◆ **G** C1
28 Parkgate St.
Dublin 8
Tel. (01) 671 93 52
Mon.–Fri.
12.30–2.30pm,
Tue.–Sat.
6–10.30pm,
Sun. 6–9.30pm
Ryan's serves delicious food with a strong Mediterranean accent.
⬚⬚

**→ ACCOMMODATION
The Clarence Hotel**
◆ **B** E4
6–8 Wellington
Quay, Temple Bar
Dublin 2
Tel. (01) 40 7 08 00
Fax (01) 407 08 18
www.theclarence.ie
reservations
@theclarence.ie
Closed for two

weeks in Jan.
Located in the fashionable Temple Bar area, the Clarence has been redecorated in an Art-Déco style by its famous owners, the rock group U2. View over the Liffey river and a restaurant, the Tea Room, that enjoys an excellent reputation. Two bars: The Octagon and The Study.
⬚⬚⬚⬚

Georgian House
◆ **B** F5
18 Baggot St. Lower
Dublin 2
Tel. (01) 634 50 00
Fax (01) 634 51 00
hotel@georgian
house.ie
Closed Dec. 24–27.
Charming brick house only 5 minutes from Trinity College, the museums and the shopping district.
⬚⬚⬚

Gresham Hotel
◆ **B** E3
23 Upper
O'Connell St.
Dublin 1
Tel. (01) 874 68 81
Fax (01) 878 71 75
sales@thegresham.
com
The prestigious Gresham Hotel, symbol of Dublin's high-society life at the end of the 19th century and mentioned by James Joyce in Dubliners, has been restored. It is still renowned for its bar, Toddys, and for its very pleasant restaurant.
⬚⬚⬚⬚⬚

Kinlay House Christchurch Hostel
◆ **B** D4
2–12 Lord Edward St.
Dublin 2
Tel. (01) 679 66 44
Fax (01) 679 74 37
kinlay.dublin@usit
world.com
Youth hostel in the heart of Temple Bar.

RESTAURANTS

- ▣ <€15/<£11
- ▣ €15–30/£11–22
- ▣ €30–45/£22–33
- ▣ >€45/>£33

Per person: around €14 in a dormitory, around €20 in a room for 4–6 people, and around €25 for a double room (continental breakfast included).
▣Ⓒ▣

Pembroke Town House
◆ G C1
90 Pembroke Rd.
Ballsbridge
Dublin 4
Tel. (01) 660 02 77
Fax (01) 660 02 91
Closed for a week at Christmas
This luxury guesthouse – formerly known as Number Eighty Eight – has been restored and is now more spacious. Facilities include a sauna.
▣ⓅⓍ▣

The Shelbourne Hotel
◆ B E5
27 St. Stephen's Green
Dublin 2
Tel. (01) 676 64 71
Fax (01) 661 60 06
shelbourneinfo@forte-hotels.com
The most elegant hotel in Dublin serves a cuisine that is both traditional and creative in its restaurant, N° 27 The Green. It has another, bistro-style, restaurant, The Side Door (entrance on Kildare St).
▣ⒸⓅ▣

Temple Bar Hotel
◆ B E4
Fleet St.
Temple Bar
Dublin 2
Tel. (01) 677 33 33
Fax (01) 677 30 88
templeb@iol.ie
Comfortable hotel in the fashionable part of the city. There is a public parking lot opposite. Hotel pub: Buskers.
▣ⒸⓍ▣

DULEEK, CO. MEATH
◆ E D6

→ ACCOMMODATION
Annesbrook
Tel. (041) 982 32 93
Fax (041) 982 30 24
sweetnan@annesbrook.com
Closed Sep.–Apr.
Neo-classical residence dating from the 18th century (King George IV stayed here) set in wooded surroundings in the heart of the Valley of the Boyne. Family atmosphere, and home-made food based on seasonal, fresh vegetables from the garden.
▣▣Ⓧ▣▣

HOWTH, CO. DUBLIN
◆ G C1

→ RESTAURANT
King Sitric Restaurant
East Pier
Tel. (01) 832 52 35
Mon.–Fri. 12.30–2.15pm, Mon.–Sat. 6.30–10pm
Seafood restaurant that also offers a fine view over the sea and 8 very comfortable rooms.
▣Ⓧ▣

KILKENNY, CO. KILKENNY
◆ G A3

→ PUBS/RESTAURANTS
Edward Langton's Pub & Restaurant
69 John St.
Tel. (056) 65133
Restaurant open daily noon–2.30pm and 6.30–10pm
Pub food served daily until 8pm
Edward Langton's Pub and Restaurant has won awards for best pub in Ireland. Popular with tourists, it offers top-quality food and entertainment. Live music on Fridays; traditional music on

---

Monday and Wednesday in summer; nightclub on Tuesday, Thursday and Saturday.
▣Ⓒ▣▣

Kyteler's Inn
(Bar and restaurant)
Kieran St.
Tel. (056) 21064
Restaurant open Mon.–Thur. 6–9pm, Sat.–Sun. 6–10pm
Pub food served until 6pm
Warm and friendly pub with traditional Irish music from Thursday until Saturday. Small terrace open in summer.
▣Ⓒ▣▣▣

→ACCOMMODATION
Lacken House
Dublin Rd.
Tel. (056) 61085
Fax (056) 62435
www.lackenhouse.ie
info@lackenhouse.ie
Closed Dec. 22–Jan. 2 and Sun.–Mon. in low season
Friendly guesthouse with an excellent restaurant (Tue.–Sat. 7–10.30pm) which has become one of the most fashionable in Kilkenny. Chef Nicolas O'Brien offers a different carte according to the fresh produce available. Specialty: seafood dishes.
▣Ⓟ▣

KILLINEY, CO. DUBLIN
◆ G C2

→ACCOMMODATION
Fitzpatrick Castle Hotel
Tel. (01) 284 07 00
Fax (01) 230 54 3O
www.fitzpatrickhotels.com
Very pleasant hotel located above Killiney. Walk over to the nearby Victoria Park to enjoy the fine view over Dublin Bay.
▣Ⓟ▣▣▣▣

MOUNTRATH, CO. LAOIS
◆ F F2

→ ACCOMMODATION
Roundwood House
Tel. (0502) 32120
Attractive 18th-century Palladian house surrounded by woods on the side of Slieve Bloom Mountains. The large dining hall, the finely furnished lounges, and the library will give you a taste of "To the manor born" life. Dinner served to residents daily at 8pm (around €37).
▣▣▣▣Ⓟ▣▣

MULLINGAR, CO. WESTMEATH
◆ G A1

→ PUB-RESTAURANT
Crooked Wood House
Crooked Wood
Tel. (044) 72165
Open Tue.–Sat. 6.30–10pm, Sun. 12.30–2.30pm
Tranquil, lakeside establishment serving delicious contemporary Irish cuisine. Speciality: game.
▣▣▣▣

→ ACCOMMODATION
Greville Arms
Pearse St.
Tel. (044) 48563
Fax (044) 48052
Former post house converted into an inn. The rooms look out over the garden. The restaurant, open for lunch and dinner, offers a fine wine list. Pub/disco every evening.
▣▣▣Ⓟ▣▣

NAVAN, CO. MEATH
◆ G B1

→ PUB-RESTAURANT
Dunderry Lodge
Dunderry
Robinstown
Tel. (046) 31671

343

Open Tue.–Sat. 7–9.30pm, Sun. 12.30–8.15pm
Restaurant surrounded by beautiful gardens and serving traditional Irish cuisine and a fine selection of wines. Piano-bar Fridays and Saturdays.
⊡🎵⊡

NEW ROSS, CO. WEXFORD

◆ **G** A4

→**RESTAURANT**
Galley Cruising Restaurant
Tel. (051) 42 17 23
Open Apr.–Oct.
Dinner-cruises on the river Barrow, with a running commentary on the history of the region, and music provided by two fiddlers. You can choose between:
– lunch at 12.30pm, and a 2-hour cruise (€17.75)
– afternoon tea at 3pm and a 1¾-hour cruise (€10.15)
– dinner at 7pm and a 2½ to 3-hour cruise (from €31.75 to €38).
⊡🎵

ROSSLARE HARBOUR, CO. WEXFORD

◆ **G** B5

→**ACCOMMODATION**
Kilrane House
Tel. (053) 33135
Fax (053) 33739
Closed Dec. 24–26.
Fine Georgian interior and six spacious comfortable rooms behind the pink façade of this Bed & Breakfast.
⊡©🍴⊡

ROUNDWOOD, CO. WICKLOW

◆ **G** C2

→**PUB-RESTAURANT**
Roundwood Inn
Tel. (01) 281 81 07

Open noon–9pm
Closed Dec. 25 and Good Friday.
Friendly bar-restaurant with a welcoming woodfire burning in the fireplace. Home-made dishes based on seafood (oysters from Galway and smoked salmon from Wicklow) as well as a few game specialties.
⊡⊡

STRAFFAN, CO. KILDARE

◆ **G** B1

→**ACCOMMODATION**
The Kildare Hotel & Country Club
Tel. (01) 6273333
Fax (01) 601 72 99
www.kclub.ie
sales@kclub.ie
Located 18½ miles from Dublin and set in a beautiful park, this hotel is one of the most luxurious in Ireland. Especially renowned for its 18-hole golf course designed by Arnold Palmer. Other activities on offer include fishing, tennis, a swimming pool and massage.
⊡🏠🛗⊡🎵♒⊞

THOMASTOWN, CO. KILKENNY

◆ **G** A4

→**RESTAURANTS**
Lady Helen Restaurant
Mount Juliet House
Tel. (056) 24455
Open daily 7.30–10pm
Sumptuous restaurant set in the magnificent Mount Juliet park. By reservation only.
⊡🛗⊞

Kendals Restaurant
Mount Juliet Clubhouse
Tel. (056) 24455
Open Mon.–Sat. 6.30–10pm, Sun. 12.30–3.30pm

Looking over Mount Juliet golf course, Kendals restaurant offers an exceptional view. Jazz concerts on Sundays.
⊡🏠♒🎵⊡

WEXFORD, CO. WEXFORD

◆ **G** B5

→**PUB-RESTAURANT**
The Wrens Nest
Commercial Quay
Tel. (053) 22359
In the heart of Wexford – famous for its opera festival – this friendly pub serves food all day.
©🏠⊡

WICKLOW, CO. WICKLOW

◆ **G** C3

→**ACCOMMODATION**
The Old Rectory Guesthouse
Tel. (0404) 67048
Open June–Aug.
This charming and comfortable B & B is open only during the high season.
⊡⊞

MUNSTER
ADARE, CO. LIMERICK

◆ **F** D3

→**ACCOMMODATION**
Adare Manor
Tel. (061) 396566
Fax (061) 396124
www.adaremanor.com
Former residence of the earls of Dunraven, this huge Neo-Gothic manor house set in a 750-acre park, houses a luxury hotel. Candle-lit dinner.
⊡🛗🏠♒🅿⊞

ARDMORE, CO. WATERFORD

◆ **F** F5

→**ACCOMMODATION**
Cliff House Hotel
Tel. (024) 94106
Fax (024) 94496

cliffhousehotel @eircom.net
Closed Nov.–Feb.
Quiet hotel with a view of the bay. Dinner served to residents and prepared with the fresh catch of the day.
⊡🏠🛗⊡♒⊡

BALLYLICKEY, CO. CORK

◆ **F** B5

→**RESTAURANT**
Sea View House
Tel. (027) 50462
Restaurant set in a small country house surrounded by a garden and with a magnificent view over Bantry Bay. Delicious fish and seafood dishes.
⊡⊡

→**ACCOMMODATION**
Ballylickey Manor House
Tel. (027) 50071
Fax (027) 50124
www.ballylickey manorhouse.com
Closed Nov.–Mar.
Built three centuries ago by Lord Kenmare, this hunting lodge overlooks Bantry Bay and the mountains beyond. Two new rooms have been added to the pre-existing 12. The house boasts a splendid garden, especially when the flowers are in full bloom.
⊡🛗🍴🏠⊡⊞

BANTRY, CO. CORK

◆ **F** B5

→**ACCOMMODATION**
Bantry House
Tel. (027) 50047
Fax (027) 50795
Closed Nov–Feb.
The property of the earls of Bantry was converted into a charming hotel in the 1980's.
⊡⊡♒⊡

RESTAURANTS

⬛ <€15/<£11
⬛ €15–30/£11–22
⬛ €30–45/£22–33
⬛ >€45/>£33

BLARNEY, CO. CORK

◆ F D5

→ **PUB-RESTAURANT**
Blair's Inn
Cloghroe, Blarney
Tel. (021) 38 14 70
Open daily
noon–midnight
Closed Dec. 25 and
Good Friday.
*Charming inn
nestling in a
wooded region.
Delightful gardens
in the summer and
log fire in the
winter. Live music
every Sunday night.*
⬛🅿⬛⬛

BUNRATTY, CO. CLARE

◆ F D3

→ **PUB-RESTAURANT**
Mews Restaurant
Bunratty House
Mews.
Tel. (061) 36 40 82
Open Tue.–Sat.
7–9.30pm
*The Mews, located
above the Bunratty
Folk Park, combines
Irish cuisine with a
few French and
Italian dishes.*
⬛⬛⬛

CAHIRCIVEEN, CO. KERRY

◆ F A4

→ **PUB-RESTAURANT**
**The Shebeen Bar
and Restaurant**
Tel. (066) 947 23 61
Open daily
noon–9.30pm
*Traditional music
all year round on
Thusdays, and at
weekends in
summer.*
🅿⬛

CASHEL, CO. TIPPERARY

◆ F E3-E4

→ **RESTAURANT**
**The Spearman
Restaurant**
97 Main St.
Tel. (062) 61143
Open daily

12.30–2.30pm
and 5.30–9pm
(Closed Sun. evening
and Mon. between
Dec. and May)
Closed Nov.
*Charming, typically
Irish place serving
fresh dishes made
exclusively with
local produce. No
alcohol license, but
all alcoholic drinks
come from the pub
in the same street!*
⬛⬛⬛

→ **ACCOMMODATION**
The Chestnuts
Kilkenny Dualla Rd.
Dualla
Tel. and fax
(062) 614694
www.thechestnuts.com
*Pleasant rooms in a
farm in the heart of
the hamlet of
Dualla. Residents
can savor the
delicious home-
made cuisine.*
⬛⬛⬛⬛

CASTLETOWNSHEND, CO. CORK

◆ F C6

→ **PUB-RESTAURANT**
Mary Ann's Bar
Tel. (028) 36146
Restaurant
open 6–9pm
Closed 3 weeks
in Jan.
*This establishment,
located above the
pretty village of
Castletownshend,
dates from 1846.
Sophisticated
seafood cuisine.*
⬛⬛⬛

CLARECASTLE, CO. CLARE

◆ F D2

→ **ACCOMMODATION**
Carnelly House
Clarecastle
Tel. (065) 682 84 42
Fax (065) 682 92 22
info@carnelly-
house.com
Closed Dec. 25
*Spacious rooms
in a fine Georgian
residence designed
by Francis Bindon
and set in a 100-acre*

park. Dinner upon
request (around
€45). Located
between Galway
and Limerick,
Carnelly House is an
ideal base for
visiting the west of
the country.
⬛🅿⬛⬛

CORK, CO. CORK

◆ F D5, A

→ **PUBS**
Bully's
◆ A B4
40 Paul St.
Tel. (021) 427 35 55
Open daily
noon–11pm
*A wide range of
small dishes
influenced by Italian
cuisine are served in
this friendly pub.
Very popular with
students.*
⬛⬛

The Office Bar
◆ A C4
5 Sullivans Quay
Tel. (021) 4317781
*A young Irish crowd
jostles by the buffet
served from
Monday to Friday
(noon– 2.30pm).
Live traditional
music on Thursday
evening.*
⬛🅿⬛

→**RESTAURANTS**
Café Paradiso
◆ A C3
16 Lancaster Quay
Tel. (021) 427 79 39
Open Tue.–Sat.
12.30–3pm and
6.30–10.30pm
*Located in the
center of Cork, Café
Paradiso serves tasty
vegetarian snacks.
Some tables on a
terrace.*
⬛⬛⬛⬛

Esaus Restaurant
◆ A B4
8 Careys Lane
Tel. (021) 427 07 25
Open Mon.–Sat.
noon–3pm, Thur.–
Sat. 6–10.15pm,
Sun.–Wed.
6–9.45pm

*Increasingly
popular modern
restaurant with a
lively atmosphere
and friendly service.*
⬛⬛⬛⬛

**Ivory Tower
Restaurant**
◆ A B5
The Exchange
Buildings
35 Princes St.
Tel. (021) 427 46 65
Open Tue.–Sat.
noon–3pm, 6.30–
10pm, Sun. 6–11pm
*Sophisticated,
creative cuisine that
includes some fine,
unusual vegetarian
dishes.*
⬛⬛

Jacobs on the Mall
◆ A B5
30A South Mall
Tel. (021) 425 15 30
Open Mon.–Sat.
12.30–2.30pm and
6.30–10pm
*This restaurant is
well worth a visit
for its contemporary
cuisine and the
original décor of
the Turkish baths in
which is it located.
Piano-bar from
noon on Saturdays.*
⬛⬛⬛

Jacques Restaurant
◆ A B5
Phoenix St.
Tel. (021) 427 73 87
Open Mon.–Fri.
noon–3pm,
Mon.–Sat. 6–10pm
*Jacques Restaurant
is renowned for its
creative fish cuisine
and its pleasant
Mediterranean
setting.*
⬛⬛

→**ACCOMMODATION**
Arbutus Lodge
◆ F D5
Montenotte
Tel. (021) 450 12 37
Fax (021) 450 28 93
www.arbutuslodge.
net
Closed 1 week for
Christmas
*Beautiful house
built in 1802 above
the river Lee and
the town. Peaceful*

HOTELS
- ⬚ <€70/<£50
- ⬚ €70–110/£50–80
- ⬚ €110–180/£80–130
- ⬚ >€180/>£130

garden and traditional music in the bar where Guinness is served on a fine old oak counter.
⬚⬚⬚⬚⬚

Killarney House
◆ A C2
Western Rd.
Tel. (021) 427 02 90
Fax (021) 427 10 10
www.killarneyhouse.com
killarneyhouse@iol.ie
Welcoming Bed & Breakfast with an ideal location (only a few steps away from the university). Tea and coffee are served in the rooms.
⬚⬚⬚⬚⬚

DINGLE, CO. KERRY

◆ F A4
→ **PUBS-RESTAURANTS**
An Cafe Liteartha
Dyke Gate St.
Tel. (066) 915 22 04
Open daily
10am–6pm
This café-cum-bookstore specializes in Irish literary works written both in English and in Irish Gaelic.
⬚

Doyle's Seafood Bar & Townhouse
John St.
Tel. (066) 51174
Open Mon.–Sat.
6–10pm
Closed Jan.
As its name indicates, the Doyles Seafood Bar serves seafood specialties that will satisfy the most demanding gourmet.
⬚⬚⬚

→ **ACCOMMODATION**
Bambury's Guest House
Mail Rd.
Tel. (066) 9151244
Fax (066) 9151786
info@bamburysguesthouse.com
Quiet, large Bed & Breakfast located only two minutes

away from the town center. The 12 spacious rooms offer all modern comforts.
⬚⬚⬚

Doyle's TownHouse
John St.
Tel. (066) 915 11 74
Fax (066) 915 18 16
cdoyles@iol.ie
Closed mid Nov.–mid Feb
Pleasant lounge and 8 cosy rooms in the house next to the restaurant of the same name.
⬚⬚⬚

DOOLIN, CO. CLARE

◆ F C1
→ **PUB-RESTAURANT**
O'Connor's Pub and Restaurant
Fisher St.
Tel. (065) 7074168
Open daily
bar: 9am–9.15pm,
restaurant:
noon–9.15pm
An absolute must! O'Connors is famous for its delicious seafood chowders and stews. The pub features live music by the best musicians in Country Clare every night from 9.30pm.
⬚⬚⬚⬚

→ **ACCOMMODATION**
Paddy Moloney's Doolin Hostel
Fisher St.
Tel. (065) 707 40 06
Fax (065) 707 44 21
doolinhostels@eircom.net
Closed Dec. 15–Jan. 10
Youth hostel especially popular in winter for its peat fire. Occasional live music in the evening. Around €10 in a dormitory, and €11 for a double room.
⬚

DUNMORE EAST, CO .WATERFORD

◆ G A5
→ **ACCOMMODATION**
Haven Hotel
Dunmore East
Tel. (051) 383150
Fax (051) 383488
www.thehavenhotel.com
Fine 19th-century mansion set in a large garden. The hotel is near the sea, in the heart of the harbor village of Dunmore East. Very friendly pub with live music, and an excellent restaurant. You can expect a warm welcome
⬚⬚⬚⬚

KANTURK, CO. CORK

◆ F C4-D4
→ **ACCOMMODATION**
Assolas Country House
Tel. (029) 50015
Fax (029) 50795
assolas@eircom.ie
Closed Nov.–Mar.
Riverside Bed & Breakfast located in a beautiful 17th-century mansion covered with ivy. Ideal for fishing enthusiasts. Excellent meals served to residents (around €40).
⬚⬚⬚⬚⬚⬚

KENMARE, CO. KERRY

◆ F B5
→ **RESTAURANT**
Packie's
Henry St.
Tel. (064) 41508
Open Tue.–Sat.
6–9.30pm
Closed Dec.–Easter
Elegant but unpretentious fish restaurant. Packie's pretty décor and traditional Irish recipes offer a touch of Mediterranean warmth.
⬚⬚⬚

→ **ACCOMMODATION**
Hawthorn House
M. & N. O'Brien
Shelburne St.
Tel. (064) 41035
Fax (064) 41932
hawthorn@eircom.net
Closed 4 days for Christmas
Charming Bed & Breakfast in the center of Kenmare with comfortable, simply furnished rooms. A generous breakfast of smoked salmon and eggs is prepared by the owner herself, who also offers her services as a baby-sitter to residents.
⬚⬚⬚⬚⬚

PUBS, RESTAURANTS AND ACCOMMODATION ◆

RESTAURANTS
- ▣ <€15/<£11
- ▣ €15–30/£11–22
- ▣ €30–45/£22–33
- ⊞ >€45/>£33

KILLARNEY, CO. KERRY

◆ **F** B4

→ **PUB**
Fáilte Pub
College St.
Tel. (064) 33404
Open daily
11.30am–11pm
This pub is true to its name (Fáilte means welcome in Irish).
▣Ⓒ♫▣

→ **ACCOMMODATION**
Muckross Park Hotel
Muckross Village
Tel. (064) 31938
Fax (064) 31965
muckrosssparkhotel
@eircom.net
Closed Dec.–Feb.
Its perfect location in the heart of Killarney National Park, makes the Muckross Park an ideal place for hikers and riding enthusiasts alike. Beautifully furnished rooms. One pub, two restaurants.
▣⬆✗▣▣

KILLMALLOCK, CO. LIMERICK

◆ **F** D4

→ **ACCOMMODATION**
Flemingstown House
Tel. (063) 98093
Fax (063) 98546
www.ils.ie/flemingstown
Closed Nov.–Feb.
(can be open by request)
Charming 18th-century farmhouse where a fine tea of home-made scones is served at milking time. Dinner is prepared with passion and talent!
▣⬆✗▣�▣

KILLORGLIN, CO. KERRY

◆ **F** B4

→ **ACCOMMODATION**
Caragh Lodge
Caragh Lake
Tel. (066) 976 91 15
Fax (066) 976 93 16
www.caraghlodge.com
Closed Oct. 15–Easter

Former hunting lodge surrounded by azaleas, camellias and magnolias right by Lake Carach. Excellent cuisine (seafood, salmon and Kerry lamb). Trout and salmon fishing available.
▣⬆♫☼▣▣

KINSALE, CO. CORK

◆ **F** D6

→ **PUBS/RESTAURANTS**
The Blue Haven
3 Pearse St.
Tel. (021) 4772209
Fax (021) 4774268
Restaurant open daily noon–3pm
The Blue Haven is one of the best restaurants in Kinsale. It also has a few very pleasant rooms for visitors who wish to stay on. Live traditional music on Thursdays.
Ⓒ♫♫▣

The Spaniards Inn
Scilly, Kinsale
Tel. (021) 4772436
Fax (021) 4773303
Open daily
7–10.30pm
Local cuisine, traditional music, darts and a peat fire... all the hallmarks of a true Irish pub!
Ⓒ♫⬆▣

→ **ACCOMMODATION**
Scilly House
Scilly, Kinsale
Tel. (021) 477 24 13
House dating from 1760, near the harbor with a warm and eclectic décor. The wine-tasting sessions in the bar-cum-library are a must.
▣⬆☼▣

MIDLETON, CO. CORK

◆ **F** E5

→ **ACCOMMODATION**
Ballymaloe House
Shanagarry
Tel. (021) 465 25 31

Fax (021) 465 20 21
res@ballimaloe.ie
Closed Dec. 24–26
This large family farm houses a cookery school and one of the best restaurants in the country. Fresh produce from the farm are used for all the meals (dinner: around €48).
▣⬆♫⊞

SNEEM, CO. KERRY

◆ **F** B5

→ **ACCOMMODATION**
Parknasilla Great Southern Hotel
Parknasilla
Tel. (064) 45122
Fax (064) 45323
Open all year round
Magnificent Victorian building surrounded by tropical vegetation. Do not miss the Shaw Library where the playwright completed Saint Joan. *Nine-hole golf course for enthusiasts.*
▣⬆▣✗☼▣▣

TRALEE, CO. KERRY

◆ **F** B3

→ **PUB-RESTAURANT**
Kirby's Brogue Inn
Rock St.
Tel. (066) 712 33 57
Open daily
10am–11pm
The bar serves food all day, while the upstairs restaurant is open for dinner between 6pm and 11pm. Live traditional music every evening in summer.
▣Ⓒ♫▣

VALENTIA ISLAND, CO. KERRY

◆ **F** A4

→ **PUB-RESTAURANT**
Boston's
Knightstown,
Valentia Island
Tel. (066) 947 61 40

Open daily
noon–9pm
Small terrace and live music in summer.
▣⬆♫▣

WATERFORD, CO. WATERFORD

◆ **G** A5

→ **PUBS-RESTAURANTS**
Dwyer's of Mary St.
8 Mary St.
Tel. (051) 87 74 78
www.dwyersrestaurant
.com
Open Mon.–Sat.
6–10pm
Closed Dec. 25–26
and Good Friday
This top-of-the-range restaurant, located in the former Royal Irish Constabulary barracks (Irish police force), opened in 1989. The chef, Martin Dwyer, defines his cuisine as Franco-Irish and only uses fresh local produce.
▣Ⓒ▣

Geoff's
9–10 John St.
Tel. (051) 87 47 87
Open Mon.–Sat.
11am–9pm
A spacious, welcoming pub that serves food all day. Tapas menu from 4.30pm.
▣

→ **ACCOMMODATION**
Granville Hotel
The Quay
Tel. (051) 30 55 55
Fax (051) 30 55 66
granvillehotel@tinet.ie
Closed Dec. 25–27
The best hotel in Waterford is located in a Georgian house by the river Suir. You can also stop for a drink at this peaceful, luxury establishment.
▣⬆♫✗▣▣

Waterford Castle
The Island, Ballinakill
Tel. (051) 87 82 03
Fax (051) 87 93 16
www.waterfordcastle.
com

◆ PUBS, RESTAURANTS AND ACCOMMODATION

CONNACHT

Small 15th-century castle on a private island with its own golf course. Only accessible by ferry, it is a small paradise!
▣◻🔧♨🔒Ⓟ▦

WATERVILLE, CO. KERRY

◆ **F** A5

→ **RESTAURANT**
The Huntsman Seafood Restaurant
Tel. (066) 947 41 24
Open Apr.–Oct.: daily 11.30–3.30pm and 6–9.30pm; Nov.–Mar.: Fri.–Sat. 11.30am–3.30pm and 6–9.30pm (may open at other times upon request. Telephone to reserve.)
Seafood specialties, as well as poultry and game. Piano-bar in summer.
▣🎵◻

YOUGHAL, CO. CORK

◆ **F** E5

→ **PUB**
Moby Dick
Market Square
Tel. (024) 92756
daily 10.30am–11pm
This place was used as general quarters by John Huston and his team during the shooting of his movie Moby Dick. You can sit outside and enjoy the view of Youghal harbor. Traditional music every Friday from June to August.
🔧🎵

CONNACHT
ARAN ISLANDS, CO. GALWAY

◆ **D** A6-B6

→ **PUB-RESTAURANT**
Dún Aonghasa Restaurant
◆ **D** C1
Kilronan
Tel. (099) 61104
The Dún Aonghasa

not only serves fine food in its dining hall, it can also prepare friendly picnics (lobster and other fine food). (around €44).
▣🔧

→ **ACCOMMODATION**
Kilmurvey House
◆ **D** C1
Kilronan
Tel. (099) 61218
Fax (099) 61397
kilmurveyhouse@eircom.net
Closed Oct.–Apr.
Bed & Breakfast.
Recently restored house at the foot of Dún Aengus. Set menu for dinner (around €20).
▣◻🔧♨▫

BALLINA, CO. MAYO

◆ **D** C3

→ **ACCOMMODATION**
Enniscoe House
Castlehill, near Crossmolina
Tel. (096) 31112
Fax (096) 31773
Closed Nov.–Mar.
Georgian house with a pale pink façade, family portraits, fireplaces and period furniture. Friendly welcome and excellent meals served to residents.
▣◻♨▫

CASHEL, CO. GALWAY

◆ **D** A5

→ **ACCOMMODATION**
Cashel House Hotel
Connemara
Tel. (095) 31001
Fax (095) 31077
info@cashel-house-hotel.com
Closed Jan. 10 to Feb. 10.
Bed & Breakfast.
A sumptuous residence overlooking Cashel Bay and surrounded by gardens that have twice been prized by the

National Garden Award. Member of the Relais et Châteaux chain.
▣◻🔧♨▦

CASTLEREA, CO. ROSCOMMON

◆ **E** A5

→ **ACCOMMODATION**
Clonalis House
Tel. and fax (0907) 20014
Closed Oct.–Apr 15
Built in the 19th century by the O'Connors, descendants of the last rulers of Ireland, this residence has an important historical heritage: manuscripts, paintings and antique furniture as well as the famous coronation stone on which, for nearly ten centuries, the kings of Ireland were crowned. Fishing and hunting on the grounds by reservation.
▣🔧◻▦

CLIFDEN, CO. GALWAY

◆ **D** A5

→ **PUB-RESTAURANT**
O'Grady's Seafood Restaurant
Market St.
Tel. (095) 21450
Open daily 12.30–10pm
Closed Nov.–Mar.
A true institution in the region, renowned for its fine seafood cuisine.
▣◻🔧

→ **ACCOMMODATION**
Rock Glen Country House Hotel
Clifden, Connemara
Tel. (095) 21035
Fax (095) 21737
www.connemara.net/rockglen-hotel
Closed Dec. 20–Feb. 12
Former hunting lodge belonging to Clifden Castle, two miles southwest of

the town. Stunning panoramic view.
▣🔧◻♨▦

COLLOONEY, CO. SLIGO

◆ **E** A4

→ **PUB-RESTAURANT**
Markree Castle
Tel. (071) 67800
Open daily noon–6pm (bar food), 7–9.30pm (restaurant)
Enjoy a walk in the magnificent gardens, after a fine gourmet meal in the restaurant.
▣🔧▦

CONG, CO. MAYO

◆ **D** B5

→ **RESTAURANT**
Echoes
Main St.
Tel. (092) 46059
Fax (092) 46665
Open Mon.–Sat. 6.30–9.30pm
Sophisticated seafood and meat dishes served in a charming setting.
▣◻🔧

→ **ACCOMMODATION**
Ashford Castle Hotel
Tel. (092) 46003
Fax (092) 46260
ashford@ashford.ie
Arthurian atmosphere in this hotel located right by Lough Corrib. Crenelated towers, age-worn wood paneling, paintings by old masters and candle-lit dinners by the fireplace give this imposing castle a definite medieval feeling.
▣🔧◻♨Ⓟ▦

GALWAY, CO. GALWAY

◆ **F** D1

→ **PUBS-RESTAURANTS**
Mc Donagh's Seafood House
22 Quay St.
Tel. (091) 565001

RESTAURANTS
- ▣ <€15/<£11
- ▣ €15–30/£11–22
- ▣ €30–45/£22–33
- ▦ >€45/>£33

Open Mon.–Sat.
noon–10pm,
Sun. 5–10pm
*Fish and Chips.
Seaside atmosphere
and a large choice
of fish dishes
(barbecues, kebabs
and mixed platters).
You can also buy
your own fish at the
store and cook it
yourself (fish shop
open Monday to
Friday between 9am
and 6pm).*
▣▣

Mc Swiggans
3 Eyre St.
Wood Quay
Tel. (091) 56 89 17
*Quaint old pub full
of charm serving
quality food.*
▣▣▣

**The Archway
Restaurant**
Victoria Place
Tel. (091) 56 36 93
Open Tue.–Sat.
noon–2.30pm,
6–9.30pm
*French-style cuisine,
served in intimate
surroundings.*
▣▣▣

**Cuba Bar
and Restaurant**
9–11 Prospect Hill
Tel. (091) 565991
Open Mon.–Sat.,
restaurant
10.30am–4pm
*Mexican restaurant
at lunchtime and
nightclub at night,
the Cuba welcomes
groups of local
musicians four
nights a week (Tue.,
Wed., Fri., Sat.).*
▣▣▣

**→ ACCOMMODATION
Ardilaun House Hotel**
Taylor's Hill
Tel. (091) 52 14 33
Fax (091) 52 15 46
ardilaun@iol.ie
Closed Dec. 22–28
*Typical Irish Bed &
Breakfast. Full of
charm and set in
splendid gardens
near a golf course
and the town
center. Neatly
decorated rooms*

*(some have a view
over the bay).*
▣▣▦▣▣▣

Brennan's Yard
Lower Merchant's Rd.
Tel. (091) 56 81 66
Fax (091) 56 82 62
Closed 1 week in
Dec.
*Peaceful and
intimate Bed &
Breakfast located in
the town center. Its
restaurant, the
Oyster, serves
reasonably-priced
traditional dishes
every day from 6pm
(around €18).*
▣▣▣▣▣▣

Norman Villa
86 Lower Salthill
Tel. and fax
(091) 521131
normanvilla@ocean.free
Closed Dec.–Jan.

*Beautiful seaside
Victorian house with
fine old furniture
and contemporary
objets d'art.*
▣▣▣▣

Quay Street House
10 Quay St.
Tel. and fax
(091) 56 86 44
www.barnacles.ie
*Friendly, well-
equipped youth
hostel (laundry
room, kitchen,
TV lounge). €14–
€23 per person.*
▣▣▣

◆ D B5

**→ PUB-RESTAURANT
Portfinn Lodge**
Tel. (095) 42265
Open May–Sep.
6.30–9.30pm

*Beautiful views of
Killary Bay. It also
has 8 rooms
available for visitors
who wish to stay on
(€57 per room,
breakfast included).*
▣▣▣▣

**→ ACCOMMODATION
Delphi Lodge**
Tel. (095) 42211
Fax (095) 42296
www.delphilodge.ie
Closed Dec. 18–
Jan. 1.
*Located between a
lake and the highest
mountains in
Connacht, the
former country
residence of the
Marquess of Sligo
offers absolute
peace and quiet.
Wild salmon fly-
fishing is available
from February until

September. Dinner
is served to all the
residents around
the fine oak table
and is traditionally
presided by the
"fisherman of the
day". (Around €35).*
▣▣▣▣

◆ D B4

**→ ACCOMMODATION
Newport House**
Tel. (098) 41222
Fax (098) 41613
kjt1@anu.ie
Closed Oct.–Mar. 19
*Elegant Georgian
country residence
located by the
Newport river.
Meals are based on
produce from the
garden and freshly
caught fish. Member
of the Relais et

Châteaux chain.*
▣▣▣▣▦▦

◆ D B5-B6

**→ ACCOMMODATION
Currarevagh House**
Tel. (091) 552312
Fax (091) 552731
currarevagh@ireland.
com
Closed Nov.–Mar.
*Romantic 19th-
century mansion
house set in 148
acres of woods
by Lough Corrib.
Friendly atmosphere.
Trout fishing and
boat outings.*
▣▣▣▦▣

◆ E A4

**→ ACCOMMODATION
Coopershill
House**
Tel. (071) 65108
Fax (071) 65466
ohara@coopershill.com
Closed Nov.–Apr.
*Set in 495 acres of
land, Coopershill
House has been
the ancestral home
of the O'Haras since
1774. It combines
old-fashioned charm
(period furniture,
four-poster beds)
with all the comfort
of modern life.
Fishing allowed on
the grounds and
restaurant open to
non-residents
according to the
space available
(dinner: from
around €37 to €40).*
▣▣▣

◆ D A5

**→ PUB-RESTAURANT
O'Dowds Seafood
Bar & Restaurant**
Tel. (095) 35809
Fax (095) 35907
Open daily
12.30–10pm
*Quality food is served
both at the bar*

HOTELS
- ⊡ <€70/<£50
- ⊡ €70–110/£50–80
- ⊞ €110–180/£80–130
- ⊞ >€180/>£130

(generously sized sandwiches) and in the restaurant *(salmon and lobster dishes). Pleasant stay guaranteed in the small port of Roundstone.*
⊟ ⋅

→ **ACCOMMODATION**
Eldons Hotel
Tel. (095) 35933
Fax (095) 35921
Closed mid Nov–mid Mar.
Fine view of the harbor and of the Twelve Pins mountain range. The famous Roundstone lobster is served by the restaurant of the hotel.
⊟ ⋅ ⋅ ⋅

SLIGO, CO. SLIGO

◆ **E** A4

→ **PUBS**
Hargadon's
O'Connell St.
Tel. (071) 70933
This excellent pub, which seems to belong to a bygone age, serves an honest, copious fare.
⋅

Mc Lynn's Bar
Old Market St.
Tel. (071) 42088
Irish music every weekend.
⋅

SPIDDAL, CO. GALWAY

◆ **D** B6

→ **PUB-RESTAURANT**
An Cruiscín Lán
Tel. (091) 553148
Restaurant open daily 12.30–10pm
International cuisine based on seafood and vegetarian dishes. Terrace overlooking Galway Bay. Mixed, live music on Fridays, and traditional bands on Saturdays.
⊟ ⋅ ⋅ ⋅

WESTPORT, CO. MAYO

◆ **D** B4

→ **PUBS**
Hoban's
The Octagon
Tel. (098) 27249
Lively crowded pub, especially on nights with live music.
♫

Matt Molloy's
Bridge St.
Tel. (098) 26655
This pub, opened by the Chieftains' flute player, offers live traditional music and a delirious atmosphere every night.
⋅ ⋅ ♫

ULSTER
ANNALONG, CO. DOWN (N.I.)

◆ **E** F5

→ **ACCOMMODATION**
Glassdrumman Lodge
85 Mill Rd.
BT34 4RH
Tel. (028) 43 76 84 51
Fax (028) 43 76 70 41
glassdrumman
@yahoo.com
Manor house located in the heart of the picturesque Mourne mountains, an area rich with history and legends. The best of Irish hospitality and courtesy. Ten rooms and a restaurant. Fishing and golf facilities nearby.
⊟ ⋅ ⋅ ⋅ ⋅

ARANMORE ISLAND, CO. DONEGAL

◆ **E** A1-B1

→ **ACCOMMODATION**
Glen Hotel
Closed Oct.–Easter
Tel. and fax
(075) 20505
The Glen Hotel is ideal for a taste of life on the island – forget all about cars and credit cards for a while!
⋅

ARMAGH, CO. ARMAGH (N.I.)

◆ **E** D4

→ **PUB-RESTAURANT**
Wheel & Lantern Cafe
Market St.
Tel. (048) 37 52 22 88
Open Mon.–Tue and Thur.–Sat.
10am–5pm
Café located in the Lennox store.

→ **ACCOMMODATION**
Charlemont Arms
English St.
BT617LB
Tel. (028) 37 52 20 28
Fax (028) 37 52 69 79
info@charlemontarms
hotel.com
Centrally located Bed & Breakfast with 18 rooms, as well as a restaurant and bar that serve food from Monday to Saturday.
⊟ ⋅ ⋅ ⋅ ⋅

BALLINAMALLARD, CO. FERMANAGH (N.I.)

◆ **E** C3

→ **ACCOMMODATION**
Jamestown House
Magheracross
Tel. (028) 66 38 82 09
Closed Dec. 25–Jan. 1.
Behind the beautiful, ivy-covered Georgian façade of Jamestown House, Helen and Arthur Stuart extend a fine welcome to their guests, who are allowed to fish and hunt – or simply relax – on the vast grounds.
⋅ ⋅ ⋅

BANGOR, CO. DOWN (N.I.)

◆ **E** F3

→ **PUB**
Clandeboye Lodge Hotel
10 Estate Rd.
Clandeboye
Tel. (048) 91 85 33 11
Open daily
noon–2.30pm

and 6–9.30pm
An outside patio can sit up to 20 people. The bar turns into a nightclub every Sat. from 9pm until 2am.
⊟ ⋅ ⋅ ⋅ ⋅

BELFAST, CO. ANTRIM (N.I.)

◆ **E** F3, A

→ **PUBS**
Bittles Bar
◆ **C** C3
70 Upper Church Lane
Tel. (028) 90 31 10 88
Open Mon.–Sat., lunch Mon.–Fri.
noon–3pm.
♫ ⋅

The Crown Liquor Saloon
◆ **C** A4
49 Great Victoria St.
Tel. (028) 90 27 99 01
www.belfasttelegraph.
co.uk/crown
Former Victorian gin temple with a magnificent façade and a very lively atmosphere. Be prepared to wait if you order oysters or the Irish stew. The frame of the Brittanic (the Titanic's sister ship), serves as décor for the upstairs restaurant, Flannigans, and is well worth a look.
⊟

Duke of York
◆ **C** B2
3 Commercial Court
Tel. (028) 90241062
Open Mon.–Sat.
10am–1am
Bar food served at lunchtime and live music on Friday and Saturday nights.
♫ ⋅

Kelly's Cellars
◆ **C** B2-B3
30 Bank St.
Tel. (028) 90 32 48 35
Pub food served
10am–7pm
Live mixed music on Fridays, jazz and blues on Saturdays.
⊟ ⋅ ♫ ⋅

RESTAURANTS
- ■ <€15/<£11
- ■ €15–30/£11–22
- ■ €30–45/£22–33
- ⊞ >€45/>£33

Kitchen Bar
◆ C C2
16–18 Victoria Square
Tel. (028) 90 32 49 01
Bar food served
11am–6pm
*Traditional music on
Friday evenings.
B&B next door.*
■ C 🍴 ▣

→ RESTAURANTS
Deanes
◆ C B3
24–40 Howard St.
Tel. (028) 90 33 11 34
Bar:
open daily
noon–2pm
and 5.30–10.45pm.
Restaurant:
Open Tue.–Sat.
7–9.30pm.
Closed 2 weeks in
Jan., 1 week in Jul.
*Both the ground
floor bar and the
upstairs restaurant
are sophisticated
and exotic, with
corresponding
service. Reservations
essential.*
■ ▣

Larrys' Piano Bar
and Restaurant
◆ C B4
21 Bedford St.
Tel. (028) 90 32 50 61
Open Tue.–Sat.
5pm–1am
*Young, friendly
atmosphere.
Piano-bar daily
6–10pm and live
music on Fridays and
Saturdays.
Reservations
recommended.*
■ 🍴 ▣

→ ACCOMMODATION
Dukes Hotel
◆ C B5
65–67 University St.
Belfast
BT7 1HL
Tel. (028) 90 23 66 66
Fax (028) 90 23 71 77
www.dukes-hotel.com
info@dukes-hotel-
belfast.co.uk
*Bed & Breakfast.
One of the most
stately Victorian
buildings in Belfast,
converted into a
luxury hotel. Only a
few steps from the
Ulster Museum*

*and the botanical
gardens. Elegant
restaurant and
friendly bar.*
■ C 🍴 ▣

Europa Hotel
◆ C A4
Great Victoria St.
Belfast
BT2 7AP
Tel. (028) 90 32 70 00
Fax (028) 90 32 78 00
jn@eur.hostinghotels.
com
*An imposing
building located
near the Opera, the
Europa Hotel is ideal
for business people.
Fine restaurant.
Parking nearby.*
■ 🍴 C ▣ ⊞

**BUSHMILLS,
CO. ANTRIM (N.I.)**

◆ E E1

→ ACCOMMODATION
The Bushmills Inn
9 Dunluce Rd.
Bushmills
BT57 8QG
Tel. (028) 20 73 23 39
Fax (028) 20 73 20 48
www.bushmillsinn.
com
mail@bushmillsinn.
com
*Only a few minutes
from the famous
distillery, this former
post house has been
superbly restored,
recreating the old
atmosphere thanks
to the gas lights and
peat fire. Don't miss
the unusual library
and its secret door.*
■ 🍴 C ▣ ♨ P ▣

The Causeway
Hotel
40 Causeway Rd.
Bushmills
BT57 8SU
Tel. (028) 20 73 12 26
Fax (028) 20 73 25 52
www.giants-causeway-
hotel.com
reception@giants-
causeway-hotel.com
*This small hotel
has overlooked
the the Giant's
Causeway since
1836. Half-board
available.*
■ ▲ ♨ ▣

**CARNLOUGH,
CO. ANTRIM (N.I.)**

◆ E F2

→ ACCOMMODATION
The Londonderry
Arms hotel
20 Harbour Rd.,
Carnlough (Glens
of Antrim)
BT44 0EU
Tel. (028) 28 88 52 55
Fax (028) 28 88 52 63
lda@glensofantrim.
com
*Former post house
built by Lady
Londonderry in
1848 and inherited
by her grandson,
Winston Churchill,
in 1921.*
■ 🍴 P ▣

**CASTLEWELLAN,
CO. DOWN (N.I.)**

◆ E E4

→ ACCOMMODATION
Chestnut Inn
28–32 Lower Sq.
Castlewellan
BT31 9DW
Tel. (028) 43 77 82 47
Fax (028) 43 77 82 47
chestnutinn@lineone.
com
*Open all year round.
Comfortable and
friendly bed &
breakfast, with a
perfect location in
the heart of the
old town near the
Dundrum Bay
beaches and forests,
and close to the
Royal County Down
Golf course.*
■ C 🍴 ▣

**DERRY,
CO. DERRY (N.I.)**

◆ E D2

→ PUB
Metro Bar
3 Bank Place
Tel. (048) 71 26 74 01
Open Mon.–Sat.
Bar food served
noon–3pm (until
4pm on Sat.).
*The Metro turns
into a feverish
place at the
weekend thanks to
its lively DJ.*
■ C 🍴 ▣

→ ACCOMMODATION
Beech Hill Country
House Hotel
32 Ardmore Rd.
BT47 3QP
Tel. (028) 71 34 92 79
Fax (028) 71 34 53 66
info@beechhill.com
Closed Dec. 25–26
*Located two miles
from Derry and set
in the grounds of a
32-acre property
dating from the
early 18th century.
Spacious rooms and
suites with Victorian
furniture. Very
generous breakfast
and fine restaurant
(from £25); the bar
is also popular
with regular local
customers.*
■ 🍴 ▲ P ▣

Waterfoot Hotel
Caw Roundabout
14 Clooney Rd.
Tel. (028) 71 34 55 00
Fax (028) 71 31 10 06
www.thewaterfoot
hotel.co.uk
Closed Dec. 25–26
*Right by the
opening of the
Inishowen peninsula,
this hotel is an ideal
base for all types of
activities: visits to the
local historical sites,
rounds of golf,
walks along the
numerous beaches,
and fishing in the
rivers. Dinner from
£15.*
■ 🍴 ⋈ P ▣

**DONEGAL,
CO. DONEGAL**

◆ E B2-B3

→ ACCOMMODATION
St Ernan's
House Hotel
Donegal
Tel. (073) 21065
Fax (073) 22098
www.sainternans.com
info@sainternans.com
Closed end
Oct.–Easter
*Very romantic
place located on a
10-acre wooded
islet accessible
only by a sea wall.
Tranquility and
privacy guaranteed.*

◆ PUBS, RESTAURANTS AND ACCOMMODATION
ULSTER

HOTELS
▪	<€70/<£50
▪▪	€70–110/£50–80
▪▪▪	€110–180/£80–130
▦	>€180/>£130

Dinner served to residents (around €24–€45).
▯▯▮▯▦ ▯▯

DUNGANNON, CO. TYRONE (N.I.)

◆ **E** D3

→ **ACCOMMODATION**
Grange Lodge Country House
N. & R. Brown
7 Grange Rd.
Dungannon
BT7 17EJ
Tel. (028877) 84212
Fax (028877) 84313
grangelodge@ireland.com
Closed
Dec. 25–Jan. 1
Located one mile from the M1 (junction 15), this small Georgian residence offers a cosy atmosphere. The rooms are full of the scent of freshly cut flowers mingling with the appetizing smell of the Brandy Snaps prepared by the owner in the kitchen. Warm, friendly welcome from Norah and Ralph Brown.
▯▯▮▯▮

ENNISKILLEN, CO. FERMANAGH

◆ **E** C4

→ **PUB**
Blake's of the Hollow
6 Church St.
Tel. (048) 66 32 21 43
Traditional music on Thur. and Fri.
▯▯♫

FAHAN, CO. DONEGAL

◆ **E** D1

→ **PUB-RESTAURANT**
St. John's Country House and Restaurant
Fahan
Inishowen
Tel. (077) 60289
stjohnsrestaurant@eircom.net
Restaurant open

Tue.–Sat. 7–9pm,
Sun. 1–2.30pm
Closed at Christmas
A dream of a place surrounded by beautiful gardens by the sea. Restaurant and 5 beautiful rooms (€89–€190).
▯▯▮▮

GIANT'S CAUSEWAY, CO. ANTRIM (N.I.)

◆ **E** E1

→ **PUB-RESTAURANT**
Smuggler's Inn Guest House and Restaurant
306 White Park Rd.
Tel. (048) 20 73 15 77
www.smugglers-inn.co.uk
Restaurant open daily 12.30–9pm
Family atmosphere and refined service in this establishment that combines restaurant, bar and guesthouse (12 rooms: €165–€190 per night, dinner included).
▯▯▯▮

GLENCOLUMBKILLE, CO. DONEGAL

◆ **E** A2

→ **PUB-RESTAURANT**
An Chistin Restaurant
Foras Cultuir Uladh
Glencolumbkille
Open daily
9.30am–9.30pm
Tel. (073) 30213
Closed Nov.–Mar.
Candle-lit dinner accompanied with pleasant traditional music in the background. Fine choice of vegetarian dishes and fish specialties.
▯▯▮

GREENCASTLE, CO. DONEGAL

◆ **E** D1

→ **PUB-RESTAURANT**
Kealy's Seafood Bar
Greencastle
Inishowen

Tel. (077) 81010
Open June–Nov.:
Tue.-Sun.;
Dec.–May:
Thur.–Sun.
Sunday lunch 1–3m
Live traditional music in summer.
▯▯♫▮

HILLSBOROUGH, CO. DOWN (N.I.)

◆ **E** E4

→ **PUB-RESTAURANT**
Hillside Bar and Restaurant
21 Main St.
Tel. (048) 92 68 27 65
Open daily
noon–10pm
Café-style menus (daily) or meals à la carte (Fri.–Sat.). Jazz on Sundays between 7.30pm and 9.30pm, and a fine range of real ales and four locally brewed beers (two English, two Irish).
▯▯▮

HOLYWOOD, CO. DOWN (N.I.)

◆ **E** F3

→ **ACCOMMODATION**
Culloden Hotel
142 Bangor Rd.
Holywood
Tel. (028) 90 42 52 23
Fax (028) 90 42 67 77
www.hastingshotels.com
res@cull.hastings
hotels.com
Closed Dec. 25.
Luxury hotel with a garden and set in 12 acres of woods only a few miles from Belfast and overlooking the bay. Ideal for those seeking peace and quiet or for tennis, sailing and golf enthusiasts.
▯▮▰▯▦

KILCAR, CO. DONEGAL

◆ **E** A2

→ **PUB**
The Piper's Rest
Main St.

Tel. (075) 38205
Pretty, thatched roof pub with live music in summer.
♫

LETTERKENNY, CO. DONEGAL

◆ **E** C2

→ **ACCOMMODATION**
Castlegrove House
Ramelton Rd.
Letterkenny
Tel. (074) 51118
Fax (074) 51384
castlegrove1@hotmail.com
Closed Dec. 23–28
17th-century residence offering spacious and comfortable rooms with a view over Lake Swilly. Dinner prepared with fresh produce from the garden is available to residents.
▯▯▮▯▦

LOUGH ESKE, CO. DONEGAL

◆ **E** B3

→ **ACCOMMODATION**
Ardnamona
Lough Eske
Tel. (073) 22650
Fax (073) 22819
www.ardnamona.com
mail@ardnamona.com
Closed for a week between Christmas and New Year
In the 19th century this house was called "one of the most picturesque in rural Ireland". Spacious rooms with a view over the classified garden famous for its rhododendrons.
▯▯▮▯▦

Harvey's Point Country Hotel
Lough Eske
Tel. (073) 22208
Fax (073) 22352
reservations@harveys
point.com
Not to be missed. Hidden behind lush vegetation in the Donegal hills and by Lake Eske, this is the

RESTAURANTS
- ■ <€15/<£11
- ■ €15–30/£11–22
- ■ €30–45/£22–33
- ⊞ >€45/>£33

---

perfect place for a tranquil, relaxing stay. French specialties.
◻♣🏠⛷🏊

OMAGH, CO. TYRONE (I. N.)

◆ E C3

→ **PUB-RESTAURANT**
Hawthorn House Hotel
72 Old Mountfield Rd.
Tel. (048) 82 25 20 05
Restaurant open daily 12.30–2.30pm and 6–10pm
Surrounded by magnificent gardens and located near a leisure park, this restaurant also has 5 rooms available for visitors wishing to stay on (£60).
◻🏊

PORTAFERRY, CO. DOWN (N.I.)

◆ E F4

→ **ACCOMMODATION**
Portaferry Hotel
10 The Strand
Portaferry
BT22 1PE
Tel. (028) 42 72 82 31
Fax (028) 42 72 89 99
info@portaferryhotel. com
Closed Dec. 25
At the mouth of Lake Stranford, this hotel is perfect for those who wish to visit the Ards peninsula. Nature lovers must not forget to bring binoculars as Stranford Bay is a renowned bird sanctuary.
◻⛷🏊

PORTBALLINTRAE, CO. ANTRIM (N.I.)

◆ F E1

→ **PUB-RESTAURANT**
Sweeney's Bar and Restaurant
6b Seaport Ave.
Tel. (048) 20 73 24 05
Open daily noon–9pm
An address well

---

worth a visit for the "best Guinness in the country"!
■

PORTRUSH, CO. ANTRIM (I. N.)

◆ E E1

→ **PUBS-RESTAURANTS**
The Coast Pizza-Pasta Bar
The Harbour
Tel. (048) 70 82 33 11
Open Wed.–Mon. 2.30–10pm
Young, relaxed atmosphere. Fine selection of pizzas and pasta.
◻■■

Ramore Wine Bar
The Harbour
Portrush
Tel. (028) 70 82 43 13
Fax (028) 70 82 31 94
Open Mon.–Sat. 12.15–2.15pm and 5–10pm,
Sun. 12.30–3pm and 5–9pm
Winebar offering reasonably-priced menus of pasta, salads and seafood, served with a good selection of wines.
◻■■

Ramore Restaurant
Next door to the Wine Bar, the

Ramore Restaurant, run by chef George Mc Alpin, was the first to serve delicious "new wave" cuisine in Northern Ireland. Prices in accordance.
◻■⊞

PORTSTEWART, CO. DERRY (N.I.)

◆ E E1

→ **PUB-RESTAURANT**
Morelli's
57 The Promenade
Tel. (048) 70 83 21 50
Open May–Sep. 9am–11pm;
Oct.–Apr. 9am–6.30pm
Snack-bar that should reopen in spring 2002, following a long restoration period.
■

RATHMULLAN, CO. DONEGAL

◆ E C1

→**PUB-RESTAURANT**
Rathmullan House
Lough Swilly
Rathmullan
Tel. (074) 58188
Open Mar.–Nov.
Visitors to the area

---

who do not stay at the beautiful Rathmullan House should at least stop for a meal or a drink and enjoy its remarkable setting.
◻♣P🏊

→ **ACCOMMODATION**
Rathmullan House
Lough Swilly
Rathmullan
Tel. (074) 58188
Fax (074) 58200
info@rathmullanhouse. com
Open Mar.–Nov.
The gardens of this graceful country house stretch all the way down to the deserted Lake Swill beach. Elegant lounges and dining room, charming rooms all furnished and decorated in different styles.
◻♣🏠⛷🏊

Shandon Hotel
Marble Hill Strand
Sheephaven Bay
Tel. (074) 36137
Fax (074) 36430
www.shandonhotel. com
shandonhotel @eircom.net
Closed Nov.–Mar. 15
Comfortable, modern hotel overlooking Sheephaven Bay. Half-board available. Dinner open to non-residents (reservations compulsory).
◻♣✖⛷P🏊

TORY ISLAND, CO. DONEGAL

◆ E B1

→ **ACCOMMODATION**
Tory Island Hotel
Tel. (074) 35920
Fax (074) 35613
ostantory@eircom. net
Closed Dec.–Mar.
This hotel offers a pleasant stay on the primitive painters' island.
◻🏊

◆ PLACES TO VISIT

Towns and cities are listed in alphabetical order.
Those located in Northern Ireland are followed by (N. I.).
The ◆ symbol refers to the map section; the ▲ symbol refers to the Itineraries section.

ADARE		◆ F D3
DESMOND CASTLE Tel. (021) 77 48 55	*Open Apr. 15–June 15 Tue.–Sat. 10am–6pm;* *June 16–Apr. 14 daily 10am–2pm.*	▲ 250
ANNAGHMORE (N.I.)		◆ E D4
ARDRESS HOUSE Tel. (028) 38 85 12 36	*Open July–Aug. daily 2–6pm;* *Sep–June Sat.–Sun. 2–6pm.*	▲ 324
ARDFERT		◆ F B3
ARDFERT CATHEDRAL	*Open June 15–Sep.15 daily 9.30am–6.30pm.*	▲ 239
ARDMORE		◆ F F5
HISTORIC SEASIDE VILLAGE Tel. (024) 94444	*Open to the public.*	▲ 221
ARKLOW		◆ G C3
MARITIME MUSEUM St Mary's Rd. Tel. (0402) 32868	*Open daily 10am–1pm and 2–5pm.*	▲ 180
ARMAGH (N.I.)		◆ E D4
ARCHBISHOP'S PALACE AND PALACE STABLES HERITAGE CENTRE Tel. (028) 37 52 96 29	*Open May 15–Sep. Mon.–Sat. 10am–5.30pm,* *Sun. 1–6pm; Sep.–May 14 Mon.–Sat. 10am–5pm,* *Sun. 2–5pm.*	▲ 323
ARMAGH COUNTY MUSEUM The Mall East Tel. (028) 37 52 30 70	*Open Mon.–Fri. 10am–5pm and Sat. 10am–1pm* *and 2–5pm.*	▲ 323
ARMAGH PLANETARIUM College Hill Tel. (028) 37523689	*Open Apr.–Aug. Mon.–Fri. 10am–4.45pm,* *Sat.–Sun. 1.15–4.45pm; Sep.–Mar. Mon.–Fri.* *10am– 4.45pm, Sat. noon–4.45pm.*	▲ 323
MUSEUM OF THE ROYAL IRISH FUSILIERS Tel. (028) 37 52 29 11	*Open Mon.–Fri. 10am–12.30pm and 1.30–4pm.*	▲ 323
NAVAN FORT & CENTRE Killkylea Rd. Tel. (028) 37 52 55 50	*Open Apr.–Sep. Mon.–Fri. 10am–6pm,* *Sat.–Sun. 11am–6pm; Oct.–Mar. Mon.–Fri.* *10am–5pm, Sat.–Sun. 11am–5pm.*	▲ 322
PEATLANDS PARK Peatlands Park, Milltown Tel. (028) 37 85 11 02	*Open daily 9am–6pm.*	▲ 324
ST PATRICK'S CATHOLIC CATHEDRAL Cathedral Rd.	*Open daily 8am–4pm.*	▲ 323
ST PATRICK'S PROTESTANT CATHEDRAL Abbey St. Tel. (028) 37 52 31 42	*Open Apr.–Oct. daily 10am–5pm and* *Nov–Mar. daily 10am–4pm.*	▲ 323
ST PATRICK'S TRIAN 40 English Street Tel. (028) 37 52 18 01	*Open Apr.–Sep. Mon.–Sat. 10am–5.30pm, Sun.* *1–6pm; Oct.–Mar. Mon.–Sat. 10am–5pm, Sun.* *2–5pm.*	▲ 323
ASHFORD		◆ G C3
MOUNT USHER GARDENS Tel. (0404) 40205	*Open Mar. 15–Oct. daily 10.30am–6pm.*	▲ 179
ATHLONE		◆ F F1
JOHN'S CASTLE Tel. (0902) 94603	*Open May–Oct.15 daily 10am–5pm.*	▲ 208
BALLINASLOE		◆ E A6, F E1
CLONTUSKERT PRIORY 3¾ miles south of Ballinasloe	*The priory is in the middle of a field. Permission* *must be requested from the farmer before crossing* *his land.*	▲ 202
BALLINCOLLIG		◆ F D5
THE ROYAL GUNPOWDER MILLS Tel. (021) 87 44 30	*Open May–Sep. daily 10am–6pm.*	▲ 215
BALLINTOY (N.I.)		◆ E F1
CARRICK-A-REDE BRIDGE Tel. (028) 20 73 11 59	*Rope bridge linking the mainland to an islet. In* *place between April and September and used by* *salmon fishermen. Free access.*	▲ 314

BALLYARNETT (N.I.)		◆ E D2
AMELIA EARHEART COTTAGE Tel. (028) 71 35 40 40	*Open Mon.–Thur. 9am–4.30pm and Fri. 9am–1pm.*	▲ 320
BALLYCASTLE (N.I.)		◆ E F1
CÉIDE FIELDS Tel. (096) 43325	*Open daily June–Sep. 9.30am–6.30pm, Mar.–May daily 9.30am–6.30pm; Nov. daily 10am–4.30pm.*	
BALLYFOYLE		◆ G A3
DUNMORE CAVES 6¼ miles from Kilkenny on the N78 Tel. (056) 67726	*Open Apr.–May daily 10am–5pm; June.–Sep. daily 9.30am–6.30pm.*	▲ 187
BALLYMAHON		◆ E B6
CORLEA BOG EXHIBITION CENTRE Tel. (043) 22386 (summer) and (01) 647 30 00 (winter)	*Open Apr.–May daily 10am–5pm; June.–Sep. daily 9.30am–6.30pm.*	
BALLYVAUGHAN		◆ F D1
AILLWEE CAVE Tel. (065) 707 70 36	*Open Oct.–Mar. daily 10am–6pm; July–Aug. daily 10am–7pm.*	▲ 243
BANBRIDGE/LISBURN (N.I.)		◆ E E4
IRISH LINEN TOUR The Linen Homelands 200 Newry Rd. Tel. (028) 40 62 33 22	*Open May–Sep. daily 10am–4pm. One-day tour.*	▲ 307
BANTRY		◆ F B5
BANTRY HOUSE Tel. (027) 50047	*Open July–Aug. 9am–7pm; Sep.–June 9am–6pm, except Mar.–Oct. 9am–5pm.*	▲ 225
BELFAST (N.I.)		◆ E F3
BELFAST CASTLE Antrim Rd. Tel. (028) 90 77 69 25	*Open Mar.–Oct. daily 9am–6pm. Closed Nov.–Feb.*	▲ 302
BELFAST ZOO Antrim Rd. Tel. (028) 90 77 62 77	*Open Apr.–Sep. daily 10am–5pm; Oct.–Mar. daily 10am–3.30pm (Fri. 2.30pm).*	
BOTANIC GARDENS Tel. (028) 90 32 49 02	*Open Mon.–Fri. 10am–5pm, Sat. 1–5pm and Sun. 2–5pm.*	◆ C B6 ▲ 302
CITY HALL Donegal Square Tel. (028) 90 27 04 56	*Guided tours June–Sep.: Mon.–Fri. at 10.30am, 11.30am, 2.30pm and Sat. at 2.30pm; Oct.–May: Mon.–Sat. at 2.30pm.*	◆ C B3 ▲ 305
GRAND OPERA HOUSE Great Victoria St. Tel. (028) 90 24 91 29	*Open Mon.–Fri. 9.30am–5.30pm.*	◆ C A3 ▲ 304
LINEN HALL LIBRARY 17 Donegall Square Tel. (028) 90 32 17 07	*Open Mon.–Fri. 9.30am–6.30pm, Thur. 9.30am–8.30pm, Sat. 9.30am–4pm.*	◆ C B3 ▲ 303
OLD MUSEUM 7 College Square North Tel. (028) 90 23 50 53	*Open Mon.–Sat. 10am–5.30pm.*	◆ C A3
ROYAL ULSTER RIFLES MUSEUM War Memorial Building Tel. (028) 90 23 20 86	*Open Mon.–Fri. 9.30am–4.30pm.*	◆ C B1
ST GEORGE'S CHURCH High St. Tel. (028) 90 23 12 75	*Open daily 9.30am–1.30pm.*	◆ C B2 ▲ 304
ST MALACHY'S CHURCH Alfred St. Tel. (028) 90 32 17 13	*Open daily 8am–6pm.*	◆ C B4 ▲ 304
ULSTER MUSEUM Botanic Gardens, Stranmilis Rd. Tel. (028) 90 38 30 00	*Open Mon.–Fri. 10am–5pm, Sat. 1–5pm, Sun. 2–5pm.*	◆ C A6 ▲ 305
BENBURB (N.I.)		◆ E D4
BENBURB CASTLE & HERITAGE CENTRE 10 Main St. Tel. (028) 37 54 81 87	*Open Mon.–Thur. 9am–5pm, Sat. 9am–1.30pm.*	▲ 324

◆ PLACES TO VISIT

CARROWMORE		◆ E A4	
CARROWMORE MEGALITHIC BURIAL SITE Tel. (071) 61534	Open May–Sep. daily 9.30am–6.30pm.		▲ 288
CASHEL		◆ F E3-E4	
ROCK OF CASHEL Tel. (062) 61437	Open June–Sep. daily 9am–6.50pm; Mar.–May daily 9.30am–4.30pm and 9.30am–4.50pm the rest of the year.		▲ 252
CASTLEISLAND		◆ F C4	
CRAG CAVE Tel. (066) 714 12 44	Open Mar. 16–Oct. daily 10am–6.30pm; July–Aug. daily 10am–6.30pm.		
CASTLECOVE		◆ F A5	
STAIGUE FORT Tel. (066) 915 11 88	Private property.		▲ 229
CASTLEREA		◆ E A5	
CLONALIS HOUSE Tel. (0907) 20014	Open June–Sep. Tue.–Sun. 11am–5pm.		▲ 290
CASTLEROCK (N.I.)		◆ E E1	
MUSSENDEN TEMPLE Mussenden Rd. Tel. (028) 70 84 87 28	Open July–Aug noon–6pm; Apr.–June and Sep. Sat.–Sun. noon–6pm.		▲ 315
CELBRIDGE		◆ G B1	
CASTLETOWN HOUSE Tel. (01) 628 82 52	Open Apr.–Sep. Mon.–Fri. 10am–6pm, Sat. 11am–6pm, Sun. and public hols. 2–6pm; Oct. Mon.–Fri. 10am–5pm, Sun. and public hols. 2–5pm; Nov.–Mar. Sun. 2–5pm.		▲ 182
CHURCH HILL		◆ E B1	
THE GLEBE HOUSE & GALLERY Tel. (074) 37071	Open May–Sep. daily except Fri. 11am–6.30pm.		▲ 298
GLENVEAGH CASTLE Tel. (074) 37090	Open Mar. 15–Nov. 15 daily 10am–6.30pm.		▲ 298
GLENVEAGH NATIONAL PARK Tel. (074) 37088	Open Mar. 15–Nov. 15 daily 10am–6.30pm; June–Aug. daily 10.30am–7.30pm.		▲ 298
CLARA		◆ F F1	
CLARA BOG Tel. (0506) 52617	Open June–Aug. daily 2–6pm.		
CLEAR ISLAND		◆ F B6	
HERITAGE CENTRE West Cork Tel. (028) 39153 or 39135	Free admission. Organized guided tours during the Heather Festival in Aug.		
CLONAKILTY		◆ F C6	
MICHAEL COLLINS MEMORIAL CENTRE	Information: Clonakilt tourist office. Tel. (023) 33226		▲ 224
WEST CORK REGIONAL MUSEUM Tel. (023) 33226 (Clonakilty tourist office)	Open Mon.–Sat. 10.30am–12.30pm and 2–5.30pm, Sun. 3–5pm.		▲ 224
CLONFERT		◆ F F1	
CLONFERT CATHEDRAL	Ask the owner of the house opposite for the key.		▲ 202
CLONMACNOIS		◆ F F1	
CLONMACNOIS & WEST OFFALY RAILWAY Tel. (0905) 74114	Open Apr.–Oct. daily 10am–5pm. Visit of a peat bog farm by train (departure: every hour, duration: 45 mins).		
CLOYNE		◆ F E5	
CLOYNE CATHEDRAL	Open May–Sep. daily 10am–6pm.		▲ 220
COBH		◆ F D5	
CATHEDRAL OF ST COLMAN Tel. (021) 481 32 22	Open daily 8am–6pm.		▲ 219

QUEENSTOWN PROJECT Tel. (021) 481 35 91	*Open 10am–6pm daily (admission until 5pm).*	▲ *218*
COLMCILLE		◆ E C2
COLMCILLE HERITAGE CENTRE Tel. (074) 37044	*Open May–Sep. daily 15 10.30am–6.30pm.* *Groups by appointment.*	▲ *298*
CONG		◆ D B5
CONG ABBEY Tel. (01) 661 31 11 (OPW)	*Open to the public.*	▲ *269*
COOKSTOWN (N.I.)		◆ E D3
WELLBROOK BEETLING MILL Tel. (016487) 51735	*Open daily except Tue. 2–6pm.*	
CORK CITY		◆ F D5, A
CORK ARTS SOCIETY GALLERY 16 Lavitts Quay Tel. (021) 427 77 49	*Open Mon.–Sat. 10am–6pm.*	◆ A B4 ▲ *212*
CORK PUBLIC MUSEUM Fitzgerald Park Tel. (021) 427 06 79	*Open Mon.–Fri. 11am–1pm and 2.15–5pm* *and Sun. 3–5pm.*	◆ A C2 ▲ *215*
CRAWFORD MUNICIPAL **ART GALLERY** Emmett Place Tel. (021) 4273377	*Open Mon.–Sat. 10am–5pm.*	◆ A B4 ▲ *214*
HOLY TRINITY CHURCH Father Matthew Quay Tel. (021) 427 08 27	*Open to the public.*	◆ A C5 ▲ *213*
HONAN CHAPEL University College Tel. (021) 427 68 71	*Open Mon.–Fri. 10am–5pm.* *On the university grounds.*	◆ A C2 ▲ *214*
ST ANNE'S ANGLICAN CHURCH Shandon Tel. (021) 50 16 72	*Open May–Oct. Mon.–Sat. 9.30am–5pm;* *Nov.–Apr. Mon.–Sat. 10am–3. 30pm.*	◆ A A4 ▲ *215*
ST FINNBARR'S CATHEDRAL Bishop St. Tel. (021) 496 33 87	*Open daily 9am–6pm.*	◆ A C5 ▲ *214*
ST MARY'S CATHEDRAL Sharman Crawford St. Tel. (021) 30 43 25	*Open daily 8am–6pm.*	◆ A A4 ▲ *215*
TRISKEL ART CENTRE Tobin St. Tel. (021) 427 20 22	*Open Mon.–Fri. 11am–4pm and Sat. 11am–5pm.*	◆ A B4 ▲ *212*
COROFIN		◆ F D2
CLARE HERITAGE CENTRE Tel. (065) 6837955	*Open Easter–Oct. 9.30am–5.30pm.*	▲ *246*
CREESLOUGH		◆ E C1
DOE CASTLE On the N 56, just before Creeslough Tel. (074) 683 79 55	*Site open to the public.*	▲ *297*
DERRY (N.I.)		◆ E D2
GUILDHALL Tel. (028) 71 37 65 06	*Open Mon.–Fri. 9am–5pm.* *Visits by appointment July–Aug.*	▲ *320*
HEZLETT HOUSE Tel. (028) 70 84 85 67	*Open July–Aug. daily noon–5pm;* *Apr.–June and Sep. Sat.–Sun. noon–5pm.*	
ST COLUMBA'S CATHEDRAL (CHURCH OF IRELAND) Tel. (028) 71 26 27 46	*Open Apr.–Oct. Mon.–Sat. 9am–5pm;* *Nov.–Mar. Mon.–Sat. 9am–4pm.*	▲ *319*
TOWER MUSEUM Union Hall Place Tel. (028) 71 37 24 1	*Open July–Aug. daily 10am–5pm;* *Sep.–June Tue.–Sat. 10am–5pm.*	▲ *320*
DONEGAL		◆ E B2-B3
DONEGAL CASTLE Tel. (073) 22405	*Open Easter–Oct. daily 9.30am–5.45pm.*	▲ *294*

PLACES TO VISIT ◆

DOWNPATRICK (N.I.) ◆ E F4

CASTLE WARD HOUSE Strangford Tel. (028) 44 88 12 04	Open June–Sep. 15 daily except Thur. 1–6pm; Oct.–May Sat.–Sun. 1–6pm.	▲ 306
CATHEDRAL OF DOWNPATRICK Tel. (028) 44 61 49 22	Open Mon.–Sat. 9am–5pm, Sun. 2–5pm.	▲ 306
ST PATRICK CENTRE 53 Lower Market St. Tel. (028) 44 61 90 00	Open June–Aug. Mon.–Sat. 9.30am–7pm, Sun. 10am–6pm; Sep.–May Mon.–Sat. 9.30am–5.30pm, Sun. 10am–6pm.	▲ 306

DROGHEDA ◆ E E6

MELLIFONT ABBEY 5 miles northwest of Drogheda Tel. (041) 26459	Open June 16–Sep. 15 daily 9.30am–6.30pm; Sep. 16–June 15 daily 10am–5pm.	▲ 198
MONASTERBOICE 6¼ miles northwest of Drogheda	Site open to the public.	▲ 198
ST PETER'S CHURCH West St.	Open daily 8.30am–8pm.	▲ 197

DRUMCLIFF ◆ E A3

| **DRUMCLIFF MONASTERY** Tel. (071) 63133 | Site open to the public. | ▲ 286 |
| **LISSADELL HOUSE** 8 miles north of Sligo Tel. (071) 63150 | Open June–Sep. 15 Mon.–Sat. 10.30am–12.15pm and 2–4.30pm. | ▲ 286 |

DUBLIN ◆ G C1, B

BANK OF IRELAND 2 College Green, Dublin 2 Tel. (01) 677 68 01	Open Mon.–Fri. 10am–4pm, Thur. 10am–5pm. Guided tours Tue. at 10.30am, 11.30am and 1.45pm.	◆ B E4 ▲ 148
CASINO MARINO Malahide Rd., Dublin 3 Tel. (01) 833 16 18	Open June–Sep. daily 10am–6.30pm.	▲ 174
CHRIST CHURCH CATHEDRAL Christ Church Place, Dublin 8 Tel. (01) 677 80 99	Open daily 10am–5pm.	◆ B D4 ▲ 168
CITY HALL Cork Hill, Dublin 2 Tel. (01) 679 61 11	Open Mon.–Fri. 9am–1pm and 2.15–5pm.	◆ B D4 ▲ 167
CUSTOM HOUSE Custom House Quay, Dublin 1 Tel. (01) 878 76 60	Open Mar. 16–Oct. Mon.–Fri. 10am–5pm, Sat.–Sun. 2–5pm; Nov.–Mar. 15 Wed.–Fri. 10am–5pm.	◆ B E4 ▲ 144
DUBLIN CASTLE Dame St., Dublin 2 Tel. (01) 671 71 29	Open Mar. 15–Nov. Mon.–Fri. 10am–5pm, Sat.–Sun. 2–5pm.	◆ B D5 ▲ 167
DUBLIN'S WRITERS' MUSEUM 18 Parnell Square North, Dublin 1 Tel. (01) 872 20 77 Fax (01) 872 22 31	Open Mon.–Sat. 10am–5pm, Sun. and public hols. 11am–5pm; June–Aug. Mon.–Fri. 10am–7pm, Sat. 10am–5pm, Sun. 11.30–6pm.	◆ B D3 ▲ 146
DUBLIN ZOO & ZOOLOGICAL SOCIETY OF IRELAND Phoenix Park, Dublin 8 Tel. (01) 677 14 25	Open Mar.–Oct. Mon.–Sat. 9.30am–6pm, Sun. 10.30am–6pm; Nov.–Feb. Mon.–Sat. 9.30am–4pm, Sun. 10.30am–4pm.	◆ B A3 ▲ 171
DUBLINIA St Michael's Hill, Dublin 8 Tel. (01) 679 46 11	Open Apr.–Sep. 10am–5pm; Oct.–Mar. Mon.–Sat. 11am–4pm, Sun. 10am–4.30pm.	
FOUR COURTS Aras Ui Dhalaigh, Inns Quay, Dublin 7 Tel. (01) 872 55 55	Open Mon.–Fri. 11am–1pm and 2–4pm.	◆ B D4 ▲ 146
GLASNEVIN CEMETARY Finglas Road, Glasnevin, Dublin 9	Open Mon.–Fri. 8am–4.30pm, Sat. 8am–1pm and 2–4pm, Sun. 10.30am–5.30pm.	
GUINNESS BREWERY St James's Gate, Crane St., Dublin 8 Tel. (01) 453 67 00	Open Mon.–Sat. 9.30am–5pm, Sun. 10.30am–4.30pm.	▲ 170

HUGH LANE MUNICIPAL GALLERY OF MODERN ART Parnell Square North, Dublin 1 Tel. (01) 874 19 03	*Open Tue.–Thur. 9.30am–6pm, Fri.–Sat. 9.30am–5pm.*	◆ **B** D3 ▲ *146*
KILMAINHAM PRISON Inchicore Rd., Dublin 8 Tel. (01) 453 59 84	*Open May–Sep. daily 9.30am–4.45pm; Oct.–Apr. Mon.–Fri. 9.30am–3.45pm, Sun. 10am–4.45pm.*	◆ **B** A5 ▲ *171*
LEINSTER HOUSE Dáil Éireann, Kildare St., Dublin 2 Tel. (01) 678 99 11	*Reservations in writing.*	◆ **B** E5 ▲ *160*
MARSH'S LIBRARY St Patrick's Close, Dublin 8 Tel. (01) 454 35 11	*Open Mon., Wed.–Fri. 10am–12.45pm and 2–5pm, Sat. 10.30am–12.45pm.*	◆ **B** D5 ▲ *169*
NATIONAL BOTANIC GARDENS Glasnevin, Dublin 9 Tel. (01) 837 43 88	*Open July–Aug. Mon.–Sat. 10am–6pm, Sun. 11am–6pm; Sep.–June Mon.–Sat. 10am–4.30pm, Sun. 11am–4.30pm.*	◆ **B** C1-D1 ▲ *173*
NATIONAL GALLERY OF IRELAND Merrion Square West, Dublin 2 Tel. (01) 661 51 33	*Open Mon.–Sat. 10am–5.30pm (Thur. 8.30pm), Sun. 2–5pm.*	◆ **B** E5 ▲ *160*
NATIONAL MUSEUM OF IRELAND Kildare St., Dublin 2 Tel. (01) 677 74 44	*Open Tue.–Sat. 10am–5pm, Sun. 2–5pm.*	◆ **B** E5 ▲ *157*
NATURAL HISTORY MUSEUM Merrion St., Dublin 2 Tel. (01) 661 88 11	*Open Tue.–Sat. 10am–5pm, Sun. 2–5pm.*	◆ **B** D5 ▲ *160*
NEWMAN HOUSE 85–86 St Stephen's Green South, Dublin 2 Tel. (01) 706 74 22	*Open June–Aug. Tue.–Fri. noon–5pm, Sat. 2–5pm, Sun. 11am–2pm.*	◆ **B** E5 ▲ *156*
NUMBER TWENTY NINE Lower Fitzwilliam St., Dublin 2 Tel. (01) 702 61 65	*Open Tue.–Sat. 10am–5pm, Sun. 2–5pm.*	◆ **B** F5
OLD JAMESON DISTILLERY ("WHISKEY CORNER") Smithfield, 77 Bow St., Dublin 7 Tel. (01) 807 23 55	*Open daily 9.30am–6pm.*	◆ **B** C4 ▲ *147*
POWERSCOURT TOWNHOUSE South William St., Dublin 2 Tel. (01) 679 41 44	*Open Mon.–Sat. 9am–6pm, Thur. 9am–7pm.*	◆ **B** E5 ▲ *149*
ROTUNDA HOSPITAL Parnell St., Dublin 1 Tel. (01) 873 07 00	*Visits by appointment.*	◆ **B** E3 ▲ *145*
ROYAL COLLEGE OF SURGEONS 123 St Stephen's Green, Dublin 2	*Closed to the public.*	◆ **B** E5 ▲ *156*
ROYAL HOSPITAL OF KILMAINHAM (IRISH MUSEUM OF MODERN ART) Kilmainham, Dublin 8 Tel. (01) 671 86 66	*Open Tue.–Sat. 10am–5.30pm, Sun. noon–5.30pm.*	◆ **B** A4-B4 ▲ *170*
ROYAL IRISH ACADEMY 19 Dawson St., Dublin 1 Tel. (01) 676 25 70	*Open Mon.–Fri. 10.30am–5.15pm. Guided tours by appointment.*	◆ **B** E5 ▲ *157*
ST AUDOEN'S CHURCH Cornmarket High Street, Dublin 1 Tel. (01) 677 00 88	*Open daily 8am–6pm.*	◆ **B** D4 ▲ *169*
ST MARY PRO CATHEDRAL 83 Marlborough St., Dublin 1 Tel. (01) 874 54 41	*Open daily 8am–6.30pm.*	◆ **B** E3 ▲ *145*
ST MARY'S ABBEY Meetinghouse Lane, Dublin 1 Tel. (01) 872 14 90	*Open June 15–Sep. 15. Wed. and Sun. 10am–5pm.*	◆ **B** D4 ▲ *147*
ST MICHAN'S CHURCH Church St., Dublin 1 Tel. (01) 872 41 54	*Open Mon.–Fri. 10am–12.45pm and 2–4.45pm, Sat. noon–12.45pm. Service at 10am on Sun.*	◆ **B** D4 ▲ *146*
ST PATRICK'S CATHEDRAL St Patrick's Close, Dublin 8 Tel. (01) 475 48 17	*Open Mon.–Fri. 9am–6pm, Sat. 9am–5pm, Sun. 10am–4.30pm.*	◆ **B** D5 ▲ *169*
ST WERBURGH'S CHURCH Werburgh St., Dublin 1 Tel. (01) 478 37 10	*Open Mon.–Fri. 10am–4pm.*	◆ **B** D4 ▲ *168*

TAILORS' GUILD HALL Back Lane, Dublin 8 Tel. (01) 454 47 94	*Open Mon.–Fri. 9.30am–4.30pm.*	▲ 169
TRINITY COLLEGE Trinity College, Dublin 2 Tel. (01) 702 10 16	*University: open daily 8am–10pm.* *Library: open Mon.–Fri. 9.30am–4.45pm,* *Sat. 9.30am–12.45pm.*	◆ B E4 ▲ 148
WATERWAYS VISITORS' CENTRE The Waterway Building, Grand Canal Quay, Dublin 2 Tel. (01) 677 75 10	*Open June–Sep. daily 9.30am–5.45pm,* *Oct.–May Wed.-Sun. 12.30–4.15pm.*	◆ B F5 ▲ 172

DUNDALK ◆ E E5

DOLMEN DE PROLEEK 3 miles from Dundalk on the Newry road	*Free access.*	
LOUTH COUNTY MUSEUM Jocelyn St. Tel. (042) 27056	*Open Mon.–Sat. 10.30am–5.30pm, Sun. 2–5pm.* *Museum of Industrial Heritage.*	

DUNDRUM (N.I.) ◆ E F4

DUNDRUM CASTLE Historic Monuments Branch (Belfast) Tel. (028) 90 23 50 00	*Visits by appointment.*	● 98 ▲ 307

DUNGANNON (N.I.) ◆ E D3

ARGORY HOUSE Derrycaw Rd., Moy Tel. (028) 87 78 47 53	*Open July–Aug. daily except Tue. 2–6pm;* *Apr.–June and Sep. daily 2–6pm.*	▲ 324
BENBURB VALLEY PARK **HERITAGE CENTRE** 89 Milltown Rd., Tullymore Etra, Benburb Tel. (028) 37 54 97 52	*Open Easter–Sep. Tue.–Sat. 10am–5pm,* *Sun. 2–5pm.*	▲ 324

DUNGIVEN (N.I.) ◆ E D2

DUNGIVEN PRIORY **& O'CAHAN TOMB** East of Dunvigen, Access on foot.	*Site open to the public.*	▲ 320

DÚN LAOGHAIRE ◆ G C2

NATIONAL MARITIME MUSEUM Old Mariner's Church, Haigh Terrace, Tel. (01) 280 09 69	*Open May–Sep. Tue.–Sun. 2.30–5.30pm.*	▲ 173

DUNQUIN ◆ F A4

DUNQUIN INTERPRETATIVE CENTRE **"IONAD AN BHLASCAOID MHÓIR"** **(BLASKET CENTRE)** Tel. (066) 915 64 44	*Open Apr.–Oct. daily 10am–6pm;* *July–Aug daily 10am–7pm.*	

DUNREE FORT ◆ E C1

MILITARY MUSEUM Tel. (077) 61817	*Open Apr.–Oct. daily 10am–6pm;* *July–Aug. daily 10am–7pm.*	

DYSERT O'DEA ◆ F D2

DYSERT O'DEA CASTLE Tel. (065) 703 77 22	*Open May–Sep. daily 10am–6pm.*	▲ 245

EMO ◆ G A2

EMO COURT & GARDENS Tel. (0502) 26573 1¼ miles from Emo on the Dublin–Cork–Limerick road	*Gardens open daily from 9am until sundown.* *House: open June 15–Sep. 15 Tue.–Sun.* *10.30am–5pm.*	▲ 182

ENNIS ◆ F D2

ENNIS FRIARY Tel. (065) 682 91 00	*Open Apr. 15–Sep. daily 9.30am–6.30pm.*	▲ 245

ENNISCORTHY		◆ G B4
ENNISCORTHY CASTLE Tel. (054) 35926	Open Mar.–Sep. daily 10am–6pm; Oct.–Feb. Sun. 2–5pm.	▲ 180

ENNISKERRY		◆ G C2
POWERSCOURT DEMESNE & WATERFALL Tel. (01) 286 76 76	Gardens: Mar.–Oct. 9.30am–5.30pm; Nov.–Feb. daily 10.30am–4.30pm. Waterfall: Mar.–Oct. 9.30am–7pm; Nov.–Feb. 10.30am–sundown.	▲ 176

ENNISKILLEN (N.I.)		◆ E C4
CASTLE COOLE Tel. (028) 66 32 26 90	Open May–Aug. daily except Thur. 1–6pm; Sep.–Apr. Sat.–Sun. 1–6pm.	▲ 326
FERMANAGH HERITAGE CENTRE & MUSEUM Tel. (028) 66 32 50 00	Open May–June and Sep. Tue.–Fri. 10am–5pm, Sat.–Mon. 2–5pm; July–Aug. Sun. 2–5pm.	
FORTHILL PARK & COLE MONUMENT Tel. (028) 32 50 50	Open May–Sep. daily 2–6pm.	
MONEA CASTLE 6¼ miles northwest of Enniskillen.	Site open to the public.	

FERRYCARRIG		◆ G B4
IRISH NATIONAL HERITAGE PARK Tel. (053) 20733	Open Mar.–Oct. daily 10am–7pm.	▲ 180

FLORENCE COURT (N.I.)		◆ E C4
FLORENCE COURT HOUSE Tel. (028) 66 34 82 49	Open May–Aug. daily except Tue. 1–6pm; Apr. and Sep. Sat.–Sun. and public hols. 1–6pm.	▲ 328
MARBLE ARCH CAVES Marlbank Scenik, Loop Rd. Tel. (028) 66 34 89 63	Open Mar. 15–Sep. daily 10am–4.30pm.	▲ 328

GALWAY CITY		◆ F D1
CATHEDRAL OF ST NICHOLAS Above Salmon Weir Bridge	Open daily 8am–9pm.	▲ 262
CITY MUSEUM Spanish Arch Tel. (091) 567641	Open Mar. 15–Sep. daily 10am–1pm and 2.15–5.15pm; Oct.–Mar. 14 Tue.–Thur. 2.15–5.15pm.	
COLLEGIATE CHURCH OF ST NICHOLAS Next to Shop St.	Open June–Sep. daily 9am–6pm, Oct.–May daily 9am–5.30pm.	▲ 260
GALWAY ART CENTRE 65 Dominick St. Tel. (091) 56 58 86	Open Mon.–Sat. 10am–5.30pm.	
LYNCH'S CASTLE Shop St.	AIB head-office. Can be visited during the bank's opening times.	▲ 260
NORA BARNACLE'S HOUSE Bowling Green Tel. (091) 56 47 43	Open May 15–Sep. 15. Mon.–Sat. 2–5pm.	▲ 262

GARINISH ISLAND		◆ F B5
ILNACULLIN GARDENS Glengarriff Bantiry Tel. (027) 63040	Open July–Aug. daily 9.30am–7pm; Apr.–June and Sep. daily 10am–6.30pm; Mar. and Oct. Mon.–Sat. 10am–4.30pm.	

GLANMIRE		◆ F D5
RIVERSTOWN HOUSE Tel. (021) 82 12 05	Open May–Aug. Wed.–Sat. 2–6pm; Sep.–Apr. by appointment.	▲ 215

GLENCOLUMBKILLE		◆ E A2
MC DYER FOLK MUSEUM Tel. (073) 30017	Open Easter–Sep. Mon.–Sat. 10am–6pm. Sun. noon–6pm.	▲ 295

GLENDALOUGH		◆ G C2-C3
GLENDALOUGH VISITORS' CENTRE Tel. (0404) 45351	Open June–Aug. daily 9.30am–6pm; Sep.–May daily 9.30am–5pm.	▲ 178
WICKLOW MOUNTAINS NATIONAL PARK Information Point, Upper Lake Tel. (0404) 45425	Open May–Aug. daily 10am–6pm; Apr.–Sep. Sat.–Sun. 10am–6pm.	▲ 177

GLIN ◆ F C3

GLIN CASTLE Tel. (068) 34173	*Open May–June 10am–noon and 2–4pm,* *or by appointment.*	▲ 250

GORT ◆ F D1

COOLE PARK Tel. (091) 63 18 04 Fax (091) 63 16 53	*Open Apr. 15–June 15 Tue.–Sun. 10am–5pm;* *June 16–Aug. daily 9.30am–6.30pm;* *Sep. daily 10am–5pm.*	▲ 247
KILMACDUAGH MONASTERY 3 miles from Gort Information from the Thoor Ballylee tourist office Tel. (091) 63 14 36 and in Kilmacduagh Tel. (091) 63 13 91	*Open Apr. 15–June 15 Tue.–Sun. 10am–5pm;* *June 16–Aug. daily 9.30am–6.30pm;* *Sep. daily 10am–5pm.*	▲ 247
THOOR BALLYLEE Tel. (091) 31436 From Gort, take the N18 for 3 miles, then take a right	*Open Easter–Sep. daily 10am–6pm.*	▲ 247

GORTIN (N.I.) ◆ E D2

SPERRIN HERITAGE CENTRE 274 Glenelly Rd., Cranagh Tel. (028) 81 64 81 42	*Open Apr.–Oct. Mon.–Fri. 11am–6pm,* *Sat. 11.30am–6pm and Sun. 2–7pm.*

HOLYWOOD (N.I.) ◆ E F3

ULSTER FOLK AND TRANSPORT **MUSEUM** Cultra Tel. (028) 90 42 84 28	*Open July–Aug. Mon.–Sat. 10.30am–6pm,* *Sun. noon–6pm;* *Apr.–June and Sep. Mon.–Fri. 9.30am–5pm,* *Sat. 10.30am–6pm, Sun. noon–6pm;* *Oct.–Mar. Mon.–Fri. 9.30am–4pm,* *Sat.–Sun. 12.30–4.30pm.*	▲ 306

INISHMORE ISLAND ◆ F C1

IONAD ARAN HERITAGE CENTRE **ARAN ISLAND HERITAGE CENTRE** Tel. (099) 61355	*Open Apr.–Oct. daily 11am–5pm;* *June–Aug. daily 10am–7pm.*

KELLS ◆ E D6

KELLS' MONASTERY & GRAVEYARD Tel. (046) 40151	*Open Apr.–May and Sep–Oct. daily 11am–5pm;* *June–Aug. daily 10am–7pm.*	▲ 192

KENMARE ◆ F B5

GOUGANE BARRA NATIONAL PARK Kenmare tourist office Tel. (064) 41233	*Open Ap.–May and Sep.–Oct. daily 11am–5pm;* *June–Aug. daily 10am–7pm.*

KILFENORA ◆ F C2-D2

BURREN DISPLAY CENTRE Tel. (065) 708 80 60	*Open June–Aug. daily 9.30am–6pm;* *Mar.–May and Sep. daily 10am–5pm.*	▲ 246

KILKEEL (N.I.) ◆ E E5

THE SILENT VALLEY Head Rd., 3 miles north of Kilkeel Tel. (028) 90 74 65 81	*Open Apr.–Sep. daily 10am–6.30pm;* *Oct.–Mar. daily 10am–4pm.*

KILKENNY ◆ G A3

BLACK ABBEY Tel. (056) 21279	*Open daily 9am–1pm and 2–4pm.*	
KILKENNY CASTLE Tel. (056) 21450	*Open Apr.–May daily 10.30am–5pm; June–Sep. daily* *10am–7pm; Oct.–Mar. Tue.–Sat. 10.30am–12.45pm* *and 2–5pm, Sun. 11am–12.45pm and 2–5pm.*	▲ 186
PICTURE GALLERY Kilkenny Castle Tel. (056) 21540	*Open daily 9am–1pm and 2–4pm.*	▲ 186
ROTHE HOUSE Parliament St. Tel. (056) 22893	*Open Apr.–Oct. Mon.–Sat. 10.30am–5pm,* *Sun. 2–5pm;* *Nov.–Feb. Mon.–Sat. 1–5pm.*	▲ 187
ST CANICE'S CATHEDRAL Church's Lane Tel. (056) 51653	*Open Easter–Oct. Mon.–Sat. 9am–1pm and 2–6pm,* *Sun. 2–7pm.*	▲ 186

SMITHWICK'S BREWERY Parliament St. Tel. (056) 21014	Open Apr.–Oct. Mon.–Sat. 10.30am–5pm, Sun. 2–5pm; Nov.–Feb. Mon.–Sat. 1–5pm.	▲ 187
KILLARNEY		◆ F B4
KILLARNEY NATIONAL PARK Tel. (064) 31440	Access to the park all year round.	▲ 234
MUCKROSS HOUSE & GARDENS Tel. (064) 31440	Open July–Aug. daily 9am–7pm; Sep.–Oct. daily 9am–6pm; Nov.–Mar. 15 daily 9am–5.30pm; Mar. 16–June daily 9am–6pm.	▲ 235
ROSS CASTLE Tel. (064) 35851	Open June–Aug. daily 9am–6.30pm; May and Sep. daily 9am–6pm; Oct. daily 9am–5pm.	▲ 235
KILLINABOY		◆ F B2
KILLINABOY CHURCH Tel. (065) 683 76 23	Open June–Aug. daily 9am–6.30pm; May and Sep. daily 9am–6pm; Oct. daily 9am–5pm.	▲ 246
KILMALKEDAR		◆ F A4
ORATORY OF GALLARUS 2 miles south of Kilmalkedar Tel. (066) 55333	Site open to the public.	▲ 239
KILMORE		◆ G B5
GUILLEMOT LIGHTSHIP MARITIME MUSEUM Kilmore Quay Tel. (053) 29655	Open May–Sep. daily noon–6pm. By appointment the rest of the year.	▲ 181
KILRUSH		◆ F C3
INFORMATION CENTRE OF SCATTERY ISLAND Merchants Quay Tel. (065) 52139	Open June 15–Sep. 15 daily 10.30am–6.30pm.	▲ 240
KINSALE		◆ F D6
CHARLES FORT Tel. (021) 477 26 84	Open June 15–Sep. 15 daily 10am–6pm; Sep. 16–Oct. Mon.–Sat. 9.30am–5.30pm.	▲ 223
CHURCH OF ST MULTOSE Tel. (021) 47 72 20	Open to the public.	▲ 223
DESMOND CASTLE Cork Street, Kinsale Tel. (021) 77 48 55	Open Apr. 15–June 15 Tue.–Sun. 10am–6pm; June 16–Sep. daily 10am–6pm.	▲ 223
REGIONAL MUSEUM Tel. (021) 477 20 44	Open Mon.–Sat. 11am–5pm and Sun. 3–5pm.	▲ 223
KINVARRA		◆ F D1
DUNGUAIRE CASTLE Tel. (091) 63 71 08	Open May–Sep. daily 9.30am–5pm. Medieval banquet at 5.45pm and 8.30pm.	▲ 243
KNOCK		◆ D C4
OUR LADY'S SHRINE FOLK MUSEUM Tel. (094) 88100 Fax (094) 88295	Open July–Aug. daily 10am–7pm; May–June and Sep.–Oct. daily 10am–6pm.	▲ 283
LETTERFRACK		◆ D A5
CONNEMARA NATIONAL PARK Renville House, Letterfrack Tel. (095) 41054	Open Easter–Oct. 15 10am–5.30pm (6.30pm in July–Aug.).	▲ 268
KYLEMORE ABBEY Tel. (095) 41146	Open Apr.–Nov. daily 9.30am–6pm.	▲ 268
LETTERKENNY		◆ E C2
DONEGAL COUNTY MUSEUM Tel. (074) 24613	Open Mon.–Sat. 1–4.30pm.	▲ 298
ST EUNAN'S CATHEDRAL Tel. (074) 21021	Open daily	▲ 298
LIMERICK		◆ F D3
HUNT MUSEUM Custom House, Rutland St. Tel. (061) 31 28 33	Open Oct.–Apr. Tue.–Sat. 10am–5pm, Sun. 2–5.30pm; May–Sep. Mon.–Sat. 10am–5pm, Sun. 2–5pm.	▲ 249

KING JOHN'S CASTLE Tel. (061) 41 12 01	*Open Apr.–Sep. daily 9.30am–5pm;* *Oct.–Mar. Sat.–Sun. 9.30am–5pm.*	▲ 249
ST MARY'S CATHEDRAL Tel. (061) 41 62 38	*Open June 15–Sep. Son et lumière shows daily at* *7pm and 8.15pm.*	▲ 249

LISBURN (N.I.) ◆ E E4

IRISH LINEN CENTRE **& LISBURN MUSEUM** Market Square, Tel. (028) 92 66 33 77	*Open Mon.–Sat. 9.30am–5pm.*	

LISMORE ◆ F E5

LISMORE CASTLE GARDENS Tel. (058) 54424	*Open daily 1.45–4.45pm.*	▲ 221

LOUGH GILL ◆ E A4

DEERPARK 5 miles from Sligo north of Lough Gill		▲ 285
PARKE'S CASTLE 4½ miles north of Lough Gill Tel. (071) 64149	*Open June–Sep. daily 9.30am–6.30pm;* *Apr–May and Oct. daily 10am–5pm.*	▲ 285

LOUGH GUR ◆ F D3

LOUGH GUR INTERPRETATIVE CENTRE Tel. (061) 36 07 88	*Open May–Sep. daily 10am–6pm.*	

LOUGH NEAGH (N.I.) ◆ E E3

ARBOE CELTIC CROSS On the east side of Lough Neagh, on the B73 road	*Site open to the public.*	▲ 324
LOUGH NEAGH DISCOVERY CENTRE Oxford Island Tel. (028) 38 32 22 05	*Open Apr.–Sep. daily 10am–7pm;* *Oct.–Mar. Wed.–Sun. 10am–5pm.*	▲ 324

LOUISBURGH ◆ D B4

GRANUAILE HERITAGE CENTRE Tel. (098) 66195	*Open Apr.–Sep. daily 10am–7pm;* *Oct.–Mar. Wed.–Sun. 10am–5pm.*	

MAGHERMORE (N.I.) ◆ E D2

BANAGHER OLD CHURCH Just under 2 miles southwest of Dungiven	*Open to the public.*	

MAGILLIGAN STRAND ◆ E D1

MARTELLO TOWER At the end of the beach, in a zone under military control	*Open Apr.–Sep. daily 10am–7pm;* *Oct.–Mar. Wed.–Sun. 10am–5pm.*	▲ 173

MALAHIDE G C1

MALAHIDE CASTLE Tel. (01) 846 21 84	*Open Apr.–Sep. Mon.–Fri. 10am–6pm,* *Sat. 11 h-18 h and Sun. 2–6pm;* *Oct.–Mar. Sat.–Sun. 2–5pm.*	▲ 174

MIDLETON ◆ E E5

JAMESON HERITAGE CENTRE Tel. (021) 461 35 94	*Open Mar.–Oct. daily 9am–4.30pm;* *Nov.–Feb. visits by appointment at 12.30pm and 3pm.*	▲ 219

MILLTOWN (N.I.) ◆ E E3-E4

PEATLANDS PARK Tel. (028) 38 85 11 02	*Open daily 9am–6pm.*	▲ 324

MOHER ◆ F C2

CLIFFS OF MOHER Visitors' Centre Tel. (065) 708 15 65	*Open July–Aug daily 9.30am–6.30pm; Feb. 15–Apr.* *daily 10am–5pm; May–June daily 10am–6pm.* *Tower and cliffs: free access.*	▲ 242

MONEEN ◆ F B3

CHURCH OF MONEEN Tel. (065) 70 84 50 08	*Open July–Aug. daily 9.30am–6.30pm;* *Feb. 15–Apr. daily 10am–5pm;* *May–June daily 10am–6pm.*	▲ 240

MURRINSTOWN		◆ **G** B5
JOHNSTOWN CASTLE PARK Tel. (053) 42888	*Open Mon.–Sat. 9am–12.30pm and 1.30–5pm, Sun. 2–5pm.*	▲ 181
NAVAN		◆ **G** B1, **E** B6
HILL OF TARA INTERPRETATIVE CENTRE Tel. (046) 25903	*Open May–June 15 and Sep. 15–Oct. daily 10am–5pm; June 16–Sep. 14 daily 9.30am–6.30pm.*	
NEWGRANGE		◆ **E** D6
DOWTH Northeast of Newgrange	*Closed to the public.*	
NEW ROSS		◆ **G** A4
JOHN F. KENNEDY ARBORETUM Tel. (051) 38 81 71	*Open daily from 10am until sundown.*	▲ 188
TINTERN ABBEY 10 miles south of New Ross on the R734 Tel. (051) 56 26 50	*Open June 15–Sep. 15. daily 9.30am–6.30pm.*	▲ 189
NEWTOWN		◆ **E** D6
LOUGHCREW 3 miles south of Newtown on the road to Earl Tree Tel. (049) 854 20 09	*Open June 15–Sep. 15 daily 10am–6pm.*	▲ 193
NEWTOWNARDS (N.I.)		◆ **E** F3
MOUNT STEWART HOUSE & TEMPLE OF THE WINDS Tel. (028) 42 78 83 87	*Open May–Sep. daily 1–6pm.*	▲ 307
SCRABO COUNTRY PARK 203a Scrabo Rd. Tel. (028) 91 81 14 91	*Open May–Sep. daily 1–6pm.*	▲ 306
NORTH SLOB		◆ **G** B4
WEXFORD WILDFOWL RESERVE Tel. (053) 23129	*Open May–Sep. 9am–6pm; Oct.–Apr. 10am–5pm.*	▲ 181
OMAGH (N.I.)		◆ **E** C3
ULSTER AMERICAN FOLK PARK Camphill Tel. (028) 82 24 32 92	*Open Apr.–Sep. Mon.–Sat. 11am–6.30pm, Sun. 11.30am–7pm.*	▲ 321
ULSTER HISTORY PARK Cullion Tel. (028) 81 64 81 88	*Open Apr.–Sep. Mon.–Sat. 11am–6.30pm, Sun. 11.30am–7pm.*	▲ 321
OUGHTERARD		◆ **F** D1, **D** B5-B6
AUGHNANURE CASTLE Aughnanure Tel. (091) 55 22 14	*Open June 15–Sep. 15 daily 9.30am–6.30pm.*	
PORTAFERRY (N.I.)		◆ **E** F4
EXPLORIS SEA AQUARIUM The Rope Walk Tel. (028) 42 72 80 62	*Open Apr.–June Mon.–Sat. 10am–6pm, Sun. 1–6pm.*	▲ 306
PORTUMNA		◆ **F** E1-E2
PORTUMNA CASTLE Tel. (0509) 41658	*Open June–Sep. 15 daily 9.30am–6.30pm.*	
QUILTY		◆ **F** C2
QUILTY CHURCH Tel. (065) 708 40 14	*Open to the public.*	▲ 241
QUIN		◆ **F** D2
		▲ 244
CRAGGAUNOWEN PROJECT Tel. (061) 36 71 78	*Open May 15–Sep. 15. daily 9am–6pm.*	
KNAPPOGUE CASTLE 6¼ miles southeast of Ennis Tel. (061) 36 81 03	*Open May–Sep. daily 9.30am–4.30pm.*	▲ 244

ST FINGHIN'S CHURCH Tel. (065) 682 56 49	*Open to the public.*	▲ 244
RATHDRUM		◆ **G** C3
AVONDALE HOUSE & **PARNELL MUSEUM** Tel. (0404) 46111	*Open May–Sep. daily 10am–6pm;* *Oct.–Apr. daily 11am–5pm.*	▲ 180
RATHFRILAND (N.I.)		◆ **E** E4
BRONTË HOMELAND **VISITORS CENTRE** Former Drumballyroney Church and School House Tel. (018206) 31152	*Open Mar.–Oct. Tue.–Fri. 11am–5pm,* *Sat.–Sun. 2–6pm.*	▲ 307
RATHKEALE		◆ **F** D3
CASTLE MATRIX Tel. (069) 64284	*Visits by appointment.*	▲ 250
ROSMUCK		◆ **D** B5-B6, **F** C1
TEACH AN PHIARSAIGH **(PEARSE' MEMORIAL COTTAGE)** Tel. (091) 57 42 92	*Open June 15–Sep. 15 daily 9.30am–6.30pm.*	▲ 265
SAINTFIELD (N.I.)		◆ **E** F4
ROWALLENE GARDENS Tel. (028) 97 51 01 31	*Open Easter–Oct. Mon.–Fri. 10am–6pm, Sat.–Sun.* *2–6pm; Nov.–Easter Mon.–Fri. 10.30am–5pm.*	▲ 307
SANDYCOVE		◆ **G** C2
JAMES JOYCE'S TOWER Tel. (01) 280 92 65	*Open Apr.–Oct. Mon.–Sat. 10am–1pm and 2–5pm,* *Sun. 2–6pm.*	▲ 173
SKIBBEREEN		◆ **F** C6
CÉIM HILL MUSEUM Near Union Hall Tel. (028) 36280	*Open Mon.–Sat. 10am–7pm.*	▲ 224
SLANE		◆ **E** D6
KNOWTH Tel. (041) 982 44 88	*Open May–Oct. daily 9am–7pm;* *Mar. and Sep. daily 9am–6.30pm.*	▲ 196
NEWGRANGE Tel. (041) 982 44 88	*Open June–Sep. daily 9am–7pm;* *Mar.–May and Oct. daily 9.30am–5.30pm.*	● 88 ▲ 196
SLANE CASTLE Tel. (041) 982 41 56	*Closed to the public.*	▲ 193
SLIGO		◆ **E** A3-A4
SLIGO ABBEY	*Site open to the public.*	▲ 284
SLIGO ART GALLERY **& COUNTY MUSEUM** Yeats Gallery Tel. (071) 45847	*Open Mon.–Sat. 10am–5.30pm.*	▲ 285
STRABANE (N.I.)		◆ **E** C2
GRAY'S PRINTING PRESS 49 Main St. Tel. (028) 71 88 40 94	*Open Apr.–Sep. daily 2–5.30pm.*	▲ 320
STRANGFORD LOUGH (N.I.)		◆ **E** F4
NENDRUM MONASTIC **SITE & MUSEUM** Mahee Island	*Site: free access.* *Museum: open Oct–Mar. Tue.–Sat. 10am–4pm,* *Sun. 2–4pm.*	▲ 306
STROKESTOWN		◆ **E** B5
STROKESTOWN PARK Tel. (078) 33013	*Open Apr.–Oct. daily 11am–5.30pm.*	▲ 290
THOMASTOWN		◆ **G** A4
JERPOINT ABBEY 1½ miles southwest of Thomastown on the N9 Tel. (056) 21755	*Open June–Sep.15 daily 9.30am–6.30pm;* *Mar. 15–May and Sep. 16–Oct. 15 daily 10am–5pm.*	▲ 187

TIPPERARY		◆ F E4	
ORMOND CASTLE Tel. (051) 64 07 87	*Open June 15–Sep. daily 9.30am–6.30pm.*	▲ 251	
TRIM		◆ G B1, E D6	
KING JOHN'S CASTLE Tel. (041) 988 03 00	*Open June 15–Sep. 15 daily 10am–6pm.*	▲ 190	
TULLY		◆ G B2	
IRISH NATIONAL STUD & **JAPANESE GARDENS** Tel. (045) 52 16 17	*Open Feb.15–Nov. 15 daily 9.30am–6pm.*	▲ 182	
VALENTIA ISLAND		◆ E A4	
SKELLIG EXPERIENCE **VISITOR CENTRE** Tel. (066) 947 63 06	*Open Apr.–June daily 9.30am–5pm,* *July–Aug. 9.30am–7pm.*	▲ 231	
WATERFORD		◆ G A5	
CHRIST CHURCH Cathedral Sq. Tel. (051) 87 41 19	*Open Mon.–Sat. 8am–7pm, Sun. 7am–6.30pm.*	▲ 189	
HOLY TRINITY CATHEDRAL Tel. (051) 75166	*Open Mon.–Sat. 8am–7pm, Sun. 7am–6.30pm.*	▲ 189	
REGINALD'S TOWER **TOWN MUSEUM** Tel. (051) 87 12 27	*Reginald's Tower:* *open June–Aug. Mon.–Fri. 8.30am–8.30pm,* *Sat. 8.30am–5pm;* *Sep.–Oct. Mon.–Fri. 10am–1pm and 2–5pm.* *Heritage Centre:* *open Apr.–May and Sep.–Oct. Mon.–Fri. 10am–1pm* *and 2–5pm; June–Aug. Mon.–Fri. 8.30am–8.30pm,* *Sat. 8.30am–5pm.*	▲ 189	
WATERFORD CRYSTAL GALLERY Tel. (051) 87 33 11	*Open Apr.–Oct. daily 8.30am–6pm,* *Nov.–Mar. Mon.–Fri. 9am–5pm. Guided tours until* *3.15pm.*	▲ 189	
WATERFORD HERITAGE CENTRE Greyfriar's Street Tel. (051) 87 12 27	*Open Apr.–Oct. daily 10am–5pm.*		
WESTPORT		◆ D B4	
HOLY TRINITY CHURCH Tel. (01) 661 31 11	*Open July–Aug. Mon.–Sat. 10.30am–6pm,* *Sun. 2–6pm.*		
YOUGHAL		◆ F E5	
COLLEGIATE CHURCH OF ST MARY	*Open daily 9am–1pm and 2–6pm.*	▲ 220	

GLOSSARY ◆

Words in brackets give the anglicized version of the Irish term.

GENERAL

Abhainn (avon, owen): river

Árd (ard): place name meaning high

Áth (ath): ford crossing

Baile (bal, bally) (Bailey): mall town, hamlet; castle courtyard

Balla: wall

Bádhún: castle enclosure

Bán: white

Beag: small

Béal (bal, bel): estuary

Bean, pl. mná: woman

Beann (ben): mountain peak

Bog: peat bog

Bóithrín (boreen): path

Bun: end of a road, mouth of a river

Cairn: stone tumulus

Caiseal, caisleán (cashel): castle

Carraig, corrig (Carrick): rock

Cath: battle

Cathair (caher): fortified enclosure

Ceann (ken, kin, can): cap

Ceilp (kelp): burned kelp used as fertilizer

Cill (kill): church

Cist: stone tomb

Clochán, pl. clocháin: dry-stone beehive hut

Clochar (clogher): convent

Cloch (clogh): rock

Cluain (clon): meadow

Cnoc (knock): hill, used in the names of approximately two thousand towns and villages

Crannóg: artificial island on a lake with a good defensive position

Cúl: back, support

Currach: primitive boat made from animal skin stretched over a wood frame

Dair, doire (derry, dare): oak, oak grove

Dearg: red

Domhnach (donagh): large church

Droim: mountain peak

Droimneach (drumlin): drumlin

Dún: fortress

Eanach: marsh

Eas (as, ess): waterfall

Éirinn (Erin): poetic synonym for Ireland

Eiscir (esker): esker

Fear, pl. fir: man

Feart (fert): tomb or burial mound

Fernagh, (ferney, fernane): alder woods

Gallán: raised stone

Gaeltacht: Irish-speaking areas

Gleann (glen): glen, valley

Gort: field

Grianán: palace, summerhouse

Inis, ennis: island

Inse: bogland

Lios (liss, lis): clay fort

Loch (lough): loch

Má, máigh: plain

Mainistir: monastery

Móin: mound

Mór: large

Mullach: rounded promontory

Poteen or poitín: illegal alcoholic drink distilled from potatoes

Ráth: circular fort

Rinn, (reen): peak

Ros: promontory or wood

Sceilg (scellig, skellig): rock, peak

Sean: old

Sheela-na-gig: female figure with exaggerated features seen on sculptures all over Ireland

Sliabh (slieve): mountain

Sráid, (strad): street, road

Teach, pl. títhe: house

Teampall: church

Tír: country

Tobar (tubber): source, well

Tochar (togher): artificial track over bogland

Tráigh, trá (strand): strand or shore

Tulach (tull, tully): small hill

Turlach: temporary lakes

Uachtar (oughter): upper

DAILY LIFE

Ar oscailt: open

Bodhrán: drum

Bord Fáilte: tourist office

Brú Óige: youth hostel

Ceol agus ól: music and drink

Dúnta: closed

Fáilte: welcome

Fógra: notice

Géill sli: give way

Go raibh maith agat: thank you

Leithreas: toilets

Ná caitear tobac: no smoking

Oifig an phoist: post office

CULTURE

Comhaltas Ceoltóirí Éireann: cultural institute founded to promote traditional music and dance

Conradh na Gaeilge: Gaelic league for the promotion of the Irish language

Fleadh Ceoil: music festival

Naomh: saint

Ogam: primitive writing using a series of hatch marks

Seanchaí: storyteller

Shebeens: illegal drinking den

Shelta: dialect spoken by the tinkers, or "travellers"

Siamsa Tíre: folk theater of Ireland

Stabht (stout): strong dark beer (stout)

Yola: ancient dialect formerly spoken at Forth and Bargy, Co. Wexford

SPORTS

G.A.A.: Gaelic Athletic Association founded in 1884 for the promotion of Irish sport (hurling and Gaelic football)

Iománaint: hurling

Peil: Gaelic football

Sliotar: hurling ball

POLITICS

Áras an Uachtaráin: residence of president, Phoenix Park, Dublin

Dáil Éireann: deputy chamber

Fianna Fáil: main political party in the Republic of Ireland, splinter group of moderates from Sinn Féin, opposed to the 1921 treaty with England

Fine Gael: the other party which is a splinter group from Sinn Féin, in favor of the 1921 treaty

Gardaí Síochána: police (Irish Republic, lit. guardians of the peace)

Seanad Éireann: high chamber of Irish legislation

Sinn Féin: "ourselves alone",

political branch of the Irish Republican Army

Taoiseach: prime minister

Teachta Dála: member of the Irish party

MYTHS AND LEGENDS

Ard rí: supreme sovereign of the Irish Gaelic people

Bean sí (banshee): lit. woman fairy, a spirit whose wail announces a death in the family

Brugh na Bóinne: burial site of the legendary kings of Ireland in the valley of the Boyne

Cú Chulainn: legendary hound, hero of the Ulster myth cycle

Diarmait and Gráinne: one of Ireland's best known love stories. It tells of the legendary flight across Ireland of two lovers: Gráinne, daughter of Cormac MacAirt, King of Tara, and her lover Diarmait, and their pursuit by Finn

Oisín (ossian): bardic warrior of the Fenian cycle

Tara: ancient capital of the Ard Rí, the country's most important political and liturgical center

Tír na-nóg: "land of eternal youth", beyond the Gaëls

Tuatha dé Danann: literally "people of the goddess Anu or Danu", divine mother of the gods and goddess of fertility. Said to have landed in Greece around 1900 BC, the Tuatha are supposed to be the fourth of six legendary races to have invaded Ireland

◆ BIBLIOGRAPHY

ESSENTIAL READING

◆ BANVILLE (J.) *Ghosts*, Secker and Warburg, London, 1993
◆ CROOKSHANK (A.) and THE KNIGHT OF GLIN: *Watercolours of Ireland*, Barrie & Jenkins, London, 1994
◆ HERITY (M.) and EOGAN (G.): *Ireland in Prehistory*, Routledge & Kegan Paul, Boston, 1976
◆ JOYCE (J.): *Dubliners*, Alfred A. Knopf, New York, 1991
◆ KEANE (M.) *Good Behaviour*, Sphere Books, London, 1982
◆ SOMERVILLE and ROSS: *Experiences of an Irish R.M.*, Everyman's Library, London
◆ TREVOR (W.): *The Stories of William Trevor*, Penguin, Harmondsworth, 1983
◆ TREVOR (W.): *A Writer's Ireland – Landscape in Literature*, Thames & Hudson, London, 1984
◆ YEATS (W.B.): *The Poems*, Everyman's Library, London, 1992

GENERAL INTEREST

◆ BÖLL (H.) TRANS. VENNEWITZ (L.): *Irish Journal*, McGraw-Hill Book Co., New York, 1967
◆ DONLEAVY (J.P.): *A Singular Country*, Ryan, Peterborough, 1989
◆ DONLEAVY (J.P.): *J.P. Donleavy's Ireland in All her Sins and Some of her Graces*, Michael Joseph, Rainbird, London, 1986
◆ FITZGIBBON (C.): *The Irish in Ireland*, David & Charles, London, 1983
◆ HILL (I.): *Northern Ireland*, Blackstaff Press, Belfast, 1986
◆ GOFF (A.): *Walled Gardens, Scenes from an Anglo-Irish Childhood*, Eland, London, 1994
◆ LORD KILLANIN and DUIGNAN (M.V.): *The Shell Guide to Ireland*, Ebury Press, London, 1962
◆ LAVELLE (D.): *Skellig – Island Outpost of Europe*, The O'Brien Press, Dublin, 1976
◆ LEHAN (B.): *Dublin*, Time Life, Amsterdam, 1978
◆ MCCABE (B.) and LE GARSMEUR (A.): *W.B. Yeats – Images of Ireland*, Little, Brown & Co., Boston; Toronto; London, 1991
◆ MCCABE (B.) and LE GARSMEUR (A.): *James Joyce – Reflections of Ireland*, Little, Brown & Co., Boston; Toronto; London, 1993
◆ MCCARTHY (J.): *Joyce's Dublin, A Walking Guide to Ulysses*, Wolfhound Press, Dublin, 1986
◆ MANNING (O.): *The Dreaming Stone*, Evans Brothers, London, 1950
◆ MARTINEAU (H.): *Letters from Ireland*, John Chapman, London, 1852
◆ NEWBY (E.): *Round Ireland in Low Gear*, Collins, London, 1987
◆ O'BRIEN (E.): *The Beckett Country: Beckett's Ireland*, Black Cat Press, Monkstown, Co. Dublin in assoc. with Faber and Faber, London, 1986
◆ O'FAOLAIN (S.): *An Irish Journey*, Longmans Green & Co., London, 1949
◆ ROLT (L.T.C.): *Green and Silver*, George Allen & Unwin, London, 1949
◆ SOMERVILLE (E.) and ROSS (M.): *Through Connemara in a Governess Cart*, W.H. Allen & Co., London, 1893
◆ YOUNG (A.): *A Tour in Ireland*, Irish University Press, Dublin, 1970

NATURE

◆ *The Book of the Burren*, Tir Eloas, Newtownlynch, 1992
◆ D'ARCY (G.): *Birds of Ireland*, Appletree Press, Belfast, 1986
◆ FEEHAN (J.): *The Landscape of Slieve Bloom*, Blackwater Press, 1979
◆ MITCHELL (G.F.): *The Shell Guide to Reading the Irish Landscape*, Country House, Dublin, 1986
◆ WALSH (W.): *An Irish Florilegium II – Wild and Garden Plants of Ireland*, Thames & Hudson, London, 1988
◆ WEBB (D.A.): *An Irish Flora*, Dundalgan Press, Dundalk, 1943
◆ WHITTOW (J.B.): *Geology and Scenery in Ireland*, Penguin, Harmondsworth, 1974

HISTORY AND LANGUAGE

◆ BARDON (J.): *A History of Ulster*, Blackstaff Press, Belfast, 1992
◆ DE BREFFNY (B.) ED.: *The Irish World – The History and Cultural Achievements of the Irish People*, Thames & Hudson, London, 1986
◆ BRENNAN (P.): *The Conflict in Northern Ireland*, Longman, France, Paris, 1991
◆ BROWN (T.): *Ireland. A Social and Cultural History*, Fontana, Glasgow, 1981
◆ COFFEY (T.M.): *Agony at Easter*, Macmillan, New York, 1969
◆ CURTIS (E.): *History of Medieval Ireland from 1086 to 1513*, Methuen, London, 1938
◆ EDGEWORTH (M.), ED. BUTLER (H.): *Tour in Connemara in 1833*, Constable, London, 1950
◆ FLOWER (R.): *The Irish Tradition*, Clarendon Press, Oxford, 1947
◆ FOSTER (R.F.): *Modern Ireland 1600–1972*, Penguin, London, 1988
◆ FOSTER (R.F.) ED.: *The Oxford Illustrated History of Modern Ireland*, Oxford University Press, London, 1989
◆ HUSSEY (D.): *Ireland today*, Penguin Books, 1995
◆ LECKY (W.E.H.): *A History of Ireland in the Eighteenth Century*, Longmans Green & Co, London, 1912
◆ LEE (J.J.): *Ireland 1912–1985. Politics and Society*, Cambridge University Press, Cambridge, 1989
◆ LYONS (F.S.L.): *Ireland since the Famine*, Collins-Fontana, Glasgow, 1973
◆ MOODY (T.W.), MARTIN (F.X.) and BYRNE (F.J.): *A New History of Ireland*, 10 vols., Oxford University Press, London, 1976
◆ MOODY (T.W.), MARTIN (F.X.) and BYRNE (F.J.): *The Oxford Illustrated History of Ireland*, Oxford University Press, Oxford, 1989
◆ PAKENHAM (T.): *The Year of Liberty*, Hodder & Stoughton, London, 1969
◆ DE PAOR (L.): *Divided Ulster*, Penguin, Harmondsworth, 1970
◆ SHAW (G.B.S.): *The Matter with Ireland*, Rupert Hart-Davis, London, 1962
◆ SPENSER (E.) ED. RENWICK (W.L.): *A View of the Present State of Ireland*, Eric Partridge, Scholastic Press, 1934
◆ THOMSON (D.): *The Great Hunger*, Hamish Hamilton, London, 1962

ART AND HERITAGE

◆ *Ancient Monuments of Northern Ireland*, 2 vols., Her Majesty's Stationery Office, Belfast, 1975
◆ BRENNAN (M .): *The Stars and the Stones – Ancient Art and Astronomy in Ireland*, Thames & Hudson, London, 1983
◆ DELARGY (J.H.): *The Gaelic Storyteller*, Cumberlege, London, 1945
◆ EOGEN (G.): *Knowth and the Passage-tombs of Ireland*, Thames & Hudson, London,1990
◆ EVANS (E.E.): *The Personality of Ireland*, Cambridge University Press, Cambridge, 1973
◆ FITZGIBBON (T.): *A Taste of Ireland in food and pictures*, Pan Books, London,1970
◆ GRAVES (R.): *The White Goddess*, Faber and Faber, London,1948
◆ HEANEY (M.): *Over Nine Waves*, Faber and Faber, London, 1994
◆ LAING (L.): *Celtic Britain and Ireland ad 200–800*, Irish Academic Press, Dublin, 1990
◆ O'DANACHAIR (C.): *Folktales of the Irish Countryside*, Mercier Press, Dublin and Cork, 1976
◆ O'KELLY (M.J.): *Newgrange – Archeology, Art & Legend*, Thames & Hudson, London,1988
◆ O'RIORDAIN (P.): *Antiquities of the Irish Countryside*, Methuen, London,1955
◆ O'RIORDAIN (P.) and DANIEL (G.): *New Grange*, Thames & Hudson, London,1964
◆ O'NEILL (T.): *Life and Tradition in Rural Ireland*, Dent, London,1977
◆ SÚILLEABHÁIN (S.): *A Handbook of Irish Folklore*, Education Company, Dublin, 1942; Singing Tree Press, Detroit, 1970
◆ SÚILLEABHÁIN (S.): *Irish Wake Amusements*, The Mercier Press, Cork, 1967
◆ SHAW-SMITH (D .): *Ireland's Traditional Crafts*, Thames & Hudson, London, 1986
◆ WILDE (LADY J.): *Ancient Legends, Mystic Charms and Superstitions of Ireland*, London, 1888

ART AND ARCHITECTURE

◆ ARNOLD (B.): *Irish Art; A Concise History*, Thames & Hudson, London, 1977
◆ ARNOLD (W.) and MORRISON (R.): *The Historic Hotels of Ireland*, Thames & Hudson, London, 1988
◆ DE BREFFNY (B.) and MOTT (G.): *Castles of Ireland*, Thames & Hudson, London, 1992
◆ DIXON (H.): *An Introduction to Ulster Architecture*, Ulster Architectural Heritage Society, 1975
◆ FINLAY (I.): *Celtic Art: An Introduction*, Faber and Faber, London, 1973
◆ GUINNESS (D.): *Georgian Dublin*, Batsford, London, 1979
◆ GUINNESS (D.) and O'BRIEN (J.): *Great Irish Houses and Castles*, Weidenfeld and Nicolson, 1992
◆ GUINNESS (D.) and RYAN (W): *Irish Homes and Castles*, Thames & Hudson, London, 1971
◆ HARBISON (P.): *Irish Art & Architecture – From Prehistory to the Present*, Thames & Hudson, London, 1993
◆ HENRY (F.): *Early Christian Irish Art*, Three Candles, Dublin, 1963

◆ HENRY (F.) ED.: *The Book of Kells*, Thames & Hudson, London, 1988
◆ LEASK (H.-G.): *Irish Castles*, Dudalgan Press, Dundalk, 1986
◆ LEASK (H.-G.): *Irish Churches and Monastic Buildings*, Dudalgan Press, Dundalk, 1987
◆ MCLAREN (D.) and MARSDEN (S.): *In Ruins – The Once Great Houses of Ireland*, Collins, London, 1980
◆ MEGAW (R.) and MEGAW (V.): *Celtic Art – From its Beginnings to the Book of Kells*, Thames & Hudson, London, 1991
◆ MORRISON (C.) and FITZ-SIMON (C.): *The Irish Village*, Thames & Hudson, London, 1986
◆ ROTHERY (S.): *Everyday Buildings of Ireland*, College of Technology, Bolton Street, Dublin, 1975
◆ ROWAN (A.): *North West Ulster – The Buildings of Ireland*, Penguin, Harmondsworth, 1979
◆ STALLEY (R.A.): *Architecture and Sculpture in Ireland 1150–1350*, Gill and Macmillan, Dublin, 1971
◆ WHITE (J.): *The National Gallery of Ireland*, Thames & Hudson, London, 1968

PAINTING

◆ BODKIN (T.): *Four Irish Landscape Painters*, The Talbot Press, Dublin, 1920
◆ BUTLER (P.): *Irish Watercolours and Drawings*, Weidenfeld & Nicolson, London, 1990
◆ PYLE (H.): *J.B. Yeats in the National Gallery of Ireland*, The National Gallery of Ireland, Dublin, 1986
◆ YEATS (J.B.): *Life in the West of Ireland*, Maunsel & Co., Dublin, 1912

LITERATURE

◆ BECKETT (S.): *All that Fall*, Faber and Faber, London, 1957
◆ BECKETT (S.): *First Love*, Calder & Boyars, London and New York, 1973
◆ BECKETT (S.): *More Pricks than Kicks*, Calder & Boyars, London, 1970
◆ BEHAN (B.): *Borstal Boy*, Hutchinson, London, 1958
◆ BEHAN (B.): *The Hostage*, Methuen, London, 1958; Grove Press, New York, 1959
◆ BEHAN (B.): *Richard's Cork Leg*, Eyre Methuen, London, 1973
◆ BELL (A.O.) ED. AND MCNEILLE (A.) ASSIST.: *The Diary of Virginia Woolf Volume Four 1931–1935*, Harcourt Brace Janovich, New York and London, 1982

◆ BÖLL (H.) TRANS. VENNEUITZ (L.): *Irish Journal*, Secker & Warburg, McGraw-Hill Book Co., New York, 1967
◆ BOWEN (E.): *A Day in the Dark*, Jonathan Cape, London, 1965
◆ BOWEN (E.): *Seven Winters. Memories of a Dublin Childhood*, Irish University Press, 1972
◆ DEANE (S.) ED.: *The Field Day Anthology of Irish Writing*, 3 vols., Field Day Publications, Derry, 1991
◆ DONAGHUE (D.): *Warrenpoint*, Jonathan Cape, London,1991
◆ DONAGHUE (D.): *We Irish*, The Harvester Press, Brighton, 1986; Alfred A. Knopf, New York, 1987
◆ DONLEAVY (J.P.): *The Gingerbread Man*, Neville Spearman, London, 1962
◆ DOYLE (R.): *Paddy Clarke Ha Ha Ha*, Secker & Warburg, London, 1993
◆ DOYLE (R.): *The Snapper*, Secker & Warburg, London, 1990
◆ EDGEWORTH (M.): *Castle Rackrent*, Macmillan London, 1970
◆ FRIEL (B.): *Aristocrats*, Gallery Press, 1983
◆ FRIEL (B.): *Translations*, Faber and Faber, London, 1982
◆ GOGARTY (O. ST. J.): *As Ireland was Going Down Sackville Street*, Harcourt, Brace & World, New York, 1937
◆ GREGORY (LADY), ED. MURPHY (D.J.): *Journals 1916–1930*, Colin Smythe, Gerrards Cross, 1978, 1987
◆ HEANEY (M.): *Over Nine Waves, A Book of Irish Legends*, Faber and Faber, London and Boston, 1994
◆ HEANEY (S.): *Door into the Dark*, Faber and Faber, London, 1969
◆ HEANEY (S.): *Field Work*, Faber and Faber, London and Boston, 1969
◆ HEANEY (S.): *Station Island*, Faber and Faber, London, 1984
◆ HEANEY (S.): *Sweeney Astray*, Field Day Theater Co., Derry, 1983
◆ HEANEY (S.): *Wintering Out*, Faber and Faber, London, 1972
◆ JOYCE (J.): *Finnegans Wake*, Faber and Faber, London, 1939
◆ JOYCE (J.): *Portrait of the Artist as a Young Man*, Alfred A. Knopf, New York, 1991
◆ JOYCE (J.): *Ulysses*, Everyman's Library, London, 1992
◆ KAVANAGH (P.): *Collected Poems*, Martin Brian & O'Keefe, London, 1972
◆ KAVANAGH (P.):

Self Portrait, 1964
u KAVANAGH (P): *Tarry Flynn*, The Pilot Press, London, 1948
◆ KEANE (M.): *The Knight of Cheerful Countenance*, Virago Modern Classics, London, 1993
◆ KEANE (M.): *The Rising Tide*, Virago Books, London, 1984
◆ KEANE (M.): *Time after Time*, Sphere Books, London, 1984
◆ KINSELLA (T.) TRANS.: *The Táin*, Dolmen Editions, Ireland, 1969
◆ LAVIN (M.): *The Shrine and Other Stories*, Houghton Mifflin, Boston, 1977
◆ LONGLEY (M.): *Poems 1963–1983*, Penguin, Harmondsworth, 1986
◆ MCGAHERN (J.): *Among Women*, Faber and Faber, London, 1990
◆ MCGAHERN (J.): *High Ground*, Faber and Faber Ltd, London, 1985
◆ MAHON (D.): *Selected Poems*, Viking/Gallery in assoc. with Oxford University Press, Oxford, 1991
◆ MOORE (B.): *The Lonely Passion of Judith Hearne*, Little Brown, Boston, 1955
◆ MOORE (B.): *Lies of Silence*, Bloomsbury, London, 1990
◆ MOORE (G.): *A Drama in Muslim*, Boni & Liveright, New York, 1922
◆ MORYSON (F.): *An Itinerary, Vol. III* James MacLehose and Sons, Glasgow, 1908
◆ MULDOON (P .): *Why Brownlee Left*, Faber and Faber, London, 1980
◆ MULDOON (P.): *Selected Poems 1968–1983*, Faber and Faber, London
◆ O'BRIEN (E.): *Mrs. Reinhardt and Other Stories*, Jonathan Cape, London, 1978
◆ O'BRIEN (E.): *Returning*, Penguin Books, London, 1983
◆ O'BRIEN (F.): *At Swim-Two-Birds*, MacGibbon & Kee, London, 1966
◆ O'CASEY (S.): *Drums under the Window*, Macmillan, London, 1945
◆ O'CASEY (S.): *Juno and the Paycock*, Macmillan London Ltd, London, 1972
◆ O'CONNOR (F.): *An Only Child*, Macmillan, London, 1961
◆ O'FAOLAIN (S.): *No Country for Young Men*, Allen Lane, London, 1980
◆ O'FAOLAIN (S.): *Foreign Affairs and Other Stories*, Penguin, Harmondsworth, 1986
◆ O'FAOLAIN (S.): *Vive Moi!*, 1964
◆ PAULIN (T.): *Ireland and the English Crisis*, Bloodaxe, Newcastle-upon-Tyne, 1984

◆ PAULIN (T.): *The Liberty Tree*, Faber and Faber, London, 1982
◆ PAULIN (T.): *A State of Justice*, Faber and Faber, London, 1977
◆ SHAW (G.B.S.): *The Complete Plays of Bernard Shaw*, Odhams Press, London, 1934
◆ SHAW (G.B.S.): *Sixteen Self Sketches*, Constable & Co., London, 1949
◆ STEPHENS (J.): *The Crock of Gold*, Macmillan, London, 1946
◆ STRABO TRANS. JONES (S.L.): *Geography*, London and New York, 1930
◆ SWIFT (J.), *Satires and personal writings*, Oxford University Press, London 1958
◆ SWIFT (J.), ED. DAVIS (H.) ET AL.,: *Prose Works*, 14 vols., Basil Blackwell, Oxford, 1939–68
◆ SYNGE (J.M.): *The Aran Islands*, Maunsel & Roberts Ltd, Dublin; and London, 1921
◆ SYNGE (J.M.S.): *The Autobiography of J.M. Synge*, Dolmen Press, Dublin; Oxford University Press, London, 1965
◆ THACKERAY (W.M.): *The Irish Sketch Book*, Smith, Elder & Co., London, 1892
◆ THACKERAY (W.M.): *The Memoirs of Barry Lyndon Esq.*, John Murray, London, 1911
◆ TREVOR (W.): *Mrs Eckdorf in O'Neill's Hotel*, Penguin, Harmondsworth, 1985
◆ TREVOR (W.): *The New Fiction from Ireland and Other Stories*, Bodley Head, London, 1986
◆ WILDE (O.): *The Works of Oscar Wilde*, Collins, London, 1948
◆ YEATS (W.B.): *Collected Plays*, Macmillan, London, 1934
◆ YEATS (W.B.), ED. DONOGHUE (D.): *Memoirs*, Macmillan, London, 1988

JOURNALS

◆ *Analecta Hibernica*, Dublin
◆ *Archeology Ireland*, Dublin
◆ *Archivium Hibernicum*, Maynooth, Co. Kildare
◆ *Collectanea Hibernica*, Dublin
◆ *Irish Economic and Social History*, Belfast
◆ *Irish Geography*, Dublin
◆ *Irish Historical Studies*, Dublin
◆ *Irish Literary Supplement*, New York
◆ *Review*, Cork
◆ *Irish University Review*, Dublin
◆ *Journal of the Cork Historical and Archeological Society*, Ballin College
◆ *Linen Hall Review*, Belfast
◆ *Studia Hibernica*, Dublin

◆ LIST OF ILLUSTRATIONS

London. *Maltese Cross in gold* from the treasures of the *Girona* © UM. *Philippe II*, Titian, oil on canvas, Pitti Gallery, Florence © Roger- Viollet
318 *Londonderry*, Jollain, engraving, in *Map of the British Isles*, 1689 © BN. *The deliverance of Derry*, William Sadler II, oil on canvas c.1830.© UM
318–9 *"Bloody Sunday", Londonderry, Feb. 1973* © Hulton Deutsch, London.
319 *Orange parades*, Derry © Chris Hill Photographic, Belfast. *Bishop Road*, lithograph early 19th century. © UM.
320 *Cathedral of Saint Columba,* Sandby, engraving © BN. *A Strabane pub* © NITO. *Amelia Earhart,* nicknamed *"Lady Lindbergh"*, photo. 1930, private
321 *Ulysses S. Grant in 1864* © Hulton Deutsch, London. *Stone circles at Beaghmore* © NITO.
322 *Tomb of Brian Boru*, Gallimard. *Royal Bastion, Fort Navan* © NITO. *Masha*, Stephen Reid, drawing, in *Myths and Legends of the Celtic Race*, Rolleston, 1912, all rights reserved
322–3 *Armagh Cathedral*, Daniel Grose, watercolor. © Irish Architectural Archives (Lord Rossmore), Dublin.
323 *Road bowling match in Castlemany*, Daniel McDonald, oil on canvas 1830 © Crawford Municipal Art Gallery, Cork. *Catholic Cathdral, Armagh* © NITO.
324 *Apple trees in flower, Ardboe Cross, Tyrone* © NITO.
325 *Enniskillen,* Sandby, engraving © BN. *Siege of Enniskillen,* manuscript 1594 © British Library, London
326 *Fishermen at Lower Lough Erne* © Chris Hill Photographic, Belfast. *Coole Castle*, tinted engraving, 1879 © Mary Evans, London
326–7 *Devenish* © Chris Hill Photographic, Belfast.
327 *Belleek porcelain* © Chris Hill Photographic, Belfast.
328 *Upper Lough Erne*, Thomas Roberts the Elder, oil on canvas © Yale Center for British Art, collection Paul Mellon, New Haven. *Lough Oughter* © BF. *Grottos of Marble Arch* © NITO.

330 *Goats on the Burren* © BF. *Kinvarra*, Cruse/ Gallimard
331 *Ruins in Castlecove* © Quéméré/Visa-Cédri
333 *Signs in Kerry* © BF *Bucylce hire in Clifden*, cl. Dominique Zintzmeyer *Bicycle tourism in County Mayo* © Holzbachova- Benet
335 *Bed and Breakfast in Westport*, cl. Dominique Zintzmeyer
336 *Dingle port; Fishing in Connemara*, cl. John Murray, Bray *Layton marina on the grand canal (co.Meath)*, cl. John Murray, Bray
337 *The Twelve Bens, Wicklow Mountains*, cl. John Murray, Bray
338 *Musicians in a Kilkenny pub* © BF *Longs bar in Ballyferriter* © BF *Guinness* advert © Sonia Dourlot
342 *Pub in Dublin* © Holzbachova-Benet
346 *Dan Foley's pub* © Sonia Dourlot
347 *Restaurant in Galway* © Lewis/Rapho
349 *Pub in Dublin* © Holzbachova-Benet
353 *"My goodness, My Guinness"*, poster by J. Gilroy
385–396 Édigraphie

ILLUSTRATORS:
Yvon Le Corre:
11, 15, 161, 178–179, 181, 186, 193, 197, 198–199, 202, 204, 216–217, 220–221, 223–225, 227–230, 236–239, 242–243, 251–253, 260–261, 264–265, 268, 271–277, 280–281, 283, 288–289, 294–299, 307, 312, 314–315, 319–321, 327, 331

Nature :
18–19 Gilbert Houbre, Jean Chevallier
20–21 Jean Chevallier, François Desbordes
22–23 François Desbordes, Jean Chevallier, Claire Felloni
24–25 Gilbert Houbre, François Desbordes, Pascal Robin
26–27 Jean Chevallier
28–29 François Desbordes, Frédérique Schwebel, Gilbert Houbre, Jean Chevallier, Frédéric Bony
30–31 François Desbordes, Claire Felloni, Jean Chevallier, Dominique Mansion
32–33 Anne Bodin, Claire Felloni
34–35 Claire Felloni, Dominique Mansion, Bernard Duhem, Jean Chevallier, François Desbordes
36–37 François Place
38–39 Jean Chevallier, Gismonde Curiace, Frédéric Bony
40–41 François Desbordes, Jean Chevallier, Claire Felloni, Dominique Mansion
42–43 François Desbordes
44–45 François Place, Pascal Robin
46 Denis Clavreul, Jean Chevallier, Anne Bodin

Arts and traditions:
71 Alban Larousse
74 Jean-Marie Guillou
83 Anne Bodin
Architecture:
Jean-Marie Guillou
Roger Hutchins
Maurice Pommier
Claude Quiec
Catherine Totems
Tony Townsend

Itineraries:
174 illustration Gallimard
201, 232 Jean Chevallier
233 Jean Chevallier, François Desbordes
317 Maurice Pommier
324 Alban Larousse
327 Pascal Robin

Maps:
Vincent Brunot
Eric Gillion
Coloring:
Claire Cormier
Jean-Marc Lanusse
Alban Larousse
Catherine Totems

Computer graphics:
Paul Coulbois
Patrick Alexandre
Kristof Chemineau
Martine Frouin-Marmouguet
Patrick Merienne

Computer maps:
Édigraphie

We should like to thank the following people and organizations for their help:
Bord Fáilte
Patricia Desseine
Dublin Corporation
Lucian Freud
Irene Halpin, of the Crawford Municipal Art Gallery
Valérie Hardy
Pierre Joannon
Kenny's Bookshop
Liebig
Simon Lincoln, of Irish Architectural Archives
Bernard Marck
Melanie McDonagh
Marie McFeely, of the National Gallery of Ireland
John and Rhona McKay
Peter Murray, of the Crawford Municipal Art Gallery
National Monuments (Northern Ireland), for the architectural reconstructions on pages 92–3 and 96–7
Northern Ireland Tourist Office
Patricia O'Gorman
RCA
Bill Rolston
John Clement Ryan, of Irish Distillers Ltd.
Eileen Tweedy
Lize Martine Van Gelderen
Anne Yeats

◆ LIST OF ILLUSTRATIONS

Acknowledgements
Grateful acknowledgment is made to the following for permission to reprint previously published material:

◆ DEVIN-ADAIR, PUBLISHERS, INC.: Excerpt from *Tarry Flynn* by Patrick Kavanagh (The Pilot Press Ltd., London, 1948), copyright by Devin-Adair, Publishers, Inc. All rights reserved. Reprinted by permission of Devin-Adair, Publishers, Inc., Old Greenwich, CT 06870.

◆ FABER AND FABER, INC. AND FABER AND FABER LIMITED: Excerpt from *Over Nine Waves: A Book of Irish Legends* by Marie Heaney, copyright © 1994 by Marie Heaney. Rights in Canada administered by Faber and Faber Limited, London. Reprinted by permission.

◆ FARRAR, STRAUS & GIROUX, INC.: Excerpts from *The Connor Girls* and *My Mother's Mother* from *A Fanatic Heart* by Edna O'Brien, copyright © 1984 by Edna O'Brien. Reprinted by permission. (In the UK by permission of Weidenfeld and Nicolson).

◆ FARRAR, STRAUS & GIROUX, INC and FABER AND FABER LIMITED: Excerpt from "The Strand at Lough Beg" from *Selected Poems 1966-1987* by Seamus Heaney, copyright © 1976, 1979, 1990 by Seamus Heaney. Rights in Canada from *Field Work* administered by Faber and Faber Limited, London. Reprinted by permission.

◆ THE GALLERY PRESS: Excerpt from *Aristocrats* by Brian Friel (1980). Reprinted by permission of The Gallery Press, County Meath, Ireland, and the author.

◆ GROVE/ATLANTIC, INC.: Excerpt from *First Love* by Samuel Beckett (Grove Press, 1974). Reprinted by permission of Grove/Atlantic, Inc.

◆ GROVE/ATLANTIC, INC.: Excerpt from *Richard's Cork Leg* by Brendan Behan, copyright © 1973 by Beatrice Behan and Alan Simpson. Reprinted by permission of Grove/Atlantic, Inc.

◆ HARCOURT BRACE & COMPANY AND THE HOGARTH PRESS: Excerpt from *The Diary of Virginia Woolf, Vol IV: 1931–1935*, edited by Anne Olivier Bell, copyright © 1982 by Quentin Bell and Angelica Garnett. Rights in Canada administered on behalf of the estate by The Hogarth Press, London. Reprinted by permission of Harcourt Brace & Company and The Hogarth Press.

◆ NORTHWESTERN UNIVERSITY PRESS AND LEILA VENNEWITZ: Excerpt from *Irish Journal* by Heinrich Böll, translated by Leila Vennewitz, copyright © 1967 by Leila Vennewitz. Reprinted by permission of Northwestern University Press and Leila Vennewitz.

◆ RANDOM HOUSE, INC. and THE ESTATE OF JAMES JOYCE: Excerpt from *Ulysses* by James Joyce, copyright © 1934, copyright renewed 1962 by Lucia and George Joyce. Rights in Canada administered by The Estate of James Joyce, Sean Sweeney, Trustee. Reprinted by permission of Random House, Inc. and The Estate of James Joyce, Sean Sweeney, Trustee.

◆ THE SAMUEL BECKETT ESTATE and THE CALDER EDUCATIONAL TRUST, LONDON: Excerpt from *First Love* by Samuel Beckett, translated by Samuel Beckett, Calder & Boyars Limited, London. Copyright © Samuel Beckett 1970. Reproduced in the UK by permission.

◆ SIMON & SCHUSTER, INC.: "The Lake Isle of Innisfree" from *The Poems of W.B. Yeats: A New Edition*, edited by Richard J. Finneran (New York: Macmillan, 1983). Reprinted by permission.

◆ THE SOCIETY OF AUTHORS: Excerpt from *Sixteen Self Sketches* by Bernard Shaw (Constable & Company Limited, London 1949). Reprinted by permission of The Society of Authors on behalf of The Bernard Shaw Estate.

◆ VIKING PENGUIN: Excerpt from "Gold Watch", copyright © 1980 by John McGahern (first appeared in *The New Yorker*), from *High Ground* by John McGahern. Reprinted by permission of Viking Penguin, a division of Penguin Books USA, Inc.

◆ WALKER AND COMPANY and A.M. HEATH & COMPANY LIMITED: Excerpt from *At Swim-Two Birds* by Flann O'Brien, copyright © 1951, 1966 by Brian Nolan. Rights in Canada, copyright © by the Estate of Flann O'Brien, administered by A.M. Heath & Company Limited, London. Reprinted by permission of A.M. Heath & Company Limited, and Walker and Company, 435 Hudson St., New York, NY 10014, 1-800-289-2553. All rights reserved.

We have tried unsuccessfully to trace the heirs or publishers of certain documents. An account has been held open for them at our publishing house.

INDEX ◆

◆ INDEX

◆ INDEX

Map section

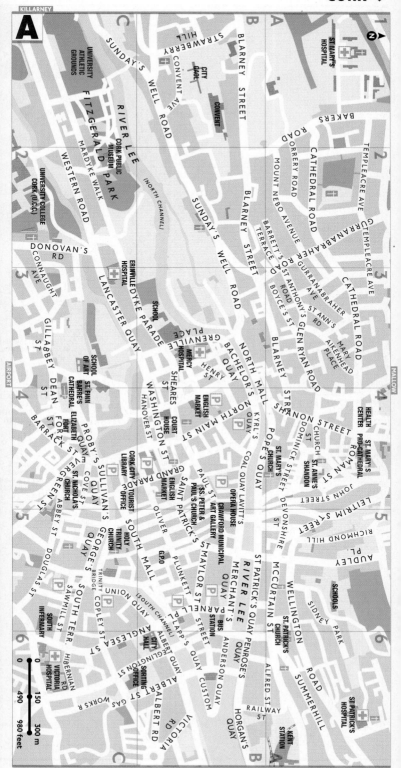

KILLARNEY

A

N ►

1

St Mary's Hospital

STRAWBERRY HILL

CONVENT AVE

CITY GAOL

CONVENT

SUNDAY'S WELL ROAD

BLARNEY STREET

BAKERS ROAD

ORRERY ROAD

CATHEDRAL ROAD

TEMPLEACRE AVE

2

UNIVERSITY ATHLETIC GROUNDS

FITZGERALD PARK

RIVER LEE

CORK PUBLIC MUSEUM

MARDYKE WALK

(NORTH CHANNEL)

SUNDAY'S WELL ROAD

BLARNEY STREET

MOUNT NEBO AVENUE

BARRETT'S BUILDINGS

ST ANTHONY'S ROAD

ST ANN'S RD

GLEN RYAN ROAD

GURRANABRAHER ROAD

GURRANABRAHER AVE

CATHEDRAL ROAD

TEMPLEACRE AVE

2

UNIVERSITY COLLEGE CORK (U.C.C.)

WESTERN ROAD

DONOVAN'S RD

CONNAUGHT AVE

GILLABBEY ST

DEAN ST

LANCASTER QUAY

ERINVILLE HOSPITAL

DYKE PARADE

SCHOOL

GRENVILLE PLACE

MERCY HOSPITAL

BACHELOR'S QUAY

NORTH MALL

BLARNEY

BOYCE'S ST

MARY AIKENHEAD PLACE

3

SCHOOL OF ART

ST FINN BARRE'S CATHEDRAL

ELIZABETH FORT

BARRACK ST

HENRY ST

SHEARES ST

WASHINGTON ST

HANOVER ST

COURT HOUSE

ENGLISH MARKET

NORTH MAIN ST

KYRL'S QUAY

POPE'S QUAY

ST MARY'S

SHANDON

CHURCH ST

DOMINICK ST

DEVONSHIRE ST

SHANON STREET

HEALTH CENTER

ST MARY'S PRO-CATHEDRAL

ROMAN ST

ST ANNE'S SHANDON

JOHN STREET

LEITRIM STREET

4

PROBY'S QUAY

SHARMAN CRAWFORD ST

ST NICHOLAS CHURCH

FORT ST

EVERGREEN ABBEY ST

DEAN ST

BARRACK ST

SULLIVAN'S QUAY

COVE ST

CORK CITY LIBRARY

TOURIST OFFICE

GRAND PARADE

ENGLISH MARKET

SAINT PATRICK'S ST

PAUL ST

SS. PETER & PAUL'S CHURCH

OLIVER PLUNKETT ST

OPERA HOUSE

CRAWFORD MUNICIPAL ART GALLERY

COAL QUAY

LAVITT'S QUAY

ST PATRICK'S QUAY

PENROSE'S QUAY

MERCHANT'S QUAY

RICHMOND HILL

AUDLEY PL

SCHOOLS

WELLINGTON ROAD

ST PATRICK'S CHURCH

MCCURTAIN ST

SIDNEY PARK

5

GILLABBEY ST

DOUGLAS ST

SAWMILL ST

SOUTH TERR

SOUTH INFIRMARY

GEORGE'S QUAY

HOLY TRINITY CHURCH

TRINITY BRIDGE

SOUTH MALL

G.P.O.

SOUTH CHANNEL

UNION QUAY

COPLEY ST

MAYLOR ST

PARNELL ST

PLUNKETT ST

BUS STATION

ANDERSON QUAY

HORGAN'S QUAY

SUMMERHILL

ALFRED ST

ST PATRICK'S HOSPITAL

6

VICTORIA HOSPITAL

HIBERNIAN RD

SAWMILL ST

SOUTH TERR

ANGLESEA ST

EGLINTON ST

CITY HALL

ALBERT QUAY

SORTING OFFICE

ALBERT ST

ALBERT RD

VICTORIA RD

GAS WORKS

ALBERT QUAY

CUSTOM

RAILWAY ST

KENT STATION

6

0   0

0   150   300 m

490   980 feet

AIRPORT

MALLOW

C   B   A

B

NEWGRANGE

NAVAN

MAYNOOTH

NAAS

FINGLA...

BANNOW ROAD

ROYAL CANAL

KILKIERAN ROAD

PROSPECT CEMETERY

FAUSSAGH AVENUE

ST. ATTRACTA RD

ST. ATTRACTA RD

INVER ROAD

QUARRY ROAD

FAUSSAGH ROAD

ROAD

CABRA

NAVAN ROAD

SKREEN ROAD

OLD CABRA ROAD

CABRA ROAD

NORTH CIRCULAR ROA...

RESIDENSE OF
THE PRESIDENCE
OF IRELAND

PRUSSIA ST.

MANOR ST.

KAVAO TERMINAL

FISH POND

BLACKHORSE AVENUE

PARK CRESCENT

MC KEE
BARRACKS

NORTH CIRCULAR RD.

AUGHRIM STREET

GRANGEGORMAN

UPPER

ST BRENDAN'S
HOSPITAL

ZOOLOGICAL
GARDENS

OXMANTOWN ROAD

MAIN ROAD

O'DEVANEY GDNS

KIRWAN ST.

ST.LAURENC...
HOSPITAL

**PHOENIX
PARK**

PEOPLE'S
GARDEN

INFIRMARY RD.

MONTPELIER
PARK

ARBOUR HILL

BRUNSWICK
STREET NORTH

COLLINS
BARRACKS

IRISH WHISKEY
CORNER
(OLD JAMESON
DISTILLERY)

CHAPELIZOD RD. CONYNGHAM RD.

PARKGATE ST.

WOLFETONE QY.

ARRAN Q

**ISLAND
BRIDGE**

CLANCY
BARRACKS

ST. JOHN'S ROAD WEST

HEUSTON
STATION

VICTORIA QY.

GUINNESS
BREWERY

USHER'S

MEMORIAL
PARK

SOUTH CIRCULAR ROAD

STEEVENS
HOSPITAL

MILITARY RD.

ST.PATRICK'S
HOSPITAL

BRAZEN
HEAD

IRISH MUSEUM OF
MODERN ART
(ROYAL HOSPITAL)

NAT. COLLEGE O
ART AND DESIG...

COLBERT RD.

INCHICORE ROAD

LANE BOW BRIDGE

MT.BROWN

JAMES'S STREET

THOMAS ST. ...

KILMAINHAM
GOAL

OLD KILMAINHAM

ST.JAMES'S
HOSPITAL

GUINNESS BREWERY
HOP STORE

EMMET RD.

ST.KEVIN'S
HOSPITAL

MARROWBONE LANE

KILMAINHAM

SIUR RD.

SOUTH

CIRCULAR

ST. JAME'S WK.

THE C

CORK STREET

GRAND CANAL

ROAD

REUBEN ST.

HERBERTON

DONORE

AVENUE

DAVITT ROAD

DOLPHIN ROAD

DOLPHIN'S BARN

**DOLPHIN'S
BARN**

MOURNE ROAD

BENBULBIN ROAD

KEEPER ROAD

SOUTH CIRCULAR ROAD

BRICKFIELDS
PARK

PARNELL ROAD

KNOCKNAREA
AV.

SUNDRIVE ROAD

RUTLAND AVENUE

CLOGHER ROAD

CRUMLIN ROAD

SPORTS
GROUND

MOUNT JEROME
CEMETERY

1
2
3
4
5
6

A B C

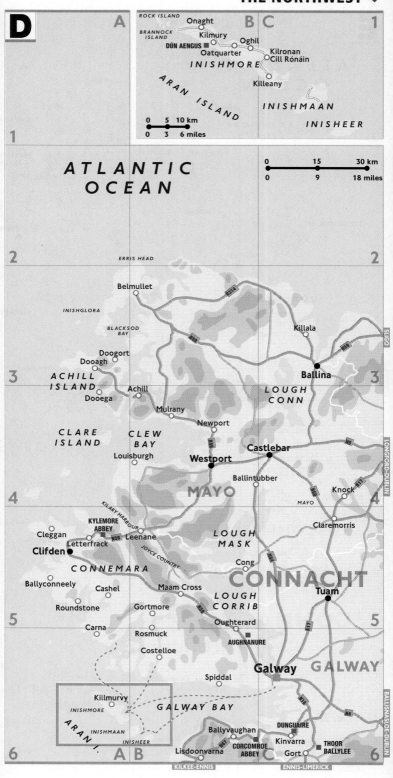

D

A | B | C

ROCK ISLAND

BRANNOCK ISLAND

Onaght

Kilmury

DÚN AENGUS ■

Oatquarter

Oghil

Kilronan

Cill Rónáin

INISHMORE

Killeany

ARAN ISLAND

INISHMAAN

INISHEER

0   5   10 km
0   3   6 miles

ATLANTIC OCEAN

0   15   30 km
0   9   18 miles

ERRIS HEAD

Belmullet

INISHGLORA

BLACKSOD BAY

Killala

Ballina

Doogort

Dooagh

ACHILL ISLAND

Achill

Dooega

Mulrany

Newport

LOUGH CONN

CLARE ISLAND

CLEW BAY

Louisburgh

Westport

Castlebar

Ballintubber

MAYO

Knock

MAYO

Claremorris

KILARY HARBOUR

Cleggan

KYLEMORE ABBEY

Letterfrack

Leenane

LOUGH MASK

Clifden

JOYCE COUNTRY

Cong

Ballyconneely

Cashel

Maam Cross

CONNEMARA

LOUGH CORRIB

CONNACHT

Roundstone

Gortmore

Tuam

Carna

Rosmuck

Oughterard

AUGHNANURE ■

Costelloe

Galway

GALWAY

Spiddal

Killmurvy

INISHMORE

GALWAY BAY

ARAN I.

INISHMAAN

INISHEER

Ballyvaughan

DUNGUAIRE ■

Kinvarra

THOOR BALLYLEE ■

Lisdoonvarna

CORCOMROE ABBEY ■

Gort

A | B | C

SLIGO

LONGFORD-DUBLIN

BALLINASLOE-DUBLIN

KILKEE-ENNIS

ENNIS-LIMERICK